D1713010

Penultimate Adventures with Britannia

I. *Adventures with Britannia* (1995)

II. *More Adventures with Britannia* (1998)

III. *Still More Adventures with Britannia* (2003)

IV. *Yet More Adventures with Britannia* (2005)

V. *Penultimate Adventures with Britannia* (2007)

and

Burnt Orange Britannia (2005)

PENULTIMATE ADVENTURES WITH

RITANNIA

Personalities, Politics and Culture in Britain

Edited by Wm. Roger Louis

I.B. TAURIS

LONDON · NEW YORK

HRC HARRY RANSOM CENTER

Published in 2008 by I.B.Tauris & Co Ltd
6 Salem Road, London W2 4BU
In the United States of America and Canada, distributed by
Palgrave Macmillan, a division of St. Martin's Press
175 Fifth Avenue, New York NY 10010
www.ibtauris.com

Harry Ransom Humanities Research Center
University of Texas at Austin
P.O. Drawer 7219
Austin, Texas 78713-7219

The paper used in this publication meets the minimum requirements of
American National Standard for Information Sciences—
Permanence of Paper for Printed Library Materials

ISBN 978-1-84511-693-4 hardcover
ISBN 978-1-84511-711-5 paperback

A full CIP record for this book is available from the British Library
A full CIP record for this book is available from the Library of Congress

Library of Congress Control Number 2007933720

Typeset, printed, and bound by Communication Specialists, Inc.
Austin, Texas

Table of Contents

List of Authors

Larry Carver, Professor of English and holder of the Doyle Professorship in Western Civilization, has taught at the University of Texas since 1973. His scholarly work focuses on Restoration and eighteenth-century British poetry and drama. His works include *The Plays of Hugh Kelly* (1990). He is Director of the Liberal Arts Honors Program. He was the curator of "Feliks Topolski" at the Humanities Research Center.

John Davis is the Warden of All Souls College, Oxford. He taught for twenty-two years at the University of Kent. In 1990 he became Professor of Social Anthropology at Oxford. He was Chairman of the European Association of Social Anthropologists, 1993–94, and President of the Royal Anthropological Institute, 1997–2001. His books include *Libyan Politics: Tribe and Revolution* (1987). He is a Fellow of the British Academy.

T. M. Devine, OBE, D.Litt, FRSE, Hon MRIA, FBA, is the Sir William Fraser Professor of Scottish History and Palaeography in the University of Edinburgh, the first-ever Chair (1908) established in the subject. He has published nearly 30 books and over 100 academic articles and chapters. In 2003 he was awarded the Royal Gold Medal by HM the Queen, Scotland's supreme academic accolade, and is currently the only historian elected to all three national academies in the British Isles.

Felipe Fernández-Armesto is Professor of History at Tufts University. His books include *Columbus* (1991), and *Millennium* (1995), an iconoclastic history of the last thousand years. He has edited *The Times Atlas of World Exploration* (1991) and is the General Editor of the *Folio History of England* (1997–2001). His recent books include *So You Think You're Human?* (2004) and *Pathfinders* (2006).

Martin Francis is Henry R. Winkler Associate Professor of Modern History at the University of Cincinnati. He is the author of *Ideas and Policies under Labour, 1945–1951* (1997) and co-editor of *The Conservatives and British Society, 1880–1990* (1996). His next book, *The Flyer: Men of the Royal Air Force and British Culture, 1939–1945*, will be published by Oxford University Press.

Sir Martin Gilbert, CBE, D.Litt, is an Honorary Fellow of Merton College, Oxford. He studied under A. J. P. Taylor, and is the author of 79 books, including the official biography of Sir Winston Churchill. His works on the Holocaust include *Auschwitz and the Allies* (1981), *Atlas of the Holocaust* (1982), *The Holocaust: A History of the Jews of Europe* (1986), and *The Righteous: The Unsung Christian Heroes of the Holocaust* (2002).

Barry Gough is Professor of History at Wilfrid Laurier University, Waterloo, Ontario. He has been Archives Fellow of Churchill College, and Fellow of King's College, London. His books include *The Royal Navy and the Northwest Coast of North America, 1810–1914* (1971), *Gunboat Frontier* (1986), *The Falkland Islands/Malvinas: Contest for Empire in the South Atlantic* (1992), and *Fighting Sail on Lake Huron and Georgian Bay* (2002). He is a former editor of the *American Neptune*.

Lord Gowrie was educated at Eton and Balliol College, Oxford. He served as Minister for the Arts in the Conservative government, 1983–85, and was Chairman of the Arts Council of England, 1994–1998. His publications include *A Postcard from Don Giovanni* (1972) and *The Genius of British Painting* (1975). His new and selected poems will appear in 2008.

Graham Greene, nephew of the novelist, has spent nearly fifty years in publishing, going from Secker and Warburg to Jonathan Cape and finally to the merged publishing houses of Cape, Chatto and Windus, and the Bodley Head, which he chaired. In 1978 he led the first delegation of Western publishers to China, and helped bring about China's accession to international copyright. He served on the Board of Trustees of the British Museum from 1978 to 2002 (Chairman, 1996–2002).

Stephen Howe is Professor of the History of Colonialism at the University of Bristol, where he is also Co-Director of the Centre for the Study of Colonial and Postcolonial Societies. His books include *Anticolonialism in British Politics* (1993), *Afrocentrism* (1998), *Ireland and Empire* (2000), and *Empire: A Very Short Introduction* (2002). He is now working on a book called *The Intellectual Consequences of Decolonisation*.

Dan Jacobson is a novelist and critic. Born and brought up in South Africa, he holds an Honorary D. Litt. from Witwatersrand University. His autobiography *Time and Time* (1985) won the J. R. Ackerley Prize. His other works include the memoir *Heshel's Kingdom* (1998), the criticism collection *Adult Pleasures* (1988), and the novels *The Confessions of Josef Baisz* (1977) and *All for Love* (2005). He has taught English for many years at University College, London.

Indivar Kamtekar studied physics at Delhi University and history at Jawaharlal Nehru University and the University of Cambridge, where he was awarded a Ph.D. for work on the partition of India. He has taught at the Indian Institute of Management in Calcutta and has been a Fellow of the Indian Institute of Advanced Study in Simla. He is the author of *What Caused the "Quit India" Movement?* (1990).

Dane Kennedy is the Elmer Louis Kayser Professor of History and International Affairs at George Washington University, in Washington, D.C. He is the author of *Islands of White: Settler Society and Culture in Kenya and Southern Rhodesia, 1890–1939* (1987), *The Magic Mountains: Hill States and the British Raj* (1996), *Britain and Empire, 1880–1945* (2002), and *The Highly Civilized Man: Richard Burton and the Victorian World* (2005).

John Lonsdale is Fellow of Trinity College, Cambridge, where he is Professor of Modern African History. He is currently completing work on the decolonization of Kenya and the political thought of the country's first President, Jomo Kenyatta. He is co-author (with Bruce Berman) of *Unhappy Valley: Conflict in Kenya and Africa* (1992). He has edited *South Africa in Question* (1988) and is General Editor of the Cambridge University Press series in African Studies.

Lord Morgan was Fellow and Tutor, The Queen's College, Oxford, 1966–89, and Vice-Chancellor, University of Wales, 1989–95. He has written 30 books on nineteenth- and twentieth-century Britain, including the *Oxford Illustrated History of Britain* (over 750,000 copies sold), a history of modern Wales, and biographies of Keir Hardie, Lloyd George, James Callaghan, and Michael Foot. He is a Fellow of the British Academy.

Guy Ortolano is Assistant Professor at Washington University in St. Louis, where he teaches British history and the history of science. *The "Two Cultures" Controversy: Science, Literature, and Cultural Politics in Postwar Britain* will be published by Cambridge University Press.

Susan Pedersen is Professor of History at Columbia University. She received her B.A. and Ph.D. at Harvard University, where she was a member of the faculty from 1988 until 2003. Her books include *Family, Dependence, and the Origins of the Welfare State: Britain and France,*

1914–1945 (1994) and *Eleanor Rathbone and the Politics of Conscience* (2004). She is now writing a history of the mandates system of the League of Nations.

Priya Satia is Assistant Professor of British History at Stanford University. She received her Ph.D. from the University of California, Berkeley, in 2004. Her forthcoming book, *The State That Couldn't See: A Cultural History of British Intelligence-Gathering in the Middle East, 1900–1932,* will be published by Oxford University Press.

Hilary Spurling is a biographer, critic, and former literary editor of the *Spectator.* Her books include a handbook to the work of Anthony Powell (1977), a two-volume biography of Ivy Compton-Burnett (1984), *Paul Scott* (1990), a biography of Sonia Orwell (2002), and a two-volume life of Henri Matisse (2005).

John H. Summers is Lecturer on Social Studies at Harvard University. He received his doctorate in American intellectual history in 2006 from the University of Rochester. His essays have appeared in the *Journal of American History, New York Times Book Review,* and *Nation.* He is writing the first full-scale biography of C. Wright Mills.

Sir Keith Thomas is Distinguished Fellow of All Souls College, Oxford, and former President of Corpus Christi College. His books include *Religion and the Decline of Magic* (1971) and *Man and the Natural World* (1983). He has edited the *Oxford Book of Work* (1999). He is a past President of the British Academy.

Geoffrey Wheatcroft is a former literary editor of the *Spectator* and "Londoner's Diary" editor of the *Evening Standard.* He now writes for the *Guardian,* the *New York Times,* and *Slate,* among others. His books include *The Randlords* (1985), *The Controversy of Zion: Jewish Nationalism, the Jewish State and the Unresolved Jewish Dilemma* (1996), which won a National Jewish Book Award, *The Strange Death of Tory England* (2005), and *Yo Blair!* (2007).

The editor, Wm. Roger Louis, is Kerr Professor of English History and Culture and Distinguished Teaching Professor at the University of Texas at Austin. He is an Honorary Fellow of St. Antony's College, Oxford. His books include *Imperialism at Bay* (1976) and *The British Empire in the Middle East* (1984). He is the Editor-in-Chief of the *Oxford History of the British Empire.* The present Director of the National History Center, he was President of the American Historical Association in 2001.

Introduction

WM. ROGER LOUIS

The word "penultimate" implies finality, but readers of *Adventures with Britannia* throughout the world may rest assured that the end is not yet in sight. Between penultimate and death are degrees of suspense and connecting links, past and future. The present volume begins, as have its predecessors, with the continuity of G. H. Hardy's affirmation that the agony of having to repeat oneself is so excruciating that it is best to end the agony by offering no apology for doing so. In the spirit of the adventurous refrain—more, still more, yet more—I again follow his example. This book consists of a representative selection of lectures given to the British Studies seminar at the University of Texas at Austin. Most of the present lectures were delivered in the years 2005–07.

Lectures are different from essays or scholarly articles. A lecture presumes an audience rather than a reader and usually has a more conversational tone. It allows greater freedom in the expression of personal or subjective views. It permits and invites greater candor. It is sometimes informally entertaining as well as anecdotally instructive. In this volume, the lecture sometimes takes the form of intellectual autobiography—an account of how the speaker has come to grips with a significant topic in the field of British Studies, which broadly defined means "things British" throughout the world as well as things that happen to be English, Irish, Scottish, or Welsh. The scope of British Studies includes all disciplines in the social sciences and humanities as well as music, architecture, and the visual arts—

for the first time, a Britannia volume includes paintings and photographs. Most of the lectures in this collection fall within the fields
of history, politics, and literature, though the dominant theme, here
as previously, is historical. The full sweep of the lectures will be apparent from the list at the end of the book, which is reproduced in
its entirety to give a comprehensive idea of the seminar's evolution
and substance.

In 2007, the British Studies seminar celebrated its thirty-second
anniversary. The circumstances for its creation were favorable because of the existence of the Humanities Research Center, now
known as the Harry Ransom Humanities Research Center, at the
University of Texas. Harry Ransom was the founder of the HRC, a
Professor of English and later Chancellor of the University, a collector of rare books, and a man of humane vision. Through the administrative and financial genius of both Ransom and the present Director, Thomas F. Staley, the HRC has developed into a great literary
archive with substantial collections, especially in English literature.
Ransom thought a weekly seminar might provide the opportunity to
learn of the original research being conducted at the HRC as well as
create common bonds of intellectual interest in a congenial setting
of overstuffed armchairs, Persian carpets, and generous libations of
sherry. This was an ingenious idea. The seminar was launched in
the fall semester of 1975. It had the dual purpose of providing a
forum for visiting scholars engaged in research at the HRC and of
enabling the members of the seminar to discuss their own work.

The sherry at the Friday seminar sessions symbolizes the attitude. The seminar meets to discuss whatever happens to be on the
agenda, Scottish or Indian, Canadian or Jamaican, English or Australian. As Oscar Wilde reportedly said, echoed by George Bernard
Shaw, England and America are two great countries divided by a
common language, but he understated the case by several countries.
The interaction of British and other societies is an endlessly fascinating subject on which points of view do not often converge. Diverse preconceptions, which are tempered by different disciplines,
help initiate and then sustain controversy, not end it. The ongoing
discussions in British Studies are engaging because of the clash of
different perspectives as well as the nuance of cultural interpretation. Though the printed page cannot capture the atmosphere of
engaged discussion, the following lectures do offer the opportunity
to savor the result of wide-ranging research and reflection.

The British Studies seminar has two University sponsors, the
College of Liberal Arts and the Humanities Research Center. We
are grateful to the Dean of Liberal Arts for allocating resources to

sustain the program of Junior Fellows—a half dozen or so assistant professors appointed each year to bring fresh blood, brash ideas, and new commitment to the program. We are equally grateful to the Director of the HRC for providing a home for the seminar. I wish also to thank Frances Terry, who has handled the week-by-week administrative detail from early on in the seminar's history. Above all I am indebted to Kip Keller for the many ways in which he has assisted the publications program of the seminar.

The seminar has been the beneficiary of generous gifts by Creekmore and Adele Fath of Austin, Baine and Mildred Kerr of Houston, John and Susan Kerr of San Antonio, Becky Gale and the late Edwin Gale of Beaumont, Custis Wright and the late Charles Alan Wright of Austin, Lowell Lebermann of Austin, Tex and Charlie Moncrief of Fort Worth, and the two dozen stouthearted members of the seminar who have generously contributed to its endowment. We are indebted to Dean Robert D. King for his help over many years. I again extend special thanks to Sam Jamot Brown and Sherry Brown of Durango, Colorado, for enabling the seminar to offer undergraduate and graduate scholarships and generally to advance the cause of the liberal arts. The students appointed to scholarships are known as Churchill Scholars. The Churchill Scholars, like the Junior Fellows, not only contribute to the vitality of the seminar but also extend its age range from those in their late teens to its oldest member, Creekmore Fath, who served in FDR's White House and has now passed his ninetieth birthday.

THE CHAPTERS—MORE PRECISELY, THE LECTURES—are clustered together around certain themes. The first two reassess David Lloyd George. **Kenneth O. Morgan** argues that Lloyd George held a consistent record in world affairs that was pro-French yet sympathetic to Germany. France appealed to the radical, anti-militarist republican in him, but he also admired the way in which the German government promoted social welfare and national efficiency. As Prime Minister during the First World War, he inevitably became close to France, especially through his relationship with its wartime premier, Georges Clemenceau. At the Paris peace conference in 1919, Lloyd George appeared to be strongly anti-German, but in fact he fought consistently for moderate peace terms while attempting to satisfy French demands for security. After falling from power in 1922, he was commonly viewed as pro-German, in part because he was critical of French intransigence on frontiers and reparations. He went to Germany to meet Hitler in 1936, a critical point in the era of appeasement. In 1941, Churchill compared him to Pétain.

Yet Lloyd George's attitude toward the French and Germans shows both consistency of purpose and statesmanship. His reputation in the 1914–1918 era as "the man who won the war" will endure, as will the negative, or at least ambiguous, legacy of his statecraft. Some of the most persistent problems in the world today are ones that Lloyd George helped create: Ireland, Palestine, and Iraq.

Susan Pedersen explains how Lloyd George's love for Frances Stevenson, his mistress and secretary, carried with it unique political advantages. She was a loyal, efficient, and effective political ally in a partnership that endured for three decades. Between 1913 and his death, Lloyd George ran several ministries, led two governments, prosecuted a major war, hammered out peace treaties for Europe, attempted to stabilize Ireland and India, and then wrote a million words of memoir. Stevenson helped at every stage and was a vital part of his success. When his wife Margaret died during the Second World War, the two could finally marry; the bride was fifty-five and the groom eighty. The unusual thing about the relationship was not so much its emotional and sexual context as the political advantages it offered to both parties. It gave her a measure of authority in a male world. But if Lloyd George set out to reshape British politics, he was not a bohemian, and had no interest in undermining the institution of marriage. Marriage remained beyond Stevenson's grasp until the end of Lloyd George's life, but her influence can be detected in Britain's social history. The female secretary, and not just the suffragist, helped open up the political world.

The feminist movement of four decades ago contributed to a fundamental reassessment of how history should be written. In reflecting on the intellectual and social currents of the 1960s, **Keith Thomas** concludes that no one at the time would have predicted the transformation of the discipline in a direction away from traditional subjects such as war and diplomacy to all aspects of human experience. It then seemed that econometric history, for example, would sweep away all that came before it and that history itself would become a social science. Yet economic history is in decline, social history has been overtaken by the new genre of cultural history, and the thrust of historical writing continues to be qualitative rather than quantitative. In the 1960s there was a plea for theory, and that demand has been met beyond expectation. But this is not surprising. What happens in one generation in economics, psychology, and literature, or anthropology, sociology, and philosophy, is reflected in the next generation of historical writing, even if historians have not read a word written by theorists themselves. In the 1980s, some academic skeptics denied the possibility of achieving any knowledge of the past, or for that matter the present. But this nihilistic doctrine has been virtually rejected, even though the nihilists were right in saying that historical work often, though not merely, reflects present-day anxieties. The passion for environmental history comes from fear of global warming and the depletion of natural resources, and the preoccupation with empire reflects anger at American involvement in Iraq—just as a hundred years earlier historians were concerned with issues of economic imperialism and British "race patriotism" against the background of the Boer War.

Dan Jacobson catches the spirit of the time at the end of the nineteenth century by inquiring into the relationship between Rudyard Kipling and Cecil Rhodes. Kipling wanted Britain to exert power over other nations and remote regions while preserving traditions in Britain—traditions so distinctive and mysterious that only those born there could understand them. Rhodes's ambitions spoke directly to Kipling's own view of Britain's imperial duty. Rhodes himself had a semi-mystical regard for British power, which he revered and at the same time tried to manipulate. The intimacy between the man of letters and the man of action and business was irresistible to both. But things did not work out as Kipling had anticipated. Rhodes died an early death, and the shock of the early Boer victories caused Kipling to realize how ill prepared Britain would be for even larger battles nearer home. He became obsessed with the thought of impending war with Germany.

For five months in 1916, J. R. R. Tolkien served on the Somme as a second lieutenant in the Lancashire Fusiliers. Nearly a half century later, **Martin Gilbert,** then a young Fellow of Merton College, Oxford, listened to his reminiscences at college dinners. Tolkien was reticent, but when he opened up, he told terrible tales of the "animal horrors" of the trenches. His job had been to supervise communications, mainly by carrier pigeons, to a command post a mile and a half behind the trenches. Many of his friends were killed. Tolkien recalled the danger of constant German artillery shells, "the screech and roar amid clouds of earth and mud." But even in hideous circumstances of pain and death there were moments of humor. Tolkien spoke German. When he once offered a German prisoner a cup of water, the fellow corrected his pronunciation. In October 1916, Tolkien was taken ill with trench fever, an infection transmitted by lice. He returned to England, but the experience of the Somme left an everlasting, haunting impression that later found expression in *The Lord of the Rings*—"dead things, dead faces in the water."

W. H. Auden loved literary works, including *The Lord of the Rings*, that effectively mix the dark with the light. As **Grey Gowrie** makes clear, Auden himself could deal with dark themes effectively by treating them lightly. In the year of the centenary of Auden's birth, he explains how the poet sustained the tradition of making poetry accessible to the common man, thereby democratizing it. While in his twenties, Auden was celebrated more than any poet since Byron. Indeed, the decade before the Second World War is the age of Auden. His poetry from the 1930s reflects the turmoil of the Spanish Civil War; with Christopher Isherwood, he witnessed Japan's invasion of China; and in a famous, and famously repudiated, poem, he memorialized the onset of the Second World War. In 1939 he left England for the United States, thereby earning the contempt of such contemporaries as Evelyn Waugh and Anthony Powell, who commented at the time of Auden's death, "I am glad that shit is dead." In New York, he met Chester Kallman, the son of a Brooklyn dentist, who became his lover and life partner. During the rest of his life, his poetry looked backward toward the T. S. Eliot of the 1920s—holding a mirror up to the wasteland and asking what are the ways of escape—and forward to Elvis Presley and the Beatles. The pain of war, beginning in the 1930s, manifests itself throughout his work. When we contemplate lands "laid waste," whether Palestine or Iraq, Auden's voice still speaks to us.

The subjugation of Iraq by the British is the subject of the lecture by **Priya Satia.** The British in the early 1920s attempted to bring the three former provinces of the Ottoman Empire under effective administrative and military control. But they faced an Iraqi insurgency at the same time that they were being confronted with resistance in Ireland, India, and Egypt. Winston Churchill, then Colonial Secretary, helped devise a system of control that was at once relatively cheap and seemingly humane. Air policing—a euphemism for strafing and bombing—was developed at a seminal period in the development of the Royal Air Force. The pilots of the RAF as well as officers of the colonial service had preconceptions of Arab society, or "Arabia," that enabled them to rationalize the killing of hundreds of Iraqis in single operations. They believed the Arabs to be chivalrous yet fanatic, to understand only force, and to possess excessive pride. Above all, they needed to save face. This was the British understanding of the "Arab mind." British officers in Iraq had served on the frontiers of India and elsewhere, and some, at least, believed Britain had become decadent. Redemption for the country could be found in the Empire, where order could be imposed, brutally if necessary, through "persuasion and love." One of the young RAF officers was Arthur Harris, later famous as "Bomber Harris" of the Second World War. Churchill was able to rationalize the British bombing of civilians in Germany in exactly the same way that the officers of the colonial service and the RAF had vindicated the bombing of Iraqis in the interwar years—with a clear conscience and with the belief that violence was inherent in the enemy's culture.

The lecture by **Barry Gough** tells the story of Arthur Marder, the doyen of historians of the Royal Navy. Marder published his first book, *The Anatomy of British Sea Power,* in 1940 and, toward the end of a distinguished career, a monograph entitled "Winston is Back" (the phrase used in a signal flashed by the Admiralty to the fleet in 1939). He was Boston born, the son of Russian Jewish immigrants. At Harvard he benefited from the supervision of William L. Langer, one of the great historians of the time. He later taught in Hawaii and California. Anti-Jewish prejudice probably prevented more distinguished appointments. As an American who had managed to unlock the secrets of the Royal Navy, he acquired a reputation as the foremost naval historian of his generation. His most famous work was the five-volume *From the Dreadnought to Scapa Flow,* which included an account of the failure of the Royal Navy to defeat the German Navy at the battle of Jutland in 1916. Jutland shattered Britain's confidence in its naval supremacy. Marder won the trust of British naval officers, who valued his fair-minded and comprehensive assessments and who helped him acquire access to secret documents. But he eventually came into conflict with Stephen Roskill, a former naval officer and one of the other principal historians of the Royal Navy. A. J. P. Taylor called the pair "Our Two Historical Dreadnoughts." Their collision marked an historiographical battle that has had repercussions to the present, not least in judging Churchill's naval policy. Marder's last work dealt with a comparative history of the Japanese and British navies, but his principal achievement goes to the heart of the First and Second World Wars.

Martin Francis deals with one of the famous photographers of the twentieth century, Cecil Beaton. In the interwar period, Beaton acquired a reputation for frivolity and artificial glamour. He was regarded as a Tory photographer who celebrated privilege and prestige. After 1939, he seemed to shift to sober realism by portraying the courage and sacrifice of ordinary soldiers and civilians. For those of his admirers who previously might have been embarrassed by Beaton's flamboyant persona as a homosexual dandy, his new depiction of everyday life and death in battle appeared to mark an abandonment of private decadence in favor of civic virtue, a public repudiation of effeminacy in favor of the robust, martial masculinity of fighting men and officers. In fact, Beaton's photography continued to evoke an elitist, imperial sensibility as well as an implicit homosexual desire that rode uneasily with wartime populism. His work came to represent "romantic Toryism." Though immensely popular, his photographs could be interpreted as portraying the opposite of the egalitarian ethos of the "people's war."

The lecture by **Indivar Kamtekar** examines the relationship between the state and social class in India and Britain during the Second World War. Of the two, the British national state was able, in its hour of crisis, to extract more resources of manpower, materials, and money from its upper classes. And while the living conditions of the British lower classes improved during the war, the condition of the Indian lower classes deteriorated, with millions dying in the Bengal famine. During the Second World War, a rich man was much more comfortable in India, while for a poor man, the wartime experience of Britain was preferable. In India, the colonial state was willing to sacrifice the interests of the poor in order to secure the cooperation of the more prosperous. In Kamtekar's view, the British thus allowed the rich to profiteer and prosper and the poor to starve and die. This interpretation has fundamental consequences for historical interpretation. Since the colonial state was gentler toward its upper classes (in comparison with much harsher treatment in Britain), the British had much less influence in molding the character of postcolonial India than is commonly believed.

Hilary Spurling also pursues themes of India during the Second World War, by reassessing the novelist Paul Scott—reassessing in the sense of taking a broad view of Scott's work since the time of her lectures on Scott to the British Studies seminar in 1986 and 1989 and her biography, *Paul Scott,* published in 1990. Scott, born in 1922, died in 1978, before he could benefit from the spectacular success of the television series *The Jewel in the Crown,* based on his set of four novels set in India in the 1940s, *The Raj Quartet.* The television series perceptively and skillfully portrayed two protagonists, Sergeant Guy Perron (based on the University of Texas classicist Peter Green, who served in India during the Second World War with Scott), and Ronald Merrick, a superintendent of police. Merrick has significance for the history of the British Empire at large. At the time, critics denied that a commissioned officer in India, whether in the police or army, could have committed such monstrous acts of brutal interrogation in the regular course of duty. Scott's genius was to penetrate into the mind of Merrick and others, and to discover the underlying motives and psychology in a way that historians, chained to their written sources, seldom can. A few historians, especially Max Beloff, noted the historical value of Scott's work early on. But no one was prepared for the wave of nostalgia for the Raj in the 1980s that accompanied

The Jewel in the Crown. Scott's aim was certainly not nostalgia but something rather different: to demonstrate the various ways in which partition was a violent conclusion to the British era in India.

In a lecture pursuing the end of British rule in Ireland, India, and Palestine, **Geoffrey Wheatcroft** discusses British motives in three of the great partitions in the twentieth century. In each he finds that the British government, contrary to common belief, attempted to avert partition. In the late nineteenth century, W. E. Gladstone believed that a political solution could not be imposed on the Irish against their will. But should the Irish majority be allowed to determine the future? In the Protestant counties in the North, the Irish did not want partition, but neither did they want to be ruled by a nationalist Parliament in Dublin. The logic led to partition, as it did in India when the same question was asked about the principle of self-determination. Self-determination for whom, the Hindu majority or the Muslim minority? The British saw it as being in their own self-interest to do everything within their power to preserve unity. Otherwise the Indian army as well as India itself would be split, and Britain's economic and strategic position in Asia would be weakened, perhaps fatally. In Palestine, one line of British thought held that the Jews and Arabs were incompatible and that the sooner partition occurred the better. But the predominant view, as put forward emphatically by the Foreign Secretary, Ernest Bevin, upheld the principle that the two communities could live together harmoniously, just as had the French and British in Canada and the two communities of European descent in South Africa. The British exhausted all possibilities before they acquiesced in partition. To them, partition represented the end of the line, the bankruptcy of policy, and the failure to achieve long-standing goals.

The name E. E. Evans-Pritchard, according to **John Davis,** is permanently associated with the Sudan. He was an anthropologist who did pioneering work in the Nile Basin, mainly with the Azande and Nuer. His study of the Nuer is the most influential account of a people who had no government, no state of their own, and who did not welcome other people's attempts to impose one. Stateless, they undermined the dominant assumption of political theory: that people without a state must necessarily live in chaos. Evans-Pritchard's second major, indeed great, contribution was his account of witchcraft, oracles, and magic as practiced by the Azande (a people with princes and social hierarchy). His account showed them to be practically minded, rational and inquiring, skeptical, yet also relying on irrational methods to explain events and to take decisions. His work thus raised questions about rationality and still shakes the self-confidence of scientific inquirers into social life. Evans-Prichard shaped the thought of future generations of political theorists and philosophers as well as social scientists. Personally, E.P., as he was known to his friends, was an archetypal Oxford Professor of the 1950s and 1960s—eccentric, outspoken, nonchalant, immensely expert, but with a generous share of the faults as well as the virtues of the species. He became Professor of Social Anthropology at Oxford in 1946 and remained there until he retired, in 1973.

In another lecture that deals with the dynamics of society, **John Summers** studies the thought of C. Wright Mills, the Texas-born sociologist who is remembered above all because of his book published in 1956, *The Power Elite*. The year 1956 might well be regarded as the beginning of the 1960s in Britain. Mills was as popular, perhaps even more so, in Britain, especially among British left-wing intellectuals, as he was in America. Summers describes him as an anarchist by temperament and a sociologist by training. He received his Ph.D. from the University of Wisconsin, and then taught at Columbia University. The key to his analytical thought was his division of society into masses and elites. His ideas had a powerful appeal for critics of the British economic and class system, including E. P. Thompson, Perry Anderson, and Robin Blackburn. Here at last, wrote Michael Foot of Mills's arrival in England, "IS THE TRUE VOICE OF AMERICAN RADICALISM." Mills seemed to embody left-wing integrity and commitment. He took on a second life as ally, tutor, and hero to British radicals of the 1960s. He died in 1962, but his inspiration lived on. The CIA paid him perhaps the ultimate tribute by identifying him, along with Herbert Marcuse and Frantz Fanon, as one of the three most influential leaders of the international Left. The *New Left Review* mourned his death and commented that he "taught what it means to be a free and humane intellect."

The 1960s, as **Guy Ortolano** comments, were characterized in Britain by anxieties about national decline. Was economic decline relative or absolute? Many economic historians now tend to be skeptical about the concept of decline itself, but it seemed clear to most contemporaries that Britain suffered from not only the humiliation of lost influence in the world but also economic stagnation and possible collapse. One of the most prominent critics of decline was Arthur Koestler, who in 1963 edited a collection of essays with the memorable title "Suicide of a Nation?" in *Encounter,* the leading intellectual journal (before the revelation that it received financial support from the CIA). Koestler himself took the lead in analyzing the causes of decline, which he saw primarily as economic as opposed to imperial. In other words, the cause of Britain's malaise was the failure to modernize the economy rather than the loss of the Empire. But there were dissenting voices, the most significant of which was Malcolm Muggeridge's. Muggeridge believed that British decline was due to spiritual impoverishment brought on by material affluence. The loss of British greatness was caused by cultural and spiritual degeneration. Despite these fundamental differences, however, Koestler and Muggeridge both expressed widespread anxieties about national decline. Whatever the verdict on economic accuracy, "decline" functioned as a powerful weapon in the cultural politics of post-war Britain.

One of the themes of the *Britannia* series is autobiography. The lecture by **Graham Greene** deals with his fifty-year career as a publisher. In the 1950s, at about the same time that his uncle, the novelist with the same name, founded the Anglo-Texas Society, our Graham Greene left Oxford to become a banker, a short but significant episode in his life, during which he issued travel money to Dag Hammarskjöld at the branch of the bank at the United Nations bearing the quaint name Chemical Corn Exchange. He began his career in publishing at Secker and Warburg, the publisher of Jomo Kenyatta's *Facing Mount Kenya*. Office legend had it that when Kenyatta delivered the manuscript, he deposited his spear in the umbrella stand. Greene remembers nearly losing his job for recommending the publication of *Lolita* as "one of funniest books I had read," but failing to warn the publisher of legal problems. In the 1960s he moved on to Jonathan Cape and began to travel, perhaps as widely as any other publisher, in Africa, the Middle East, and the white Dominions. At one point he had the impression that the good days were finally over when the Peace Corps, followed by hippies, arrived in Nepal. In the 1970s he began to work toward Chinese accession to international copyright, which was eventually achieved in 1992. The high point of his career was the publication of the *Crossman Diaries,* which revealed the inner secrets of the Wilson government of the 1960s; their appearance marked a signal achievement in the battle against excessive governmental confidentiality.

In the 1960s, the Humanities Research Center acquired a collection of twenty paintings by Feliks Topolski. **Larry Carver** relates the story of the controversial acquisition and assesses the stature of the artist. Early in his career, he acquired a reputation as a caricaturist, but gradually he has become acknowledged as a portrait artist of the first rank. Born in Poland in 1907, he visited England for the first time in 1935. During the Second World War, he became an official war artist, made drawings of the Blitz, witnessed the liberation of the Bergen-Belsen concentration camp, and attended the

Nuremberg trials. He traveled throughout the world from the 1940s to the 1970s. His paintings depicted Indian independence, the Chinese and Cuban revolutions, chaos in the Congo, and the war in Vietnam. The Chancellor of the University of Texas, and founder of the Humanities Research Center, Harry Ransom, recognized his genius and set about acquiring "twenty great" portraits. But unfortunately for Ransom, many of Topolski's subjects felt victimized and humiliated. Those close to Aldous Huxley even claimed that Topolski's painting had hastened his death. Topolski was not invited to the University of Texas to celebrate his work. But admiration for his portraits grew over time, and his son and daughter, Daniel and Teresa Topolski, gave a joint lecture to the British Studies seminar in 2006. They successfully argued his claim to distinction as an artist who not only had the powers of a sociologist but also the compassion of a humane observer.

"Suez and All Souls," the lecture by **Roger Louis,** is a study of an Oxford college and Oxford itself during a period of national and international crisis. In 1936, All Souls had been associated with the appeasement of the Nazi government. But at that time the College represented the connection between academic influence and public affairs. In 1956, it no longer seemed to be a nexus of power and intellect. At this level, the lecture addresses itself to the myth and reality of All Souls. At another level, it establishes the meaning of the Suez crisis not only for All Souls, but also more generally for Oxford and indeed all of Britain, by commenting on Suez as a moment in the history of the British people. Through the examples of three members of All Souls involved in the crisis, Roger Makins, Patrick Reilly, and Quintin Hailsham, one can see quite clearly that points of honor were at stake. All of them believed that entering into a secret alliance with France and Israel had tarnished the good name of England. All Souls thus becomes a microcosm of Oxford and the country at large. The College itself in 1956 still resembled the College of 1936, but it was entering tempestuous times. A decade later, in 1966, it appeared to some to be on the brink of dissolution, or deserved to be, but All Souls survived, demonstrating not only resilience but also renewed purpose.

At the time of the Suez crisis, the British were fighting a counterinsurgency battle in Kenya against the movement called Mau Mau—described by **John Lonsdale** as a rising that mobilized Kenya's largest ethnic group, the Kikuyu, who were themselves about 20 percent of the total population. The British viewed Mau Mau as irrational and lacking legitimate grievance; they also mistakenly believed that Jomo Kenyatta was its leader. What caused Mau Mau was the illusion of white settler strength in the Second World War, when the white farmers curtailed the rights of African peasant farmers in the area called the White Highlands. Tenants (or "squatters") no longer enjoyed the freedom of cultivating crops or raising stock. British counterinsurgency consisted of a brutal attempt to impose institutions on a rebellious peasantry to make it governable. The British appeared to succeed, in the sense of making Kenya safe for white settlers in the years to come, when British rule ended. The irony was that this civilian aspect of British counterinsurgency, in making possible a prosperous peasantry, made Kenya safe for the rule of President Jomo Kenyatta, whom the British had convicted for managing Mau Mau.

In 2007 there were four anniversaries dealing with the legacy of the British Empire and Britain's influence in world: the 200th anniversary of Britain's abolition of the Atlantic slave trade, the 50th of Ghana's independence, the 25th of the war with Argentina over the Falkland Islands, and one of the most important of all in British history, the 300th of the Union of England and Scotland. These anniversaries provide the context of the lecture by **Stephen Howe,** who explores the "imaginative afterlife" of the imperial past in Britain today. The "English question" comes to the fore because of the fear that a revived English sense of nationality may prove to be inward looking, even xenophobic or racist. England created "Britishness" through the conquest and integration of Wales, Scotland, and, less successfully, Ireland. There emerged a centralized, increasingly powerful, monarchical state and, later, an overseas Empire cemented together by the sense of Britishness. But in recent decades the English, Scots, and Welsh have appeared to be growing further apart. How will the English, whose separate identity was submerged by an expansionist, even globalized, Britishness, define themselves? And what of the immigrants from former colonies, especially from South Asia and the Caribbean, who have little difficulty considering themselves British but look on "English" as a less accessible identity? If Britishness continues to decline, what form of "Englishness" will emerge and whom will it encompass? There are indications that the answer will not necessarily be negative, as the fear of an inward-looking England might suggest. In the words of the rock singer Billy Bragg, the only way out is "to grasp the thorny rose of our English identity and start drawing inspiration from contemporary, multicultural England."

The lecture by **T. M. Devine** is concerned with the background to decolonization and specifically with its Scottish dimension. From beginning to end, the Empire provided the Scots remarkable

opportunities in trade, the professions, military service, and administration, while the structure of Scottish industry was built around
imperial markets. During the period of dissolution, however, some
Scots began to speculate that without the Empire, the Union of
Scotland and England would not hold: "Now that the Empire is
dead many Scots feel cramped and restricted at home." But more
than fifty years after the independence of India, the predictions of
the disintegration of the Union have not been fulfilled. The reasons
are to be found in historical circumstances. The British Empire had
a powerful influence on Scottish national consciousness and identity. Scottish regiments, for example, were a source of pride, and the
fame and significance of the Scottish military tradition lives on even
to the present. How then can the apparent equanimity with which
Scotland accepted decolonization be explained? There was no single cause that eroded Scotland's emotional attachment to the Empire, but it is remarkable that, though the business and professional
classes benefited immensely from imperial connections, Scottish society as a whole remained grossly unequal. The abysmal conditions
of working-class housing, mass poverty, and unemployment were
marked features of Scotland during the era of empire. After 1945,
state intervention in industry, political commitment to full employment, and the welfare state slowly brought security and material improvement. The age of empire was passing at the same time that the
Union was becoming even more important than before. Social and
economic benefits became the new anchor of the Union.

The lecture by **Dane Kennedy** considers the case to be made for
describing the United States as an empire. The concept has an ambiguous connotation, positive and negative, depending on one's vision of the part Americans should, or should not, be playing in the
world today. These views are often polemical rather than analytical. What can be learned from a straightforward comparison of the
old British Empire and the present American position in the world?
Though the United States is often described as a superpower, the
Royal Navy was as dominant in its day as American air power is today. While the American army is far more powerful relative to its
rivals than the British army ever was, the latter could deal effectively
with colonial warfare. In the economic sphere, both Britain and the
United States espoused doctrines that sometimes brought about the
transformation of other societies, and both manifested a nexus of
forces that Eisenhower described as the "military-industrial complex." The British pursued a civilizing mission—a "dual mandate" to
develop the colonies for the benefit of the inhabitants as well as the
British themselves—while the Americans, through a combination

of neoconservative and Christian fundamentalist forces, have also justified intervention on moral grounds: for example, to improve the status of women. There may be vast differences in the relative economic and military strength of the old British Empire and the United States in the world today, but there are also remarkable historical similarities.

The last lecture is short but defies summary. Read it for a humane British (or Spanish) view of American society in the wake of appalling behavior by the Atlanta police in early 2007. As of the present writing, there still has been no apology from the Mayor of Atlanta. **Felipe Fernández-Armesto** proves himself, in more ways than one, to be a latter-day Tocqueville, who visited America in the 1830s to make a study of the penal system.

1

Lloyd George, the French,
and the Germans

KENNETH O. MORGAN

"Rooted in nothing": thus Keynes's devastating critique of David Lloyd George, included in an account of the peace conference in Paris in 1919 but destined to remain unpublished for the next fourteen years. Ever since then, the wartime premier has been characterized as mercurial and erratic, variously described as a "chameleon," a "goat-footed bard," a "vampire and medium in one."[1] To the wider public, he was often seen as a man who destroyed his own Liberal Party and betrayed promises of building a land fit for heroes afterward. However, this lecture suggests that one major aspect of Lloyd George's career does in fact convey a sense of consistency, even of honor. This is his record in international affairs. At home, he was often the most baffling and kaleidoscopic of politicians. There were paradoxes aplenty in foreign affairs as well. The great warlord, the advocate of a "fight to the finish" and a "knock out blow" against Germany, was also the man who sought reconciliation at Versailles and the appeasement of Adolf Hitler. Yet even here there is some continuity, most of all in his relations with two great peoples, the French and the Germans. It was they who gave his international perspectives a sense of direction. After all, to him, as to many others, it was with France and Germany, not with the United States, that Britain enjoyed her "special relationships."

From the start, Lloyd George saw himself as a very pro-French politician. He admired Napoleon; he was greatly moved by Victor Hugo's *Les Misérables*. He enjoyed French culture, French towns on the Côte d'Azur, French men—and indeed French women whom he might encounter on the Promenade des Anglais in Nice. Like many on the British Left, from William Hazlitt to Michael Foot, he had a view of the past that was partly defined by the French Revolution, which he acclaimed as marking the downfall of feudalism. France appealed to the radical in him—democratic, republican, anti-militarist, anti-clerical. During the crisis with France over the Fashoda affair in the Sudan, in 1898, he urged that maintaining good relations with France should be the paramount consideration. He strongly supported the 1904 Entente Cordiale with France, on ideological grounds. He was much excited by the disestablishment of the church in France, in 1905, and it gave him zest in pressing for the disestablishment of the Church of England in his own Wales.

One French politician he particularly admired was Georges Clemenceau, not least for his prolonged campaign on behalf of Captain Alfred Dreyfus, a Jewish officer falsely accused of treason and sent to Devil's Island amidst a torrent of Catholic, militarist anti-Semitism. Lloyd George had an early meeting with Clemenceau in 1910, while the former was at the Treasury. It was arranged by T. P. O'Connor, the Irish Nationalist MP. But it does not seem to have gone well once their conversation switched from domestic issues to questions of Anglo-German relationships. While Lloyd George tells us in his memoirs how impressed he was, Clemenceau seems to have found the Welshman ignorant of foreign affairs and dangerously inclined to favor appeasement of Germany on naval and colonial questions. They even had different versions of how long the conversation lasted, Clemenceau believing that it was a relatively brief encounter.[2] It was symptomatic of difficulties to come.

But the pro-French Lloyd George was also very sympathetic to Germany—an enterprising, modernizing, industrializing, and, not least, Protestant Germany. The Welsh more generally admired Germany as the home of the great reformer Martin Luther, the source of several famous Welsh hymn tunes, the land of the great oratorios of Bach, Mendelssohn, and Beethoven, and the site of great universities like Heidelberg and Göttingen. Some of this was brought out in a short travel book in 1889, *Tro yn yr Almaen* (Visit to Germany), by the late-Victorian Welsh man of letters and historian Owen M. Edwards. But Lloyd George also admired a far more contemporary Germany. He hailed its nonsectarian, comprehensive, technically sophisticated education system: like others, he honored the legendary "Prussian schoolmaster," a model for many such in Wales. Lloyd

George's early political hero, Joseph Chamberlain, father of Neville, was a strong advocate of a rapprochement with Germany, and tried to create one in 1897. A vital change came when Lloyd George, in his first ministerial post, became President of the Board of Trade, between December 1905 and April 1908, a centrally important and still under-researched period of his career. Here he was hugely impressed by German commercial enterprise and technical expertise, all underpinned by a robust system of social welfare since the time of Bismarck. Lloyd George was also far less hostile to German protectionism than the more doctrinaire free-trade Liberals, and his own Patents Act (1907) and Merchant Shipping Act (1906) alarmed some purists with their nods toward the protection of British products and services. He made particular use at the Board of Trade of W. H. Dawson, a famous expert on Bismarckian Germany and the author of nearly thirty books on aspects of German social, economic, and intellectual life.[3]

France and Germany appealed to different aspects of David Lloyd George's outlook and, perhaps, personality. France appealed to the Old Liberal him with its liberal democracy and republican and egalitarian values. This chimed in with the Lloyd George of late-Victorian politics in Wales, who denounced the "unholy Trinity" of the "bishop, the brewer and the squire." Germany, by contrast, attracted the New Liberal in him—the New Liberalism of national efficiency and social welfare. There was this eternal dualism within him—and perhaps within the Welsh more generally. Increasingly throughout his career, this legendary Celt, so hailed or condemned by Keynes, thought not as a Latin but as a northern European. At some risk in the principality, perhaps, one could almost see Lloyd George as an honorary Anglo-Saxon.

Lloyd George's growing affinity with Germany, and with German rather than French values, was reinforced in his important visit to Germany in August–September 1908. It is not an episode that is well documented—the only account is a brief one in the Liberal journalist Harold Spender's autobiography, *The Fire of Life*.[4] Since going to the Treasury in April 1908, Lloyd George had been working closely with Winston Churchill, Charles Masterman, and others on an imaginative program of social reform—in part, as he made explicit, so that the Liberal government could face the challenge from Labour and the revolutionary appeal of socialism. Lloyd George then moved on to more ambitious schemes for comprehensive social insurance, invalidity pensions, health and educational reform, and labor exchanges in the employment market. He traveled from Bavaria, in the south, to Hamburg, in the far north, using one of the newfangled motorcars for the purpose. Intriguingly, the car was lent him by a Liberal MP, Sir Charles Henry, whose beautiful wife, Julia, was one of Lloyd George's parliamentary mistresses.

Lloyd George was fascinated and excited by what he saw in Germany, especially over pensions: "I had never realised before on what a gigantic scale the German pension system is conducted. . . . It touches the great mass of German people in well-nigh every walk of life."[5] He saw there a land of industrial enterprise and social cohesion. Like the Liberal Imperialists, he regarded Germany as the very embodiment of the idea of national efficiency. There were national compulsory insurance schemes, but they did not undermine voluntary effort in social provision. Germany, incidentally, made a similar impression on the former American president Theodore Roosevelt, whose New Nationalism of 1912, combining progressive reform with a strong program for national defense, Lloyd George was to find very compelling. Roosevelt was one of Lloyd George's heroes, unlike Roosevelt's old adversary Woodrow Wilson, who seemed to him inhuman: Lloyd George's *Truth about the Peace Treaties* notes bitterly Wilson's lack of compassion in Paris in 1919 when the news came through of Roosevelt's death: "I was aghast at the outburst of acrid detestation that flowed from Wilson's lips."[6] Lloyd George's own great National Insurance Act of 1911, covering comprehensive health insurance along with an initial limited program for unemployment insurance, was heavily influenced by the German model, even though Lloyd George breezily claimed that the British system ("ninepence for fourpence") actually gave better value than the German system and contained far less regimentation as well. He continued to follow up German ideas for social reform right down to the outbreak of war. Thus, with his lieutenant Dr. Christopher Addison, he was working in the summer of 1914 on ideas for building up the health centers of the national insurance system in a way that might have anticipated the efforts of another Welshman, Aneurin Bevan, in launching the National Health Service thirty-four years later.

Lloyd George's visit of 1908 pushed him in a strongly pro-German direction. But the mood of his visit changed when he turned to consider Anglo-German naval rivalry. He had a meeting with the German vice-chancellor, Bethmann Hollweg. Here he heard echoes of a different Germany—the voice of the Junker class and the military Prussian caste.[7] There was no meeting of minds between them. Lloyd George thus pressed on with reinforcing the alliance with the French. During the Agadir crisis in Morocco, in July 1911, he talked tough in the Mansion House speech, which appears to have been specifically directed against Germany. Yet even then the legacy of his early pro-Germanism could shine through. On 17 July 1914, after the Sarajevo assassination and barely a fortnight before war broke out, Lloyd George could proclaim to the world, "The sky has never seemed more relatively blue."

DURING THE FIRST WORLD WAR, AFTER AN INITIAL UNCERTAINTY when journalists wondered whether he might revert to his anti-war position from the Boer War in 1899–1902, Lloyd George became the most committed of war leaders. He drew on Liberal values and the principle of nationality to justify all-out war on behalf of "gallant little Belgium," gallant little Serbia and Montenegro, and, by extension, gallant little Wales, another of the world's "little five-foot-five nations."[8] He underlined this approach when he went to the new Ministry of Munitions in May 1915; to the War Office, in July 1916; and above all when he entered 10 Downing Street, after a famous putsch to remove Asquith, in December 1916. In the years 1917–18 he became extremely close to the French view of international affairs. There were certainly major differences. The French, naturally, were "westerners," focusing on the war in western Europe, since it was their homeland that had been invaded by the Boche. Their leaders repeatedly urged a concentration of Allied resources to defend their territorial base. Lloyd George was far more of an "easterner," favoring a more peripheral strategy, one aimed at the Balkans and eastern Mediterranean. He felt that the French did not see the importance of naval power in the war. After the catastrophic loss of life at Passchendaele in August–September 1917, Lloyd George pursued a covert policy of holding back British forces from the western front in France, partly because of his lack of trust in the competence and even the word of the British commander in chief, General Haig. But he was also very sensitive to French security needs, and for a time became a kind of hero in France. One powerful episode was his speech on 3 September 1916 during the battle of Verdun, when he delivered a moving tribute to French courage in the Verdun Citadelle itself. He spoke in English, and his French listeners found his Welsh accent hard to follow. But, said one French military observer, moved to tears by the speech, "We had no need to understand what he said."[9]

When Clemenceau became French prime minister in November 1917, he and Lloyd George began a fascinating relationship that largely dictated Anglo-French relations for the next two years. As was indicated earlier, the two premiers had, indeed, many resemblances. Clemenceau was greatly influenced by the ideas and values of English liberalism: his early inspirations were John Stuart Mill and the

positivist philosopher Herbert Spencer. He spoke good English after his visits to the United States, which began in July 1865, just after the end of the American Civil War, when he witnessed the aftermath of the funeral of Abraham Lincoln and acquired (unhappily)
a young American wife. He was accused in France of being a pro-
English politician and was heckled at political meetings with cries of
"Aoh, yes." He and Lloyd George shared similar approaches to the
world—republican values, left-wing ideas on democracy and social
reform. It should be said, though, that whereas Lloyd George showed
himself to be a great patron of the trade unions, both at the Board
of Trade and when he concluded the famous "Treasury Agreement"
with labor in 1915, Clemenceau emerged in his first premiership
(1906–09) as a fierce strikebreaker and a passionate anti-socialist
and anti-syndicalist.

Clemenceau and Lloyd George were both free spirits in political
life. Both were very image conscious, Lloyd George with his inverness
cloak and long mane of hair, Clemenceau with his cape, boots, and
cane, as depicted in his statue in Paris (also gloves to hide the eczema
on his hands). Both were acutely sensitive to the role played by the
press and other media. Clemenceau actually ran his own newspapers,
La Justice, L'Homme Libre, and (after wartime censorship) *L'Homme
Enchainé.* Lloyd George always kept up close relationships with journalists (e.g., A. G. Gardiner or Robert Donald), used his close associations with editors (e.g., C. P. Scott of the *Manchester Guardian*) and
proprietors (e.g., George Riddell of the *News of the World*), and was
always suspected of using the press during the political vacuum of
the war years to promote his designs. It was press intrigues that many
felt led to his becoming Prime Minister in December 1916. He was
even involved in the buying of newspapers (as with the *Daily News*
takeover by the anti-war Cadbury family in 1901, during the second
Boer War).[10] In August 1922, after the death of Lord Northcliffe, the
Prime Minister, astonishingly, contemplated buying up *The Times.*

Both were fairly unfussy in monetary matters. Lloyd George almost ruined his career in the share-purchase scandal of the Mar-
coni case, in 1912; earlier, Clemenceau had been heavily implicated
in the Panama Canal scandal, in 1893. Both had unusual friends,
including the wealthy arms manufacturer and international go-
between Sir Basil Zaharoff, and suffered to a degree from Jewish as-
sociates (the Isaacs brothers with Lloyd George, Cornelius Herz and
Joseph Reinach with Clemenceau). Both were to a degree woman-
izers, Lloyd George, "the Welsh goat," very conspicuously so with his
various mistresses, Clemenceau with his *amitié amoureuse* with Ma-
dame Baldensperger. And to an overwhelming degree, both were

political outsiders. Lloyd George was always a volatile party figure, with his secret proposals for an interparty coalition in 1910 and his heading an actual coalition in 1916–22. Clemenceau excluded himself from high office after losing the premiership in 1909. In 1917–18, Lloyd George and Clemenceau were effectively Prime Ministers without a party.

There were, however, marked differences of style between them. The Tiger and the Goat were both big beasts but of very different types. Clemenceau was a genuine intellectual. He actually wrote a novel, of which Maurice Barrès caustically observed, "All he needs to be successful as a novelist is to find something to say."[11] He was a close friend and patron of the painter Claude Monet: indeed, he revived Monet's career in his old age by arranging for him to have the contract to paint the *Nymphéas* (Waterlilies) cycle for the Paris Orangerie. In retirement he wrote a long book about Demosthenes, which was particularly fascinating on his oratorical style. Lloyd George, by contrast, although immensely fertile in ideas, was mercurial and intuitive, not an intellectual. He did not really share Clemenceau's cultural interests, artistic or literary. In his methods he was beguiling, whether with deputations or individuals. Keynes's essay sees him as a seductive, beautiful woman, a femme fatale.[12] In the famous phrase, Lloyd George could "charm a bird off a bough." Clemenceau, by contrast, was brusque, aggressive, confrontational. His weaponry was not merely verbal. He inspired physical fear in his opponents after fighting several duels with pistol or sabre; he was equally adept at either. He engaged in a brief sabre duel with Paul Deschanel, whom he blooded before the latter wisely fled the scene, accompanied by Clemenceau's derisive comment, "Monsieur is leaving us."[13] Deschanel was to get his own back with a vengeance in 1919, when he defeated Clemenceau in the election for the post of president of the republic. This personal and temperamental divergence between Lloyd George and Clemenceau was often to prove a source of contention over time.

They came most closely together in 1918. This was, indeed, the high point of the Entente Cordiale throughout its first hundred years. Certainly, there were many sharp passages between the two Prime Ministers, from the Abbeville conference of April 1918, with Clemenceau insistently pressing Lloyd George for more British manpower to be sent to the western front, and Lloyd George threatening to withhold naval transport from ferrying British and, later, American troops to France. This dispute remained unresolved at the armistice.[14] Yet in spite of this, Lloyd George and Clemenceau enjoyed a far better relationship than Churchill and de Gaulle were to have in 1940–45 (admittedly, in the latter case, Franklin D. Roosevelt's attitude toward the French added to the difficulties). In particular, Lloyd George and Clemenceau campaigned successfully for unity of command on the western front. They made war against an agreed-upon common enemy—the British generals, whom Lloyd George distrusted for military incompetence and for maneuvering with King George V and others to interfere politically. In the end, Marshal Foch was promoted over the Scotsman General Haig. (Incidentally, Lloyd George is quite wrong in saying in his *War Memoirs* that Clemenceau, anti-clerical and a free thinker in religion, was hostile to Foch on grounds of that general's staunch Catholicism.)[15] In the last few months of the war, after the failure of the final German push on the Amiens sector in April 1918, the impact of the American army, and the final Anglo-French advance to victory from August, the relation between Lloyd George and the French was especially close. They prepared, with some difficulty, plans for a post-war European and colonial settlement. This was notably so in the Middle East, where France took Syria, and Britain acquired as its mandate the new, artificial state of Mesopotamia, with its possibly immense oil reserves in the Mosul region. Two oil pipelines would be built across Syria from Mosul. One thing on which Lloyd George and Clemenceau agreed was that they did not want the Americans muscling in, as they threatened to do. More generally, there was joint wariness toward Woodrow Wilson's utopian schemes for reshaping the world order. Indeed, the French felt that Woodrow Wilson's Fourteen Points were inferior to Lloyd George's own proposals, delivered two days earlier, since the latter demonstrated far more realism. When war ended, in November 1918, France and Britain were comrades in arms as never before or since in history.

AT THE TIME OF THE ARMISTICE, LLOYD GEORGE was apparently in strongly anti-German mode. During the "coupon" general election, in December 1918, he referred to the need for reparations to ensure that Germany would meet the cost of the war, and urged the need for the Kaiser to face trial. But Keynes exaggerated this in his *Economic Consequences of the Peace.* The election campaign in Britain was not just a vindictive call for a Carthaginian peace. Most of what Lloyd George had to say in his few election speeches was a call for reconstruction and a better society at home. Internationally, he sought reconciliation with the Germans. The early stages of the peace conference in Paris, heavily colored by Clemenceau's urge for territorial and financial penalties to be imposed on Germany, alienated Lloyd George profoundly. Even during the war years, he had always drawn a distinction between the German Junker caste and the civilized and cultured German people. In Bangor in his Caernarfon Boroughs constituency in February 1915, he had made the contrast between "the best Germany, the Germany of sweet songs and inspiring noble thought. . . . the Germany of a virile philosophy that helped to break the shackles of superstition in Europe" and a very different Germany, which "talked through the raucous voice of Krupp's artillery, a Germany that harnessed science to the chariot of destruction and death."[16] Against the latter alone would he wage "a holy war." He offered nothing remotely like the notorious Morgenthau Plan of 1944, in which the U.S. Secretary of the Treasury, given some backing by the former Foreign Office mandarin Lord Vansittart, proposed the deindustrialization of postwar Germany and its reduction to a pastoral economy. Lloyd George wanted to restore and rebuild a secure Germany after 1918, partly out of national self-interest and not least because of his fear that otherwise this giant nation, in the very heart of Europe, would be driven into the arms of Russian Bolshevism. Indeed, the various German revolutionary upheavals in the immediate post-war period seemed to confirm Lloyd George's view of the essential need for a constructive, non-vindictive post-war settlement with the post-imperial Weimar Republic.

In the early stages of the Paris conference, the famous Fontainebleau Memorandum, of March 1919, was a high point of Lloyd George's pro-Germanism.[17] It was devised in a hotel close to the forest of Fontainebleau near Paris in consultation with a few private advisers: Maurice Hankey, Philip Kerr, General Sir Henry Wilson, and, perhaps the most influential, General Smuts of South Africa. It was the first document to place on public display the British desire for appeasement, at least in the nonpejorative sense of that many-sided term. Clemenceau noted ironically that it slid over all the problems that related to Britain itself: for instance, it specifically endorsed the contentious British right of "freedom of the seas," including the right to search vessels of foreign origin. It was without doubt a highly personal document that goes to the very heart of many of Lloyd George's preconceptions about the French and the Germans.

It made two main points. First, it urged that it was crucial for world peace that German-speaking peoples in the Saarland, Upper Silesia, Danzig, and above all the so-called "Polish Corridor" should not be placed under alien rule. There should be no more Alsace-Lorraines. A demilitarized Rhineland should remain as part of Germany, as should the Saarland. Lloyd George showed a consistent sympathy with German grievances in this respect. He was successful in arranging for a local plebiscite in Upper Silesia (where the vote

went in favor of remaining in Germany) and was always responsive
to the German population in the Sudetenland. In 1938, before and
after Munich, he showed scant regard for the Czech (as opposed to
the Slovak) point of view. This was not least because of his animosity
toward the Czech premier Benes—"that little swine Benes"—whom
he felt had been deceitful during the peace conference and at Genoa.[18] He linked this protection for ethnic minorities with a wider
call for arms limitation.

Second, although this was a lesser aspect at first, he urged that
reparation payments by Germany be kept flexible and bearable so as
not to undermine the new German republic as a trading and manufacturing nation. Lloyd George was certainly erratic on this aspect:
for instance, he insisted that reparations should include payments
of pensions to widows and orphans, which almost doubled the bill.
But during the conference negotiations in Paris, he succeeded in
handing the entire reparations issue over to a long-drawn-out technical commission, which was to try to produce a precise total for
reparations in accordance with Germany's capacity to pay. This in
effect kicked the question into the long grass and helped ensure
that most of the money sought would never be paid. The subsequent
odium fell on Lords Cunliffe and Sumner on the commission, not
on Lloyd George. Keynes could never fathom Lloyd George's tactics
here—but, then, Keynes was famously not a politician.

From the time of the signing of the Treaty of Versailles, in July
1919, Lloyd George was constantly engaged in fundamental revision of the peace treaties. He was in fact the only survivor able to
do so. Woodrow Wilson lost a compliant Congress when the Republicans triumphed in the midterm elections; he then suffered a
stroke, and the peace treaty was voted down by a heavily isolationist
Senate. In his last two years, Wilson was president in name only, and
his country remained aloof from the League of Nations thereafter.
In France, Clemenceau, now nearly eighty, resigned, and was then
defeated in the presidential election by his old dueling adversary
Deschanel. Lloyd George, however, took a long view of international
reconciliation—a view that Keynes, his sternest critic earlier, now
came to applaud.[19] Both Lloyd George and Keynes saw the vital need
for revision of the Treaty of Versailles. It was a process, not an event.

But he was also the only one of the peacemakers to attempt to
deal with French security concerns while trying to settle with Germany. In March 1919 during the conference in Paris, he offered
Clemenceau a proposal for a long-term military guarantee by Britain, which included the remarkably prescient idea of a Channel
tunnel to aid in defense collaboration.[20] In return, Clemenceau

dropped his insistence that the Rhineland be detached from Germany. But the idea of a guarantee fell through, ostensibly because the Americans, mired in isolationism, refused to involve themselves. Clemenceau felt duped and betrayed: "England is the disillusion of my life." In fairness to Lloyd George, the French had their own brand of duplicity, since Clemenceau concealed their plans for a military occupation of the Rhineland for years to come. But Lloyd George's was still a remarkably visionary idea, one that challenged old British conceptions about a continental military commitment. In peace conferences in 1920–21, he seemed to be moving toward both the objectives of Fontainebleau for international appeasement and the agreed-upon needs of French territorial security necessary to avoid a repetition of 1870 and 1914. Joined together with both was the idea of bringing newly communist Russia into the comity of nations. Here, despite much opposition from his Unionist (Conservative) coalition partners, Lloyd George succeeded in withdrawing British forces from Russia by the end of 1919, and later in concluding an Anglo-Russian trade treaty, with the prospect of full diplomatic recognition. In late 1921, he and the new French prime minister, Aristide Briand, a Breton with whom he also struck up a good working relationship, were again having serious talks about a British military and naval guarantee. At the Cannes conference, in early January 1922, there appeared to be a real prospect of a British continental commitment, of a kind not seen since Wellington wound up the Peninsula War in 1813. It was hoped that the proposal would be accepted by the French Chamber of Deputies and ratified as part of a broad European package at a large international conference to be convened in Genoa in April 1922.

In fact, the unexpected downfall of Briand's government destroyed everything. The French deputies were not amused by Briand's larking about with Lloyd George on the golf course at Cannes, and suspected Albion's usual perfidy. The conference at Genoa produced little of substance; partly it was undermined before it began by the Treaty of Rapallo, concluded between Russia and Germany through the secret diplomacy of the German foreign minister, Walter Rathenau. Things now turned very sour as the entente became anything but cordial; Lloyd George found the new French premier, Raymond Poincaré, a man from Lorraine, intransigent and nationalistic. The last phase of Lloyd George's relationship with Clemenceau also had been disagreeable. In June 1921, the old Frenchman, over in England to receive an honorary degree from Oxford University, called on the Prime Minister in his private room in the Commons. It was not a success. Clemenceau bluntly told Lloyd George, "*Dès le lendemain d'armistice je vous ai trouvé l'ennemi de France.*" Lloyd George laughed and cheerfully responded, "*Eh bien, n'est-ce pas notre politique traditionelle?*"[21] The Frenchman was not amused. Afterward, he commented that he enjoyed his solitary walks in the Vendée forests because he would not see Lloyd George there—only squirrels. Lloyd George was attacked by the French for being a peacemaker toward Germany and a warmonger toward Turkey. Poincaré shouted at Lord Curzon, the British Foreign Secretary; Curzon retaliated by bursting into tears. When Lloyd George fell from office on 19 October 1922, there was immense French rejoicing. In fact, he never returned to government again.

HENCEFORTH, LLOYD GEORGE, OUT OF POWER but still an influential voice, was seen in France as consistently pro-German. He was very critical of French policy both in the Franco-Belgian invasion of the Ruhr, with its coal and steel resources, in 1923 and in their punitive attitude toward reparation payments from Germany. In the thirties he took a more lenient view of German objectives than Churchill ever did. In 1936 he offered only mild criticism of Hitler when his armies occupied the Rhineland. Some of Lloyd George's former ministerial aides were more pro-German than he was. His former private adviser in his personal secretariat (the "Garden Suburb"), Philip Kerr, Lord Lothian, a Christian Scientist, wanted a fresh basis for Anglo-German relations founded on a long-term security pact. W. H. Dawson's pro-Germanism, even pro-Hitlerism, forced him into retirement. The former deputy secretary of the Cabinet, Lloyd George's fellow Welsh-speaking Welshman, Thomas Jones, became friendly with Ribbentrop while the latter was ambassador to Britain, and with others in All Souls, Oxford, worked assiduously to promote the appeasement of Germany.[22]

It was Jones who largely arranged Lloyd George's ominous visit to Hitler at Berchtesgaden in September 1936. It may be seen as bracketing his career, along with the very different visit to Germany back in 1908. This time Lloyd George went to the top—literally so, since he met Hitler in the Berghof, close to what later became his "Eagles' Nest" retreat at Berchtesgaden, where he enjoyed a stunning overview of the Bavarian Alps. Lloyd George was accompanied by several fellow countrymen: Thomas Jones; a somewhat mysterious Germanophile Welsh academic, Dr. T. P. Conwell-Evans; and his distinctly reluctant daughter, Megan Lloyd George.[23] Why on earth did Lloyd George go? Was it the product of his disdain for the national government of Stanley Baldwin, which refused to take Lloyd George's "New Deal" plans for economic recovery seriously?

Was it dismay at the failure to deal with the legitimate territorial grievances of the Germans, notably in the Sudetenland? Was it the simple vanity of an old man of seventy-three who felt that, yet again, he could use his authority to save the world? Lloyd George did some touring, looked at German public-works schemes, admired roads and schools, even met a few German fellow Baptists. He said nothing about the travails of the Jews, already being savagely persecuted. He had long talks with Hitler in which each flattered the other at length, and received a signed photo from the genial Führer. In the newspaper of the pro-appeasement Lord Beaverbrook, the *Daily Express,* Lloyd George called for a long-term pact of mutual guarantee with Germany. He wrote of the "new spirit of gaiety and cheerfulness" that he detected in Hitler's Germany. Hitler himself, in a phrase that was to haunt Lloyd George's reputation thereafter, he described as "the George Washington of Germany."[24]

Lloyd George, always unsympathetic to Benes and the cause of Czechoslovakia, was a late convert to confronting Hitler, although he did vote against the Munich agreement, whereas Churchill only abstained. In 1939, Lloyd George was a powerful critic of a guarantee to Poland, but after conversations with the Russian ambassador, Ivan Maisky, he presciently commented that it would mean little enough without an alliance with the Soviet Union. Long after war had been declared, he called for peace negotiations with the Germans. His talks with the American Under Secretary of State, Sumner Welles, in March 1940 focused on the Allies' failure to revise the peace treaties of 1919–23 and to offer Germany a secure guaranteed role commensurate with its power. It was, said Lloyd George, irrational to fight a great country that had thrown off its Hohenzollern past. The war was "the most unnecessary, the most insanely stupid that had ever been forced upon England."[25] In May 1940, his powerful onslaught on his old adversary Neville Chamberlain helped considerably to sway Commons opinion and install Churchill as Prime Minister. Yet Lloyd George was still thought of as a difficult, perhaps defeatist, figure. He would not join the Churchill government, nor take the post of Ambassador to Washington when Lord Lothian died. It simply was not his war. He now condemned the policy of "unconditional surrender" that he himself had eloquently championed in 1917.

At the end of his career, Lloyd George was again identified with France—but the wrong France. After a particularly negative speech in the Commons, his last major one there, on 7 May 1941, Lloyd George found himself condemned by Churchill as "Old Papa Pétain," undermining British morale with defeatist utterances as "the illustrious and venerable Marshal Pétain" had done during the Ramadier government in France in June 1940. It was said that the German Abwehr, absurdly, even saw him as a possible gauleiter for an occupied Wales.

In many of his attitudes on foreign and imperial policy, Lloyd George was distinctly erratic—toward the League of Nations or India, for example. But on Anglo-French and Anglo-German relations, greater consistency can be detected, even if qualifications are needed here too. He was a strong champion both of the Entente Cordiale, which reached its zenith during his premiership, and of seeing Germany as a natural ally. He genuinely tried, especially in 1919–22, to reconcile the French need for homeland security with the territorial and economic aspirations of a re-emergent, ethnically united Germany. In the event, like everyone else, including Churchill, he failed. The world in the later twentieth century of Franco-German reconciliation was the work of de Gaulle and Adenauer after 1945. Ours is not the world Lloyd George made.

Or is it? Let us look beyond the ancient feuds of the Teuton and the Gaul. In the past thirty years, successive British governments have encountered supreme problems in three countries above all—Northern Ireland, Palestine, Iraq. They all have one thing in common. Like all things wise and wonderful, Lloyd George made them all.

Spring Semester 2007

1. J. M.Keynes, *Essays in Biography* (London, 1961 edn.), pp. 35–36.

2. David Lloyd George, *War Memoirs* (London, 1938), Vol. II, pp. 1608–10.

3. *Oxford Dictionary of National Biography*, s.v. "W. H. Dawson," (Oxford, 2004).

4. Harold Spender, *The Fire of Life* (London, n.d. [1920]), pp. 161–66.

5. E. P. Hennock, *British Social Reform and German Precedents* (Oxford, 1987), pp. 149–50.

6. David Lloyd George, *The Truth about the Peace Treaties* (London, 1938), Vol. 1, p. 232.

7. Lloyd George, *War Memoirs*, Vol. I, pp. 17–19.

8. Queen's Hall speech, 19 Sept. 1914, printed in David Lloyd George, *From Terror to Triumph* (London, 1915), pp. 8–9.

9. Ian Ousby, *The Road to Verdun* (London, 2003), p. 256.

10. Stephen Koss, *The Rise and Fall of the Political Press* (London, 1981), Vol. I, pp. 397–400.

11. William Logue, *Leon Blum: The Formative Years, 1872–1914* (De Kalb, Ill.), p. 91.

12. Keynes, *Essays in Biography*, p. 34.

13. Jean Baptiste Duroselle, *Clemenceau* (Paris, 1988), pp. 432–37.

14. Elizabeth Grenhalgh, *Victory through Coalition: Britain and France during the First World War* (Cambridge, 2005), and "David Lloyd George, Georges Clemenceau, and the 1918 Manpower Crisis," *Historical Journal*, 50, 2 (June 2007), pp. 397–421. See also David Dutton, *The Politics of Diplomacy: Britain and France in the First World War* (London, 1998), pp. 170–80.

15. Lloyd George, *War Memoirs*, Vol. II, pp. 1717–18.

16. Lloyd George, *From Terror to Triumph*, p. 88 (Bangor speech, 28 Feb. 1915).

17. Printed in Lloyd George, *The Truth about the Peace Treaties*, Vol. 1, pp. 404–16.

18. Colin Cross (ed.), *A. J. Sylvester: Life with Lloyd George* (London, 1975), p. 219 (entry of 5 Oct. 1938).

19. See J. M. Keynes, *A Revision of the Treaty* (London, 1922).

20. Georges Clemenceau, *Grandeurs et Miseres d'une Victoire* (Paris, 1928), pp. 200ff.

21. Duroselle, *Clemenceau*, p. 879.

22. E. L. Ellis, *A Life of Dr. Thomas Jones, C.H.* (Cardiff, 1992), pp. 402–03.

23. A. Lentin, *Lloyd George and the Lost Peace* (Basingstoke, 2001), p. 93.

24. *Daily Express*, 17 Sept. 1936.

25. *Foreign Relations of the United States, Diplomatic Papers, 1940:* special mission to Europe of Sumner Welles, pp. 85–86: meeting with David Lloyd George, 13 Mar. 1940.

2

The Story of Frances Stevenson
and David Lloyd George

SUSAN PEDERSEN

Imagine you are hired, fresh out of college at the age of twenty-one, as tutor to the teenage daughter of the Chancellor of the Exchequer. The Chancellor's wife is away in the country much of the time; her husband wanders about 11 Downing Street in his carpet slippers. He looks at you a lot, and brushes up against you in the hallway when he passes. He has a terrible reputation, you know, but if you are honest with yourself, you have to admit you quite fancy him. The tension in the house becomes palpable (although your charge, convinced that her father loves her alone, is thankfully oblivious of it), and after some months the Chancellor pops the question. Will you be his secretary, on the understanding that he gets to sleep with you as well? He will not leave his wife for you, he will not destroy his career, but as the confidante and adviser of one of the government's brightest stars, you will share a good slice of his life.

What woman would agree to this unequal bargain? Well, early in 1913, when Lloyd George was the Chancellor making the proposal, Frances Stevenson, the daughter of a Scots accountant and his part-French, part-Italian wife, did so. And I, for one, can understand her. It is not just that I have always had a soft spot for Lloyd George, who was a flesh and blood human, thank the Lord, and not one of those conscience-laden stick figures in morning coats that the Edwardian Liberal Party produced in such numbers. It is also that so few real opportunities were open to a young woman with a head for politics in that era. There was the suffrage movement, of course, but the exalted martyrdom of the Pankhurst-led militants did not appeal to everyone, and a slightly older cabal of Newnham and Somerville graduates already had the leadership of the more sensible constitutionalist wing sewn up. The few elected women in local government were usually middle-aged spinsters with impressive records of volunteer work; even when suffrage was granted and a few women entered Parliament, they rarely gained entree to the clubby, masculine heart of political life. Only a few wives or daughters saw much of that world, and even they withdrew when, say, the Foreign Secretary and his German counterpart had a chat about naval requirements. A private secretary might be there, though, taking a few notes in the corner. Not without a moral struggle, Stevenson said yes.

Thus began a partnership that would last until Lloyd George's death, thirty-two years later. Stevenson acted as Lloyd George's private secretary through the second half of his Chancellorship, his periods at the Ministry of Munitions and the War Office, his six years as Prime Minister, and his subsequent decades in opposition. She accompanied him on official travels, including to Paris for the peace negotiations and to San Remo in 1920, headed up his private office after his fall in 1922, shared in planning his many opposition initiatives and campaigns, and prepared material for his multivolume *War Memoirs*—a project that absorbed considerable time in the mid-1930s. Through these years, she was also his mistress, maintaining a London flat but often staying at Lloyd George's house in Surrey whenever his wife, Margaret, was (as she often was) in Wales. Neither Stevenson nor Lloyd George was entirely faithful: he had a notoriously roving eye, and she a serious relationship with Colonel Thomas F. Tweed, a political associate of Lloyd George's, in the late 1920s. The relationship was, however, passionate and lasting, bringing happiness to both. It also burdened Frances with as many as three abortions before she finally insisted on bearing a child (which Lloyd George certainly thought his own) in 1929, when she was forty. The two finally married, over his daughters' implacable opposition, in 1943, two years after Margaret's death; the bride was fifty-five and the groom eighty.

A fair number of people—from key members of Lloyd George's political and personal staff to, from 1916, his wife—knew of this liaison, and a great many others must have suspected it, but in Lloyd George's lifetime it never was publicly exposed. Margaret and David Lloyd George continued to share houses, vacations, family cares, and political duties, and Stevenson's very proper demeanor and genuine competence at her job warded off suspicion. But the real reason this triangular relationship endured unmolested was surely that all three principals, in some crucial sense, played by the rules. Today, allegations of sexual infidelity can wreck ministerial careers and (nearly) bring Presidents down; three-quarters of a century ago, a nicely pragmatic hypocrisy prevailed. As John Grigg remarked, discussing just this relationship, the view was that marriage "was an institution whose maintenance was in the public interest," one that politicians were expected to uphold in public—the compensation being that private arrangements (provided they were kept out of the divorce courts and the scandal sheets) were discreetly overlooked.[1] Herbert Henry Asquith, Lloyd George's arch-rival and then boss, pouring out epistolary love and war secrets in equal measure to the young Venetia Stanley in 1915, certainly understood this, and Stevenson did as well. "So long as a man, or a woman, kept the conventions outwardly, the public would excuse or ignore his private behaviour," she wrote in a blunt comment about Edward VIII's decision to renounce the throne to marry his mistress—an act Lloyd George found ridiculous and unpatriotic in equal measure.[2] Frances rather agreed.

THAT ERA IS DEFINITELY BEHIND US. Today, we profess to hold politicians to the most stringent standards of marital fidelity while relishing every salacious detail when they fall short. The appearance of *If Love Were All: The Story of Frances Stevenson and David Lloyd George,* a new book by the historian and biographer John Campbell, makes it clear just how far we have come. Little of the book's content is a revelation, for the basic contours of this relationship became known with the publication of Stevenson's memoir and then of A. J. P. Taylor's editions of Stevenson's diary and the couple's letters in the early 1970s.[3] The emphasis has, however, shifted. A story that Stevenson told as one of love and devotion ("nothing I could ever do would be so worth while as to help this man")[4] and that Taylor's editions treat partly as a great political partnership becomes, in Campbell's hands, something more tempestuous—"a romantic adventure, made up of love, sacrifice and destiny." Everything about this book—its powder-blue dustjacket illustrated with composite cameos, its cloying title, its forensic attention to the timetable of clandestine meetings—places it within the genre of popular romance.

Now, there is certainly something to this. Letters from "your old Pop" to "my girl" or from "Pussy" to "my own darling little man," scraps of doggerel verse, occasional erotic meditations, and Stevenson's unpublished but heartfelt fiction all attest to the strength of the pair's emotional and sexual bond. Although Stevenson's diary and

letters were mostly about politics, by extracting particular passages
and mining some additional sources—notably the memoirs of Lloyd
George's creepily prurient assistant A. J. Sylvester and Stevenson's
stabs at fiction—Campbell has plenty of material to write a behind-
the-front-door (though not quite beneath-the-sheets) account of
this particular love. Yet reading my way through love letters, family
arguments, speculations about the parentage of Stevenson's daughter, Jennifer, and observations on Lloyd George's sexual obsessions,
I felt a mounting sense of unease. It is not that the details Campbell
dwells on are, taken individually, inaccurate, but taken together they
add up to a very partial portrait of these two people—and, I would
suggest, of their relationship as well.

To begin with, a portrait of Lloyd George that leaves politics out
effaces almost everything that made him Lloyd George. Rather like
Bill Clinton, Lloyd George lived for politics: it was, from his early
manhood, the arena in which he ruthlessly pursued personal ambitions and radical political goals. The years with Frances Stevenson were, moreover, his years of greatest achievement and power.
Between 1913 and his death, Lloyd George ran several ministries;
led two governments; prosecuted a major war; dealt with serious
social insurrection; hammered out peace treaties or stabilization
strategies for Europe, Ireland and India; broke, then remade, and
then broke with his party; launched a number of recovery plans,
"new deals," and comeback schemes—and when most of this was
over, wrote something like a million words of memoir. Campbell,
author of an excellent earlier study of Lloyd George in opposition,
is well aware of all this hyperactivity: indeed, it may have been out
of a scrupulous historian's wish to refrain from revisiting pastures
already plowed that he pays so little mind to it here.[5]

Yet however well meant, this was a poor choice, for the simple reason that Lloyd George has become, in the thirty years since that earlier book, something less than a household name. Simply telling the
reader to "be aware that LG was the dominant personality on the
political stage from the turbulent Edwardian period of the People's
Budget and the House of Lords crisis (1909–11), right through his
wartime and postwar premiership (1916–22) and well into the interwar period" just will not suffice, especially when we more often see
him shuttling between his women or pinching the odd farmgirl at
Churt than struggling to rebuild the Liberal Party or (even in opposition) keeping a research and political staff of twenty hard at work.
Campbell does pause over the depressing and disturbing story of
Lloyd George's cowardice and defeatism during the Second World
War, but fails to put it in the context of his record in office and

of his unwearying opposition campaigns in favor of a more activist economic and foreign policy in the twenties and thirties. As a result, we get a rather skewed sense of the man as a whole.

And the same can be said for Stevenson. We hear a great deal about her flirtations, pregnancies, vacations, and social life; much less about the political work that absorbed her, daily, for almost thirty years. Campbell, indeed, seems rather uncertain about what she actually *did,* but anyone who has used the Lloyd George papers, and discovered therein Stevenson's letters to Lloyd George's collaborators and admirers, should have little trouble answering that question. Frances was a consummate political secretary, with the emphasis on "political" quite as much as "secretary": she acted as gatekeeper but also as surrogate, flattering and placating suppliants and dispensing the soothing impression that their views were Lloyd George's own. Over the years, she developed acute political judgment, which she deployed while handling politicians, leaking information, and anonymously writing for the *Sunday Times* ("very proud of myself," she uncharacteristically wrote in her diary about her series on international statesmen).[6] Campbell notes the depth of her involvement in every plan and crisis, registering that, for example, her diary for November 1921 is devoted almost entirely to Irish affairs, but he tells us almost nothing about those concerns. Instead, by lingering over the spectacle of Stevenson flirting with the Quai d'Orsay's Philippe Berthelot or dining with the Prince of Wales, he makes her appear more frivolous or power-seeking—in a word, more *mistressy*—than she was.

Our eyes relentlessly trained on the personal, we also fail to catch just how central politics was to the emotional economy of the relationship itself. Yes, it was based on love, but politics—the hard, daily work of politics—was the soil for that love's thriving. "Beloved let us love so well, / Our work shall still be better for our love, / And still our love be sweeter for our work, / And both, commended for the sake of each, / By all true workers and true lovers born," Lloyd George wrote, leadenly but with foresight, at the outset of their long affair. He was certainly besotted with Stevenson and made her his secretary in order to make her his lover, but it is fair to say that she would not have remained his mistress for forty years had she not been his very competent secretary as well. As John Grigg bluntly but quite accurately wrote, although it suited Lloyd George to be in love, he was too politically driven and too busy to tolerate "a serious love affair involving a lot of to-ing and fro-ing" for long;[7] it was, then, a great convenience for him to have a mistress who was in the next office and also took excellent notes. But if Lloyd George shaped his love to suit his ambitions, so too did Stevenson. It was not that she slept with a man old enough to be her father in order to get ahead (although plenty of women have done so); it is that she found his power erotic and loved to share it. She felt the humiliation of having to duck out of sight when Lloyd George's wife or his fiercely jealous daughter Megan arrived, but she loved her "front-row seat in the theatre of politics" and knew that she shared his life more fully as his secretary-mistress than she would have done as his wife.[8] She was more devastated than he was when he fell, and she was just as determined to see him climb back.

CAMPBELL SEES THE TENSIONS AND CONFLICTS; he tracks the passions and reconciliations. But the framework he has chosen constricts him, making him surprisingly incurious about how the thousands of hours the two spent in meetings and cabals affected their relationship and Lloyd George's political course alike. This is a shame, for their romance was moderate and in many ways conventional; it was the cross-generational, cross-gender political collaboration that was atypical and remains inadequately explored. Plenty of Lloyd George's contemporaries had mistresses, while both of his great prime ministerial rivals—H. H. Asquith and Stanley Baldwin—maintained complex emotional relationships with young women while keeping their marriages intact.[9] Lloyd George was unusual in that he integrated his young lover, entirely and forever, into his political establishment, providing himself with a more loyal and effective ally that any of his contemporaries had. Frances Stevenson may have been the most influential female political secretary until Harold Wilson's right-hand woman, Marcia Williams, but you would never know it from this book.

Does that matter? I think it does. Stevenson's conquest of the role of secretary seems much less momentous and interesting than her conquest of a Prime Minister's heart, but, historically speaking, it is the former achievement that may have been more significant. Women had begun entering the civil service before 1914, but mainly as stenographers and typists; only with the call-up of men did large numbers enter government service. Most of those women were drummed out to make space for ex-servicemen after 1918, but a few willing to forgo marriage (which resulted in dismissal) and battle their way up the ranks clung on. And some of those dismissed looked elsewhere—including, after 1919, to Geneva, where their efficiency, literate prose, impeccable social skills, and correct French (not to mention their willingness to do political and administrative work while holding clerical posts and receiving clerical rates of pay) made them indispensable to the running of the League of Nations, the International Labour Organization, and a welter of other international humanitarian lobbies and groups. A mix of curiosity, ideals, and ambition drove these women, and if the men on whose doors they knocked let them in mostly out of desperation or (in Lloyd George's case) desire, that move toward desegregation was more consequential than anyone could imagine. The female secretary, and not just the suffragist, opened up the political world.[10]

If we want to find the mother lode of attraction and excitement in this most political relationship, then we might do better to look in the office rather than the bedroom. Instead, by focusing so relentlessly on the private, Campbell unintentionally succeeds in making Lloyd George what he never was in life: boring. Love letters are riveting, no doubt, when written to oneself, but except in the hands of especially anguished and literary lovers, they tend to be repetitive and tedious. Lloyd George's are distinctly commonplace and often trail off incomprehensibly (to me, but also—less forgivably—to Stevenson) into Welsh. "Yours is the tenderest & purest love of my life Pussy *bach anwyl aur*," he writes in 1915; "I do want to get back to Pussy *bach anwyl aur chus melyn siwgr mel yn gariad I gyd bob tamaid o honi* & all the rest which I dare not commit to writing," he adds in 1920. Thanks to the zeal of the gutter press, we know that Prince Charles harbored a desire to be a tampon; Lloyd George, in the summer of 1918, wanted to be a cold: "I have been envying that cold and wishing I were in it. In the dead of night I should have crept down to the lips & had a great time—pressing their softness & then scampering along those pearly teeth—then touching the top of the tongue—then back to the lip." Campbell mourns the many letters that passed between the two that were destroyed, but given the very full tranche quoted here, it is hard to share his grief. As it is, one leaves the book with the slightly soiled feeling of the voyeur without the compensatory thrill of having at least seen something especially interesting.

Stevenson, who watched Lloyd George persuade trade unionists into no-strike pledges and Irish nationalists into loyalty oaths, did not mind his limitations as a writer of love letters—although she did read more gifted practitioners with pleasure. "Have you read the love-letters of Abelard & Héloise?" she wrote him in July 1919, when he was in Wales with his wife. The letters were wonderful, she thought, but rather sad; she would not advise him to read them. "They did not manage things very well," she concluded rather smugly, "& I think I know two people who would have arranged things better."

Lloyd George and Stevenson did arrange things rather better, satisfying not only themselves but also, in some measure, Margaret, who did not like the relationship but preferred it to living year-round in London with her exhausting husband. This arrangement was both politically and personally functional, but only on a political level was it consequential (or indeed very interesting). That is as it should be, for although Lloyd George set out to remake British politics, he was neither a sex reformer nor a bohemian, and had no interest in remaking the institution of marriage. International borders and British political institutions still bear traces of the forms that Lloyd George (with Stevenson at his side) pressed upon them; marriage, by contrast, survived their discreet private arrangements intact. I, then, am rather relieved that Campbell found himself unable to turn this story into a bodice ripper. Lloyd George—a man who could charm birds off trees, who could make rural allotments interesting, and who, for my money, is still the most significant twentieth-century Prime Minister—may not now be well remembered, but at least he will not be remembered mostly for having slept with his secretary.

Summer 2007

A version of this lecture appeared in the *London Review of Books,* 25 January 2007.

1. John Grigg, *Lloyd George: From Peace to War, 1912–1916* (London, 1985), p. 84.

2. Quoted in John Campbell, *If Love Were All: The Story of Frances Stevenson and David Lloyd George* (London, 2006), p. 162.

3. Frances Stevenson, *The Years That Are Past* (London, 1967) and *Lloyd George: A Diary by Frances Stevenson,* ed. A. J. P. Taylor (New York, 1971); Taylor also published an edition of the letters as *My Darling Pussy: The Letters of Lloyd George and Frances Stevenson, 1913–1941* (London, 1975).

4. Quoted in Campbell, *If Love Were All,* p. 46.

5. John Campbell, *Lloyd George: The Goat in the Wilderness, 1922–1931* (London, 1977).

6. Stevenson, *Lloyd George: A Diary,* p. 223.

7. Grigg, *From Peace to War,* p. 80.

8. Campbell, *If Love Were All,* p. 269.

9. H. H. Asquith's passionate attachment to Venetia Stanley is displayed in Michael and Eleanor Brocks, eds., *H. H. Asquith: Letters to Venetia Stanley* (Oxford, 1982). Stanley Baldwin's close relationship with Joan Dickinson can be traced through Philip Williamson and Edward Baldwin, eds., *Baldwin Papers* (Cambridge, 2004).

10. Little has been written on the rise and role of the secretary, but see Meta Zimmeck, "Strategies and Stratagems for the Employment of Women in the British Civil Service, 1919–1939," *Historical Journal,* 27, 4 (1984), pp. 901–24.

3

The Changing Shape
of Historical Interpretation

KEITH THOMAS

In 1966 the *Times Literary Supplement* devoted three issues to "New Ways in History." They were orchestrated by the restless medievalist Geoffrey Barraclough, who had turned from the Middle Ages to contemporary history in the belief that recent world events had made irrelevant the austerely remote tradition of scholarship in which he had been raised. Many of the contributors must have been chosen in the hope that they would adopt an aggressively forward-looking tone, and they did not disappoint. M. I. Finley, one of the few classical historians in those days whom modern historians would have recognized as deserving the name, deplored his colleagues' intellectual isolation, their ignorance of sociology, and their failure to confront "central human problems." E. P. Thompson, whose book *The Making of the English Working Class* had appeared in 1963, attacked "the established constitutional and parliamentary-political Thing" in the name of history from below. The anonymous author of the leading article (Barraclough himself) asserted that historians should align themselves with the social sciences by tackling the questions "which ordinary people wanted answering." Sir Isaiah Berlin, he added unkindly, was wrong to dismiss "scientific" history as a "chimera"; a younger generation of historians had passed him by.

The opening article was even more confrontational. It asserted that the first half of the twentieth century was "a time when most historians temporarily lost their bearings," and declared that "academic history, for all its scholarly rigour, had succeeded in explaining remarkably little about the workings of human society or the fluctuations in human affairs." The remedy, it suggested, was not to "grub away in the old empirical tradition," but to forge a closer relationship with the social sciences, especially social anthropology, sociology, and social psychology, to develop a more sophisticated conceptual vocabulary, and to employ statistical techniques. The future lay with the computer, which would replace the "stout boots" worn by the advanced historians of the previous generation. In the United States, the new econometric history was already "sweeping all before it."

Forty years later, the author of those brash words still bears the scars inflicted in the resulting furor. Not only did Isaiah Berlin take some convincing that I was not the anonymous leader writer, but by an unfortunate piece of timing, I had invited that outstanding grubber in the empirical tradition, G. R. Elton, to an Oxford college dinner in the week after my article appeared. It was a chilly evening. My guest went back to Cambridge to write *The Practice of History* (1967), a robust rejection of all new ways in history in general and of my views in particular. It was a faint consolation to find, in the "index of historians" appended to that work, the name Thomas making an incongruous appearance between those of Tacitus and Thucydides.

HOW DO THE CONFIDENT PREDICTIONS AND PRESCRIPTIONS of 1966 look now? Some were patently off target. Econometric history has not swept all before it; on the contrary, its intimidating formulae and rebarbative style have been partly responsible for the regrettable lack of interest shown by many of today's historians in economic history of any kind. Social history has not become a central subject around which other branches of history are organized, but has in its turn been overtaken by the newer genre of cultural history. There is more cooperative scholarship and organized research than there used to be, but the "individualist, prima donna tradition" against which the polemicists of 1966 inveighed is, in the age of stars like Simon Schama and Niall Ferguson, more alive than ever.

On the other hand, the computer has outperformed all expectations. Who in 1966 would have guessed that today's historians would order their library books online, take their laptops to the archives, scroll through searchable databases, and become highly dependent upon such electronic aids as Early English Books on Line (EEBO) and Eighteenth Century Collections Online (ECCO)?

Quantitative history has some spectacular achievements to its credit, like the anthropometric studies of changes over time in human height and weight, or the reconstruction of British population history in the pre-census era by the Cambridge Group for the History of Population and Social Structure. William St Clair's work *The Reading Nation in the Romantic Period* (2004) shows that counting can illuminate the history of culture no less than that of the economy. Nevertheless, it is obvious that only limited aspects of the past can be understood in this way and that the precision offered by figures is often spurious. The thrust of most modern historical writing is qualitative rather than quantitative. The dream that historians in white coats would bring scientific certainty to the study of the past now seems just another delusion of the 1960s, that optimistic decade when Harold Wilson invoked the "white heat" of technology.

Yet though history has not become a social science, it is much closer to adjacent disciplines than it used to be. Roderick Floud and Pat Thane recently lamented that "there is little sign of the partnership between history and sociology which seemed in prospect forty years ago." But even if sociologists remain resolutely unhistorical, many historians are firmly sociological. In his *Classes and Cultures: England, 1918–1951* (1998), for example, Ross McKibbin draws on the work of almost every prominent British sociologist from Ralf Dahrendorf and J. H. Goldthorpe to A. H. Halsey and W. G. Runciman.

Social and cultural anthropology are now accepted as part of the everyday equipment for investigating the history of such subjects as religion, kinship, ritual, or gift exchange. There is a greater sense of the otherness of the past, and many historians conceive of their subject as a kind of retrospective ethnography. Who would have guessed in 1966 that the history of witchcraft would become a staple topic on the undergraduate curriculum? The influence of social anthropology is equally evident in the widespread preoccupation with "the native's point of view." Instead of trying to classify and order human experience from the outside—as if historical actors were butterflies, and historians entomologists—much imaginative effort has gone into the re-creation of the way things appeared to people at the time. This shift from the etic to the emic, as the linguists would call it, involves an enhanced concern with the meaning of events for those who participated in them and a new respect for what people in the past thought and felt. Back in the 1950s, it was common to disparage ideas as mere rationalizations of self-interest. Today, even the hardest-nosed historians seek to recapture the vocabulary, categories, and subjective experiences of historical actors, rather than anachronistically viewing their behavior through modern spectacles.

This approach has been reinforced by the declining appeal of Marxism, with its tendency to dismiss conscious thought as mere "superstructure," and by a revived interest in the philosophy of R. G. Collingwood, who saw history as the reenactment of past experience. It is as evident in the enterprising attempts of social historians to reconstruct the values of the semi-literate as it is in the historical study of political thought by Quentin Skinner and J. G. A. Pocock and the high intellectual history of scholarship practiced by polymaths like Anthony Grafton, Ian Maclean, and Noel Malcolm.

During the last forty years, historians have learned from many other disciplines. Geographers have taught them to study the physical environment and to map patterns of human settlement. Archaeologists have stimulated students of all periods into looking beyond written sources to the physical remains of the past, whether artifacts, buildings, or landscape. Art historians who have moved from high art to the study of visual culture have fostered a much greater sensitivity to history's visual dimension than was evident forty years ago, when it was highly unusual for a serious history book to carry any illustrations at all, let alone the colored ones we expect nowadays. Literary scholars have accustomed historians to the notion that plays, poems, and novels, sensitively employed, can yield insights just as rewarding as those derived from state papers or parish registers.

The plea made in 1966 for greater use of theory has also been abundantly answered. Much of the historiography of the late twentieth century can be explained as a response to the delayed impact of Malthus, Marx, Durkheim, Weber, Keynes, Freud, Collingwood, Evans-Pritchard, J. L.Austin, Lévi-Strauss, Bakhtin, Elias, Geertz, Kuhn, Foucault, Habermas, Bourdieu, Benedict Anderson, and others. This is unsurprising, for what happens in one generation in economics, psychology, sociology, philosophy, or anthropology will usually be reflected in the history writing of the next, even if its authors have never read a word by the theorists concerned. The great change during the last forty years is that historians have become much more self-conscious about their borrowings. It is difficult to open a work of academic history these days without encountering a reference to "discourse" or "thick description" or "paradigms" or "bricolage" or "the public sphere" or "path dependency" or "the civilizing process" or "imagined communities," none of them terms that would have meant very much in 1966. Nowadays, when young practitioners review the works of their elders, their most frequent criticism is that they are "under-theorized," a charge that would once have evoked mere puzzlement.

No one in 1966 foresaw the impact of the various linguistic and literary theories known as post-structuralism and post-modernism. Their adherents caused some perturbation in the 1980s, when it seemed that these modern skeptics were denying the possibility of achieving any certain knowledge of the past. But that nihilistic doctrine has been tacitly rejected. Most practicing historians today take a commonsensical view. They are critical of their sources and do not need to be told that they are not a mirror of reality. They know that the categories they use and the periods into which they divide up history are expository devices, not intrinsic features of the past. They are aware that many so-called facts are contestable and that events look different to different observers. But they also know that things really did happen in the past and that historians can often find out what they were. The outcome can be seen in acute methodological self-consciousness of the kind displayed by C. J. Wickham in his prize-winning *Framing the Middle Ages* (2005). Every term employed is carefully defined; the first person singular is frequently used, by way of disclaiming any pretense to oracular authority; and the very title indicates that the book records a continuing process of "construction."

British historians have been less afflicted than some of their North American colleagues by epistemological uncertainties about the difference between fact and fiction. But the so-called linguistic turn has made them more sensitive to the rhetorical conventions and ideological presuppositions that shape the books they write and the documents they study. The boom in studies of past historiography has alerted them to the way that self-interested groups construct versions of the past to serve partisan objectives. *The Invention of Tradition,* edited by Eric Hobsbawm and Terence Ranger (1983), and Pierre Nora's *Les lieux de mémoire* (1984–92) are the two great landmarks here.

Many historians now believe, perhaps rather perversely, that what happened in the past is less important than what people thought had happened. This conviction helps account for the decline of "hard" economic history. It is also the reason that social history, once envisaged as the detached study of supposedly objective groupings like families, households, communities, and classes, has, since the 1980s, been mutating into cultural history, seen as an account of the mental assumptions and linguistic practices of the people involved. The change, lucidly chronicled by Cambridge's first professor of cultural history, Peter Burke, is admirably exemplified in Stuart

Clark's meticulous study of a totally vanished system of thought, *Thinking With Demons* (1997).

All this helps explain the reluctance of most present-day historians to embark upon large-scale narratives mapping the course of historical change over long periods. Despite the efforts of today's television historians, the genre has been discredited by the teleological triumphalism and ideological intent with which such narratives are usually infused. An even greater discouragement is an enhanced sense of the sheer complexity of the past and the impossibility of embodying in a single, selective account the infinitely numerous points of view from which it can be legitimately surveyed. Few manage to achieve the magisterial objectivity of J. H. Elliott's *Empires of the Atlantic World* (2006), a comparative history of the British and Spanish empires over more than three centuries. Hence the recourse to microhistory, the attempt to see the world in a grain of sand by intensively studying small communities, single events, or even individuals, on the model of Emmanuel Le Roy Ladurie's *Montaillou* (1975) or *The Great Cat Massacre* by Robert Darnton (1984).

The greatest triumph for the polemicists of 1966 has been the way that the subject matter of history has broadened beyond recognition, so that it now embraces all those topics of human concern about whose neglect they complained. In the early 1960s, history still meant politics, the constitution, war, and diplomacy, with economic history a poor relation, often in a separate department. (When I examined in the Oxford History School in 1961, one of my co-examiners, Dame Lucy Sutherland, set a paper on modern British history that was almost entirely political. I pointed out that there was nothing on the industrial revolution. "No," she said, "that came up last year.") Today, political history has survived, but only by broadening its focus to include the study of political culture and extending its range to include the politics of smaller units, like the factory or the family. Military and naval history are exceptionally vigorous, with a huge lay following for accounts of battles and campaigns, not all of them intellectually demanding. But every aspect of human experience now has its historians, from childhood to old age, from dress to table manners, from smells to laughter, from sport to shopping, from barbed wire to masturbation.

An instructive comparison is afforded by the volume on the Normans and Angevins in the old and new Oxford histories of England. In 1951, A. L. Poole offered an essentially political narrative, with some chapters on the economic and social background. In 2000, Robert Bartlett started with politics, but then embarked on a retrospective ethnography, covering everything from concepts of the holy to hairstyles, with a whole page on attitudes to crocodiles.

WHERE, THEN, DO WE LOOK FOR TODAY'S NEW WAYS IN HISTORY? There can be no single answer, for history has become a crowded and heterogeneous field, characterized by an astonishing diversity of approach. There is no agreement about what is central and what is peripheral, and little sense of participation in a common intellectual enterprise. The historical profession is enormous; each year, some ten thousand people publish books or articles on British and Irish history alone. The Stakhanovite ethos prevailing in research-driven universities has resulted in a torrent of publications that threaten to overwhelm anyone who attempts to study more than the tiniest area of the past. Writing serious history is a much more difficult undertaking than it was in the 1960s, when there were so many unexplored areas and when gifted writers like Eric Hobsbawm or Lawrence Stone could sketch out bold synoptic articles in *Past and Present*. Today, the crippling accumulation of specialized knowledge means that one has to work very much harder to say anything new.

If past experience is any guide, future innovations will come from one of two sources: first, new theories about human nature and human behavior, most of them developed in adjacent disciplines; second, the impact of contemporary events. The former are hard to predict, but the latter can be seen all around us. Until 1950 or so, academic history was written within the conceptual framework created by the nineteenth-century's great invention, the nation-state. But as the world has changed, so have historical perspectives. In the United Kingdom, the end of empire and the growth of Asian and Caribbean immigration have engendered the postcolonial outlook. Less attention is now given to proconsuls and generals and more to those on the receiving end of empire: slaves, convicts, poor whites, and indigenous peoples. The agonies of Northern Ireland and the granting of devolution to Scotland and Wales have made historians less Anglocentric. The old English history courses are now labeled British history, and the English Civil War has turned into the War of the Three Kingdoms. National identity and "Englishness" have become central issues in historical debate.

The formation of the European Union has stimulated some slightly strained attempts at writing histories of the continent that transcend national frontiers. But the shift of political and economic power to the United States and the Far East has encouraged historians everywhere to be less Eurocentric. In the United States, the belief that American liberties stemmed from the Magna Carta and the House of Commons once gave English history a central place in the curriculum. Today, the diminished international importance of Britain, and the changing ethnic composition of the American population, have made British history an increasingly unsuccessful competitor with the history of Latin America, China, Japan, and the Middle East. It retains a place only because of its imperial dimension. Meanwhile, the history of anything to do with Islam has, for obvious reasons, become the dernier cri, and is likely to remain so for some time.

Despite the professional drift to intense specialization, modern realities encourage the study of ever larger units; hence the vogue for Mediterranean history, Atlantic history, and Pacific history. Yet even they now seem parochial as the globalization of economies and communications inexorably generates the conviction that the only true history has to be a history of the world. That is the animating doctrine behind the London School of Economics' new *Journal of Global History;* and it is admirably exemplified in *The Birth of the Modern World* by C. A. Bayly (2004), a genuinely global history of the nineteenth century. It seems certain that for the next generation of historians, the relationships among the world's different cultures will be a central concern.

Just as contemporary developments alter our geographical horizons, so they point us to previously neglected aspects of the past. Some of the reasons for the widening of history's subject matter in the last forty years have been adventitious, like the munificence of the Wellcome Trust, which has elevated the history of medicine from a harmless hobby for retired physicians into a dynamic and creative field. Credit must also be given to purely internal campaigns, like Lucien Febvre's strenuous advocacy in *Annales* of a broader historical coverage. But the decisive cause has been the impact of present-day concerns.

In the United States, the civil rights movement of the 1960s focused attention on the history of African Americans. In Britain, the democratization of the historical profession, the founding of new universities, and the influence of the Left all helped shift interest away from cabinets and chanceries to the experience of ordinary people, the main concern of the History Workshop movement led by Raphael Samuel.

Above all, it has become mandatory for all historians to consider the gender aspect of their topic, whatever it may be, with the strong implication that not to do so is as much a moral failure as an intellectual one. When, in 1957, I gave a course of lectures at Oxford on the relations between the sexes in England from the Reformation to the First World War, the general reaction was of bewildered amusement. No one had anything to say about the history of women in the *TLS* of 1966. It was the feminism of the 1970s that brought about a fundamental reassessment of how history should be written. More recently, the claims of gays and lesbians to social and legal recognition look as if they will make the histories of masculinity and female friendship as central to the undergraduate syllabus as was Stubbs's *Charters* in my day.

Nearly all the fashionable historical topics of the present time owe their vogue to essentially non-academic preoccupations. The countless studies of memory and forgetting are in part a legacy of the Holocaust. The passion for environmental history stems from anxiety about global warming and the depletion of natural resources. The renewed concern with empire is closely related to U.S. foreign policy. The obsessive interest in the history of the body has been fuelled by the AIDS epidemic; it also reflects the concerns of a secular and hedonistic age, preoccupied with physical health and sensual gratification. Similar concerns underlie the current popularity of such topics as the history of consumer goods as well as the study of the emotions, personal identity, and the emergence of the self.

History has always embodied the hopes and fears of those who write it. Its future character depends on what those hopes and fears will prove to be.

Summer 2007

A version of this lecture appeared in the *Times Literary Supplement,* 13 October 2006.

4

Kipling in South Africa

DAN JACOBSON

T o begin with, a reminiscence. The first piece of verse by
Rudyard Kipling I committed to memory—without even
knowing I was doing so—was incised in large roman capitals on a wall of the Honoured Dead Memorial in Kimberley, South
Africa. During the Anglo-Boer War (1899–1902), Kimberley was besieged for some months by forces from the two independent Boer
republics, the Transvaal (De Zuid Afrikaansche Republiek) and
the Orange Free State. Among those trapped in the city during the
siege was the arch-imperialist Cecil John Rhodes, a former Prime
Minister of the Cape Colony, the eponymous founder of the British colony of Rhodesia, to the north, and the most prominent of
the mining magnates who had been drawn to South Africa by the
discovery of diamonds in Kimberley and subsequently of gold in
Johannesburg. Rhodes had in fact deliberately moved from Cape
Town to Kimberley once it became clear to him that war between
Britain and the two "Dutch," or Boer, republics was imminent: this
he did out of a sense of noblesse oblige to the city in which he had
made his first and greatest fortune and which he felt to be peculiarly "his" thereafter. (Many other people, the Boer leaders among
them, felt the same way about it, which was why they had made Kimberley one of their prime targets.) Once the siege was lifted, Rhodes
returned to his house and estate just outside Cape Town and immediately commissioned his favorite architect, Herbert Baker, to find
a prominent site in Kimberley and to design for it a memorial to

the imperial troops and local militiamen who had lost their lives defending the city.

Built entirely out of ruddy yellow granite brought down from Rhodesia, and complete with a massive cannon manufactured locally during the siege, the Honoured Dead Memorial is an imposing flat-topped affair, half fortress and half Doric temple in appearance. It stands in the middle of a grassed-over traffic circle just outside the grounds of the Kimberley Boys' High School, which I attended for a full ten years. So I had ample opportunity to study the memorial and its inscription as I trudged back and forth between school and home. Not until much later did I learn that the incised words stretching across several yards of stonework had been composed by Rudyard Kipling at Rhodes's request. The names of both these men had been familiar to me almost as far back as I could remember. In Kimberley—then still a company town dominated by the De Beers Consolidated Mines—Rhodes continued to be regarded as a kind of demigod; Kipling I knew chiefly as the author of "Rikki-Tikki-Tavi," a story about a mongoose battling cobras in an Indian garden, which, like an addict, I had read and reread at frequent intervals over many years. But I knew nothing of the close friendship that had sprung up between the author and the empire builder; nothing of the three brief visits Kipling had made to Kimberley (during one of which he had enjoyed watching the City Hall burn down); nothing of the fact that Rhodes had formally passed over to Kipling a house (also built by Baker) in the exquisite grounds of the estate he had laid out just under Table Mountain. It was in this house—dubbed The Woolsack, to which Rhodes had granted Kipling a life tenancy—that the latter resided with his family during all but two of the lengthy annual visits he made to South Africa between 1898 and 1908.

The direct alliance between the two men was to be of brief duration, however, for Rhodes died (of heart failure, at the age of forty-nine) some months before the surrender of the Boer republics in November 1902. Thus he never had the opportunity to see in its completed state the memorial he had commissioned for Kimberley, though he would certainly have read the inscription Kipling composed for it:

> THIS FOR A CHARGE TO OUR CHILDREN IN SIGN OF THE PRICE WE PAID
> THE PRICE WE PAID FOR FREEDOM THAT COMES UNSOILED TO YOUR HAND
> READ REVERE AND UNCOVER FOR HERE ARE THE VICTORS LAID
> THEY THAT DIED FOR THE CITY BEING SONS OF THE LAND

These chiselled, unpunctuated words made a great impression on my schoolboy mind: not least because of their obscurity. I did not know what a "charge" meant here; plainly it did not refer to something that people did on battlefields or in games of rugby. And who exactly were the "you," "we," and "they" that the lines evoked with such confidence? Most mysterious of all, however, was the command to "read revere and uncover." *Uncover?* At school the boys sometimes talked in spooky voices about the massive, never-to-be-opened steel door lodged in one of the monument's walls, behind which (it was said) there was a flight of stairs leading down to a place where all the "Honoured Dead" from the siege were interred. But if that were the case, who would think of going down there to uncover them? To what end? And what gruesome spectacle would meet their eyes if they actually did it?

By the time I left school, some of these puzzles had been resolved; but other, more grown-up ones had taken their place. I knew, for instance, that the "freedom" proclaimed in the inscription had nothing to do with the ambitions of the Nationalist Afrikaners, the defeated "children" of the Boers, of whom relatively few had been living in Kimberley when I had entered school, but who in the ten years since then had grown to be a significant minority of its white population. And sure enough, just two or three years later there were enough of them in Kimberley and elsewhere, countrywide, to vote the Afrikaner Nationalist Party into power—which it exercised zealously for the next half century, until its notorious policy of apartheid collapsed both from its own inner contradictions and from the pressure put on it by the country's ever more restive black population. I was also aware that neither the English-speaking nor the Afrikaans-speaking whites had the slightest intention (in those days) of extending the "freedom" they enjoyed to the black-skinned "sons of the land," who had always greatly outnumbered both white groups put together. Considerations like these had for me turned the inscription on the monument into a kind of ponderous joke, a warning to all monument builders never to take for granted anything about a future they would not live to see.

Remarkably enough, it was in South Africa, near an inconsequential place in the Orange Free State by the name of Karree Siding, that Kipling actually found himself under fire for the first time. His readers would have been much surprised had they learned that this was the case, for by then he had won worldwide fame for what he had written about soldiers and soldiering in India, Burma, and Afghanistan. In his last book, *Something of Myself*, a "partial autobiography" published in 1936, he devoted three or four vividly skittish pages to that baptism of fire near Karree Siding, and in so doing produced a more satisfying piece of prose than anything to be found in the formally composed fictions he had set in South Africa. (Some critics have made big claims for a few of the South African stories, especially for "A Sahib's War" and the famously mysterious "Mrs. Bathurst"—a tale I have never been able to understand, with or without its admirers' helpful notes.) However, the poems he wrote on South African themes are another matter. They vary in merit of course; the two starkly entitled "South Africa" are hardly more than doggerel; but the best ("Bridge-Guard in the Karroo," say, or "The Old Issue") are much superior to the comparable prose pieces. The reason for this, I believe, is that poetry actually lends itself more readily to expressing political passions than fiction ever can. A poet is able to speak directly to the reader, even when he adopts a mask to do so, whereas the conflicts at the heart of any successful piece of fiction have to be acted out by seemingly autonomous characters possessing an interior life of their own.

But it is exactly that kind of autonomy that the politically engaged—and enraged—Kipling could grant to none of the characters who appear in his stories about South Africa. With very few exceptions, he regarded the Boers as his personal enemies, and particularly sneaky ones at that, irrespective of whether they lived as British subjects in the Cape Colony or had taken up arms in the Transvaal and the Free State. He felt much the same about the vociferous liberals back "home," whom he accused of flagrant sentimentality about the Boers and a criminal indifference to the fate of the Empire as a whole. Even less forgivable, perhaps, were all the complacent, well-bred, games-playing English amateurs occupying high positions in Parliament and the colonies, in the civil service and the army—the flannelled fools and muddied oafs, as he famously described them in his poem "The Islanders"—who imagined that wars could be won and overseas possessions held without the exercise of ruthlessness and professional skill. In the hands of such idlers, he believed, one government after another had succeeded in putting at risk British interests not just in southern Africa but everywhere else too—above all in India. As Umr Singh, the Sikh mouthpiece of "A Sahib's War," dutifully puts it, in speaking of what he has witnessed during the war: "It is for Hind [India] that the Sahibs are fighting this war [in South Africa]. Ye cannot rule in one place and in another bear service. Either ye must everywhere rule or everywhere obey." [1]

THE GEOPOLITICAL MISGIVINGS EXPRESSED HERE by Umr Singh take one back to Rhodes, to Kipling, and to the curious intensity of their relationship. As it happened, the two men became intimate when each was more or less at the height of his fame. True, Rhodes's reputation had been tarnished by his complicity in the Jameson Raid, a failed attempt to overthrow the government of the Transvaal by organizing a military coup from outside the country's borders. (Hence his enforced surrender of the premiership of the Cape Colony four years before the outbreak of the war.)[2] It was true also that Kipling, the younger of the pair by about a dozen years, still had to write several of what would become his most widely admired books (*Kim* among them, as well as *Puck of Pook's Hill* and *Just So Stories*); yet his work had already secured for him a degree of popular esteem that was almost Dickens-like in its fervor. Each of the two men could therefore take the eminence of the other for granted, just as they did their belief that the English or British "race" was more qualified than any other to rule over peoples and territories incapable of governing themselves.

To these affinities were added a few mutually supportive differences. For all the success Rhodes had achieved as a financier and politician, he had difficulty in finding the words in which to express his ambitions: he was "as inarticulate as a schoolboy of fifteen," according to Kipling, whose own fluency (almost from birth, it seems) was phenomenal. Yet Kipling himself remained a schoolboy of a kind, too, not least in his perpetual hunt for heroes to worship— men of action, almost invariably, who set about shaping the world to their own ends, whether as soldiers, sailors, camel drivers, district commissioners, surgeons, engineers, painters, gardeners, empire builders. And here in Cape Town he found himself the friend and confidant of the greatest empire builder of all, whom he had admired for many years (long before meeting Rhodes, he had written of him as "one of the adventurers and captains courageous of old"), and who candidly revealed how much he relied on this newfound confidant to become his "purveyor of words." (The phrase is quoted by Kipling in *Something of Myself*.)

Equally significant to their fellowship was their shared conviction that the world could best be understood—and best mastered, therefore—as "an aggregation of secret and semi-secret societies, a pattern of circles, intersecting indeed, but closed."[3] These half ideas— megalomaniac from one aspect and paranoid from another—were to lead each of them in some strange directions, among which their shared ardent interest in Freemasonry was probably the most innocent. Kipling's hunger always to be in the know, and to make sure that everyone else knew him to be in the know, is manifest almost everywhere in his writings, sometimes to their advantage, often not. (Especially when he indulges in his unique capacity for picking up specialized jargons of all kinds.) As for Rhodes, his schemes ranged from forming a secret society with the object of "furthering the British Empire" and thus "bringing the whole uncivilised world under British rule" (in his first will) to the slightly more modest plan (in his seventh will) to "rejoin" the United States to the Empire and thus to found "so great a power as to . . . render wars impossible." By the time he and Kipling got together, these ambitions had been greatly scaled down, publicly at any rate, to establishing the Rhodes scholarships at Oxford, a scheme of which Kipling duly became a trustee.

Within a week or two of Rhodes's death, Kipling wrote to a friend, "No words could give you any idea of that great spirit's power . . . It seems absurd to speak of one's own petty loss in the face of such a calamity but I feel as though half of the horizon of my life had dropped away."[4] This outburst is all the more striking when one thinks of the shattered silence with which he had met the death of his adored older daughter, Josephine ("my little Maid") three years before, not to speak of the even grimmer silence he was plunged into by the second great loss of his life: the death of his only son on the western front barely a dozen years later. The grief he felt for his daughter eventually found expression—of a deliberately distanced kind—in one of his most touching stories, "They"; his son, John, he mourned as openly as he ever did in the poem "My Son Jack," written as if the boy had been lost at sea and not in the mud of the trenches. On the death of Rhodes, on the other hand, he immediately wrote two memorial poems, one of them specifically to be read at the funeral in the Matopos Hills outside Bulawayo. Declamatory and prophetic in style (and utterly mistaken, as time was to show, about what lay ahead), there is a touch of unintended pathos in the final verse of the poem, with its covert allusion to the exchanges between the poet and the politician:

> There, till the vision he foresaw
>   Splendid and whole arise,
> And unimagined Empires draw
>   To council 'neath his skies,
> The immense and brooding Spirit still
>   Shall quicken and control.
> Living he was the land, and dead,
>   His soul shall be her soul!

That stanza appears on the wall of the grandiose Rhodes Memorial, designed once again by Herbert Baker, just below Table Mountain. It was Baker who chose to use the lines quoted above rather than the verses Kipling had specifically written for the memorial, which are more dramatic in tone and looser in form and grammar:

> As tho' again—yea, even once again,
>> We should rewelcome to our stewardship
> The rider with the loose-flung bridle-rein,
>> And chance-plucked twig for whip,
>
> The down-turned hat-brim, and the eyes beneath
>> Alert, devouring—and the imperious hand
> Ordaining matters swiftly to bequeath
>> Perfect the work he ordained.

Yet another poem, written by Kipling before he and Rhodes had met, and slightly rephrased after the great man's death, was later still pressed into service as the inscription on a seated bronze of Rhodes overlooking the rugby fields of the University of Cape Town. It too speaks of "empire to the northward . . . / Ay, one land / from Lion's Head to the Line."[5]

WITH RHODES DEAD and "half the horizon" of Kipling's life "dropped away," it might have been expected that his interest in South Africa would diminish sharply. In fact, for another seven years he continued to make protracted annual visits to the Cape, during which time he went on publishing, among much else, poems and stories with a South African setting or derived from his experiences there. In many of these poems he excoriated British complacency and softness of mind, which, he insisted, were on display once again in the payments for damages being made to the Boer inhabitants of the two defeated republics, not to speak of the relatively early return to them of a measure of self-government. This last move he described as putting the Boers "into a position to uphold and expand their primitive lust for racial domination"[6]—a statement seized on by various British biographers and essayists as evidence of how concerned he was about the fate of South Africa's blacks, should they be left to the mercies of the Boers. Unfortunately, these writers have misunderstood what Kipling meant. From beginning to end of his South African sojourns, he took remarkably little interest in black Africans; and I have little doubt that it was Boer domination of the British in southern Africa that was on his mind when he wrote the words quoted above. During the earlier decades of the twentieth century, the term "race" was habitually used in South Africa to

refer to the quarrel between Boer and Briton, and *not* between white
and black—however bizarre that exclusion may seem to us today—
and it was repeatedly used in this sense by Kipling in his letters and
Rhodes in his speeches.[7]

After inspecting the living conditions of the black mine workers in Kimberley, who were kept in close confinement by the De
Beers Corporation in so-called compounds for their entire term of
hire (usually for six months at a time), Kipling noted merely that,
"Kaffirs steal diamonds." About the Boers, he wrote in his letters
in even more hostile fashion after the war had been won than he
did while it was still being waged. Occasionally he acknowledges an
honorable exception among them; more often he refers to them by
such terms as "idle dirty Dutch animals," "a creolised race," "speak-
ers of a hideous taal-patois," and so forth. Outbursts of this kind may
properly be compared with his half-mad imprecations against the
Germans ("Huns," "Boche," etc.) during the First World War: "[T]he
idea begins to dawn upon the German mind that this is not a war of
victories but a war of extermination for their race . . . There can only
be killing, butchery, and three nations, at least, desire ardently that
the Boche be killed—at retail, since he can't be killed wholesale."[8]
Admittedly, the letter containing that passage was written on the last
day of 1915, just months after the death of his son in the Battle of
Loos, and one hesitates to pass judgment on what any bereaved father might say, in private, in such circumstances. But it was not untypical of much else in his correspondence before and after 1918.

In his post-war published writings on South Africa, Kipling did
indeed write several reconciliatory poems, such as "Half-Ballade of
Waterval," "Piet," "Chant-Pagan," and "The Settler." These and others were clearly intended to promote a process of healing between
the two "races," and the affecting and reverberating passages that
appear in them—descriptions of landscape, evocations of states of
mind, renderings of poignant details that only an eye as sharp as
Kipling's would register—show how genuinely the prospect of reconciliation appealed to his imagination. What is troubling about these
poems, however, is that they are all *victors'* poems: by which I mean
that in each case the suppositious speaker of the poem is a Briton
speaking either to his fellow Britons or to one of his defeated enemies; in none are the latter permitted to utter a phrase or even a single word for themselves. They are pitied for their death in battle or
their plight in being shipped off as captives to Ceylon or St. Helena;
they are congratulated in sportsmanlike fashion for having put up a
good fight (and no hard feelings—mind!). Yet the imbalance between

the speaker and the spoken-to or spoken-about is never rectified; in the following lines, for example, the intention to honor the dead Boer is plain, yet implicitly the poem honors more highly still the rough, patronizing generosity of the British soldier mourning him.

> Ah, there, Piet! whose time 'as come to die.
> 'Is carcass past rebellion, but 'is eyes still enquiring why.
> Though dressed in stolen uniform with badge o' rank
>   complete,
> I've known a lot of fellers go a damn sight worse than Piet.

AS A MAN AND A WRITER, KIPLING was by nature both obsessional and protean: two modes of responding to the world that for him were less at odds with each other than one would expect them to be. Intermittently at least, he was a driven, tormented man who had been subject to one major nervous breakdown and other, lesser collapses; haunted by fears of madness and cancer; frequently given to dwelling with manifest pleasure on the pain inflicted upon—or suffered by—his invented characters; insistent on hammering moral lessons into other people's heads (though capable at times of doing the job far more effectively with a single witty phrase). He was also a master at dramatizing certain localized forms of obsession, as in his extraordinary story "The Disturber of the Traffic," in which a lighthouse keeper becomes convinced that the waves in the straits he watches over are running lengthways in sinister parallel "streaks"; these distress him so much he eventually takes it into his "pore sick head" that the only way to stop them is to forbid all ships from passing his light. The story is, in effect, about a man whose thoughts are incessantly driven down narrow channels—straits indeed—from which he cannot escape.

Unlike the single idée fixe in the mind of this unfortunate creature, Kipling's obsessions were themselves protean in nature: they moved in many directions at once. His need to show that he knew more about everything (mechanical, social, linguistic, religious, historical, Masonic etc.) than other people knew about anything was in itself an obsession. So was the ferocity with which he attacked those whom he believed to be his country's enemies: first the Boers, then the Germans (whom he had deeply mistrusted long before the outbreak of the First World War), then the Americans (before they entered the war on Britain's side, in 1917), then the Irish republicans (of course), then the Jews (about whom he wrote in increasingly paranoid fashion as he grew older—choosing to forget that the collaboration of the Beits and Rothschilds had been indispensable to the success of his great hero, Rhodes). As a result of his South African experiences, an urgency of a related kind took command of his preoccupation with the future of the British Empire. During his startlingly precocious and productive years in India, he had been able to regard the Empire, by and large, as a given fact, as a demanding yet thoroughly well-deserved piece of good fortune that no one would ever be able to take from his people or himself. But this he could no longer do. Now he was inclined to see the Empire both as a grand, evolving project that no bounds could contain, and at the same time as a besieged enterprise under threat from powerful enemies of many kinds.

All this cohabited in his mind with a late-developed passion for England itself, which he described as "the most marvellous of all the foreign countries I have ever been in," and which inspired some of his most thrilled and eloquent writing. What Kipling found so glamorous about England overall, and about the landscapes of southern England especially, was that its topography was inseparable from its human history. Unlike the South African veld, which he admired for other reasons, this landscape was coded, reclusive, idiosyncratic; its hills and fields continually spoke to him of unforgotten historical events and social intimacies impenetrable by outsiders. (See, for example, *Puck of Pook's Hill,* as well as many of the other stories and poems set in the Sussex countryside, where he finally made his home.)[9]

But if an immemorial bonding together of land and people was what he loved most about England, how could that same people in another guise go about claiming for themselves perpetual title to a vast amorphous empire that had no natural boundaries whatever? How could England be at once "An Habitation Enforced," to quote the title of one of his most famous stories, while at the same time serving as a springboard to the seizure and occupation of so many distant parts of the world? And what would happen to all those eager Britons whom he urged for empire's sake to turn themselves into Australians and New Zealanders, say, or South Africans and Canadians—or even, as some had done long before, into Americans, like the leading characters of "An Habitation Enforced"? In such poems as "A Song of the English," "The Houses (A Song of the Dominions)," "Our Lady of the Snows," "The Native-Born," and many others, one can see Kipling trying with a certain desperation to resolve the conflict between his simultaneous enthusiasm for the world-straddling greatness of Britain, on the one hand, and, on the other, for all that was distinctive and allusive about England. Would "the Blood" and "the Race" and "the Heritage" (his terms—and his capital letters) be enough to keep in place these two poles of his imagined world? Would the ties between motherland and (white) empire that his poems insisted on be strong enough for the task? Could "The hush of our dread high altar / Where the Abbey makes us We," as he bathetically put it in "The Native-Born," really sustain as one people the Britons at home and the British "natives" yet to be born in countries so geographically remote?[10]

The contrary tug of these impulses led him up many political and poetical blind alleys, but he could never have managed without them. They sustained his extraordinarily prolific and various output almost to the end of his life; they drove him restlessly from one self-assumed public duty to another, from one mode of writing to the next, from one stern exhortation to yet another reproachful outburst against those who let him down, as they so often tended to do. Everything he wrote, all his urgings in prose and verse, he put before the public with a seemingly indiscriminate haste, a shamelessness even, that led him in later years to be mocked as well as honored for the sheer copiousness of his output. He wrote for adults; he wrote for children; he cajoled and bullied young and old alike; he insulted them, flattered them, warned them, made them laugh, spoke up tenderly for the humblest of them, made their flesh creep with intimations of uncanny forms of life and death, and, when nothing else would do, he bewildered them by retreats into taciturnity, blank refusals either to abandon or to explain the mysterious omniscience his writing so often hinted at.

Protean indeed. He was like a figure from a fairy story: at one moment a noisy bullfrog, at the next, a prince. And something of a prophet too. He had never understood, or even tried to understand, some of the bedrock certainties of South African life, the most prominent among them being the sheer weight of numbers that the indigenous inhabitants of the country would eventually bring to bear on every aspect of its political life. (To be fair, the same could be said about almost all other whites, the novelist Anthony Trollope aside, who visited the country after the great diamond and gold rushes of the 1870s and 1880s.) But Kipling never forgot the crushing defeats the Boers had inflicted on British forces during the first few months of hostilities in South Africa: episodes that had left him with the conviction that since Britain's military and moral unpreparedness for a major war had been revealed to all, an Armageddon must now lie ahead. Thus, ironically enough, it was in England that he set the finest of the poems to emerge from his South African experiences; it was out of the Romney Marsh, some miles from his beloved house, Batemans, in East Sussex that he drew the poem's imagery; and it was written with a directly political, propagandist, even warlike purpose. His aim in this long poem, "The Dykes," was to incite the British government to introduce universal military training—of a kind similar to that which circumstances had always enjoined on the Boers—for the young men of the United Kingdom. From this distance, it could be said that the program of wholesale conscription and rearmament he was urging on Britain might not have averted the European war he feared, but merely hastened its onset. Yet, from this distance again, who can tell?

One thing we can be certain of is that the language he used in "The Dykes" survives the occasion of its writing and the motives of the writer himself. As these verses plucked from it go to show:

> Far off, the full tide clambers and slips, mouthing and tasting all,
> Nipping the flanks of the water-gates, baying along the wall,
> Turning the shingle, returning the shingle, changing the set of the sand . . .
> We are too far from the beach, men say, to know how the outworks stand.
>
> So we come down to the beach, uneasy, to look; uneasily pacing the beach.
> These are the dykes our fathers made: we have never known a breach.
> Time and again the gale has blown by and we were not afraid;
> Now we come only to look at the dykes—at the dykes our fathers made.
>
> O'er the marsh where the homesteads cower apart the harried sunlight flies,
> Shifts and considers, wanes and recovers, scatters and sickens and dies—
> An evil ember bedded in ash—a spark blown west by the wind . . .
> We are surrendered to night and the sea—the gale and the tide behind!

Spring Semester 2006

1. In this story, Umr Singh constantly parrots the official line that the Anglo-Boer war was "a white man's war," with the local blacks—and Umr Singh himself—wholly excluded from combat because of the color of their skin. Hence the story's title ("A Sahib's War") and various developments of its plot too. The fact is that throughout the war both sides used large numbers of blacks as spies, scouts, porters, and personal servants; and, more to the point here, the British also put significant units of armed blacks into the field. (This the Boers never dared to do, lest the guns they distributed be turned against them.) Only by assiduously blocking their ears and closing their eyes could Kipling and his imaginary Umr Singh have remained ignorant of this fact.

2. In *Following the Line* (1897), Mark Twain wrote of him: "In the opinion of many people Mr Rhodes *is* South Africa; others think he is only a large part of it. These latter consider that South Africa consists of Table Mountain, the diamond mines, the Johannesburg goldfields, and Cecil Rhodes . . . I admire him, I frankly confess it, and when his time comes I shall buy a piece of the rope for a keepsake."

3. See W. L. Renwick in Andrew Rutherford, ed., *Kipling's Mind and Art* (London, 1964).

4. *The Letters of Rudyard Kipling,* edited by Thomas Pinney, Vol. VI: *1931–1936,* p. 26 (London, 2004).

5. The Lion's Head is a peak guarding the western flank of Table Mountain; "the Line" of course refers to the Equator, some two thousand miles to the north. Though he did not revisit South Africa after 1908, in later years Kipling steadfastly declined the requests of the executors of Rhodes's estate to return The Woolsack to them—presumably because he could not bear to make this symbolic break with his friendship with Rhodes and his memories of the time he and his family had spent in the country. After Kipling's death, in 1936, The Woolsack did finally fall into the hands of the executors, who passed it on to the University of Cape Town. Today it is used as one of the many administrative buildings on the campus.

6. Rudyard Kipling, *Something of Myself* (London, 1937), p. 166.

7. Presumably the blacks were too far outside the realm of politics, as the term was commonly understood, to be brought into consideration. More than twenty years after the end of the Anglo-Boer War, Roy Campbell, who remains the finest lyric poet in English that South Africa has yet produced, and who was as sensitive to the local idiom as anyone could be, wrote a lengthy satire in rhyming couplets about the country's political and intellectual life. Entitled *The Wayzgoose,* it focuses on two typically South African simpletons, Johnny (the English speaker) and Piet (the Afrikaner). "Think not that I on racial questions touch," the refrain of the poem runs, "For the one was Durban-born and the other Dutch." (Durban in those days was the most British, the most true-blue Tory, of all South African cities.)

8. *Letters,* ed. Pinney, Vol. IV: *1911–1919,* p. 352.

9. When T. S. Eliot went public with his admiration for Kipling by producing *A Choice of Kipling's Verse* (1941), readers who regarded Eliot as the high priest of austere, highbrow modernism were surprised to learn of his enthusiasm for a poet written off by most intellectuals of the day as little better than a music-hall balladeer. In fact, Kipling's influence on Eliot (himself far more of a self-made Englishman than Kipling ever was) had by 1941 already shown itself in two of his own "historical" or "country house" poems, "Burnt Norton" and "Little Gidding."

10. The reference in the second line of the quotation is to Westminster Abbey.

5

Tolkien in the First World War

MARTIN GILBERT

J. R. R. Tolkien and the Somme were inextricably linked. I learned this forty-four years ago, in 1962, shortly after I was elected to my first university appointment, as a Junior Research Fellow at Merton College, Oxford. I was twenty-six years old.

In those days there was a strict seating order at college dinners. The head of the college sat in the center, the senior fellows on either side of him, and the junior fellows at the far ends of the table. Also at the ends were the Emeritus Fellows, long retired, venerable, distinguished guardians of the college name. Several of them had served in the First World War. When they discovered at their end of the table a historian, new to his craft, filled with the keenness of a youngster amid his elders, they were happy to talk about those distant days, already more than forty years in the past.

Some enjoyed singing the songs of the trenches, in versions far ruder than those sung today. Tolkien was more reticent, yet when he did open up, he was full of terrible tales. There was never any boasting. The war's scars were too many, its reality was too grim, to lead to self-glorification or even to embellishment.

In 1916, the twenty-four-year-old Tolkien was a second lieutenant in the Lancashire Fusiliers. On the evening of 14 July—two weeks after the start of the Battle of the Somme—his battalion went into the line. He had never seen action before. What he later called the "animal horror" of the trenches was as yet unknown to him. But

he already knew that one of his closest friends, Robert Gilson, had
been killed on the first day of the battle, two weeks earlier.

Gilson, two years younger than Tolkien, had written home two
nights before he was killed: "Guns firing at night are beautiful—if
they were not so terrible. They have the grandeur of thunderstorms.
But how one clutches at the glimpses of peaceful scenes. It would be
wonderful to be a hundred miles from the firing line once again."

Tolkien was to experience many such nights. He was also to lose
more friends. On 22 July, three days after his first five-day spell
in the trenches, his friend Ralph Payton was killed in action. Payton's body was never identified; his name is inscribed today on the
Thiepval Memorial to the Missing.

Two days after Payton was killed, Tolkien returned to the trenches
for a second five-day spell of front-line duty. As battalion signals officer, his task each time he went "up the line" was to supervise the
communications to the brigade command post a mile and a half
behind the trenches. The main method of communication was by
pigeon.

As we talked of those far off times, Tolkien remembered, as vividly as if it were yesterday, the constant danger of German artillery
shells ranging throughout the area, falling with their screech and
roar amid clouds of earth and mud, and the fearful cries of men
who had been hit.

Like all the First World War soldiers at dinner in college, Tolkien knew that his stories seemed antique compared to the more recent memories of those who had fought in the Second World War.
Several times he told me, in words he was later to use in his introduction to the second edition of *The Lord of the Rings:* "It seems now
often forgotten that to be caught by youth in 1914 was no less hideous an experience than to have been involved in 1939 and the following years."

Forty-four years after my Merton conversations with Tolkien, I
passed the Roman Catholic church at Bertrancourt, three miles behind the old front line. There, on 6 August, he attended Mass before setting off, the following morning, for the front-line trenches.
It was his third spell up the line, and he was fortunate. During the
five days that he ran the communications there, no British forward
assault took place, and only four men were killed. One writes "only"
because, at the time, the death of four soldiers on a battalion front
seemed a small toll.

Like many old soldiers, Tolkien spoke of the stark, dull ordinari-
ness of much of life on the battlefield. But there was no lack of action. On 27 September he was back in the front line, organizing

communications through the splintered maze of Thiepval Wood as his battalion struggled in vain to enter the Schwaben Redoubt, a German strong point that had resisted all efforts to capture it since 1 July. On the following day, when the battalion carried out a successful raid on a German machine-gun position that had caused havoc for the attackers, more than thirty Germans were taken prisoner.

Tolkien, who spoke German, later recalled with wry amusement how, when he offered a drink of water to a wounded German officer, the prisoner, while accepting the water, corrected him on his German pronunciation.

Tolkien and his signallers were always vulnerable. One of them, Private Sydney Sumner, had disappeared during intense shellfire on 9 July. For two months no trace of him could be found. "Dear Sir," his wife wrote to Tolkien in hope and despair, "I would not care if only I knew how he went," and she added, "I know that they cannot all be saved to come home."

Sumner had left a one-year-old daughter at home. His name is on the Thiepval Memorial to the Missing: a memorial with more than 73,335 names on it. No one of those men was ever identified amid the cruel carnage of the battlefield, another facet of Tolkien's "animal horror" of the trenches.

On 21 October, Tolkien was again in the front line with his signallers, following the first wave of infantrymen, who captured the German trench in front of them. During the attack, a German shell hit one of his signallers. Another rescued the signaller's pigeon basket. On the following day, the battalion chaplain, Captain Evers, who had disappeared during the fighting, returned to the British lines covered in blood. He has spent the night in no-man's-land, under German artillery fire, tending the wounded.

On 26 October, while in reserve, Tolkien's battalion was inspected by General Sir Douglas Haig. The next day, Tolkien was taken ill. He had contracted trench fever, a blood-borne bacterium spread through the burrowing of the ever-active lice. He was not to see active service again.

On 18 November 1916, the final day of the Battle of the Somme, Tolkien was struck off his battalion's strength and evacuated to Britain. He was never to forget his five months on the Somme. In *The Lord of the Rings*, Sam Gamgee—whom Tolkien said was "a reflection of the English soldiers, of the privates and batmen I knew in the 1914 war, and recognized as so far superior to myself"—trips, "catching his foot in some old root or tussock. He fell and came heavily on his hands, which sank into the sticky ooze, so that his face was brought close to the surface of the dark mere. There was a faint hiss, a noisome smell went up. . . . Wrenching his hands out of the bog, he sprang back with a cry. 'There are dead things, dead faces in the water,' he said with horror."

I feel proud to have told the story of a battle of which Tolkien was my first eyewitness. *The Battle of the Somme: The Heroism and Horror of War* is my tribute to all who fought on that battlefield just over ninety years ago.

Summer 2007

A version of this lecture appeared in the *Financial Times,* 29 July 2006.

6

The Age of Auden

GREY GOWRIE

The week of 21 February 2007 saw the centenary of the birth in York of W. H. Auden. All over the world, at 1755 hours precisely, Audenites prepared very cold, very dry martinis and at 1800 hours, six o'clock, again precisely, downed them in praise and memory of a giant of English letters. Vital to have been meticulous about the hour. As he said of himself in an autobiographical sketch:

> So obsessive a ritualist
> a pleasant surprise
> makes him cross.
> Without a watch
> he would never know when
> to feel hungry or horny.

Like many Oxford undergraduates of my generation (he was Professor of Poetry when I went up), I knew Auden slightly and dined with him a few times. He had aged prematurely, become repetitive and, away from the page, fairly boring. Like his friend and contemporary John Betjeman, he had long invented a persona—dotty vicar in his case—but Auden got trapped by it. Prone to chant curious mantras—"Yeats was not *my* idea of a gentleman" or "Peeing in the washbasin is a male privilege"—he smelt like a forgotten cheese. Yet it was impossible to doubt his genius for a moment. Though the word may have now dwindled into hyperbole, it can nevertheless be defined, and when Auden died in 1973, it was defined by his friend

V. S. Yanofsky: "There was in him some communion with the great human reality, as there was in Tolstoy—a trait characteristic of all geniuses, despite their fantasies." In conversation, another friend of Auden, Isaiah Berlin, assented. Berlin thought there were two twentieth-century Englishmen of genius, the other being Churchill.

An American scholar, Samuel Hines, called the 1930s the Age of Auden. It is important, three-quarters of a century later, to be aware of how celebrated Auden became as a young man—more so than any poet since Byron. Allowing for immense differences in the means of communication and what was then a smaller, though more expert, educational base, you have to think of someone like John Lennon to get the feel of Auden's fame in his twenties. Like others, he had fallen for T. S. Eliot's vivid depiction of a civilization breaking up: the fragments "shored against my ruins" in *The Waste Land*. But as a disciple of poets older than Eliot, like Hardy, Frost, and Edward Thomas, Auden translated the modern movement into the language of ordinary educated men and thereby democratized it. Patriotic, about the English industrial landscape in particular, Auden became an exemplar of Ezra Pound's dictum (though he never much cared for Pound) that poets are the antennae of the race. His rhythms and imagery orchestrated an appropriate foreboding for what, in a great, later repudiated, poem about the outbreak of the Second World War, he called a low, dishonest decade. Like Churchill, Auden had read the writing on the wall long before the full text was revealed in all its horror. He immersed himself in psychology, for he believed that holding a mirror up to the wasteland was not enough. You had to examine the behavioral pathways out.

Auden domesticated the modern movement for the English, therefore, rather in the way Elvis Presley domesticated black rhythm and blues for white Americans, or the Beatles (whom Auden admired) anglicized rock and roll in their early years. He was a hit. His versatility—plays, verse dramas, prose poems, songs and musical pieces, verbal charades, versified essays, doggerel, "straight" poems in the great pentametrical tradition—served only to draw attention to his antennae, the early warning sign he contrived by taking familiar toys out of the English middle-class cupboard and arranging them in ominous patterns to fit his unique, authoritative tone.

> It is time for the destruction of error.
> The chairs are being brought in from the garden

And in a poem completed several months later:

> It is later than you think; nearer that day
> Far other than that distant afternoon

> Amid rustle of frocks and stamping feet
> They gave the prizes to the ruined boys.

A synoptic 1938 sonnet about League of Nations diplomats ends:

> Far off, no matter what good they intended,
> The armies waited for a verbal error
> With all the instruments for causing pain.
> And on the issue of their charm depended
> A land laid waste with all its young men slain,
> The women weeping and the towns in terror.

In the context of Palestine, Kosovo, or Iraq, this still speaks to us, and poignantly.

By the end of the 1930s, Auden was, as he described Freud in his 1939 elegy, no longer a person now, but a climate of opinion. His intense lyrical gifts—remember the electrifying effect of the young gay man reading "Funeral Blues" in the hit film *Four Weddings and a Funeral*—propelled his fame. If you want to know what he was like, or re-create the sheer effect of him, read the long poem *Letter to Lord Byron,* which he wrote on a 1936 trip to Iceland with the Ulster poet Louis MacNeice, another fine centenarian. Written in emulation of Byron's *Don Juan,* the English poem Auden found both comic and sublime, it is self-knowing and self-critical. It is also an astonishingly assured autobiographical performance for someone not yet thirty, and uses wit in the way of Clive James or Alan Bennett today. Next year Auden wrote a great (and again later repudiated) poem on the Spanish Civil War. With Christopher Isherwood, he "covered" the Sino-Japanese conflict; imagine the *Daily Mail* sending Simon Armitage, say, to report, in verse, on current Baghdad. Auden won the King's Medal for poetry. John Masefield may have held the title, but Auden in the 1930s was as much the Laureate of English *society* as Phillip Larkin became two decades later. I emphasize the word because poets as different as Robert Graves, David Jones, and Ted Hughes reveal that there is more to poetry than social preoccupations or an ability to hit a particular mood at a particular time. Auden would have agreed with them. He was becoming most unhappy with his political role as the spokesman of a generation.

A political thunderclap, Auden's celebrated departure for New York in January 1939 changed things. This was partly on account of rage at what some felt was an attempt to save his skin. Evelyn Waugh's phony-war novel *Put Out More Flags* satirized Parsnip and Pimpernel (Auden and Isherwood) for, somewhat literally, buggering off. "I am glad that shit is dead," Anthony Powell is reported (by Kingsley Amis) as saying when Auden died. The timing was wrong for such criticism. During the winter of 1938–39, appeasement was still the order of the day. And indeed after war broke out and Auden had written "September 1, 1939"—"in one of the dives on Fifty-second Street"—he volunteered to return to Britain and join up. He was told he would be called when needed. The Americans first rejected him as a GI for being homosexual, but after he had taken citizenship, they commissioned him and contrived a task in occupied Germany. Isherwood was a pacifist; Auden was not. Nevertheless, Auden's status as a public figure made him a target, and to a degree it still does. This centenary is unlikely to be celebrated as warmly in Britain as Betjeman's a year ago.

In New York, Auden cultivated a spiritual and sexual life that did not even, like Graham Greene's 1951 novel *The End of the Affair,* elevate renunciation into a principle, but instead insisted on happiness and personal fulfillment as valid objectives for society as well as for individuals. A liberal conservative through background and disposition, Auden had come to loathe being treated as a Marxist intellectual in Britain. It was one of the reasons he left, though less important than the need to make a living by writing full-time. Given his fame, this was possible in the United States. What also made the abandoned Auden generation—leftist, at best agnostic—so angry was his return in New York to the High Anglican Christianity of his upbringing. It deregulated senses and disappointed expectations. Auden did not give a fig. He had fallen in love with Chester Kallman, the eighteen-year-old son of a Brooklyn dentist. A streetwise kid used to vamping older males, Chester knew all about opera and educated Wystan in its ways. Amazingly, for that society and that time, Chester's father encouraged the friendship. As an affair, it was sexual for a year or two only. As a relationship (Auden said he managed to combine the role of anxious mum with jealous lover), it lasted for life. Chester confirmed for Auden that vision of eros without which social or brotherly love degenerates into an unsustainable piety, and religion likewise. In common with John Updike in our own day, Auden is one of the few twentieth-century writers untroubled by the connection between sexual and religious feelings. As he had written in another 1938 sonnet, about Macao:

> Churches beside the brothels testify
> That faith can pardon natural behaviour.

In time of war, Auden wrote four long poems: *New Year Letter, For the Time Being, The Sea and the Mirror,* and *The Age of Anxiety.* They may not live up to Eliot's *Four Quartets* or Pound's *Pisan Cantos* as war works or even, in Auden's estimation, to his beloved Tolkien's epic,

The Lord of the Rings. But it is well worth a general reader visiting or revisiting them, *The Sea and the Mirror,* Auden's take on *The Tempest,* especially. No dialogue between a living writer and two dead ones (Shakespeare and Henry James) could be more entertaining; Shakespeare's spirit comes alive in the poem in a way Virgil's never can in Dante. And, as always, there are sensational lyrics: "Miranda's Song" and the duet between the Master and the Boatswain.

Making poems lively and fun became a post-Kallman imperative. Auden had learned, too, from Robert Frost that the darkest themes can be rhetorically most authentic when you treat them lightly. He was a conventional modern (American perhaps only in this) in seeking to create a conversational, even gossipy, style and turn his back on Romantic portentousness. Yeats and Rilke were influences he strove to jettison, not least because he had the technical ability to compete with them. For mastery of the tricks of his particular trade, Auden compares with Picasso rather than with any other writer.

Although he was now a U.S. citizen, for the rest of his life Auden wrote most of his poems in Europe: first in Ischia, then, after purchasing it with a $30,000 Italian literary award, in the only home he ever owned, at Kirchstetten, near Vienna. He wanted a German-speaking wine-drinking country with opera nearby. There he died, drinking and chain-smoking to the end. His Christianity was thoroughly European (lots of jolly local saints) and light years from the American habit of enthusiastic fundamentalism. It was Dantesque, also, in being informed by his acute perception, in the 1930s, of the Inferno to come; by his vision of a Paradisal or beatific love when he met the young Kallman; and by his humane affection for the Purgatory of our common life here on "middle earth." He was never a mystic, and the tone of his greatest poems, which I believe were written between 1947 and 1955, is conversational, sunlit, unhurried, Mediterranean. He looked at the natural world through overlapping filters of human culture, something hard to do in America, where the tradition is to make it new. The coda of "In Praise of Limestone," which Stephen Spender rightly called one of the century's greatest poems, is a summation of this vision and reveals Auden's unique, even Shakespearian, comprehendingness:

> Dear, I know nothing of
> Either, but when I try to imagine a faultless love
> Or the life to come, what I hear is the murmur
> Of underground streams, what I see is a limestone landscape.

How wonderful, too, that "Nones," another work of the period and perhaps the best Crucifixion poem since the Anglo-Saxon *Dream of the Rood,* should have been written not by a Herbert or a Newman or a Hopkins, but by a middle-aged homosexual on an Italian island who would stop work in mid-line or mid-stanza when the exact hour struck for his martini.

Summer 2007

A version of this lecture appeared in the *Spectator,* 24 February 2007.

7

Air Control in Iraq and the British Idea of Arabia

PRIYA SATIA

W hen Marx said, "History repeats itself, first as tragedy, then as farce," he was underscoring the notion that history cannot in fact repeat, that it is always developing, dialectically. Tragic and often farcical as the current U.S. involvement in Iraq is, it is not a mere repetition of the British attempt to impose colonial control violently over Iraq in the 1920s. Nevertheless, that earlier episode can shed light on the present discontents, to the extent that it produced their "conditions of possibility," including a mode of modern statecraft designed to secure imperial ends in an anti-imperial world.

Britain first obtained control of the former Ottoman provinces that make up Iraq during the Great War. By then, the growth of anti-imperial international opinion made it necessary to dress the Iraqi colony up in more respectable clothes. So the mandate system inaugurated by the new League of Nations assigned newly freed "immature" countries to long-term and generally unsupervised tutelage under more "advanced" powers. Now, to Iraqis, as to many others, "mandate" was nothing but a flimsy imperial disguise, not least because the British had, through a mixture of careless idealism and careful shrewdness, repeatedly promised them independence during the war. Writhing under a protracted military occupation, they mounted a violent insurgency in 1920, at a moment when the British were already facing massive nationalist resistance in Egypt, India, Ireland, and elsewhere.

Militarily and financially overstretched, the imperial state fumbled for creative solutions to counterinsurgency. Early in 1921, Colonial Secretary Winston Churchill called a conference at Cairo. There various experts and officials decided, among other things, to establish an Iraqi constitutional monarchy under the Hashemite prince Feisal (recently booted from Syria by the French) and to police Iraq through a new system known as "air control": the fledgling Royal Air Force would patrol over the country, coordinate information from agents on the ground, and then bombard subversive villages and tribes. Airpower had been used spasmodically elsewhere in the Empire in 1919, but in Iraq the British would rigorously practice bombardment as a permanent method of colonial administration as well as evaluate the air force as an independent arm of the military.

As many scholars have noted, air control was cheap; here, in large measure, lay its attractiveness. But it also served other purposes: its theoretically panoptical power seemed capable of solving the peculiar information problems the British associated with Iraq—in their eyes, a vast desert of mirage, haze, and lying natives. To the intelligence community, Iraq was almost destined for aerial control, for aesthetic as much as practical reasons: the infrastructural austerity of air control seemed suited to a theoretically horizonless desert that allowed power to "radiate" untrammeled "in every part of the protectorate [*sic*]."[1] The region's actual topographical diversity—its mountains, labyrinthine marshes, and varied deserts—when acknowledged, was held up as yet further proof of Iraq's suitability as a training ground for the RAF. Then there was the much-touted "natural fellow-feeling between . . . nomad arabs and the Air Force . . . both . . . in conflict with the vast elemental forces of nature." There were, in short, cultural reasons, related to British imaginings about the region, why air control was first devised in Iraq. After all, reasons of cost and efficiency would have applied equally elsewhere, and indeed, after a brief incubatory period in Iraq, air control was exported elsewhere in the Empire, albeit in modified fashion. But the invention of this unprecedented scheme, which relied on a new technology whose uses had yet to be fully imagined, depended in the first instance on the inspiration provided by notions of Iraq's peculiar suitability to aerial surveillance. T. E. Lawrence, who was closely involved in the plan's formulation, insisted at the outset that it was "*not* capable of universal application." But a decade later, after the scheme had been exported to other parts of the Empire,

experts were disparaging as "absurd" the contention that "some peculiar quality about the country . . . has enabled aircraft to achieve
in Iraq what they could not achieve anywhere else." Nevertheless,
notions of some such "peculiar quality" sustained faith in the Iraqi
scheme throughout the interwar period, despite often vocal skepticism about its efficiency and humanity.

In short, cultural representations shaped the practical organization of surveillance in the Middle East—and its violent excesses.
Hannah Arendt observed: "When the British Intelligence Services
(especially after the First World War) began to attract England's
best sons, who preferred serving mysterious forces all over the world
to serving the common good of their country, the stage seemed to
be set for all possible horrors," but, happily, "cruelty played a lesser
role [in the British Empire] between the two World Wars than ever
before and a minimum of human rights was always safeguarded."[2]
It is time to re-examine received wisdom about the relatively benign
nature of the interwar British state and to try to understand how
British officials reconciled genuine ethical scruples with the actual
violence of imperial policing in the Middle East.

INTENSE BRITISH SURVEILLANCE OF OTTOMAN ARABIA began at
the turn of the century when the effects of rivalry with Germany,
nationalist movements within the Ottoman Empire, and the intelligence failures of the Boer War combined to recommend more energetic intelligence-gathering in the region. Britain's obligations to
the Ottomans under their official alliance meant that military officers on leave, diplomats, gentlemanly scholars, archaeologists, journalists, and other sorts of informal agents were the primary sources
of intelligence.

Once there, these agents complained of the great difficulty of
gathering intelligence in a proverbially inscrutable land, "peopled,"
as one put it, "mainly by the spirits of the Arabian Nights, where
little surprise would be occasioned in . . . seeing a genie floating . . .
out of a magic bottle." It was so "uncanny" that another felt "suddenly transplanted to the . . . moon." The fundamentals of cartog-
raphy in an infamous "white spot," an uncharted blank, remained
a challenge for distracted and dreamy agents, who often had great
difficulty simply determining where they were. Unsurprisingly, they
concluded the region was "very much the same everywhere." In any
case, "in keeping with the country," the local population was so
prone to exaggeration that, in the words of Captain Gerard Leachman, "one cannot believe a word . . . one hears."

Despite all this, "Arabia"—as they referred to this geographic and

cultural imaginary—did seem to possess certain virtues lost to an
increasingly decadent and bourgeois Britain—as the difficulties
of the Boer War had made clear. Indeed, many of these informal
agents had been drawn to the work as a means of venturing to an
antique and romantic land under cover of patriotic duty. In Arabia,
one agent wrote, "one may step straight from this modern age of
bustle and chicanery into an era of elemental conditions . . . back
into the pages of history to mediaeval times." Extending their ro-
manticization of the noble Arab to themselves, they saw the desert as
a haven for individuals who prized "boundless liberty," whether they
had been born there or had fled there to escape civilization's relent-
less smothering of their instincts. As one of the few places the Royal
Geographical Society ranked "Still Unknown," Arabia also offered
the chance to revive the heroic pioneer spirit of Victorian exploration. Informality, a libertarian ethic, and a nostalgic hankering after
imperial fame kept intelligence in the Middle East distinct from the
discreet intelligence activity afoot elsewhere. Arabia was considered
a kind of "spy-space" in its very essence, where professional methodological and ethical standards simply did not apply: "Crossing the
Mediterranean," explained an agent, "one entered a new realm of
espionage . . . full of Eastern . . . cunning and subterfuge . . . in
which the spy no longer emerged bogey-like as in the West."

Indeed, intelligence in "Arabia" seemed delightfully to resemble
the intelligence world of the emerging genre of spy fiction, with
whose development it neatly dovetailed. Deeply conscious of working in the region of the Bible and the *Odyssey*, where espionage had
always been an integral part of the epic struggle for knowledge of
the self, these agents self-consciously followed their fictional contemporary, Kipling's Kim, in seeing "no contradiction between being
a spy and being a spiritual disciple."[3] (Indeed, H. St. John Philby,
who ultimately fell out with the government and defected to Saudi
Arabia, named his even more notorious son after Kipling's protagonist.) In the "infinitely mysterious" desert, faith, rather than facts
or visual data, seemed a reasonably practical objective. They embraced a new anti-empiricist epistemology: if travel in blank Arabia
numbed the senses, it did, as one traveler put it, allow one to "see,
hear, feel, *outside the senses* (emphasis added)." Indeed, many agents
wanted the job precisely for a chance to escape the existential dilemmas then being unleashed by Western science; the very forces fuel-
ing the turn-of-the-century mystical revival drove these adventurers
to the ancient seats of occultism, then being excavated by affiliates
of the intelligence community. The apparent limitations on empirical intelligence-gathering in Arabia tended to open the door to a
breed of explorer-agents willing, like the contemporary philosophi-

cal and artistic avant-garde, to experiment with new theories of perception and more "unscientific" ways of knowing.

As a basis of knowledge, faith could at once solve agents' intelligence-gathering difficulties and provide an antidote to their spiritual cravings. To them, Arabia, of all magical, mysterious places, was *the* place for miraculous conviction: in the words of the informal spy and infamous future secret diplomat Mark Sykes, "the desert is of God and in the desert no man may deny Him." Despite the sway of the secular discourse of Orientalism, there remained a lingering perception that Arabia was a biblical homeland to which Britons could return in search of the "perfection of mental content" that Arabs "alone, even among Asiatics," seemed to possess. Primitivism was trendy, however racist. Arab "wisdom" was intuitive rather than intellectual, as beyond scientific check as all things Arabian: "The European thinks, the Oriental only reflects," theorized the journalist Meredith Townsend, "and if left to himself the idea, turned over and over endlessly . . . is part of the fibre of his mind." This was as much a product of place as race: a traveler in Mesopotamia echoed, "In . . . desert countries . . . the essential facts . . . sink into you imperceptibly, until . . . they are . . . woven into the fibres of your nature."

Thus, agents' distraction from empirical intelligence gathering also offered a way forward through an intuitive strategy. By intuition, they meant the acquired ability to think like an Arab, an empathetic mimicry of the "Arab mind," for, they held, "Only by Orientals—or by those whose long sojourn in the East has formed their minds after the Oriental pattern—can the Orient be adequately described." Agents like Norman Bray determined to "merge . . . in the Oriental . . . absorb his ideas, see with his eyes, and hear with his ears, to the fullest extent possible to one bred in British traditions." And, of course, the powers of T. E. Lawrence, then an archaeologist with ties to the intelligence community, were later traced to what Basil Liddell Hart called an "immersion in [the Arabs], by sympathetic projection."

Agents prized the intuitive ability to discern truth from the dross of Arabian deception. What made Arabist experts *expert* was their ability to see, like Arabs, beyond surface deceptions, to discern the real from the unreal, the mirage, the lie. Knowing Arabia was a matter of genius. "Book knowledge" mattered little, for, Bray explained, "we 'sensed' the essence of a matter." The gifted few seemed, to contemporaries, preternaturally omniscient: "Leachman . . . knew everything." Thus, at the outbreak of war they exercised a remarkable influence over the intelligence and military tactics employed in the Middle East, not least the innovative use of airpower. Besides its uses in desert mapping and communication, the intelligence community praised its "enormous political possibilities," discovered when the Iraqi tribes the British liberated got "out of hand and require[d] a lesson" in the form of an "aerial raid with bombs and machine guns."

It was to these agents that the petrified British government turned during the post-war Iraqi rebellion, and it was with their help that Churchill obtained approval of the scheme at Cairo. The RAF officially took over in October 1922. The full-fledged force eventually consisted of eight squadrons of fighters and light bombers, four armored-car units, and several thousand Iraq Levies. Army garrisons were gradually reduced until they protected only the nine air bases equipped with wireless telegraphy. In a single two-day operation, a squadron might drop several dozen tons of bombs and thousands of incendiaries and fire thousands of rounds of small-arms ammunition.

Despite the agents' hopes, the dream of omniscience remained a dream: the regime was plagued by reports of pilot disorientation, visibility problems, and instances "of quite inexplicable failures to identify . . . whole sections of bedouin tribes on the move." It was not uncommon for aircraft to make a "demonstration" over or bomb the wrong town. Bafflingly, "hostile parties" found cover in watercourses, hillocks, and other features of the allegedly "featureless" landscape. Assessing the effect of operations was itself "a matter of guesswork." (Some historians nevertheless claim aerial control actually worked against the desert's "clearly defined, completely visible targets.")[4]

But in an infamously deceptive land, all this inaccuracy was easily dismissed: the Civil Commissioner and head of political intelligence, Arnold Wilson, explained that complaints about RAF observation failures were, like all information, necessarily exaggerated, not least because mirages prevented fair judgment of pilots from the ground. In any case, accuracy itself was moot, since aircraft were meant to be everywhere at once, "conveying a silent warning." "Terror," grounded in notions of Arab exaggeration, was the scheme's explicit tactical principle: where there was one plane, Arabs would spread news of dozens; a few casualties would instill fear of hundreds. Air control would work like the classic panopticon, for, an official memo explained, "from the ground every inhabitant of a village is under the impression that the occupant of an aeroplane is actually looking at *him* . . . that all their movements are being watched and reported." If pilots could not be sure whether they were looking at "warlike" or "ordinary" tribes, neither could tribes discriminate "between bombing and reconnaissance expeditions." In its Iraqi co-

coon, the RAF was safe from criticism of inaccuracy, protected by the notorious fallibility of all news from Arabia.

Moreover, the foundation in "terror" was held up as the regime's ingenious proof *against* inhumanity. In theory, invisible airpower would bloodlessly awe tribes into submission, just as guerrilla warfare exploited what Lawrence called the "silent threat of a vast unknown desert."[5] Alternatively, interference with its victims' daily lives, through the destruction of homes, villages, fuel, crops, and livestock, would produce the desired result. Of course, the system's inhumanity stemmed from its inability to distinguish between combatants and noncombatants, in its violent destruction of their possessions as much as their lives. And as early RAF statements openly acknowledged, the "moral effect" depended on demonstrations of exemplary violence, which could hardly be accomplished without loss of life. In any case, theory aside, however diligent the RAF may have been in giving warnings by loudspeaker, leaflets, and "demonstration flights," the "pacification" of Iraq proved horrifically costly in Iraqi lives—a hundred casualties was not unusual in a single operation, not to mention those lost to starvation and the burning of villages. Whether for attacking British communications, refusing to pay taxes at crushing rates, or harboring wanted rebels, many tribes and villages were ultimately bombed into submission.

In the wake of all this slaughter, critical voices began to emerge in Whitehall. The new War Secretary wrote witheringly, "If the Arab population realize that the peaceful control of Mesopotamia depends on our intention of bombing women and children, I am very doubtful if we shall gain that acquiescence of the fathers and husbands of Mesopotamia as a whole to which the Secretary of State for the Colonies looks forward." This critique was amplified in the press and Parliament, where many had looked upon the Iraqi venture as outdated imperial foolishness from the very outset.

All this official displeasure quickly elicited explanatory memoranda from the Air Ministry, arguing in the main that "all war is not only brutal but indiscriminate in its brutality." The Air Staff pointed to the comparative effects on civilians of naval bombardment, shelling, blockading, trampling by invading armies, and so on, urging that at least the lives of attackers were safer in air operations. Speaking as unsentimental realists, they insisted paradoxically on "the great humanity of bombing," for, however "ghastly"—indeed, because so ghastly—it forced the enemy to give up quickly, thereby preventing untold further losses.

The Great War had certainly shifted notions about humanity and warfare; to many military thinkers, the moral imperative was to minimize casualties as a whole rather than civilian deaths in particular, since modern combatants were merely civilians in uniform. Nevertheless, the Air Staff did not really address the concerns of those who were equally offended by modern war's general brutality or of those who considered aerial bombardment, in its all-seeing omnipotence, more lethal and terrible than older forms of barbarity. But most saliently, their counterexamples—naval bombardment, blockades, and the like—were all wartime measures. The Air Staff paper was meant to discuss bombing as a peacetime policing technique. What was permissible only in wartime elsewhere turned out to be always permissible in Iraq. The Air Secretary acknowledged that there things happened "which, if they had happened before the world war, would have been undoubtedly acts of war."

This military permissiveness drew not only on racism—indeed, many airpower theorists based their faith in the bomber on the notion that people were the same everywhere and would respond in the same manner to its power. It drew, more importantly, on the agents' ideas about the nature of Iraq, a mystical and romantic land existing somewhere beyond the pale of worldly and bourgeois "convention," a place where honor and bravery (however mindless) were enacted in a theatre of perennial conflict. The RAF intelligence officer John Glubb, later "Glubb Pasha" of the Arab Legion, insisted, "Life in the desert is a continuous guerilla warfare," and this meant striking hard and fast because that was the way of "Bedouin war." To Bedouin, war was a "romantic excitement" whose production of "tragedies, bereavements, widows and orphans" was a "normal way of life," "natural and inevitable." Their appetite for war was the source of their belief that they were "elites of the human race." In this view, it would almost be a cultural offense *not* to bomb them with all the might of the Empire. For their part, as "knights of the air," airmen had brought chivalry, in the sense of honorable combat between elite warriors, back into an otherwise thoroughly grim and "vulgarised" modern warfare. Arnold Wilson assured the Air Ministry that the problem was one only of British public perception, that Iraqis were used to a state of constant warfare, expected justice without kid gloves, had no patience with sentimental distinctions between combatants and noncombatants, and viewed air action as entirely "legitimate and proper." "The natives of a lot of these tribes love fighting for fighting's sake," the former Chief of Air Staff, Hugh Trenchard, assured Parliament in 1930; "They have no objection to being killed." In a place long romanticized as an oasis of prelapsarian egalitarianism and liberty, defenders of air control could rest assured that bomb victims retained their dignity even under bombardment and were not miserable wretches deserving of a condescending pity. After all, according to the military theorist J. M. Spaight, chivalry was an influence quite distinct from "the humanitarian one," which regarded with compassion "those whom chivalry despised."

Thus, Iraqi women and children need not trouble the conscience, for, the British Commander observed, "[Iraqi sheikhs] . . . do not seem to resent . . . that women and children are accidentally killed by bombs." To them, women and children were "negligible" casualties compared to those of "really important men," elaborated Lawrence, conceding this was "too oriental a mood for us to feel very clearly." In 1932 the British High Commissioner warned against clipping the "claws" of the RAF in post-mandatory Iraq because "the term 'civilian population' has a very different meaning in Iraq from what it has in Europe." This was a population at once so orientally backward and so admirably manly and phlegmatic that, to a postwar imperium increasingly in thrall to cultural-relativistic notions, all principles of *ius in bello* were irrelevant. The austerity of tribal existence, a condition imagined to extend to all Iraqis, rendered even concern about destruction of "property" irrelevant—despite the targeting of livestock, camels, and villages.

Moreover, data of any kind was so notoriously difficult to find in Arabia that there seemed little point in worrying about precisely who was killed in the bombings. From the Colonial Office, former agents Richard Meinertzhagen and Reader Bullard assured their colleagues in Iraq that their bombs had little effect beyond fright and that excessive concern over "results" was needless, since both aerial and ground observation of casualties was "always misleading" and "news as to casualties [would] drift in from the desert gradually." This cavalier attitude rendered casualties entirely, well, casual: "If the Civil Commissioner is going on to Mosul," read a general-headquarters telegram to Wilson, "will he be so kind as to drop a bomb on Batas"—and this was apparently the sort of kindness he never objected to. Striking at a phantom enemy and enjoying the bliss of willful ignorance at the outcome allowed air control to sit more easily in the official mind. Only in Arabia, about which the British had long decided nothing could ever be really known, did such fecklessness make sense and thus make air control acceptable.

Air control also seemed to fit comfortably in a biblical land. In 1932, when the inhumanity of air control was of some pressing importance at the world disarmament conference in Geneva, the High

Commissioner in Iraq argued that unlike the outrages inevitably committed by ground troops, "bombing from the air is regarded almost as an act of God to which there is no effective reply but immediate submission." Lawrence similarly translated the "impersonally fateful" nature of bombing in the Arab's eyes: "It is not punishment, but a misfortune from heaven striking the community." Arabia was a biblical place, and Arabs knew that; they expected periodic calamity and continual news of life and death. Bombardment was to them yet another kind of visitation. Air control played on their presumed fatalism, their faith in the incontrovertible "will of God." Such people could bear random acts of violence in a way that Europeans, coddled by secular notions of justice and human rights, could not. Hence, the frequent emphasis on not breeding too much familiarity with aircraft, lest the Arabs cease to view them as vehicles of divine retribution.

As a biblical space, Arabia was also a place of elemental clashes between good and evil, out of the realm of ordinary, mortal law. Living in a "world of violence, bloodshed and war," the chivalrous Bedouin were held to possess "depths of hatred . . . of which our lukewarm natures seem no longer capable . . . deeds of generosity worthy of fairy-tales and acts of treachery of extraordinary baseness." Their "love of dramatic actions" outweighed "the dictates of reason or the material needs," and even, the General Staff affirmed, overcame the "inherent dislike of getting killed." In this last bastion of authentic experience, bombardment could be accommodated as yet another vitalizing experience—one shared equally by airmen. No group did more to fulfill this romantic vision of air control than the Ikhwan, Abdul Aziz ibn Saud's puritanical avant-garde forces, which continually raided into Iraq from Najd. Gertrude Bell, then a powerful intelligence and administrative force in Iraq, was fiercely proud of "our power to strike back" at the Ikhwan, who, "with their horrible fanatical appeal to a medieval faith, rouse in me the blackest hatred." Bloodlust was the way of the place, and the mantra was "When in Rome . . ."

These clashes between good and evil transformed "pacification" into a series of episodes of cosmic significance. Living in constant fear of assassination during the rebellion, Political Officer Leachman "reveled in dropping bombs on Arabs concealed in a hollow," according to his adoring fellow officer Bray. The transposition of real Arabia into the Arabia of myth, the consummate spy-space, made bombing palatable, even to those who believed they would revile it any other context. The vindication of air control grew out of long-circulating ideas about Arabia as a place somehow exempt from the this-worldliness that constrained human activity in other parts of the world. There heroes could reach the most exalted heights and villains the profoundest depths; there, as in literature, agents could find escape from the pitiful reality of human suffering into an exalted sphere in which everything possessed a cosmic significance. There, where each soul was free to work out its cosmic destiny, violence was entirely personal: Leachman's murderer, Dhari, was the single exception to the general amnesty granted after the rebellion. He was not seen as a member of that uprising, but as someone who had violated the honor between two men; the Iraqi unrest was reconfigured as an episode of medieval battle in which the mettle of chivalric men was tested and rewarded. In this "supreme crisis," Bray wrote, "every quality [Leachman] possessed, *even his faults,* served the cause of England" (emphasis added).

Ordering bombardment was thus entirely consonant with the sensibility of the Arabist agent enchanted with notions of Arabian liberty. The agents loved Arabia for its otherworldliness, and it was that quality that also made it fit to bear the unearthly destruction wreaked by bombers. Britons considered the moral world of Arabia distinct from their own. From the outset, the intelligence project in Arabia had been infused with a philosophical spirit, which did not depart it at this stage.

The Arabian window of acceptability opened the door to wider uses of aerial bombardment: in 1921 the Air Staff deemed it better, for fear of allegations of "barbarity," "to preserve appearances . . . by still nominally confining bombardment to targets which are strictly military . . . [and] avoid emphasizing the truth that air warfare has made such restrictions obsolete and impossible. It may be some time until another war occurs and meanwhile the public may become educated as to the meaning of air power." Iraq offered the Air Staff a romantic theatre in which to sell the new warfare. It worked. Eventually, British bombs fell frictionlessly all over the world, including in Europe. The gruesome relish evident in a 1924 report by the officer commanding Squadron 45 in Iraq is striking in this regard: "The Arab and Kurd . . . now know what real bombing means, in casualties and damage; they now know that within 45 minutes a full sized village . . . can be practically wiped out and a third of its inhabitants killed or injured by four or five machines which offer them no real target, no opportunity for glory as warriors, no effective means of escape." This officer later achieved distinction, and, writes David Omissi, "in the ruins of this dying village one can dimly perceive the horrific firestorms of Hamburg and Dresden," for the officer was none other than Arthur Harris, head of Bomber

Command in the Second World War.[6] It was largely under his influence that Prime Minister Churchill warded off pangs of conscience
about bombing Germany by putting his faith in the "higher poetic
justice" that "those who have loosed these horrors upon mankind
will now in their homes and persons feel the shattering stroke of
retribution."[7] It was the Ikhwan all over again, and Europe itself
had become the scene of a clash between good and evil—a gradual
transposition that dated to the days before Hitler's seizure of power,
when "fascist" was an epithet hurled against the Saudi government
and Britons began to fear that bombs would not so much secure the
Empire as turn Britain into a desert.

IDEAS ABOUT "ARABIA" EXONERATED AIR CONTROL from charges of
inhumanity, but the regime also projected an actively humane image. This public relations coup was largely a product of the regime's
much-touted reliance on political officers on the ground, whose supposed intuitive understanding of the place carried within it a claim
to an empathetic style of colonial control. From the outset, despite
their fondness for the aerial regime, the community of agents insisted on the enduring need for "men who are specially gifted, who
have got the feeling of the Middle East in their blood." They had
little to fear: the RAF quickly realized it needed such agents on the
ground to ascertain just when the desired "moral effect" had been
achieved. They were also crucial for coping with the visibility problems that plagued the supposedly all-seeing regime.

The RAF's Special Service Officers worked closely with pilots and
regular political officers, quickly absorbing the latter's tactics. Intuitive ability and a canny knowledge of local custom were deemed
indispensable to acquiring the information required for bombardment, given the "peculiar mentality" of tribesmen, "who," in Glubb's
words, "deemed it a duty to . . . welcome a guest, although he was
mapping their villages with a view to bombing them and told them
so." The RAF trusted these officers to accurately "sense impending
events" (even if not to "dig down to the facts"). Successful bombardment was often attributed to their genius, wireless technology allowing them to communicate swiftly with aircraft—from their mouths
to God's ears.

In theory, these agents facilitated the work of the pilots, and the
latter in turn enabled them to roam freely and achieve greater intimacy with the local population. Backed by the skeletal air regime,
these men on the spot, in the eyes of the ever-nostalgic former agents
in the Colonial Office, were akin to those intrepid Britons of an
older, braver age who had served in frontier zones at the bidding of

"an adventurous spirit." For all its modernity, the austere air-control regime strengthened the feeling that in Arabia they could be as imperialists of old. It was the agents' proximity to the local population that ensured the RAF could, the Air Staff explained, "[pick] out the right villages . . . to hit . . . when trouble comes." By this ironic logic, the RAF's successful persecution of a village testified to the regime's benevolent intimacy with people on the ground, without which they would not have been able to strike it accurately.

Indeed, the claim to empathy ultimately underwrote the entire air-control system with its authoritative reassurances that bombardment was a culturally suitable tactic in this region. As late as 1957, RAF Marshal Sir John Slessor defended the regime by pointing to the Special Service Officers, who "became so attached to their tribesmen that they sometimes almost 'went native.'" Well into the 1980s, Glubb insisted, "The basis of our desert control was not force but . . . love."[8] In 1989, a military historian—cited even by American air force officers—again vindicated the regime by pointing to Glubb, since, "no European was ever closer and more sympathetic to the Arabs than [he]."[9] And in 2003, Captain Todd Brown, an American, defended brutal policing in Iraq thus: "You have to understand the Arab mind. . . . The only thing they understand is . . . force, pride and saving face."[10]

At the end of the day, the claim to empathy was built on sand. From its Edwardian invention as an intelligence epistemology, it signalled not the recognition of a common humanity but a self-alienating strategy for coping in an alternate physical and moral universe. After the war, aspiring agents, inspired partly by the legends surrounding their predecessors, continued to venture to enchanted, biblical Arabia to escape the bonds of too much civilization, to recover a noble, free spirit lost to "utilitarian" England. Travel in the desert was still understood as an escape into the blue, a truant fulfillment of patriotic duty. Glubb knew that "in the desert I was alone. The government was indifferent." To enter Arabia was still to exit the customary world, in both senses of the word, since "the desert is a world in itself."

The "extraordinary and romantic" world of the RAF in Iraq compounded this feeling of being in a world apart. Its tenuous links to "civilisation" through a miraculous wireless infrastructure, and rumors of Lawrence's presence in the ranks, only fed its Arabian mystique. If flight over the austere biblical terrain reached new heights of sublimity and divinity, it also produced "quite a bad effect upon one's nerves," a feeling that "the end of the world had really come," according to one RAF official. For new pilots, this "sense of being

lost at sea" was deemed a critical "mental factor." Pilots could identify "that air of quiet weariness which comes to those who have been
in the desert too long." They fell prey to a "nameless terror" that
made them go mad as time passed. This was not a place for empathy, but for total psychic breakdown; without some kind of bracing,
Britons risked losing their minds. Emulation of Arabs was intended
to enable their survival in this extraterrestrial space, but did not
produce compassion for the Arab victims of the surreal world of
bombardment they actually created. Thus did Iraq actually become
a place beyond the reach of secular and humanitarian law.

THE BRITISH CONCESSION OF IRAQI INDEPENDENCE in 1932 was con-
fessedly "nominal"; the Air Staff made it clear that the change upon
Iraqi admission to the League would be "more apparent than real."
Special Service Officers remained on the loose, despite the Iraqi
government's objections. The Air Ministry defended such continuities by reminding Parliament that this was "an oriental country
where intrigue is rife." Making it just that themselves, they privately
conceded, "We really have no defence."

   Air control was a mechanism of control for a region where more
overt colonial rule was a political impossibility, since, as the Air
Ministry theorized, "in countries of this sort . . . the impersonal
drone of an aeroplane . . . is not so obtrusive as . . . soldiers." Even
British public opinion was irrelevant: the scheme's cheapness was
explicitly intended to elude the democratic check of taxpayers. It
allowed the covert pursuit of empire in an increasingly anti-imperial
world—indeed, today's drawdown plans for Iraq apparently also include a plan to replace American troops with airpower that could
"strike everywhere—and at once," in the ominous words of a Pentagon consultant.[11]

   After reoccupying the country during the Second World War, the
RAF finally left Iraq in 1958. Two years later, Glubb reflected on how
humans justify their actions: Saud had unleashed the massacring
Ikhwan to consolidate his power, all the while "breathing the . . .
service of God," and the United States, breathing its own lofty ideals, had dropped the atomic bomb on Hiroshima. Neither, he explains, was guilty of hypocrisy, for "the human mind is a surprising mechanism." "Hypocrisy" is indeed useless as an explanation,
however useful it may be as a description, of the failures of avowedly
enlightened regimes. This lecture has attempted to lay bare the
"surprising mechanism" of the British official mind that enabled it,
with mostly clear conscience, indeed with confidence in a consistent
paternalism, to invent and implement the world's first air-control re-

gime. The "idea of Arabia" circulated by agents over the previous two decades had provided them with a key for evading all charges of hypocrisy and brutality. Criticism was never totally silenced, but enough people were convinced, indeed impressed, for the regime to remain viable for the entire interwar period.

Fall Semester 2006

1. All references to archival sources can be found in my forthcoming book, *Spies in Arabia: The Great War and the Cultural Foundations of Britain's Covert Empire in the Middle East* (Oxford University Press).

2. Hannah Arendt, *Imperialism: Part Two of "The Origins of Totalitarianism"* (1951; New York, 1968 edn.), p. 101.

3. Jon Thompson, *Fiction, Crime, and Empire: Clues to Modernity and Postmodernism* (Urbana, Ill., 1993), p. 87.

4. Sven Lindqvist, *A History of Bombing,* trans. Linda Haverty Rugg (2000; trans., New York, 2001), p. 68.

5. T. E. Lawrence, *The Seven Pillars of Wisdom: A Triumph* (1926; New York, 1991 edn.), p. 196.

6. David Omissi, *Air Power and Colonial Control: The Royal Air Force, 1919–1939* (Manchester, 1990), p. 154.

7. W. G. Sebald, *On the Natural History of Destruction,* trans. Anthea Bell (1999; trans., New York, 2003), pp. 19–24.

8. John Glubb, *The Changing Scenes of Life: An Autobiography* (London, 1983), p. 105.

9. Philip Towle, *Pilots and Rebels: The Use of Aircraft in Unconventional Warfare, 1918–1988* (Washington, D.C., 1989), p. 54.

10. Dexter Filkins, "Tough New Tactics by U.S. Tighten Grip on Iraq Towns," *New York Times,* 7 Dec. 2003.

11. Quoted in Seymour M. Hersh, "Up in the Air: Where is the Iraq War Headed Next?" *New Yorker,* 5 Dec. 2005, http://www.newyorker.com/fact/content/articles/051205fa_fact.

8

Arthur Marder and the Battles for British Naval History

BARRY GOUGH

The battle of Jutland—fought 31 May and 1 June 1916 between fleets of the famed Royal Navy and the aspiring Imperial German Navy—remains to this day one of the most puzzling and hotly disputed topics of modern history. Arguably the finest analysis of the event and its participants, including those in command at sea as well as those who directed the course of fleets from the admiralties, was written by the unlikeliest of persons. That historian was Arthur Jacob Marder, the Boston-born eldest child of Russian Jewish immigrant parents, and a young scholar who had entered Harvard College on the sole merit of high school achievement. He surmounted difficulties thrown up by the Depression and earned a traveling fellowship to visit London so as to complete research for his dissertation. By accident or fate, by dint of dedication and energy, and by intellectual curiosity and historical training, he became a master of British naval history of the First World War and of the battle of Jutland in particular.

On 31 May 1966, fifty years after the event that rocked British confidence in its sea supremacy, a reporter and a photographer from London's *Evening Standard* found Marder, age fifty-five, lounging in a canvas chair in sunny Hyde Park. The headline of the feature column "Londoner's Diary" noted that Marder was the ranking authority on Jutland and that his book *Jutland and After* had been published on that precise date to mark the anniversary. In answer

to the reporter's questions, Marder glibly replied that he was the
world's expert on Emma Hamilton, Nelson's love. As to his discussion of Jutland, it was the interrelationship of the remarkable persons involved and how they had directed the course of the war that
was most compelling, he explained. The Royal Navy had retained
mastery of the seas despite considerable mauling of its assets by
the Germans. Winston Churchill, wearing his historian's hat, was
quoted to the effect that it would take another war to display with
success the abilities of British admirals and their ships.

The photograph showed Marder to be middle aged, balding,
chubby, and bespectacled. His relaxed composure, revealing a
friendly, gregarious nature, belied his seriousness and, perhaps
most, his complete dedication to his task. None of the hardships
that he had endured—in getting to his exalted station as the principal historian of the British navy of that period or in surmount-
ing numerous difficulties to obtain access to the documents and
private papers upon which such a monumental history could be
constructed—were revealed in the thousand words the newspaper
devoted to Marder and his Jutland book. But for an American to
be so featured surely gave the wide British readership cause for
wonder, perhaps even concern: how was it that an American had
come to tell the innermost secrets of that famous battle? This was
Marder's mystery. And there were echoes, too, of Admiral Alfred
Thayer Mahan's explanation to the British in 1890 that their greatness depended on the British fleet, British seaborne trade, and colonies and bases that "locked up the world," as Admiral Lord ("Jacky")
Fisher proclaimed.

That same day BBC television featured Marder as an authority
on Jutland. The after-action viewers' survey showed high approval
ratings for the program and for Marder's part in it. That evening,
too, Oxford University Press gave its acclaimed author a party at its
London office and invited many of the famed admirals and historians who had helped Marder. All in all, the fiftieth anniversary of
Jutland was a Marder triumph. And subsequent reviews of the book
in newspapers and journals testified to Marder's greatness.

Among those giving unqualified praise was Captain Stephen
Roskill, Royal Navy, who in retirement had become an historian
working for the Cabinet Office. Soon Roskill's work was to become
the only serious rival to Marder's. Within two years, Roskill, since
named official biographer of the late Colonel Maurice Hankey,
the celebrated "man of secrets" of the Committee of Imperial
Defence and the Cabinet secretariat, came forward to challenge
Marder's right to use the Hankey diaries for 1918. Marder became

irritated by Roskill's obstruction, for previously Hankey's heir had granted Marder unfettered use of the diaries. But Marder lost this battle, and his original text, which contained extracts from the diary, had to be changed in proofs. Marder was hurt by Roskill's action, for it was his view that scholars should help one another. The ensuing rivalry became increasingly heated: the two quarreled in pages of the *Times Literary Supplement* and in the text, footnotes, and appendices of their subsequent books. Their private correspondence to third parties is peppered with slights and accusations about the other.

The dispute became celebrated. A. J. P. Taylor, himself a stormy petrel of historical studies, referred to the disputants as "Our Historical Dreadnoughts." Brian Ranft and other naval historians referred to the squabble in their publications. Michael Howard dubbed them "sparring partners." Marder and Roskill were more than pugilists in training: something more serious underscored their rivalry. The protagonist was Roskill. He was of the service, that is, a former officer in the Royal Navy. He knew the navy from within, and he held strong views about those he had served with and served under. Marder, by contrast, came to his topic and task as an outsider: everything he learned about the navy he discovered as a student of history—by examining records; reading reports of proceedings, signals, and correspondence; culling through memoirs; interviewing admirals and captains; and sifting through mounds of periodicals and newspapers. Marder, trained at a premier university in historical methods, kept his judgments under tight rein. Caution ruled, though he demonstrated a clear analytical instinct and he liked the prospect of examining the anatomies, so to speak, of institutions. In fact, the first book he wrote on the Royal Navy bore the title *Anatomy of British Sea Power, 1880–1905* (1940).

That an American had unlocked Britannia's secrets always remained a subject of wonder, surprise, and even consternation. But that he was based at universities in faraway Honolulu and, later, Southern California added an exotic twist to the story. Marder had ventured to the remote and isolated University of Hawaii in 1944, fresh from work in the Research and Analysis division of the Office of Strategic Services, precursor of the CIA, in Washington, D.C., and U.S. Army intelligence-personnel education at Hamilton College in Clinton, New York. Marder made the best of it. Rising to senior professorial rank, he showed outstanding abilities as a teacher, launching the first-ever courses on world history at Hawaii. He studied Japanese and Japanese history, a subject to which he later reverted when he examined the comparative, intertwining histories of the Royal Navy and the Imperial Japanese Navy from 1936 to 1945 for the two volumes of *Old Friends, New Enemies*. Travel from his distant places of domicile to London was as time-consuming as it was expensive. But from student days, Marder had learned how to travel inexpensively.

Once arrived in London, he toiled intensively, barely stopping for a sandwich at lunchtime (when admirals and admiralty secretaries would head for their clubs for extended periods of dining and chat). On days when libraries and repositories were closed to researchers, Marder would journey by train or country bus to visit an admiral or his widow in some remote manor, there often to find pure literary gold in a trunk in an attic. Between teaching terms, Marder would fetch up at, say, the Penn Club or the Langham Hotel, Bloomsbury, hard by the British Museum Library and not far by foot from White-hall or the National Archives' old Public Record Office in Chancery Lane. His list of documents to read seemed long, even endless. Time was of the essence. The story soon got about that Marder, freshly arrived from Heathrow, rushed to the order counter of the British Museum Library Reading Room, presented his requests, and told the serving officer that he had only four months to complete his work and not a moment to lose. All of this is probably true, for even if an admiral of the fleet asked Marder to dine with him at his club on his next visit to town, the historian surely would decline. Instead, he could be found toiling over a newly released file in the National Archives or examining, by special arrangement with the secretary and the Board of Admiralty, certain dockets normally held under lock and key in "the cage," specifically precious papers of the First Lord and First Sea Lord of the Admiralty not yet "released" to the National Archives.

Marder's dervish-like visits to, say, the Admiralty Library were something remarkable for a young student like me to witness. The librarian would have all the documents set out systematically in a closed room, one usually open to others on any day other than that designated for Marder. Judicial appraisals of the glittering historical jewels would take place, arrangements for copying speedily finalized, and new needs for remaining work assayed. By this time, Marder's "sweeps" had got the attention of staff members: they sharpened an otherwise enervate atmosphere.

Marder's supreme aide, Lieutenant-Commander Peter Kemp, ran the Admiralty Library. He became one of three devoted helpers who enabled Marder to find the details he needed. The others were Vice-Admiral Sir Peter Gretton and Captain John Creswell, who, like Kemp, were veterans of the sea and the navy and who became interlocutors, so to speak, between the British naval past and the sort of naval history Marder was writing. All were naval historians of stature. Creswell, who admired Marder's talents and objected to Roskill's judgments, toiled for ten pleasant years on Marder's work. Creswell had "barged in," that is, volunteered his knowledge and his time, he told Marder in one of his last letters, for it occurred to him when reading *From the Dreadnought to Scapa Flow: The Road to War, 1904–1914,* an introductory volume, what a pity it would be if, when Marder got to writing about the war at sea in 1914 and after, he should not be able to check his views by the opinions of someone who had been brought up to seafaring and had known war at first-hand. Put another way, by bringing these experiences to Marder's attention, he could minimize the perils that Marder faced as an historian without a naval background. (Marder helped Kemp, Gretton, and Creswell with their books, but this was small recompense for their generous and mighty assistance to Marder.) On each of the five volumes that compose Marder's *From the Dreadnought to Scapa Flow: The Royal Navy in the Fisher Era, 1904–19,* this committee of arch-Marderites toiled tirelessly.[1] Loyal and generous without counting the cost to themselves, they worked as a loose team, circulating drafts and answering the author's stream of queries. On occasion they corrected Marder's mistakes and misapprehensions, notably Marder's overly strong criticism of Jellicoe.

Not least in Marder's favor was a professional and avuncular publisher, Oxford University Press, which lured Marder away from Jonathan Cape and made Marder into one of its pre-eminent authors. In total, Marder produced an astonishing fourteen volumes: one by Knopf, four by Cape, and nine by OUP. Marder kept up a torrid pace, one that left scant time for anything but business. "But that's your affair," Roskill chided in reference to Marder's planned Saturday-afternoon visit to Roskill's country residence, noting that Marder moved at the speed of an intercontinental ballistic missile.[2]

Adding to Marder's mystery and the wonder of his achievement is the story of how he became a naval historian in the first place. It was a matter of chance or, as Marder would have it, fate. When rushing down the stairs of Harvard's Widener Library to keep a lunch date, Marder, then a young undergraduate, barged into Professor William Langer, the up-and-coming dean of international diplomatic historians and the intended supervisor of Marder's undergraduate thesis. Langer took the occasion to ask the embarrassed Marder what topic he had selected. Marder blurted out something about the Kaiser's generals. No, said Langer, that had been done; besides, new documents on the mission of the minister of the War Office,

Lord Haldane, to Berlin in 1912, the last serious attempt of the British government to end the Anglo-German naval race, had just been released. That settled it. His imagination fired by this glimpse of naval rivalry, Marder concentrated on the Royal Navy, beginning with the year 1880, in all subsequent seminar papers and theses. No serious academic writing was being done on this subject at the time, especially on the links between the navy and foreign policy. It was a vacuum waiting to be filled, he told Taylor in an interview for BBC TV, and nature abhorred a vacuum, he added.[3] Why had he not chosen the U.S. Navy for his subject, some wanted to know. It seemed less interesting, Marder replied, and besides, Admiral Samuel Eliot Morison was writing the big American naval history. These were offhand answers and only slightly credible: the fact of the matter was that Marder found in British naval history a means of writing about recent European naval histories and rivalries in times of peace and war. He provided the naval and maritime dimensions of larger cataclysmic events and circumstances, perspectives that other professionals in the historical line could not master.

But the road that Marder had to travel to get to his destination was always rocky and tortuous, especially in his quest for documentation. His years at Harvard, where his training, largely in the school of Leopold von Ranke, taught him that all materials needed to be collected and examined before a proper estimation of their contents and merits could be made, instilled in him the need to master his sources. Langer, who marveled at his student's unfailing progress and brilliant reception at the hands of various critics, including Taylor's rhapsodizing of Marder, once joked that he thought Marder would have to hire a vessel the size of the liner *Queen Elizabeth* to bring home all the documents collected on one long sortie in the British records.[4] But Marder always repaid Langer's lovely comments, for his mentor had set the highest standards and was himself a brilliant teacher and role model.

IF FATE OR CHANCE BROUGHT MARDER TO NAVAL HISTORY, it also played a second role, in how he continued his research. In 1938, when he ventured to London to get the inside details on naval policy-making necessary to complete his *Anatomy of British Sea Power,* he found the doors barred to private researchers, like himself, trying to get access to Admiralty papers. In London, Marder wrote to the Admiralty Records Office Holdings and made his case, saying that he needed to return to the United States before too long. The official in charge replied that it was a pity he had so little time to devote to research on the topic in question. Marder, seeing a weakness, immediately replied that there had been a misunderstanding and that he did not have to return as soon as stated. Marder was then asked to provide a list of topics, and in the end the Admiralty agreed to make available for viewing all but two. At that time there was no thirty-year rule, or fifty-year rule, for that matter, and access to departmental records was possible only by private arrangement. G. P. Gooch, the venerable historian, told Marder that he had tried to see the Admiralty papers but without success, so there was no need for the young American to bother about it. But Marder, seeing the chance, got through. He went to the Admiralty Records Office, where a naval officer instructed to read all the requested documents in advance—to prevent the revelation of state secrets—had barely perused them. After three days of plowing through the documents, the officer gave up, leaving Marder to decide what papers he should not see.[5] Joyfully, Marder ransacked the files. His use of these papers required that he not cite them specifically, only as "Admiralty MSS," and Marder kept to this obligation, never violating the trust. His typescripts had to be vetted by the Admiralty secretariat, and he faced possible censorship only with the second volume of *From the Dreadnought to Scapa Flow,* in the sections dealing with the escape of the enemy cruisers *Goeben* and *Breslau* to Constantinople, which helped bring Turkey into the war on the side of the Central Powers, and with the subsequent court-martial of Admiral Troubridge, who was seen to have been capable of preventing the same. In fact, as details in his publisher's files reveal, Marder trenchantly defended himself against what now appears to be an embarrassing attempt by the Admiralty to protect its own reputation.

A third instance of fate playing a role in Marder's rise—and the advance of British naval history more generally—occurred twenty years later. Access to documents in 1938 gave him no advantage after 1945 when he returned to London to resume his work. A stronger door now barred the way. Chilling winds of the Cold War blew though Whitehall. Annually he wrote supplicating letters without result. Marder marked time and turned his talents elsewhere—editing the diaries and letters of Admiral Sir Herbert Richmond, the notedly caustic critic of naval affairs, and gathering the letters of Admiral Lord Fisher, the greatest British sailor since Nelson, the person, Marder argued, who saved the Royal Navy from disaster in the First World War. These works were literary triumphs, and they broadened Marder's reputation. Even so, they were a stopgap for Marder's talents until he could get back to the mother lode of Admiralty documents about how the war at sea was planned and waged.

Late one evening in May 1955, a sleepy Marder answered a call at his Honolulu residence from the president of the University of Hawaii, his close friend Paul Bachman. A British admiral was in town as part of the British naval mission to Washington. He had heard about Marder and knew his important work. Could he meet the historian? Yes, was Marder's reply, and so lunch was arranged for the next day. The conversation went well, and as the admiral walked to his waiting car to take his leave, he asked Marder if there was anything he could do to help him with his histories. Marder seized the day. Yes, he said, as a matter of fact there was. He explained. "Leave it to me," was the way the admiral, Sir Geoffrey Barnard, put it, "I know just the man in Whitehall to ask."[6] Months passed, and then a welcome telegram arrived from Washington, saying that when Marder was next in London he was to see so-and-so to make arrangements for the viewing and copying of documents. Barnard, who reviewed the first book of the resulting *From the Dreadnought to Scapa Flow* in *Punch*, wrote of Marder: "His high reputation has been built by devotion to research." Barnard held Marder in the highest regard, and he assisted him in other ways and on other projects—for instance, on Marder's "WC Project," that is, a portrait of Winston Churchill as a naval lord in the Second World War.

Fate dealt Marder a terrible blow just at the time he was completing that first volume of *From the Dreadnought to Scapa Flow*. In an event strangely reminiscent of Thomas Carlyle's loss by fire of the first volume of his *History of the French Revolution*, Marder's notes and drafts for the period 1915 to 1919 were incinerated when three janitors at the University of Hawaii mistook two boxes of research notes for two cartons of marked examinations. Marder was crestfallen. At one stage he decided to abandon the subject of his history beyond the date of the commencement of war; his publisher nevertheless ended up issuing a truncated version of the first volume. Meanwhile, Marder, gingerly pressed by Gretton and others on grounds that he was the only person who could write a frank and unbiased appraisal of the battle of Jutland and subsequent events of the naval war, including the shipping crisis of 1917 (one that led to the introduction of convoys to counter U-boat depredations), had started to redo his research. He won damages from the university, obtained a special release from his teaching duties, and secured a grant from the American Philosophical Society to cover the cost of recopying documents lost in the flames. A person of lesser courage would have abandoned the project. At the end of the day, volume II, entitled *The War Years: To the Eve of Jutland*, was better than ever it could have been, for two new document collections had recently been made available to him. In the preface, he thanked the janitors of imperishable memory for their inadvertent actions, which, in the end, made the final result better than could have been imagined. This was a kind gesture. Not least, the First Lord of the Admiralty, Lord Selkirk, hearing of the tragedy, came to Marder's aid, promising renewed assistance, even though the documents he needed to consult one more time were in the process of being shipped to the National Archives. That meant that Marder would not get the kind of special treatment he had experienced earlier. In any event, Marder got to the documents, his progress expedited by willing aides who not only had heard of his plight but also knew of his sterling research and writing.

Three volumes were to follow in short order, *Jutland and After, 1917: The Year of Crisis* (about the shipping saga), and *Victory and Aftermath* (the end of the naval war, including the surrender and scuttling of the High Seas Fleet). A perceptive, hard-hitting analysis of Admiralty naval policy and staff planning, an assessment of naval commanders afloat, and sure judgments about training, manpower, and materiel concluded the work. An extensive annotated bibliography indicated the breadth and depth of the research and nicely pointed the way for future scholars. Though Roskill thought Marder should have stopped in 1918, with the end of the war—Marder had to remind him that the original intention had always been to bring the story through to the peace treaties—and though he thought Marder ought not to undertake a grand analytical conclusion, and said so, Marder was not to be deterred. In fact, Marder's conclusion was masterly. It also indicated the sorts of subjects he intended to explore in subsequent years, including a challenging examination of what lessons the Royal Navy learned from the study of the history of the late war—sadly too little, in Marder's estimation, especially about convoys.

Honors and glory now came steadily to Marder. He was named Commander of the British Empire, awarded the Chesney Medal of the Royal United Services Institution for Defence Studies, and named George Eastman Professor at Balliol College, Oxford, for the academic year 1969–70. Oxford University subsequently awarded him a D.Litt. for outstanding historical achievement. The Board of Admiralty, in an unheard-of gesture (for it had always been suspicious of historians and had given Sir Julian Corbett a wrap on the knuckles for the volume on Jutland that he had done for the First World War official history of naval operations), issued a special minute of commendation to Marder. It also gave him a special dinner in the famed Painted Hall at Greenwich. Marder's star shone brightly in the firmament in the early 1970s, and he was the wonder of the naval-history world.

News of his fame spread in historical circles in the United States, but in a climate of academic change that mirrored the political ferment of the times, Marder's achievement had less credibility, particularly among younger colleagues. Now a professor at the new University of California, Irvine, where he was appointed the first non-administrative faculty member in 1964, his rigorous views on curriculum, historiography, and methodology were easy targets for proponents of theory, demography, statistical analysis, and social science. Student rebelliousness and rudeness he could not stomach. But all this time he kept to his historical tasks. He was named a fellow of the American Philosophical Society. He served as president of the Pacific Coast Branch of the American Historical Association. He retired in 1977 and moved to the pleasant community of Montecito, near Santa Barbara.

THE 1970S WERE TIMES OF INTENSE CHALLENGE from Roskill. Marder was encroaching on his epoch of study, the interwar years. Roskill was anxious that his official history, *The War at Sea* (1954–61), not be opened for reappraisal: the time was not ripe for such, he opined. Marder, however, was restless. He sought new subjects in the naval line. In earlier days he had published on Churchill as First Lord of the Admiralty in 1911–15. He now decided to see what Churchill had done when he again became First Lord, in 1939. Employing a new technique—writing to those who had worked directly with Churchill, either as civilians or serving officers—Marder accumulated his own archive. His inquiries brought him into close cooperation with Sir Basil Liddell Hart, Sir Ian Jacob, and Sir Eric Seal, the last two of whom had worked very closely with Churchill and who denied any overbearing intervention by Churchill in the affairs of the Admiralty's running of the war at sea. Many others were interviewed or corresponded with, and the Marder method, conducted from distant California, allowed a new interpretation to emerge of how the sea war was waged. This was one that Roskill had not been able to touch on in *The War at Sea*. Marder launched the first fruits of this new research under the heading "Winston is Back," a special supplement of the *English Historical Review* in 1972. Roskill was alarmed, and because he held the opposite view of Churchill, and had argued for it in several articles as a features writer for the *Sunday Telegraph*—these became the basis of his later book *Churchill and the Admirals* (1977)—all the makings of an historians' battle existed. In an unkind critique of Marder's rapid progress, stated in *The*

Times on the eve of Marder's Oxford degree ceremony, Roskill said that he would have been able to do as well had he not been obliged to read and critique the draft volumes of Marder's five-volume magnum opus. Newspaper editors and the reading public were on to the spat immediately, and they eagerly awaited further eruptions. They did not have to wait long.

Roskill's complaining reply to the *English Historical Review* was declined by the editor, so Roskill turned to the *Journal of Royal United Services Institution for Defence Studies,* where it duly was published in the issue for December 1972. When Marder's next book, *From the Dardanelles to Oran: Studies of the Royal Navy in War and Peace, 1915–1940,* appeared in 1974, Marder answered Roskill's charges with an extended appendix to the reprinted and enlarged "Winston is Back." "Musings on a Bolt from Olympus," as Marder titled it, took Roskill to task on a number of grounds, and had, from Roskill's unfortunate point of view, the deleterious effect of further drawing attention to the claim made by Seal that he could not find in the Admiralty signals dockets any evidence of undue interference from Churchill in the conduct of the naval war while Churchill was First Lord. It was Seal who in 1953 had been ordered by Churchill, then writing his own account of the Second World War, to stamp out any suggestion by Roskill in the official history that Churchill had interfered unnecessarily.

The struggle between Marder and Roskill did not rest there. It continued through Marder's analysis of the destruction of the French Navy at Oran, the sacking of Admiral Sir Dudley North over matters tangentially related to "Operation Menace," Marder's appreciations of Admiral Sir Dudley Pound when he was First Sea Lord, and Marder's account of the sending and loss of the battleship *Prince of Wales* and the battle cruiser *Repulse.* Marder never said that Churchill was faultless in the way the war at sea was waged after he became Prime Minister in 1940, but he stoutly defended Churchill's actions before that date. Roskill could never appreciate this. Nor could he defend Pound, whom he thought medically unfit for the job as well as a centralizer and a control artist, though he was far more pliable than Marder had portrayed. Letters were exchanged in the *Times Literary Supplement* for a time, but Marder was now on to his last project, the challenging business of comparative naval history (here he was an initiator) of the Royal Navy and the Imperial Japanese Navy. His research took him again to London but more extensively to Japan, twice, in a gallant attempt to find surviving naval records, interview participants, and gain an appreciation of Japanese strategic, military, and political thought. In the first volume of *Old Friends, New Enemies,* he returned to Churchill. He argued, and this was one of his favorite themes, that historians ought not to judge unfolding events by what they later learned to have transpired. He liked to cite Homer's "After the event any fool can be wise." This was a polite and tangential jibe at Roskill, whose judgments, as Creswell and others observed, were often colored by later evaluations.

And right to the end Marder defended his historical method of using details and particulars to sustain a powerful narrative. Resisting any desire to tilt at historical windmills or take on the theories of other historians, Marder stuck to the historical records. Of course, he was not faultless in the selection of materials, and on occasion he failed to weigh correctly the testimony of various informants; in certain cases or episodes, he may be said to have gone overboard by the needless recounting of supporting evidence. But these, his critics noted, did not appreciably weaken his great work.

Marder died Christmas Day 1980, age seventy, in a hospital in Santa Barbara, of pancreatic cancer. His widow, Jan, agreed to the pressing suggestion of Marder's Irvine colleague, the military historian Henry Cord Meyer, that two of Marder's former Ph.D. students, John Horsfield and Mark Jacobsen, should complete the second volume of *Old Friends, New Enemies,* several chapters of which had been completed by Marder before his death. That volume appeared in 1990. In fact, Marder did not live to see the first volume appear. Kemp, in a memoir of his departed friend, paid him the great compliment of calling Marder the supreme historian, which he was. What Kemp identified in Marder, many others had witnessed firsthand: first, Marder's great courage in redoing the work lost to the incinerator, and, second, Marder's great happiness in his work, a happiness that flowed from his marriage to Jan, from his family, and from his students. Kemp stated that Marder demonstrated a marked modesty, a characteristic that others may not have so easily identified, knowing as they did Marder's dogged and even forceful ways in the pursuit of evidence. But Kemp was right, for modesty was the handmaiden of Marder's simplicity of approach and his insistence on forming no preconceived notions, let alone conclusions.

NOWADAYS NAVAL HISTORY CLASSIFIES MARDER'S WORK as core history, while the search continues for a form of cognate history that involves a firmer appreciation of technology, state finance, and industrial infrastructure than Marder could provide in his narrative. But if present-day critics would look at the *Anatomy of British Sea Power,* they would see the origins of what they proclaim as the new naval history. And if they would look at his study of the Royal Navy and the Imperial Japanese Navy, they would see the first example of comparative naval history of the modern era. Marder holds enduring fascination. He demonstrated in his lifetime a supreme commitment to task. Like many of the generation that William Palmer has called the World War II generation of historians, he lived through the Depression, was well educated at the post-graduate level, served in government or military service, and flourished as a publishing scholar in the abundance offered by the expanding American university world after 1945. But Marder faced innumerable problems: the anti-Semitism that plagued his early academic career and marginalized him to Hawaii, innumerable obstacles in getting at Admiralty and other records, attempted Admiralty censorship of his literary texts, the incineration of his research notes, student and faculty disaffection, and, of public notoriety, the backfires lit by Roskill and fanned into flames in the papers and periodicals of the day.

Always in the background was Marder's account of Jutland. Marder liked to quote Admiral Scheer, the German commander at Jutland: "In itself, Jellicoe's slow blockade strategy was correct and accomplished its purpose."[7] But Churchill was right on another score, and this became Marder's underlying theme of analysis, that the navy had a not untypical prejudice against brains. In Churchill's summation: "We had competent administrators, brilliant experts of every description, fine sea-officers, brave and devoted hearts: but at the outset of the conflict we had more captains of ships than captains of war. In this will be found the explanation of many untoward events."[8]

The factor that counted most was the tradition of the Royal Navy. Thus Marder's dispassionate analysis came down to an intangible: "What saw the Navy through was tradition, tradition based upon knowledge of victories won." The Germans had no such tradition, for theirs was a new and untried navy. They never looked for a fight, rather the opposite. And had they not been caught by surprise at Jutland—Royal Navy ships spotted them coming over the horizon with no prior indication that they were at sea—they would have avoided a naval Armageddon. The last thing they wanted, Marder held, was a stand-up fight, even if they had, or thought they had, a numerical and material advantage. "It was the ghost of Nelson," said Marder. But the reason why the Royal Navy had not crushed its opponent also came within Marder's understanding. By carefully tracing the signals intelligence that directed the movements of Jellicoe's and Beatty's fleet units, he discovered the undeniable fact that the foul-up occurred in the Admiralty. A simple mistake—failing to realize that the German naval command had shifted its center of signals reception from the fixed station on the continental shore to the moving fleet at sea—cost a Nelsonic victory of annihilation of the enemy. Lessons there were to be learned. When the fifth volume of *From the Dreadnought to Scapa Flow* was published, in 1970, this unlikely historian of the Royal Navy had made the story of Britain's supremacy at sea his own.

Fate and chance played decisive parts in Marder's rise. From fate and chance had derived order and system. In later years, Marder mused that but for that encounter on the steps of the Widener Library he might well have pursued his interest in the Kaiser's generals—disagreeable characters, he thought. Instead, he took on, though without knowing the consequences, the delightful task, hardly to him a burden, of writing the history of the officers and men of the Admiralty and the Navy who held the trident of Neptune. Let them say what they will, Marder used to say, echoing the *Times* writer who recorded Jacky Fisher's funeral, held within a year of the final destruction of the German High Seas Fleet, "his place is safe with history." And so is Marder's in the Valhalla of historians—not that he is unassailable, mind, for no historian is without fault, but because he combined scholarship of the first order with compulsive readability, and the virtues of simplicity with those of impartiality. He set a standard that few others historians can approach. Not least, as Taylor once commented, historians often write books that are too long, but of Marder "we can never have enough."

Spring Semester 2006

1. Arthur J. Marder, *From the Dreadnought to Scapa Flow: The Royal Navy in the Fisher Era, 1904–1919* (5 vols., London, 1961–1970).

2. Marder Papers, University of California, Irvine.

3. Arthur Marder, interview with A. J. P. Taylor, *Listener*, 88, 2221 (21 Oct. 1971).

4. Marder Papers.

5. Arthur J. Marder, "Fate Knocks Three Times," undated and unpaginated MS, Marder Papers. This typescript appears in various states and in various places in Marder's files. It seems to have originated as Marder's answers to queries raised in various quarters, and Marder, though modest in style and manner, did nothing to check the growing public fascination with the origins and progress of his naval histories.

6. Ibid.

7. This and subsequent quotations are from Marder's interview with Taylor, *Listener*, 88 (21 Oct. 1971).

8. Winston S. Churchill, *The World Crisis, 1911–1918* (abridged, rev. ed., 1931; New York, 2005 edn.), 59.

Churchill at home in his office, No. 10 Downing Street. Wartime photograph by Cecil Beaton. IWM, MH 26392 (see p. 121).

British sailors as if in a stage musical. Wartime photograph by Cecil Beaton. IWM, CBM 2475 (see p. 111).

A study in legendary courage: Lt.-Gen. Carton de Wiart VC. Wartime photograph by Cecil Beaton. IWM, IB 3449C (see p. 119).

Ghurka with wounded comrade. Wartime photograph by Cecil Beaton.
IWM, IB 291 (see p. 119).

9

Cecil Beaton's Wartime Art

MARTIN FRANCIS

In 1943 the reviewer Henry Saville declared, "As far as any one man typifies any one thing, Cecil Beaton can be considered today to symbolize the revolution the war has brought to Britain." In the 1930s, Saville alleged, Beaton had been "amusing" and "clever," but wartime commissions had transformed him into a serious "reporter" of the human experience.[1] In the 1920s and 1930s, Beaton was Britain's leading chronicler of the worlds of theatre, fashion, high society, and royalty, what Beaton himself termed "the pleasure class," or what others were to label "the plutography." However, during the Second World War, Beaton's work appeared to undergo a change in direction. He was commissioned to take portraits not of movie stars and debutantes at costume balls, but of prominent politicians and military leaders. Languid and spangly images of the rich at play gave way to sombre photographs of the destruction caused by the London Blitz. His employment by the Ministry of Information led to assignments with the Royal Air Force and the British army in North Africa, India, Burma, and China.[2] Beaton's wartime work appeared to represent a shift from playful frivolity to the seriousness of literally life-and-death situations, from artificial glamour to sober realism, and, most critically of all, from a celebration of privilege to a lionization of the courage and sacrifice of ordinary soldiers and civilians. In this narrative, Beaton underwent a secular redemption, and his work was brought into alignment with the populist and collectivist strictures of the "people's war."[3] Moreover, for those admirers who might previously have been embarrassed by Beaton's flamboyant self-fashioning as a homosexual dandy, his new direction could be presented as an abandonment of private decadence in favor of civic virtue, or a public eschewing of effeminacy in favor of celebrating the robust and martial masculinity of the fighting man and those who commanded him.

In fact, any attempt to sequester Beaton's wartime photographs within the dominant narratives of the "people's war" can be only partially successful. Beaton's pictures and diaries represent the continued significance, especially (although not exclusively) in the realm of the imagined and the fantastic, of a flamboyant, elitist, and imperial sensibility that coexisted uneasily with the democratic discourses of wartime populism. While never explicitly party political, they represent a visual rendering of what can be termed "romantic Toryism," a set of political and cultural possibilities that proved to be a not insignificant part of Britain's wartime symbolic economy.[4] Moreover the homosexual sensibility latent in his photographs destabilizes any readings of his wartime photographs that imply a shift from frivolous and fantasied "feminine" fashion photography to serious, "masculine" documentary realism.

The notion of Beaton's war as marking an artistic progress from artifice to realism, a visual encapsulation of his own path from privilege to participation, is a "before and after" story that belies complex continuities between the 1930s and 1940s. Beaton's prewar photography certainly celebrated a world of privilege, leisure, and conspicuous consumption. As befitted the temper of the times, Beaton's field of vision took in the plutocratic rather than the aristocratic, a gilded world in which the titled elite partied and posed with fashion models, writers, artists, stage and screen actors. However, Beaton's prewar work was not all stylized portraiture of the smart set. His experiments in grotesque, pastiche, and caricature revealed considerable virtuosity. The man who constructed elaborate backcloths for his society portraits also took candid travel photographs, documentary images of Haiti, Tangiers, Mexico, Greece, Russia, Italy, and New York, which anticipated his more spontaneous war images. He also sought a dialogue with surrealism, placing his fashion models among piles of debris or next to an inverted bucket of whitewash. Beaton was no dilettante in the 1930s, and he clearly took seriously the duty of establishing photography as an artistic endeavor of the highest status.[5]

Just as Beaton's photography in the 1930s was not merely an exercise in flamboyant fancy, the war years did not necessarily produce an unqualified shift toward an aura of austerity and authenticity appropriate to the life-and-death struggle against Nazism. Beaton's theatrical proclivities persisted long after 1940. In 1942 he took time out from his Ministry of Information duties to design costumes for a revival of Shaw's *Heartbreak House* starring Edith Evans. Some of his war photographs were self-consciously theatrical. A group of identically dressed sailors in the Middle East are photographed from above in a choreographed ensemble reminiscent of a dance routine from a stage musical. Groups of civilians or military personnel are frequently spread across Beaton's photographs in what look like informal chorus lines. Nor did Beaton turn his back on fashion photography during the war, even if a wartime motif was never far away. He continued to work for *Vogue*, providing images such as that published in 1941 of Mrs. Reginald Fellowes wearing a Paquin hat and firefighting gloves. In January 1943, Beaton portrayed the new uniforms of the women's auxiliary services in a highly stylized and glamorized set of poses.

Beaton did not become a documentary realist during the Second World War. His photographs remained a mix of invention and reality, a fusion of fantasy and documentation. Screens and frames, a distinctive element in his 1930s fashion studies, recurred in the staging of his wartime portraits. The Chinese police department at Chengtu, for example, is viewed through a cutout circle in the wall. Strong geometric shapes—circles or squares—were incorporated into a photograph wherever possible. The most successful example of this is a photograph of burnt-out tank remains after the battle of Halfaya Pass ("Hellfire" Pass, in northwest Egypt near the Libyan border), in which an alignment of metal disks create a macabre yet decorative landscape of war. Beaton saw battle sites as an affirmation of the mutually enriching dialogue between surrealism and photography. Casting his gaze over the carcasses of blackened aircraft, cars ripped apart by machine-gun bullets—"their underparts pouring out in grotesque, tortured shapes,"—or the bizarre sight of "some unaccountable clothing blown into telephone wires," Beaton concluded that "the Surrealists have anticipated this battle ground."[6]

The stylistic continuity between Beaton's prewar and wartime photographs mirrors the failure of the class politics within them to undergo a dramatic realignment. It is true that the field of Beaton's subjects was dramatically broadened to include not just senior military and political figures but also ordinary British civilians and regular servicemen. However, his photographs of the home front (including his most widely reproduced image, the sentimental image of the child Blitz victim Eileen Dunne) were among his least successful wartime commissions. The heroic productivity of miners and foundry workers (celebrated by artists such as Stanley Spencer and Henry Moore) or the mystical fortitude of Londoners sheltering in the Underground (captured by both Henry Moore's sketchbook and Bill Brandt's camera) failed to inspire him. Beaton lacked empathy for both industrial labor and patriotic communalism, key ingredients in dominant constructions of the "people's war." Beaton's belief in an intrinsic and rightful social hierarchy was not shaken by his wartime experience. When changes within the corridors of power suggested a new populist standard, Beaton endeavored to refashion wartime political images along more reactionary lines. Photographing the unimpeachably plebeian Ernest Bevin, whose appointment as Minister of Labour in 1940 embodied the wartime centrality of the working class (at least in its unionized, masculine formation), Beaton attempted to ensnare his sitter within the trappings of refinement by posing him against a grand staircase in his Whitehall offices. Bevin, clearly troubled by the potential association of prewar aesthetics with prewar social and political hierarchies, chided Beaton for "trying to make me look more Royalist than the King! I suppose you think America expects me to have the Duke of Buccleuch's background."[7]

The apogee of Beaton's wartime romantic Toryism came in his photographs of the royal family, especially the highly idealized studies of Elizabeth, the Queen Consort. Beaton's success as a royal portrait photographer was far from inevitable. For all his snobbery, his exposure to social privilege in the 1930s had largely been confined to mixing with a fashionable "fast set" to which the majority of the royal family (with the exception of the Duke and Duchess of Kent and Edward, Prince of Wales) did not, and did not want to, belong. However, Beaton possessed a genuine reverence for the crown and what he felt to be the intrinsic radiance of its female members. Portraying the Queen Consort in evening dress and jewels in a state of halcyon serenity might have appeared perverse within the mythos of a "people's war," but these images of pageantry and the theatricality of dynastic power were hugely popular and widely reproduced during the war years. Beaton used lighting to invest his portraits of the House of Windsor with "royal auras," implying a sacralized regality, perhaps even a full-blown divine right of monarchy.

It has been argued that the success of the British crown in the twentieth century was based on a powerful synthesis of private probity and public grandeur. Beaton, by contrast, as a romantic Tory in the Disraelian mold, was committed to emphasizing the extraordinary, rather than the ordinary, aspects of monarchy. He never quite overcame the essential banality of George VI, expressing his frustration that his portraits of the king lacked mystery and magic. However, this disappointment was more than compensated for by the critical acclaim accorded his fairy-book portraits of the Queen Consort. Beaton's personal belief in the matchless qualities of a hereditary monarchy was genuine and heartfelt, but it should also be remembered that his romantic-Tory valuation of the monarchy was widely shared, even by those caught up in the people's war. To broad swaths of the population, the royal family represented stability and continuity, a reassuringly steadfast presence amidst the violent dislocation of total war. For all the wartime pronouncements about participatory citizenship, Britons still fought the Second World War as loyal subjects of the British imperial crown.

When dealing with military culture, Beaton was drawn to glamorous individuals rather than to the understated fortitude of the citizen-soldier. Indeed, Beaton was never more lyrical than when describing the "romantic daring" of the Royal Air Force officers whom he spent several weeks with during 1941. Typically, he assigned them to a gentlemanly and chivalric past rather than to the technological modernity suggested by the aircraft they flew. He cited with approval the group captain who organized archery practice for his aircrew, so that "these champions of the most modern of all long-range weapons are adepts at the bow and arrow, through which the English archers won the Battle of Agincourt." He eulogized "Digger," a Rhodesian flyer who "looks like the traditional hero thrown back from a romantic novel," and "Mac," who "looks like a pale Van Dyck cavalier."[8] In North Africa, Beaton was fascinated by the founder of the Special Air Service, the "daring highwayman" David Stirling, one of the "most romantic figures of this war." He also lunched with the irregular soldiers of the Long Range Desert Group, whose adventures behind enemy lines were "as brightly coloured as any pirate story."[9]

THE ENTWINING OF BEATON'S SOCIAL CONSERVATISM WITH his sexual self-fashioning had significant consequences for his representation of British masculinity during the war. In the 1920s, Beaton had rejected the middle-class patriarchy of his father's Hampstead home in favor of the quasi-aristocratic matriarchy of high bohemia and, for all intents and purposes, never returned. His public performances as a dandy and his private homosexual passions in the decades to come could therefore be seen as an obliteration of both bourgeois and hegemonic masculine conventions.

Before the war, Beaton had occasionally openly flirted with transvestism (in 1934 he had photographed himself impersonating Elsie de Wolfe at a ball in New York) and androgyny (as in the portraits of

Countess Castega or Oliver Messel). However, like Noel Coward, his contemporary, he usually preferred to deploy his bohemian-queer aesthetic more covertly, using camp theatricality to create a "high style" that was taken up by both gay men and lesbians, but that also amounted to a successful homosexual infiltration of mainstream culture in the 1920s and 1930s. By contrast, more palpable renderings of same-sex desire were not on Beaton's agenda. There are distinct similarities between Beaton's photographs and those of George Platt Lynes, an American. Lynes, like Beaton, was a fashion and portrait photographer and also shared the latter's interest in dance, performance, and theatrical staging. Indeed, the two men were good friends from the 1920s, and both worked for *Vogue*. However, while Lynes's stylized images of high glamour and Hollywood celebrity are remarkably similar to Beaton's, Lynes simultaneously produced a series of male nudes that, in their extraordinarily blatant homoeroticism, anticipate the work of Robert Mapplethorpe. There is, by contrast, no testimony to gay eroticism as overt as this in Beaton's opus.

However, the potentially destabilizing impact of Beaton's prewar queer aesthetic on his wartime photographs was ever present. If Beaton's studies of military life in the Middle and Far East are rarely overtly homoeroticized, they are nonetheless not entirely unproblematic. His photographs are of men waiting or resting and of the routine of daily life, not records of front-line combat action. He made no effort to compete with the visceral images of fighting and dying offered up by the photojournalism of Robert Capa. Indeed, it is not unreasonable to categorize his studies of officers and men attending lectures and briefings, reading letters from home, or spending their leisure time in the mess as essentially domestic. Beaton's diaries are full of domestic referents, even in the context of a homosocial military life from which the female and the familial were ostensibly banished. He described Derek Adkins, his Royal Air Force conducting officer in Egypt, buying provisions for their desert assignment, items as diverse as saucepans, towels, goggles, and toilet tissue: "There was so much to buy that it seemed like marriage, getting a trousseau and setting up house." Beaton spoke admiringly of mess secretaries who, "like housewives on shopping expeditions," swapped sugar and tea for eggs with local tribesmen, or of squadron leaders who used wildflowers and old Chianti bottles to create improvised floral displays in the mess tent. He noted the presence on the desk of Air Vice Marshal Arthur Coningham of leather frames containing photographs of his "good-looking wife, like Norma Shearer, and family." [10]

Beaton certainly chronicled the hard bodies fighting the desert war—for example, the toned torso of a Long Range Desert Group member stripped to the waist—or buffed sailors exercising on the deck of a battleship. However, it was a sensitive and slightly built bomber pilot, rather than the squadron's hearties, who most impressed Beaton during his time chronicling the Royal Air Force. For Beaton, nineteen-year-old Hughie Tring, described as "the son of a clergyman, aesthetic-looking, with strong, rather feminine features, lean, with the long well-formed hands of a violinist, and the dark quiet voice of a scholar," represented "the nobility of our cause."[11] Beaton's aesthetically derived conception of male beauty makes it impossible for him to valorize masculinity solely in terms of physical strength, even when his subject is a warrior rather than a fashion model or a matinee idol. Moreover, Beaton's only significant image taken near a combat zone (more precisely, the Chin Hills on the Burma front) is a study not of male aggression but of masculine tenderness, as a wounded Gurkha lays his cheek on the head of the comrade who is carrying him to safety.

Nor do Beaton's photographs of senior military figures always seem particularly martial. Air Marshal Arthur Tedder appears puckish and playful. "Glubb Pasha" looks wistful rather than self-possessed, and his manly authority is undermined by a heavy black telephone that looms in the foreground, implying that power is a product of technological rather than human agency. Victoria Cross recipient Lieutenant-General Adrian Carton de Wiart stands bolt upright and stares into the distance with a steely gaze and a firmly set jaw. However, even this fierceness is mitigated by the fact that he possesses only one eye, his eyeless socket hidden under a black eye patch. His scarred face is thereby a reminder of the vulnerability of masculinity under fire. De Wiart preserves the boundary of his body with his rigid poise, ensuring it cannot be registered as leaky or abject. Nevertheless, his wound makes it impossible not to be reminded that the male body is never impenetrable, thereby compromising his performance of martial masculinity. When preparing for his portrait, Admiral Lord Louis Mountbatten was desperate to give an impression of toughness appropriate to his status as Supreme Allied Commander in Southeast Asia. However, the ghosts of his past as a dynastic paladin and bisexual playboy haunt Beaton's image of what remains an elegant and dapper officer. Beaton renders him as little more than a mannequin, an androgynous fashion plate, an object of mere fascination, incapable of the agency and autonomy that hegemonic masculinity required.

The relation of Beaton's homosexuality to the construct of the people's war is far from straightforward, especially when it is so entangled with his social self-fashioning. One of the reasons Beaton may have been so eager to preserve social hierarchy at a time when this was being called into question by the imperatives of wartime populism was that his class allegiances protected his sexual affinities. After all, the democratizing aspects of wartime culture certainly did not imply a more egalitarian attitude toward alternative sexualities. While the dislocations of war and military service created increased opportunities for same-sex relationships, the immediate post-war years were characterized by a dramatic deterioration in the position of gay men: the queer became a scapegoat for anxieties about the viability of family life, juvenile crime, and the decline of Britain's imperial status. The failure of wartime egalitarianism to extend to the sexual domain might suggest that the queer presence in Beaton's photographs established him as a social insider but, equally, a sexual outsider. Beaton's romantic Toryism, while rooted in class politics that were decidedly reactionary, also contained affective elements that might be judged distinctly subversive. What is critical here, however, is that whether as an unapologetic snob or as a circumspect queer, Beaton emblematizes aspects of wartime culture that cannot be easily accommodated within established conceptualizations of the people's war.

RACIAL DIFFERENCES AND BRITAIN'S DESIRE to remain an imperial power disturbed the predominant populist conceptions of national identity and citizenship. Given the obvious inconsistency between a war to defend democracy and the continued denial of self-determination to Britain's colonial territories, the British government was obliged to repair relations with its imperial subjects by refashioning paternalism into the more flexible conception of "partnership." Beaton's brief for his visit to India, in 1944, was to produce images that would show the Empire to best advantage, a task given increased urgency by the growing confidence of Indian nationalism in the wake of Britain's earlier military setbacks in the Far East. However, Beaton's Indian photographs made little effort to envisage the Empire as anything other than a fixed hierarchy of both race and class. His photographs of Indian women looking "like lotus flowers" or of the dancer Pam Gopal, while graceful and dignified, could easily be accommodated within the discourses of Orientalism and the imperialist travelogue. This was not surprising, since Beaton's first exposure to Asian culture had been mediated through the extravagantly caricatured Orientalist fictions of the London theatre of the early 1920s; Beaton was a particular devotee of plays and musicals such as *The Garden of Allah*, *The Geisha*, and *The Cingalee*.[12] His studies of British rulers and Indian nobility are an even clearer demonstration of how a rigidly hierarchical conception of the Empire was cardinal to the romantic-Tory imaginary. Lady Wavell was photographed in court dress on the stairs of Viceroy House in Delhi; Sir John and Lady Colville were pictured enthroned in majesty in the magnificent reception room of the Governor's mansion in Bombay; the Maharajah and Maharani of Jaipur were placed in a delicately ornamental wing of their palace. Beaton's images are of the Raj at its most elegant, its most ornamental, and its haughtiest. If they seemed to be shot for the society pages of the *Tatler*, they also exemplified the Raj's salience to a romantic-conservative vision of Britain that had first been articulated by Benjamin Disraeli in the 1870s.

While Beaton photographed Indian princes and princesses as well as British grandees, the hierarchy he celebrated was always as much racial as social. One of the most obvious examples of the racialized basis of Beaton's wartime imaginary is an image of the pallid and physically delicate Felicity Wavell (the viceroy's daughter) seated on a rickshaw and attended by six Indian soldiers, their dark skins and uniforms a dramatic contrast to the young woman's ghostly whiteness. Often, though, Beaton's racial politics are covert and coded. The photograph of Lieutenant Antony Liddell enjoying a bath at the leave camp on the viceroy's estate at Simla might seem, on first impression, innocuous. It presents the image of Liddell's head, photographed from below, peering over the rim of a bathtub with, in the background, a wash basin, its external plumbing in clear view, and a shelf on which is arranged a shaving brush and a bottle of antiseptic solution. However, as Anne McClintock, among others, has suggested, cleanliness was regularly deployed as a signifier of racial superiority, the white man's body protected by the commodities of European hygiene manufacturers from the contamination of the colonial other.[13] Many of Beaton's images feature this motif of European hygiene in a colonial context. He photographed soldiers' laundry drying on clotheslines in the Egyptian desert, the crisp white uniforms of sailors on the decks of ships, and the spotless dressings of wounded soldiers in hospital. On visiting Air Vice-Marshal Coningham's "immaculate trailer" in the desert, Beaton waxed lyrical about its interior, of which Coningham was "justifiably proud": "no grain of sand has penetrated past the meat-safe mesh of the entrance."[14]

It seems reasonable at this point to return to Beaton's emphasis on the domestic once again, although this time investing it with its imperial as well as its gendered connotations. In his India photographs, imperial destiny is conceived not as a result of military aggression, but in the form of a daily life and domestic peace from which the violence of colonial encounters has been erased. Beaton puts domestic sentimentalism to work as an imperial instrument, and not just in his photography. During his tour of India, he could not resist the temptation to direct both Mrs. Casey, the wife of the governor of Bengal, and Lady Colville, the wife of the governor of Bombay, to redesign their living quarters. Beaton wrote of his pride in transforming the private rooms at Government House in Calcutta so that they "became slightly Edwardian, very feminine and almost human. I strewed many books around, a few sweet dishes and even a dessert plate." [15] Such aesthetic diversions in the nominally private sphere, inscribed as they are with concealed racial and social signifiers, need to be recognized as fundamentally political and registered as an intrinsic part of imperial life.

For all Beaton's desire to look backward, his romantic Toryism also contained a strong element of what has elsewhere been termed "conservative modernity." [16] His photograph of Lieutenant Philip Ashley being visited in the hospital by the actress Doreen Lawrence presents a perfect romantic hero, poised with an open book and holding a cigarette, his strong facial features in profile and a young woman seated at the foot of his bed. It has been often remarked how similar this photograph is to a still from a Hollywood movie. Indeed, Hollywood cinematic styles afforded Beaton a means for reconciling his belief in the superiority of glamour and exclusivity with the modernizing imperatives of mass society. The imperial and dynastic worlds were also to be revitalized by using the Hollywood referent as a corroboration of their compatibility with modernity. For example, Beaton went to Tehran in 1942 to photograph the young Shah of Iran, Mohammed Reza Pahlavi, and his glamorous wife, Queen Fawzieh. Beaton described their summer palace as being "as new as any Hollywood picture palace," with "modernistic" decorations, a California-style swimming pool, and "geometric furniture." Aesthetics, typically, embodied politics, the Shah's modern palace being appropriate to a ruler who, Beaton claimed, despite his destiny to "sit upon the jewel-studded, peacock throne of Aurangzebe," supported liberal reform. He noted that the Queen was wearing a knee-length dress, "probably from Shaftesbury Avenue," and was "very pretty, even beautiful, and more photogenic than most film stars. If ever . . . the Queen had any desire for a more histrionic career, her Botticellian plumpness of features, her piercing blue eyes, the dark chestnut hair that grows so beautifully from the forehead, the sex appeal of the Asiatic cherub, would land her plumb in the centre of the Hollywood Screen." [17]

In this description of the young royal couple, Beaton attempts to blend Hollywood glamour, the oriental exotic, and the majesty of a hereditary monarchy, oblivious of the potential incompatibilities between these elements. Indeed, he had to abandon an effort to photograph the Queen in a version of the sixteenth-century miniatures of the Age of Shah Abbas when she informed him she possessed only a Westernized wardrobe of contemporary dresses and negligees. Nevertheless, the ultimately elitist sensibility that Beaton expressed here was clearly light years from the democratic and collective imperatives of the people's war.

BEATON'S ROMANTIC TORYISM WAS NOT JUST an idiosyncratic posture against wartime populism by a man regularly identified, even by his admirers, as a monumental snob. The popularity of his wartime photographs and writings suggests he was disclosing sensibilities that had considerable purchase in the symbolic economy of the 1940s. Moreover, similar structures of desire were associated with a number of other contemporary genres and individuals, drawn from across the widely different (yet frequently interconnected) domains of the arts and entertainment, the military and politics. The cinematic costume melodramas of the Gainsborough studios have been read as a yearning for hierarchy and expressivity that subliminally challenged official wartime discourses of egalitarianism and self-restraint. However, conservative images of glamour on screen were not confined to Gainsborough, but were also a critical element of Alexander Korda's romances and historical dramas. Laurence Olivier's screen adaptation of Shakespeare's *Henry V* celebrated a dynastic vision of British patriotism and suggested Beaton was not alone in detecting an affinity between the officer heroes of the Royal Air Force and a romanticized image of medieval chivalry. Michael Powell and Emeric Pressburger's movie *I Know Where I'm Going* located authenticity in the hierarchical world of a dashing Scottish laird and presented modern mass society as materialistic and soulless. Film star Leslie Howard's popularity rested on serving as a paradigm of the debonair English gentleman and amateur, an image that in wartime was fused with a lyrical, almost ethereal, patriotism. Beaton's theatricality found an echo in the suave elegance and showmanship of conductor Sir Malcolm Sargent, who, in evening dress, defiantly led classical concerts in the midst of the Blitz. Noel Coward, who shared both Beaton's sexuality and his snobbery, succeeded in aligning his drawing-room elitism with a celebration of the national character at war in his incursion into moviemaking, *In Which We Serve*. If Coward's vision of wartime mobilization implied that equality of sacrifice did not have to entail the dismantling of prewar social hierarchies, it should not be forgotten that *In Which*

We Serve (rather than Carol Reed's much more egalitarian *The Way Ahead,* which used the same metaphor of a self-contained military unit as a personification of the nation at war) was one of the most popular cinematic releases of the entire war. That these personifications of romantic Toryism often obscured more complex social realities (both Coward and Beaton adopted an elite sophistication which belied their suburban origins, while Korda and Pressburger were émigré Hungarian Jews, as was Leslie Howard's father, the future "Englishman's Englishman" having spent part of his childhood in Vienna) should not be allowed to detract from their purchase in the wartime popular imagination.

In Which We Serve was based on the early wartime career of Lord Louis Mountbatten. With his royal blood, glamorous social life, impeccable dress sense, and heroic war record, Mountbatten was an obvious candidate for incorporation into the romantic-Tory pantheon. However, such an appropriation required a little wishful thinking, given Mountbatten's self-proclaimed support of the Labour Party, and his role, as the last Viceroy, in presiding over the dismantling of Britain's Indian empire, in 1947. His predecessor as Viceroy, Archibald Wavell, had ultimately proved a failure as a military commander, but he still attracted considerable adulation during the war, both Beaton and Coward presenting him as a romantic cavalier, a valiant soldier who also wrote poetry and appeared to them as the reincarnation of a Jacobite prince. Younger military men also offered the opportunity to highlight splendid individualism and gentlemanly codes of honor. Wing-Commander Guy Gibson, bomber pilot and leader of "Operation Chastise" in 1943, was taken by Churchill to North America to advertise the finest qualities of the English officer class. Irregular warfare provided particular scope for escaping the regularization and professed meritocracy of Britain's "citizen army." Gentlemen soldiers such as Sir Fitzroy Maclean carried out daring raids behind enemy lines in Yugoslavia. Perhaps the finest exemplar of romantic Toryism in the wartime military was Simon Christopher Joseph Fraser, 17th Lord Lovat, the handsome "Damascus blade" who led commandos at Dieppe and on D-Day, singing "Jerusalem" as enemy shells whizzed over his landing craft. "Shimi" Lovat should have been a splendid anachronism, a Highland chief, a territorial magnate, or the head of a worldwide clan, but this decidedly feudal figure proved a compelling version of noblesse oblige, his exploits regularly chronicled in the otherwise decidedly populist *Daily Mirror.*

While wartime romantic Toryism did not necessarily imply fealty to, or even association with, the Conservative Party, Lovat served as Under-Secretary at the Foreign Office in Churchill's short-lived caretaker government in 1945, and Guy Gibson was briefly a Conservative candidate for Macclesfield. This fusion between the heroic soldier and the Tory paternalist was also revealed in tributes paid to Ronald Cartland, a young anti-appeasement Conservative MP who enlisted in 1939 and was killed at Dunkirk. Obituaries of Cartland portrayed him not merely as a gallant Christian gentleman, but as one whose idealistic life and noble death transcended the squalid years of appeasement and the slump.[18] The memorialization of Cartland in the summer of 1940 is a reminder that romantic Toryism benefited just as much as Priestley-style populism (which dominates established narratives of the war) from the hostility to the prewar order that welled up following Dunkirk. Moreover, among those paying heartfelt tribute to Cartland was Winston Churchill, whose patrician high-mindedness, sentimental patriotism, historic reverence for the monarchy, flamboyant style, and haughty imperialism all delineated him as the romantic Tory par excellence. Beaton was the author of one of the most widely reproduced photographic images of Churchill, a study of the typically pugnacious Prime Minister posed behind his Downing Street desk; Beaton immodestly claimed that the image could be found "in the place of honour . . . on the walls of nearly every public house in the country."[19] The wartime premier seemed to share with Beaton a sense of the war as requiring the presence of both tradition and theatricality. Certainly, for all their obvious differences, both Churchill and Beaton were equally suspect conscripts in a national endeavor that eventually came to be understood as a struggle to ensure that a new, more democratic, and more equitable society would rise out of the ruins of war. Beaton's romantic Toryism was therefore far from unique, and serves as a testimony to the resilience of conservative structures of feeling in Britain during the 1940s: patterns of desire whose presence in the wartime imagination ensured that the meritocratic, technocratic, and populist themes of 1939–45 would not go unchallenged, either during the war itself or in the years that followed.

One epilogue to Beaton's wartime story might depict the photographer, alienated from the political settlement that brought the Labour Party to power in 1945, retreating once again into the world of high style and high fashion, seeking out the comfort of nostalgia by designing costumes for Edwardian-set films such as *Lady Windermere's Fan,* produced by that other romantic idealist-imperialist, Alexander Korda. In this poignant postscript, Beaton's prewar aesthetics and their associated political connotations are interpreted as being unwelcome or redundant in the postwar New Jerusalem. The

problem with such a narrative is twofold. First, it implies an inflex-
ibility in Beaton's photography that is belied by his post-war work.
In the late 1950s, Beaton returned to the more spontaneous and
candid images of much of his wartime photography—for example,
in his famous portraits of a weary and haunted Marilyn Monroe.
Second, and much more significantly, if Beaton's romantic Toryism
could register so powerfully during the people's war, why should it
not remain equally cogent during the "people's peace," when the
wartime imperatives of collectivism and egalitarianism were rendered less urgent and less appealing? In 1953, the coronation of
Queen Elizabeth II celebrated a forward-looking reconceptualiza-
tion of the Empire as the British Commonwealth. However, it also
drew upon motifs of imperial, social, and dynastic continuity that
were anything but democratic or modern. Romantic Toryism remained an essential constituent of the British cultural imagination
at the beginning of what was being termed the New Elizabethan
Age, as the rather overdrawn appellation itself all too clearly revealed. One of its most notable exemplars, Winston Churchill, had
recently returned to Downing Street, while another was responsible for what became, despite its potential anachronism, one of the
iconic images of postwar Britain. The official coronation portrait
(taken in a studio against a screen image of Westminster Abbey) was
simultaneously theatrical, opulent, noble, and sacred. The author of
this romantic study in pageantry and deference, it almost goes without saying, was Cecil Walter Hardy Beaton.

Spring Semester 2007

1. Quoted in Philippe Garner and David Alan Mellor, *Cecil Beaton* (London, 1994), p. 45.

2. Many of these photographs (including those discussed in this lecture) are reproduced in Gail Buckland, *Cecil Beaton: War Photographs, 1939–1945* (London, 1981). A selection of Beaton's wartime photographs in the collection of the Imperial War Museum can be viewed online at http://www.iwm.org.uk.

3. For different perspectives on the Second World War as a "people's war," particularly the implication of its having had a leveling effect on British society, see Angus Calder, *The People's War: Britain, 1939–1945* (London, 1969); Harold L. Smith, ed., *War and Social Change: British Society in the Second World War* (Manchester, 1986); James Hinton, *Women, Social Leadership, and the Second World War: Continuities of Class* (Oxford, 2002); Sonya O. Rose, *Which People's War? National Identity and Citizenship in Wartime Britain, 1939–1945* (Oxford, 2003).

4. For further elaboration of this argument, see Martin Francis, "Cecil Beaton's Romantic Toryism and the Symbolic Economy of Wartime Britain," *Journal of British Studies*, 45, 1 (2006), pp. 90–117.

5. For assessments of Beaton's career, see Roy Strong, *Beaton Portraits* (London, 1968); James Danziger, *Beaton* (New York, 1980); and Hugo Vickers, *Cecil Beaton* (London, 1985).

6. Cecil Beaton, *Near East* (London, 1943), p. 57.

7. Buckland, *War Photographs*, p. 16.

8. Cecil Beaton, *Winged Squadrons* (London, 1942), pp. 6, 18.

9. Beaton, *Near East*, pp. 43, 74–75.

10. Ibid., pp. 39, 40–41, 58.

11. Beaton, *Winged Squadrons*, p. 30.

12. Cecil Beaton, *India* (London, 1945); Cecil Beaton, *Cecil Beaton's Indian Album* (London, 1946).

13. Anne McClintock, *Imperial Leather: Race, Gender, and Sexuality in the Colonial Context* (London, 1995).

14. Beaton, *Near East*, p. 58.

15. Vickers, *Beaton*, pp. 278–80.

16. This phrase is from Alison Light, *Forever England: Femininity, Literature, and Conservatism between the Wars* (London, 1991), p. 10.

17. Beaton, *Near East*, pp. 100–01.

18. Barbara Cartland, *Ronald Cartland, by His Sister* (London, 1941), pp. 7–15.

19. Cecil Beaton, *Photobiography* (New York, 1951), p. 139.

10

England and India, 1939–1945

INDIVAR KAMTEKAR

Much modern history has been written under the influence of imperialism and nationalism. These intoxicants, so often successful in instilling solidarity and pride, have often also blurred historical views in ways easy to identify but difficult to rectify. This lecture attempts to bring into focus some blurred issues within modern Indian history by making two comparisons: first, between the activities of state power in India and in Britain during the Second World War; second, between the trajectories—the fortunes and misfortunes over the same period of time—of social classes and regions within India. A look at history from above and below the unit of a single country or nation can reveal views that the category "nation" obstructs.

This new look involves a shift of emphasis. After the publication of the multivolume *Official History of the Indian Armed Forces in the Second World War,* historians who dealt with the 1940s in India turned their attention toward Indian independence and partition.[1] They dissected the details of constitutional negotiations and political mass mobilizations.[2] Histories mentioned the huge strains the war imposed on India, particularly inflation and shortages, culminating in the horrendous Bengal famine of 1943. A nuanced textbook by Sumit Sarkar recognized that business profiteering meant "a major step forward for the Indian bourgeoisie"; however, the overall impact of the war was depicted as being disastrous for other social groups.[3] *The New Cambridge History of India* took the line that "the Second World War had a devastating effect on economic life in India."[4] The present lecture, apart from severely qualifying this picture—by presenting an untapped vein of data about rural India—analyzes the 1940s in India not from the perspective of political negotiations or mass mobilization, but as a period of enhanced resource extraction.

States inaugurate wars and then try to make them the business of the people they govern. Modern wars therefore test states on the home front as well as the battlefront. During wartime, a state's appetite for resources increases. How, and to what extent, a state can extract greater resources than usual from society can be instructive: the state's new burst of energy and activity provides a flare of light enabling its features to be seen more clearly.

THE SECOND WORLD WAR CAUGHT INDIA looking the wrong way. For decades, defense policy had assumed that the attackers would be Russian and that the attack would come from the northwest, through Afghanistan; but the attackers turned out to be Japanese, and they came from the east, through Burma. Although Assam was the only province actually invaded, its neighbor, Bengal, was also severely affected. Many war factories were concentrated in Bengal; many thousands of troops from Britain, the United States, African countries, Australia, and China were stationed there. Only the eastern fringe of India became an active center of operations, but the whole country was sucked into the war effort. India became a major supply base in the Second World War, contributing enormous quantities of men, materials, and money.

More than two million Indian men joined the Indian Armed Forces, serving in Africa, the Middle East, Burma, and Europe.[5] The government of India boasted that the Indian Army was the largest volunteer force in history. Though indeed volunteers, most of these men, desperate for jobs, were forced to join up by need. To meet the army's increased demand for manpower, recruiting officers were allowed to enlist men who were underweight. Army doctors who monitored the weight of the new recruits found that in northwest India, "irrespective of age or initial weight every recruit gained 5 to 10 lb of weight on basic [army] ration alone, within 4 months of enlistment and this gain continued at a diminishing rate thereafter."[6] This is what it meant, as far as access to food and medicine, for the poor to "volunteer" for the army.

The malnourished young men who enlisted bore little resemblance to the ideal soldier of the British Indian Army. Ever since the late nineteenth century, the best Indian soldier was supposed to be a tall, fair-skinned, wheat-eating, healthy, handsome, loyal, simple-minded, and strong peasant from the northwest of the country—a peculiar assortment of attributes, dignified by the grand rubric of martial race theory. In peacetime, this theory of recruitment ensured that the Punjabi peasant provided the backbone of the army. During the Second World War, while the largest number of recruits continued to come from Punjab, the second-highest number of recruits came from the province of Madras, the antithesis of Punjab in the Indian imagination.[8] Unlike the Punjabis, the Madrassis who joined—and there were more than a quarter of a million of them— were mostly agricultural laborers. They became drivers, carpenters, cooks, and electricians. The recruits from Bengal came mostly from towns, and about a third of them were technical men.

A new type of army produced a new set of problems. It could be difficult even to get people from the same region to work together: the refusal of the Jats to serve with lower castes from their own region led to the creation of separate low-caste regiments.[9] Problems arose not just because men had to work with one another, but because they had to operate modern equipment with which they were totally unfamiliar. Cavalrymen, used to horses, were in the Middle East given trucks instead. The number of accidents was large.

Regarding war production, the official version trumpeted: "At the outbreak of war, our industries, established—as were all the factories of the United Nations—for the pursuit of peaceful trade, directed their endeavors to the grim business of war. At first their output was but a mere trickle, but as the months passed, the flow of war materials, of supplies, of essentials to arm and sustain men on the battlefields, grew into a mighty flood."[10] The Indian army required and received supplies of guns, ammunition, food, uniforms, sheets, blankets, tents, boots, medicines, drink, and tobacco as well as a whole range of other stores. India was an important arsenal for the Middle East operations and for the war in Burma. The British and American armies also received supplies from India, including nearly 400 million tailored items, 25 million shoes, 37,000 silk parachutes, and 4 million cotton supply-dropping parachutes.[11] At one stage, India was providing 1.2 billion yards of cloth annually to the defense forces. It was said in 1947 that "India clothed the armies east of Suez."[12]

While huge increases in production were called for in India, in reality the production of necessary commodities remained obstinately immobile or increased only slightly. The production of coal, on which the railways and the steel industry depended, actually fell during the war.[13] Mill-made cloth production in India, some 4 billion yards before the war, went up to about 4.6 billion yards, using virtually the same equipment. The importing of machinery, on which Indian industry depended, was restrained by the wartime shortage of shipping.[14] The war showed that an economy without a capital-goods sector was incapable of robustness. As for agriculture, the "Grow More Food" campaign was announced, but the amount of food grown remained more or less the same.[15]

By contrast, British production increased considerably, even in agriculture. The agricultural labor force was expanded by one-fifth, while land under cultivation rose from twelve million to eighteen million acres. Industry accelerated much faster. By 1943, British production of bullets, tanks, and ships was more than eight times greater than in the first three months of the war. Between 1939 and 1942, the production of machine tools rose threefold.[16] The British war effort reached a limit in 1943 because manpower was unavailable to expand either the armed forces or the labor pool.

To regulate consumption, items in short supply were strictly rationed in Britain. While food grains were the focus of rationing in India, British rationing involved meat, eggs, and butter—bread, flour, potatoes, and oatmeal were available in unlimited quantities. British rationing covered the vast majority of the population; rationing in India, centered on urban areas, covered only a fraction of the total population. In Britain, the ration merely determined what a person ate; in India, it might determine whether a person ate. For the rich in India, almost all items of consumption remained easily available.[17]

War finance posed two problems. How were Indian resources to be put at British disposal? And how were the resources to be raised from Indian society?

No doubt the simplest financial arrangement would have been to confiscate Indian revenues, but the era of Clive was over. At the end of the First World War, India had paid a substantial lump sum to Britain toward the costs of the war, but during the Second World War, it seemed to Keynes, who mentioned the option, that "politically this is perhaps the least easy to bring off."[18] This was because the opinion of Indian officials and industrialists could not be ignored. The troops in India from Australia, New Zealand, and Canada would be paid for entirely by their own countries, but Indian troops would have to be paid for, in some measure, by Britain; in some shape or form, money would have to be credited to the government of India.

A financial agreement reached early in the war divided the costs between the government of India and the British Exchequer.[19] The payments due to India would be made in sterling in London, but credited to a restricted account: in other words, a forced loan. By the end of the war, over two billion pounds had been spent by the Indian government; on the basis of the financial agreement, about half the amount was attributable to each party. Thus, the war transformed India from a debtor to a creditor nation, with sterling balances of well over a billion pounds.[20] During the Second World War, while Britain stripped herself of overseas assets, India overcame her foreign debts.

But during the war, the government of India had to raise all the money. The war, roughly speaking, "witnessed a threefold increase in the intensity of fiscal pressure."[21] In other words, in real terms, compared to its prewar expenditures, the colonial state spent three times as much by the end of the war. This posed a huge problem. The colonial state was not good at raising financial resources. Even when it came to meeting its normal expenses in peacetime, it had proved inept. While ruling over the same territory, the Mughal state had extracted proportionately much higher taxes than the colonial state did. Western states expanded their fiscal girth in the twentieth century, while the fiscal size of the colonial state in India remained stubbornly slender.[22] Financing the war effort demanded profligacy from a creature of limited means.

The British state raised resources from the British people through taxation and borrowing. The excess-profits tax, 60 percent at the beginning of the war, was raised to a confiscatory 100 percent in May 1940. Lending money to the state in its hour of peril, through savings certificates, the post office savings bank, and defense bonds, was projected as a patriotic virtue. The amounts borrowed were substantial, almost three billion pounds annually, a figure roughly equal to the total amount of annual taxation.[23]

Similar expedients were tried in India: levels of taxation were raised and savings schemes announced. But Indians who could afford to pay high taxes proved unwilling to do so. The Indian public showed no urge whatever to contribute to the state's finances. On the contrary, there was actually a withdrawal of savings from post office banks.[24] There was also a panicky scramble to exchange currency notes for silver one-rupee coins, which were drained out of the Reserve Bank, and practically disappeared from circulation.[25] Keynes described the crucial problem of Indian war finance as early as 1940: "On balance, more loan money has been lost to the public than has been gained from it."[26] When taxes and loans failed to raise enough money to meet war expenditures in India, that left one solution: the money-printing press.[27] There was an outpouring of paper currency. The amount of currency in circulation multiplied about six and a half times during the war years.[28] The printing press became perhaps the most productive machine in India.[29]

Inflation was the inevitable result. In May 1943, Keynes wrote about the dangerous extent to which the large British military expenditures in India were being uncompensated for by either taxation or loans: "We have carried to breaking point the policy of financing the war in India and the Middle East by printing paper money, whilst . . . actually diminishing the goods to be purchased."[30] The price index in 1945 was about two and a half times its value at the beginning of the war.[31] Food prices in wartime Britain, kept in check by a system of subsidies, rose only about 18 percent; in India, the price rise was, in one estimate, about 300 percent for *rationed* foods.[32]

WHAT WAS THE SOCIAL IMPACT OF THESE ACTIVITIES of the colonial state? The picture that emerges varies with both region and social class. The war gave a boost to the Indian business class. Stocks of textiles, for example, had accumulated in a prewar slump; after the war began, there were substantial orders from the government, and the stocks were quickly sold. The Income-Tax Investigation Commission set up after the war noted: "The conditions created by the war brought about a serious breakdown in the working of the [Income Tax] Department. Businessmen and speculators were able to make large profits by legal as well as illegal means; the control regulations led dealers to conceal their most profitable transactions from the knowledge of the authorities."[33] The war was no time to bother with a balance sheet.

There was a wave of enthusiasm and enterprise among industrialists, and industry did well for several reasons: imports were curtailed by lack of shipping; Japan, formerly a major exporter, became an enemy; large purchases were made on government account; and purchasing power expanded for some sections of the public. Contractors were inundated with contracts for military construction.[34] Big new companies were floated in areas like chemicals, machinery, and automobiles. Shortages of every kind of commodity meant that there were opportunities to make large profits in numerous areas.

This prosperity is also explained by the conditions under which Indian industry sold its products. Before the government intervened, the price of cloth increased to more than five times the prewar level. Since the intervention required the cooperation of the industrialists, profits remained high even after the price rise was checked somewhat. The government of India claimed that price controls operated in the interests of the common man; as one study countered, if public benefit was indeed intended, then "the control-ling authority should have consisted of people who could take a dis-passionate and impartial view of the situation and act in the best interests of the community as a whole. [Instead it] was packed with the representatives of vested interests."[35] The price of coal was de-termined in a similarly collusive way.

The situation in Britain was very different. Profits could not be of the same order, for the British businessman, operating in a more formally organized economy, could not evade taxes so easily. A black market existed, of course, but in the view of one authority, "The black market was never very large, and people did not treat the war as an opportunity for a great display of dishonesty."[36] In India, production increased slightly, yet profits increased a great deal; in Britain, pro-duction increased a great deal, but profits did not increase much.

For much of India's peasantry, the Second World War meant awak-ening from the nightmare of the 1930s, which had been dominated by the Great Depression. Then, the prices of agricultural products had fallen catastrophically, and peasant earnings with them; peas-ants' assets had often been sold in distress sales. But in the 1940s, agricultural prices rose, and with them rose the spirit of much of the countryside.

Inflation lightened the burden of debts, money rents, and land revenue.[37] In the early 1940s, the same amount of produce fetched two or three times what it would have earned five years earlier. Old obligations, which remained monetarily fixed, could therefore be met by selling a half or a third of the produce previously required to meet them. The problem of rural indebtedness, hitherto a focus of government attention and legislation, was "relegated to the back-ground almost to the point of being forgotten" by August 1943.[38] In a pamphlet titled *War-time Prices,* the economist P. J. Thomas wrote: "In India, owing to the wide prevalence of small-scale production, the number of producers is large, and the advantage of high prices is reaped by a very great number of persons."[39] Such opportunities came to them only once in a blue moon. Suddenly, a large section of the peasantry received more prosperity than its political leaders might have dared to promise.

In various ways, the black market made rural life in some parts of India more colorful. There was extra money to spend. Villagers traveled to town more often: bus travel became more popular. Sons were packed off more frequently than earlier for an education in urban areas. Urban contacts changed rural values. Earlier, surplus cash among the rural rich would have been invested in jewelry and land; after the war, it provided capital for new enterprises like shops and rice mills. Men who would otherwise have remained landlords became "incipient capitalists."[40] The war changed not just the rich villager's income but his outlook as well.[41]

The Indian middle class's experience of wartime was mixed. For the young, life became easier. Middle-class jobs had always been scarce, and in the 1930s they had become scarcer still—as various provincial reports on the problem of educated unemployment testified. For a college or high school graduate, getting a job, preferably by clambering aboard the ship of state, was the biggest test of life. A government job provided, in addition to income, the triple gift of protection against dismissal, a reasonable pension, and, usually, an entitlement to idleness. With the onset of the war, middle-class jobs suddenly became available in plenty. At first the unemployed looked for jobs, and then the employers looked for them. College dormitories, where many young men had been condemned to education for want of employment, began to empty. Middle-class youths were recruited by the military or by the mushrooming governmental departments handling civilian and military supplies. The problem of educated unemployment was solved for well over a decade.[42]

But for those already employed, the war meant a falling standard of living. Inflation wounds the recipients of fixed incomes. Among the middle class of Calcutta, the consumption of meat and fish was halved, that of milk more than halved, and the consumption of eggs fell to a quarter of the prewar figure. More of the middle-class salary was now spent on food, but the food seemed less palatable. Moreover, higher expenditures on food meant that there was less available for everything else.[43] The number of servants, a badge of membership in this class, was halved, as were budgets for clothes. There grew, especially at the lower levels of government service, "a bitterness which belated and grudging measures of relief have not by any means helped to assuage."[44] The young were happy to have jobs, but people like clerks and teachers, who had already been employed for some time, became increasingly impoverished and enraged.

These years proved unpleasant for the industrial working class as well. Although the war was a time of unprecedented industrial profits, the urban industrial labor force did not, as a whole, benefit from this prosperity. Employment increased, and longer hours were worked, but real wages fell nevertheless, declining by as much as 30 percent in the period 1939–43.[45] The highest industrial profits and the lowest real wages both occurred in 1943. This was contrary to the trend in Britain, where the wages of labor rose by 80 percent, while the cost of living increased by 31 percent.[46] The Indian working class regained its prewar standard of living only in 1949.

The first detailed survey of agricultural labor revealed that on average 85 percent of a farm laborer's wages were spent on food, and yet in 96 percent of the cases this provided less than the minimum number of calories considered nutritionally adequate. The economist V. M. Dandekar, reflecting on this data, commented: "What is poverty if not this?"[47] During the war, over most of India, grain prices rose faster than incomes; hungry agricultural laborers became hungrier still.[48]

This process of impoverishment reached its height in Bengal, which displayed, during what came to be known as the great Bengal famine of 1943, the country's most gruesome misery. Food in Bengal primarily meant rice.[49] And rice was, even for most people living in rural Bengal, an item that had to be purchased.[50]

The price of rice rose phenomenally, becoming too high for the poor to afford. Then stocks vanished from the markets. While agricultural laborers were by far the worst sufferers across Bengal, fishermen, transport workers, and rural artisans were also badly affected. In the countryside, buyers of food suffered terribly, while peasants who had food grains to sell tended to escape calamity. The famine began in rural areas early in 1943. By July 1943, starvation in the districts was on the increase, driving those who had become destitute to board trains for places where food might be available. Many of them went to Calcutta. The governor of Bengal sent alarming reports, which the Viceroy initially read with skepticism.[51] In due course, everyone had to face the fact that a cataclysm was occurring: military personnel had to take over the daily removal of corpses from streets and houses. After starvation came the epidemics. Malaria killed the most, followed by cholera, dysentery, diarrhea, various enteric fevers, and smallpox. More people were killed by disease than outright starvation.[52] In sheer scale, the tragedy of the Bengal famine bears comparison with any other of the Second World War, and dwarfs other incidents in India. The dead outnumbered the entire Indian industrial working class, and surpassed the number of Indian soldiers killed during the war by a factor of 100.

British social history followed an opposite trajectory. The British government initially expected that food rationing, long hours of work, and the general worries of war would damage public health. Exactly the opposite happened. Aware that a healthy workforce was important to the war effort, the state watched over its health anxiously. Food supplies were controlled as never before. Prices remained relatively stable: the rise in the cost of living was low (one estimate was 31 percent). Food was adequately available to farm laborers and industrial workers, who were increasing their earnings, with unequivocally positive results. The year 1942 saw a decrease in major infections and "record-breaking in vital statistics": the maternal and infant mortality rates, the proportion of stillbirths, and the standardized death rate among civilians were the lowest ever recorded in England.[53] The British National Food Survey Committee later remarked that "from a nutritional point of view the working class diet was probably more satisfactory in 1944 than at any time before the war."[54] While starvation deaths occurred in India, the less privileged classes in Britain improved their quality of life.[55]

Rationing, which covered the whole country and used the slogan of equal shares for all, became a symbol of the state's fair play. The controlled economy, with full employment and a strict rationing of basic foods, led to "a great reduction in group differences of all kinds."[56] As A. J. P. Taylor reasoned: "Broadly speaking, the entire population settled at the standard of the skilled artisan. This was a come-down for the wealthier classes . . . It was security for the masses such as they had not known before."[57] If the distribution of property was seen as a marker of class, then the leveling of class was slight; if income was considered, then the change was greater; and if everyday consumption was taken as an index, then leveling was much more in evidence. Such a debate would be unthinkable for Indian history. Indian society during the Second World War saw both starvation and prosperity on new, unprecedented scales.

IN 1943, R. H. TAWNEY PUBLISHED A CLASSIC ARTICLE on the aftermath of the First World War, in which he remarked that it was "of the nature of modern war to cause a sensational increase, both of range and of intensity, in the authority exercised by the state over economic life."[58] The transformations in state power brought about by war were widely recognized. Independent India's economic policies bore the imprint of the war. A civil servant wrote over four decades later: "Practically every control which has been practised in India since Independence, every control which continues even today, was started during the War."[59] Michael Howard commented that a lasting result of the Second World War for Britain was "a great and accepted increase in both governmental power over the community and sense of responsibility for the community."[60]

Military recruitment, the provisioning of the Allied armies, requisitioning, and rationing caused the state to penetrate more deeply than ever before into Indian society. Yet the terms of India's participation in the war show a pronounced lack of self-confidence on the part of the colonial state. The official history of British war finance stressed the constraints on the government of India: "Official advice from India threw cold water on any suggestion of a general re-opening of the [financial] settlement . . . the co-operation of Indian industrialists and business men, on which war production depended, would be forfeited."[61] The price levels told the real story. There was no attempt to fix prices according to objective considerations like costs or profits; the prices of commodities became those that producers or manufacturers were "not reluctant to accept."[62] Pricing policy discloses the power (or lack of power) of various social classes in India. War discloses who calls the shots.

The wartime economic boom, especially the agrarian boom in Punjab, which is neglected in the historiography, was politically relevant, providing in the short run some bags of cement to fortify the citadel of state power. By contrast, the tragedy of the Bengal famine was widely publicized. Arguments over causes and numbers have persisted over the years. The official Famine Enquiry Commission estimated a mortality of 1.5 million; later, the economist A. K. Sen calculated that 3 million was likely nearer the mark; and a subsequent study concluded that 2.1 million would be more accurate.[63] In one view, the cessation of rice imports from Burma and the need to feed an expanding army precipitated a shortage of rice. In another view, as Sen neatly put it, "A moderate short-fall in *production* had . . . been translated into an exceptional short-fall in *market release.*"[64] Whereas earlier famines might be attributed to drought, the great Bengal famine was attributable to wartime inflation. In this sense it was man-made. And despite all the statistical fanfare, the number of dead could still easily be wrong by a million.

This may be the aspect worth pondering. So little was known about the victims. They lay beyond the colonial state's myopic gaze. If the significance of an event is judged by the mortality involved, then the Bengal famine must unquestionably rank as the most important event of the 1940s in India. If judged by its impact on state power, however, the famine plummets to a lower place. Those who died were mainly agricultural laborers. Since franchise was based on property and education, they were not on the provincial voters lists. The famine was a colossal human tragedy, but, cynically, no cause for political panic. Its victims could not even be counted properly, because they counted for so little.

So India did not suffer during the war, although many Indians did. The premise for this conclusion: there is much more to Indian history than meets the imperialist or nationalist eye. Nationalist and imperialist history, even when regional in scope, take the region as representative, as a microcosm. India is always, in a sense, the unit of analysis. But the experiences of different regions and of different social classes could diverge dramatically. A national category can easily generate much outrage; regional and class analysis—as well as international comparisons—can sometimes generate more insight.

The thread running through this lecture has been the stark contrast during the Second World War between the war effort of the state in Britain and that of the colonial state in India. Seen separately, each nation's account can, no doubt, be qualified. But if the pictures are contrasted, two different types of relationships between the state and social classes are clarified. The claims that colonial rule was civilizing and good, or the cries that it was exploitative and cruel, leave this unsaid.

During the Second World War, the British upper classes were forced to send their children to the battlefront, to curb their own consumption, and to contribute large amounts to the national treasury. The Indian upper classes could not be conscripted, their consumption could not easily be curtailed, and their profits could not effectively be taxed. In fact, they often benefited substantially from the war. Both states worked desperately to extract resources, but they could not select identical targets for resource extraction. Faced with the emergency of war, the British state squeezed the British upper classes, whereas the colonial state starved the Indian lower classes. Moreover, in Britain a successful war effort required the state to satisfy the sectional interest of the lower classes; in India it required the state to appease the upper classes. Overall, the war effort in India was run on the terms of, and indeed to the benefit of, the upper classes; this was not the case in Britain.

What does it suggest when a state fighting a prolonged war and desperate for additional resources fails to squeeze much out of the wealthy or powerful classes? A relationship of power between the state and social classes is revealed with unusual clarity, showing that in its relation to the upper classes of society, the late-colonial state in India was a weak creature. This relationship has left a legacy.[65] Since independence, the Indian state has swollen enormously, employing many times more people and spending many times more money than it did during the Second World War; but the time when it can effectively extract resources from the dominant classes has not yet come.

Spring Semester 2007

A version of this lecture first appeard in *Past and Present,* 176, 1, 2002.

1. Bisheshwar Prasad, gen. ed., *Official History of the Indian Armed Forces in the Second World War, 1939–45,* 25 vols. (Delhi, 1952–66). Exceptions were Johannes Voigt, *India in the Second World War* (Delhi, 1987), and Judith Brown, "India," in I. C. Dear, ed., *The Oxford Companion to World War II* (Oxford, 1995).

2. For a survey, see R. J. Moore, "India in the 1940s," in Robin Winks, ed., *The Oxford History of the British Empire,* Vol. V: *Historiography* (Oxford, 1999).

3. Sumit Sarkar, *Modern India, 1885–1947* (Delhi, 1983), pp. 383–84, 393, 405–08.

4. B. R. Tomlinson, *The Economy of Modern India, 1860–1970* (Cambridge, 1998), p. 160.

5. The numbers in the Indian armed forces serving in India on 1 September 1945 were as follows: army, 1,906,700; navy, 30,200; and air force, 22,900. The numbers have been rounded off from Government of India, *Statistics Relating to India's War Effort* (Delhi, 1947) [hereafter *SWE*], p. 2. The total number serving in India's armed forces, inside and outside India, was 2,128,000 on 1 September 1945.

6. A. G. Fernandes and K. Someswara Rao, "Nutrition Work in the Indian Army," Indian Council of Medical Research, Special Report Series, no. 36, *Review of Nutrition Surveys Carried Out in India* (Delhi, 1961), pp. 73–78, 94.

7. Stephen P. Cohen, *The Indian Army: Its Contribution to the Development of a Nation* (Bombay, 1971), p. 140.

8. One author gave the following figures for the percentage of the Indian armed forces recruited from selected provinces: Punjab, 29.9; Madras, 22.0; Uttar Pradesh, 13.8; Bengal, 6.6, and Bombay, 6.1 (P. S. Lokanathan, *Transition to Peace Economy* [Delhi, 1945], pp. 44–45).

9. Interview with Lt. Gen. Harbaksh Singh, Delhi, 22 Oct. 1996.

10. S. C. Aggarwal, *History of the Supply Department, 1939–46* (Delhi, 1947), preface.

11. *SWE,* pp. 7, 11.

12. M. K. Vellodi, "Cotton Textile Control in India," *Asiatic Review,* 43 (Jan. 1947), pp. 10–22.

13. H. Crookshank, "War and the Indian Mineral Industry," *Proceedings of the Indian Science Congress,* 33rd sess. (Bangalore, 1946), pp. 85–96.

14. Vellodi, "Cotton Textile Control in India."

15. *SWE,* p. 15.

16. Arthur Marwick, *Britain in the Century of Total War: Peace and Social Change, 1900–1967* (London, 1968), pp. 276–77.

17. Rabindranath Chatterji, "Food Rationing in India," *Indian Journal of Economics,* 26, 103, pt. IV (1946), p. 626.

18. Note by J. M. Keynes dated 20 Jan. 1942, in Donald Moggridge, ed., *The Collected Writings of John Maynard Keynes,* Vol. XXIII (London, 1979), p. 329.

19. For details, see R. S. Sayers, *Financial Policy, 1939–45* (London, 1956), pp. 252–73.

20. The sterling debt extinguished by India during the war was about 300–350 million pounds; the sterling balances, which accumulated to India's credit, stood at 1.321 billion pounds at the end of 1945 (Sayers, *Financial Policy,* pp. 256–59).

21. Lokanathan, *Transition to Peace Economy,* p. 10.

22. Dharma Kumar, *Colonialism, Property and the State* (Delhi, 1998), pp. 207–08.

23. W. K. Hancock and M. M. Gowing, *British War Economy* (London, 1949), pp. 163, 348, 502.

24. *Report on the Work of the Indian Posts and Telegraphs Department, 1945–46* (Calcutta, 1948).

25. M. D. Joshi, "Currency," in V. B. Singh, ed., *Economic History of India, 1857–1956* (Delhi, 1965), p. 404.

26. Keynes to Waley, 19 Nov. 1940, in Moggridge, ed., *Collected Writings,* Vol. XXIII, pp. 325–26.

27. Lokanathan, *Transition to Peace Economy,* p. 12.

28. "The inflation in war time was due to the large increases in currency circulation (from Rs. 172 crores in 1939 to over Rs. 1200 crores at the end of 1945) without any tangible increase in the supply of goods" (Shanmukham Chetty, *Speeches of Union Finance Ministers, 1947–48 to 1984–85* [Delhi, 1984], p. 3). One crore equals ten million rupees. The exact figures are in *SWE,* p. 45.

29. The economist K. N. Raj calculated that of the total deficit of Rs 3,300 crores incurred in India between September 1939 and March 1946, not more than Rs 800 crores (24 percent) was met by borrowing from the public (K. N. Raj, *The Monetary Policy of the Reserve Bank of India* [Bombay, 1948], p. 160).

30. Note by Keynes dated 11 May 1943, in Moggridge, ed., *Collected Writings,* Vol. XXIII, p. 270; see also p. 265.

31. If August 1939 is taken as the base, in July 1943 the general index of prices was 239, and the index for food and tobacco was 294, but these indices ignored the "black markets which were flourishing all over the country" (Raj, *Monetary Policy,* pp. 153–54).

32. Chatterji, "Food Rationing," pp. 622–630. The contrast holds for the 1940s as a whole. "The food cost index was 311 in April, 1949 (1937=100), while it was 193 in the U.S.A. and 108 in the U.K." (B. N. Ganguli, *Devaluation of the Rupee: What It Means to India* [Delhi, 1949], p. 44).

33. *Report of the Income-Tax Investigation Commission, 1948* (Delhi, 1949), p. 4.

34. Patwant Singh, *Of Dreams and Demons: An Indian Memoir* (Delhi, 1994), p. 23.

35. J. J. Anjaria, D. T. Lakdawala, and D. R. Samant, *Price Control in India* (Bombay, 1946), p. 129.

36. T. O. Lloyd, *Empire to Welfare State: English History, 1906–1985,* 3rd edn. (Oxford, 1986), p. 265.

37. Ministry of Finance, *Taxation Enquiry Commission: Summary of Report* (Delhi, 1955), p. 100.

38. *All-India Rural Credit Survey: Report of the Committee of Direction,* Vol. II: *The General Report* (Bombay, 1954), p. 2.

39. P. J. Thomas, *War-Time Prices* (London, 1943), p. 11.

40. M. N. Srinivas, "The Industrialization and Urbanization of Rural Areas," *Sociological Bulletin,* 5, 2 (1956), pp. 86–87.

41. M. N. Srinivas, *The Remembered Village* (Delhi, 1976), pp. 70, 129, 233–36, 239, 282.

42. Planning Commission, *Outline Report of the Study Group on Educated Unemployed, 1955* (Delhi, 1956).

43. S. Bhattacharyya, "World War II and the Consumption Pattern of the Calcutta Middleclass," *Sankhya,* 8, 2 (Mar. 1947), pp. 197–200.

44. *Report of the Central Pay Commission, 1947* (Delhi, 1947), p. 27.

45. S. A. Palekar, "Real Wages in India, 1939–50," *Economic Weekly,* annual no. (Jan. 1957), pp. 151–60; "Real Wages and Profits in India, 1939–50," *Indian Economic Review,* 3, 4 (1957), pp. 34–45.

46. Arthur Marwick, *War and Social Change in the Twentieth Century: A Comparative Study of Britain, France, Germany, Russia and the United States* (London, 1974), p. 162.

47. V. M. Dandekar, "Agricultural Labour Enquiry, 1950–51," in Dandekar, *The Indian Economy 1947–92*, Vol. II (Delhi, 1996), pp. 127–55, esp. 134–38, 145.

48. It is true that many from this class found work due to the war effort—as soldiers, as laborers constructing airfields and barracks, as miners, or as factory workers—and this gave them resources they would otherwise not have had. To estimate the overall consequences of this employment, compare the figures in B. N. Datar and I. G. Patel, "Employment during the Second World War," *Indian Economic Review*, 2, 1 (Feb. 1956), with the number of agricultural laborers in India, calculated in S. J. Patel, *Agricultural Labourers in Modern India and Pakistan* (Bombay, 1952), pp. 30, 148. It would seem that contact with the government and military contractors sustained many laborers, but the impact of inflation damaged many more of them. For agricultural labor as a class, the war was, on the whole, catastrophic.

49. "Paddy [i.e., rice] is the main crop of the province, being sown on about 88% of the total cultivated area of Bengal" (Ramkrishna Mukherjee, "Economic Structure of Rural Bengal: A Survey of Six Villages," *American Sociological Review*, 13 [1948], p. 666).

50. In rural Bengal, about 36.2 percent of all rural families did not own any rice land, while about 40.5 percent owned less than two acres. In the opinion of many economists and agricultural experts, the subsistence level was two acres of rice land per family. Thus, about three-fourths of all rural families owned rice land below the subsistence level. See P. C. Mahalanobis, "The Bengal Famine: The Background and Basic Facts," *Asiatic Review*, 42, 4 (Oct. 1946), p. 312.

51. Herbert to Linlithgow, 2 July 1943, in Nicholas Mansergh, editor-in-chief, *Constitutional Relations between Britain and India: The Transfer of Power, 1942–47*, Vol. IV (12 vols., London, 1970–83), doc. 27.

52. "Very substantially more than half the deaths attributable to the famine of 1943 took place *after* 1943" (Amartya Sen, *Poverty and Famines: An Essay on Entitlement and Deprivation* [Delhi, 1981], p. 215; see also p. 203).

53. W. P. D. Logan and E. M. Brooke, *The Survey of Sickness, 1943 to 1952*, General Registrar Office, Studies on Medical and Population Subjects (London, 1957), p. 11.

54. Ministry of Agriculture, Fisheries and Food, *Studies in Urban Household Diets, 1944–49*, Second Report of the National Food Survey Committee (London, 1956), p. 7.

55. "From 1942 onwards, in spite of the war, the general health of British society began to improve strikingly" (Alan Milward, *The Economic Effects of the Two World Wars on Britain* [London, 1970], p. 22).

56. Ministry of Agriculture, *Studies in Urban Household Diets*, p. 4.

57. A. J. P. Taylor, *English History, 1914–1945* (London, 1965), p. 550.

58. R. H. Tawney, "The Abolition of Economic Controls, 1918–1921," *Economic History Review*, 13 (1943), p. 23.

59. S. Bhoothalingam, *Reflections on an Era: Memoirs of a Civil Servant* (Delhi, 1993), p. 26.

60. Michael Howard, "Total War in the Twentieth Century: Participation and Consensus in the Second World War," in Brian Bond and Ian Roy, eds., *War and Society* (London, 1976), p. 224.

61. Sayers, *Financial Policy*, p. 261.

62. D. R. Gadgil, "Wartime Controls and Peacetime Ends," in *Problems of Indian Labour: A Symposium* (Delhi, 1947), pp. 2–3.

63. Sen, *Poverty and Famines,* pp. 196–202; Arup Maharatna, *The Demography of Famines: An Indian Historical Perspective* (Delhi, 1996), p. 175.

64. Sen, *Poverty and Famines,* pp. 63, 76, original emphasis; see also pp. 57–62.

65. According to an official report, in an entire decade—the 1950s—not one person was convicted for tax evasion in the whole of India (*Report of the Direct Taxes Enquiry Committee, 1958–59* [Delhi, 1960], p. 150).

11

Reassessing Paul Scott

HILARY SPURLING

In 1964, Paul Scott set out across India on a journey that he knew would make or break him as a novelist. He was forty-three years old with eight published novels behind him, none of which had done more than scratch the surface of the kind of book he had been struggling for twenty years to write about India. This journey was a last, desperate gamble that brought him to the verge of mental and physical collapse. At the same time, it strengthened and expanded his creative grasp, enabling him to break through as a writer to levels of emotional and intuitive understanding inaccessible to the conscious mind. It led directly to the *Raj Quartet,* the four linked novels he produced as soon as he got back from what became a voyage of self-discovery, a way of confronting his own inner demons and, through them, the dark, hidden underside of British imperial India.

Scott put himself into the first of his four books as its narrator, the nameless stranger who turns up near the beginning without introduction or explanation in the luxuriant garden of the MacGregor house in Mayapore. The writer at that stage was still groping his way forward, absorbing impressions, probing, and piecing his narrative together, like the observant stranger in his fictional garden with its cascades of bougainvillea, its jasmine and canna lilies, its patches of brilliant sunlight heightened by the dense blue-black shadows of neem, peepul, tamarind, and banyan trees: "The range of greens is extraordinary, palest lime, bitter emerald, mid-tones, neutral tints. The textures of the leaves are many and varied, they communicate themselves through sight to imaginary touch, exciting the finger-tips: leaves coming into the tenderest flesh, superbly in their prime, crisping to old age . . . In the shadows there are . . . odours of sweet and necessary decay, numerous places layered with the cast-off fruit of other years softened into compost, feeding the living roots that lie under the garden massively, in hungry immobility."

On one level, this passage grew from memories of a real garden belonging to the Indian couple who were Scott's hosts in Calcutta in 1964. On another, it explores the garden of the mind, where the novelist broods and ponders, ranging back and forth over the present and the past, sensing underlying shapes and patterns, watching new life stir in the tangled undergrowth of the subject as it begins at last to come within his imaginative reach. It is a potent and accurate image of the writer at work.

On his return from India in 1964, Scott sat down at once to write *The Jewel in the Crown,* the opening movement of the *Raj Quartet.* The whole sequence covers the final, inglorious phase of Britain's imperial dominion in India, from the arrest of Congress Party leaders in the Second World War to the handover of power in 1947, the speedy retreat of the British, and the massacres precipitated by the division of India from Pakistan as both countries became independent. The *Quartet* starts with the rape of a white woman during the Quit India riots that mobilized resentment against the British in 1942. It ends five years later with the murder of a Muslim—a body falling from a railway carriage, butchered by Hindu terrorists on an ambushed train that moves off again, after a brief, bloody interval, to complete its interrupted journey across the subcontinent: "It was the smooth gliding motion away from a violent situation which one witness never forgot. 'Suddenly you had the feeling that the train, the wheels, the lines weren't made of metal but of something greasy and evasive.'"

Railway journeys play a vital part in the *Raj Quartet.* Trains make connections, they move through time and space, they may be used to ferry themes as well as people. This particular train, with its cargo of dead or dying Muslims, also carries, in separate carriages, a party of British imperialists heading for home in August 1947: civil servants, police and army personnel, sahibs and memsahibs fleeing Indian Independence, the splendid ceremonial dissolution of the Raj, the breakdown of civil authority, and the terrible consequences visited upon countless unofficial victims. The observer in the passage quoted above—the witness uneasily aware of the greasiness and evasion inherent in this process—is a young British conscript posted to India in wartime, Sergeant Guy Perron, who provides a linking commentary, or consciousness, in the last of the four novels, *A Division of the Spoils*. Perron is a professional historian who becomes, like the anonymous stranger in the first novel, a spokesman or stand-in for the author himself. He represents, so to speak, the historian in Scott.

Scott's own first contact with India had come when he was drafted into the Indian Army as an officer cadet in 1943. He knew nothing about the country, didn't particularly want to go there, and responded, as soon as he landed, with shock and revulsion. He felt lonely, homesick, and ill. He loathed the heat, the dirt, and the poverty, disliked the army, and was so appalled by the arrogant complacency of the British that he would in the end spend the greater part of his adult life unraveling its implications (his imaginative engagement in *The Raj Quartet* was with the British, not the Indians, who—apart from the key figure of Hari Kumar—remain more or less on the sidelines). Scott in those days knew exactly where he stood, politically speaking. Young, liberal minded, and highly critical, he never doubted the wisdom of handing India straight back to its inhabitants, a conviction that deepened over the next three years as he became steadily more fascinated by the place and its people. He sailed home to England in May 1946, and by August he was getting worrying letters from friends left behind, both Indian and English, containing news of riots in Calcutta, looting, rape, murder, and even more alarming premonitions of what might come in case of partition.

It would be nearly another twenty years before he returned to try to make sense of a process his younger self had seen, or glimpsed, coming to an end. By this time, he had come to recognize the end of empire as unfinished business. His wholesale contempt for the Raj had grown less confident, and so had his initial conviction that the behavior and attitudes of British India had nothing whatsoever to do with him. On the face of it, Scott had little or no connection with the imperial ruling elite. He was born in London into a family of shabby gentility on his father's side and, on his mother's, the same working-class background as that of the sleeping soldiers contemplated by Perron in a Bombay guardroom in the last volume of the *Quartet:* "The faces were those of urban Londoners and belonged to streets of terraced houses that ended in one-man shops: newsagent-tobacconist, fish and chip shop, family grocer, and a pub at the corner where the high road was. What could such a face know of India? And yet India was there, in the skull, and the bones of the body. Its possession had helped nourish the flesh, warm the blood of every man in the room, sleeping and waking."

Scott himself quoted this passage to show that his link with India ran through his mother's people as well as his father's, and
that the British withdrawal was part of what he called his personal
luggage. He was thinking of a character named Barbie Batchelor,
an elderly, retired missionary in *The Towers of Silence,* the *Quartet*'s
third volume, who turns up at the hill station of Pankot with a large
tin trunk from which she cannot be parted. As Barbie herself is
shunted round Pankot from house to house and from one family to
the next, the trunk becomes a fearful nuisance, constantly having
to be sent for, stowed away, brought out again, and sorted through,
ending up capsized in transit with its contents spilled all over the
road. "I see now," Scott wrote afterward, "that her trunk of missionary relics, which gives her so much trouble throughout the book . . .
is really a symbol for the luggage I am conscious of carrying with
me every day of my life—the luggage of my past, of my personal
history and of the world's history." This is what made him a writer.
It is why he always insisted he was not a historical novelist, and why
his books still reverberate so insistently for readers today: "One is
not ruled by the past, one does not rule or re-order it, one simply
is it, in the same way that one is as well the present and part of the
future."

At the end of his life, Scott attempted to define his achievement
for a class of postgraduate students at a university in the American
Midwest. He drew up a chart on the blackboard, beginning before
the First World War, when Britain, at the height of its power, wealth,
and influence, was in possession of an empire that covered a quarter
of the globe, and ending after the Second World War with the election of a British Labour government, the creation of a welfare
state at home, and the abandonment of empire abroad. He saw the
changes signalled by these two events—each promoted in its day as a
glorious liberation, each producing with time increasingly sour and
disruptive consequences—reflected consciously or unconsciously in
the contemporary novel. He defined post-war British fiction as "the
end of the party and the beginning of the washing up." For a hard-
drinking heavy-smoking host like Scott, the end of a party meant
stacking the dirty dishes, rounding up the empties, finishing off the
whisky bottle, holding some sort of inquest over broken glasses and
cigarette burns on the carpet, going over any rows that had blown
up, working out who had come (and who had left) with whom, who
was on speaking terms and who wasn't. It is a characteristically un-
romantic image of what Scott himself was doing in the *Raj Quartet.*
"You write for an age," he told his students, indicating his chart on
the blackboard, "and this is my age."

He came in the end to see the precipitate, unprepared hand-over of power by the British as a disaster, the final, tragic failure of a long relationship between the two countries. Its root causes run underground through the *Raj Quartet.* As the novels appeared, Scott's persistence was unwelcome, indeed virtually unheard-of, in Britain, where for many years after independence, people refused to think about India. His novels were attacked or dismissed almost unanimously from opposite directions. On the one hand, his younger, more fashion-conscious contemporaries complained that he glamorized the past, apparently by the very act of recognizing its existence and writing about it. On the other hand, an older generation of readers saw him as a troublemaker hell-bent on raking over dead embers of rancor, bitterness, and betrayal. By 1975, when Scott completed the last of his four novels, the Raj and its repercussions seemed to most people to be safely consigned to ancient history.

A quarter of a century after Scott's return journey to India, when, as his biographer, I crossed the subcontinent in his footsteps, I often felt like ancient history myself. At one point I stayed alone in a small town high in the Western Ghats of the Deccan at the hotel immortalized by Scott in his last novel, *Staying On,* a kind of afterthought or pendant to the *Quartet.* He had first gone there as a young conscript in 1943, when it was a smart little outfit beside the parade ground, full of British army officers, the center of social life in a bustling garrison town. Long before I got there, it had become a ghost hotel. My high bare dusty room contained nothing but a chest and a bed shrouded in an elephant-grey mosquito net the size of a small marquee. The only woman on the premises, probably the only English visitor anyone there could remember, I seemed to have stepped into a world peopled by ghosts—the ghosts of the British and their former glory in an obsolete hotel. In fact, the place turned out not to be dead at all. Its life had simply shifted to the bar in the compound outside, where, amid piped-in music and lights strung in the trees, a crowd of young Indian men came and went, drank and talked, paying no attention to the phantoms forgotten in the silent, unvisited rooms.

Subsequent events have proved Scott right when he said that the ghosts of the past can neither be ignored nor forgotten. His driving principle as a novelist was what he called a vigorous sense of history, "vigorous because it pruned ruthlessly that other weakening sense so often found with the first, the sense of nostalgia, the desire to *live* in the past." Scott feared and mistrusted nostalgia. He said the denial of memory was a terrible thing, but its opposite—the tendency to romanticize the past—could be just as destructive. The *Quartet* took him a decade to write, and twenty years' preparation before that. "Imagination is not enough," he said. "You have to have knowledge too." But knowledge was not easily available at that stage. Official records were blocked, documentary evidence was largely inaccessible, and people in both countries proved reluctant to talk.

Scott's struggle in this kind of limbo paralleled that of men like Sir Conrad Corfield, a former head of the Political Department in India, who had been strongly critical of government policy, and General Mohan Singh, founder of the Indian National Army, a patriotic resistance force proscribed and suppressed by the British. Both had written memoirs (both gave copies to Scott) that were repeatedly rejected by publishers on the grounds that the subject was of no public interest. A whole generation of retired British colonial administrators found themselves treated as figures of fun and their views for all practical purposes suppressed. In India, Scott's attempts to find out more about the activities of the INA met with closed doors. "My not very thrusting attempts in Delhi to be shown pertinent archives were not successful," he explained, adding unexpectedly, "I didn't persist because as a novelist . . . the reluctance interested me almost as much, if not more than the archives would have done."

The novelist in Scott was transfixed by the widespread and deep-rooted amnesia that confronted him on all sides. The end of the Raj had been an abrupt and humiliating defeat for the British, who reacted by turning away from what was generally agreed to be a closed chapter and vehemently resisting any attempt to re-open it. During and after the writing of the *Quartet,* Scott was accused of harboring a sneaking desire to return to the bad old days of colonial supremacy. "To forget strikes me as the quickest way of making the same mistakes again," he responded austerely. "I'm not sure that there is any such thing as forgetting, but there are tender conspiracies of silence—and these may engender ignorance, always a dangerous thing."

Scott did not condone the Raj. He looked long and hard at its many failures: its inhumanity, smugness, self-righteousness, and rigidity. His treatment of individual characters in the *Quartet* may be sympathetic, but his collective portrayal of the British is far from flattering. When an Indian friend asked him what he meant by the title of the second of the four novels, *The Day of the Scorpion,* he explained that scorpions live under stones because they are sensitive to heat: "There was an old belief that, if you surrounded them with a ring of fire, they committed suicide. But actually they are shrivelled by the heat, and when they dart their tails, they're not committing suicide but trying to attack. Well, that's what so much of the British in India was all about. They were driven out of their places in the end by a number of pressures—and were scorched by fires they had really set fire to themselves."

The fires the British lit have been smoldering ever since. In the 1960s, Scott was already tracing the growing racial tensions in contemporary Britain back to much earlier failures of foresight and strategic planning. "History seems to have overtaken me," he wrote to an Indian friend in Bombay when war broke out between India and Pakistan, adding sadly as the fighting dragged on: "All this is in my book, you know." He struggled long and hard against the collective inertia cloaking British determination to disclaim responsibility for the consequences of imperial collapse: the greasy, evasive, perennial human instinct to glide smoothly away from violent disturbance. He addressed unpopular issues in the *Raj Quartet* and reached unpalatable conclusions. He said it was part of the novelist's job to confront what he saw as a pervasive, obstinate, and pusillanimous spirit of withdrawal from the problems of the modern world.

Scott got small thanks for his pains, relatively grudging critical esteem, and little public recognition until he won the Booker Prize for *Staying On* in 1977, a few months before he died. He would surely have raised a sardonic eyebrow to see the *Quartet*, so widely underrated in his lifetime, turned after his death into one of the most successful television adaptations ever made, under the overall title *The Jewel in the Crown*. The series precipitated a wave of overwhelming nostalgia for the Raj in the early 1980s: trendy Raj restaurants and pubs sprang up all over Britain, serving Raj drinks in Raj interiors—potted palms, brass fittings, rattan furniture—to customers wearing Raj clothes in white or biscuit-coloured linen. Scott himself would have been the first to recognize this wave of fakery, masquerade, and make-believe, however absurd in rational terms, as a perfectly natural human instinct to sidestep the implications of too much clear-sightedness.

Granada TV's *Jewel in the Crown*, sensitive and scrupulously faithful though it was, remained at bottom a superbly directed and acted family saga. What it lacked was the majestic breadth and sweep of the novelist's imagination, the shifting temporal and spatial perspectives that give such richness of tone and color to Scott's panorama of unheroic characters pursuing prosaic occupations in mundane settings. The domestic concerns of the human figures occupying the foreground of the *Raj Quartet*—the wrecked lives of Hari Kumar and his lover in the first of the four novels, the rifts and tensions threatening the shaky equilibrium of the Layton family in the last—acquire depth and gravity from the sense of historical and political tides turning in the background.

Professional historians like Max Beloff and Wm. Roger Louis recognized from the start the intellectual force and originality of the *Raj Quartet*. Scott's portrait of modern British India penetrated deeper and further than anyone else had gone (or indeed could go) at the time. In the early years of the civil rights movement in the United States, he was the first to confront directly the nature and extent of British colonial racism, the unacknowledged color bar that was as much a reality in imperial India as in the American South. His exposure of routine, secret brutality and coercion within the British police and security forces was generally dismissed in Scott's day, by even his greatest admirers, as more or less preposterous fictional license. Documentary evidence, forthcoming only long after his death, led to the kind of widespread historical reappraisal already forestalled in essence by the *Raj Quartet*.

If Scott saw history as an active force for the promotion of understanding, tolerance, and freedom, his strength as a novelist was imaginative rather than analytical. The emotional heart of the *Raj Quartet* lies not with objective observers like Guy Perron, but with their opposite number, the least theoretical and most practical of men, a character whom Perron initially distrusts, subsequently despises, and eventually detests with unqualified venom. This is the formidable Major Merrick, whose career progresses steadily throughout the four volumes, raising him from one rung to the next up the official ladder of command and trust until he reaches his high point (and his dreadful end) in *A Division of the Spoils*. Insofar as the *Quartet* may be said to have a villain, it is Ronald Merrick, who believes implicitly in the Raj and its panoply of racial privilege and power. "He believes we've abandoned the principles we used to live by," Perron explains, "what he would call the English upper-and-ruling class principle of knowing oneself superior to all other races, especially black, and having a duty to guide and correct them. He's been sucked in by all that kiplingesque talk that transformed India from a place where ordinary greedy Englishmen carved something out for themselves . . . into one where they appeared to go voluntarily into exile for the good of their souls and the uplift of the native."

Merrick is a man of the past as well as a man of action. His insistence on the virtues of a world that no longer exists, perhaps never existed, makes him dangerously attractive in times of trouble, when "his absolutely inflexible and unshakable sense of his own authority" comes as a relief even to people who mistrust his methods. The kind of man always welcome in a tight spot, Merrick slowly comes to seem (as someone said of a similar character in one of Scott's earlier novels) more like *the man who brings the tight spot with him*. For all his impressive public reputation, he is in private a sadistic bully and blackmailer. He wins the confidence of his victims before driving them to despair and, in at least one case, to suicide. He lacks entirely what Perron calls "that liberal instinct which is so dear to historians that they lay it out like a guideline through the unmapped forests of prejudice and self-interest as though this line, and not the forest, is our history."

Scott explores that dark unvisited forest principally through Merrick: through glimpses of his background and upbringing, his social and emotional deprivation, his private obsessions, the sources of his indomitable will, and his undoubted power to charm. This is by no means an unsympathetic portrait. On the contrary, Scott somehow manages to make the reader look through Merrick's eyes and, seeing the world in the same light as Merrick sees it, understand how his conduct might have appeared to him to be a series of sound, bold, eminently justifiable moves in pursuit of honorable ends. Merrick's baleful influence is chiefly apparent through the ruined lives of his prisoners—Hari Kumar, Corporal Pinker, Havildar Khan (the "poor weary shagged-out shamed and insulted havildar" who hangs himself in *A Division of the Spoils* in the course of interrogation at Merrick's hands). Each represents a landmark in Scott's attempt to map the irrational impulses that operate in regions far from the historian's searchlight of conscious understanding.

He said that the original seeds of *The Jewel in the Crown* were planted in his mind by the affair of the Jallianwallah Bagh, when British troops fired on a trapped and helpless Indian crowd in 1919. The two related fictional incidents that set the *Quartet* in motion— the attacks on Edwina Crane and Daphne Manners, each of whom eventually dies in consequence—had a historical precedent from the same period. The roots of vengeance, repression, and inhumanity, running invisibly underground through time and space, are massively present even in the quietest, least eventful, and most elegiac of the four novels, the third in the sequence, *The Towers of Silence*. It takes place largely in 1943-44 among the isolated Anglo-Indian community of Pankot, mostly spinsters, widows, and wives with sons or husbands away at the front. It is set against the background of the distant European war, the Japanese invasion of the subcontinent, defeat and dispersal on all sides; and it charts the gradual, reluctant acceptance by one small section of the British civilian population in India that its time is up: "This sense of danger, of the sea-level rising, swamping the plains, threatening the hills, this sense of imminent inundation, was one to which people were now not unaccustomed."

It was Beloff who pointed out that Scott spoke for the other half, the wives and daughters of British India in places like Pankot, passive watchers who play no part in the decision-making process, who remain often barely conscious of its existence, let alone of its ramifications behind the scenes, and who yet must gather their energies to receive and absorb its impact. The whole novel is focused through the eyes of the missionary Barbie Batchelor, the obscure elderly owner of the battered tin trunk, who finds herself professionally redundant at the beginning of the book, and who spirals slowly downwards in the course of it through successive circles of loneliness, rejection, homelessness, and humiliation to madness and death. Barbie ends up a speechless outcast with no recollection of the past, forcibly restrained by cold water and winding sheets in the Samaritan Hospital at Ranpur. It is a grim and graphic image of the denial or suppression of memory. Barbie's fate is paralleled by the experience of Susan Layton, the younger and prettier of the two Layton sisters, who starts the book as a radiant bride, and who also finishes by succumbing, though only temporarily, to insanity and incarceration. Susan's dog, which has pined in its mistress's absence, causes perturbation when glimpsed by a guest at a garden party given to mark the first of many enforced departures from Pankot:

> She . . . was staring, horrified, at a patch of petal-strewn grass, a corridor between long rectangular beds of rose-trees, bush and standard, vagrant-looking with green reversionary shoots pale and erectile, already sucking the life out of the roots. Along this path the creature crawled, slunk, towards them; a black spectre of famine worn to its hooped rib cage and the arched column of its backbone. A thin dribble of saliva hung from its open mouth . . .
> The others stayed where they were, watching the apparition approach the verandah steps slowly, dragging one leg, pausing every few paces to rest, droop-headed, before struggling on, its eyes upturned . . . showing blood-shot whites.

Images like this horrifying hound help bear the weight of a novel that comes down in the end with an almost Shakespearian sense of ordinary people: people who have no individual existence for the historian: shallow, cowardly, small-minded people activated by prejudice and self-interest: the sort of people who provide the casualties and mop up the damage when greater men, like Mark Antony, cry havoc and let slip the dogs of war.

Scott's first stop on reaching India in 1964 in search of what eventually became the *Raj Quartet* was a flat with a balcony overlooking the nineteenth-century law courts on the Oval Maidan, or parade ground, in Bombay. If there is one particular passage in which Perron may be said to stand for his creator, it is near the beginning of *A Division of the Spoils* when he, too, looks across from a Bombay balcony to the dark bulk of the law courts: "For a moment—perhaps under the influence of that symbol of the one thing the British could point to if asked in what way and by what means they had unified the country, the single rule of law—he felt a pressure, as soft and close to his cheek as a sigh: the combined sigh of countless unknown Indians and of past and present members of the glittering insufferable *raj*."

This was what Scott tried to do: to speak for (or catch the sigh of) countless unknown, unrepresented, insignificant members of the Raj: to preserve them from the dangers of misrepresentation, the denial of memory, the distortions of nostalgia—to insist that their history was neither disposable nor detachable from the present and the future. He was, as he once said of E. M. Forster in reference to *A Passage to India,* a prophetic writer. He foresaw what others preferred not to see, and often he did not like what he saw. Sometimes he found it unbearable. It was this stern, insistent, prophetic vision that dismayed his contemporaries and made him in the end one of the most powerful and perceptive novelists of the twentieth century.

Summer 2007

A version of this lecture appears as the introduction to the Everyman's Library edition of Paul Scott's *Raj Quartet.*

12

The Myth of Malicious Partition

GEOFFREY WHEATCROFT

A few years ago, a story in the London newspapers was not so
much a nine days' wonder as a nine-minute stir. The personal
effects had come to light of an army officer killed on the western front in 1915, among them his dressing case and a tetchy note
telling his soldier-servant to get the shaving things in order. But no
one remarked on the identity of this officer or its significance. He
was Captain the Honourable T. C. Agar-Robartes, MP, Coldstream
Guards, son and heir of Lord Clifden and heir also to Lanhydrock,
a beautiful house in Cornwall that now belongs to the National
Trust. When the war began he was a Member of Parliament, but he
joined the army, and became one of twenty-two sitting MPs killed in
the war, along with eighty-five sons of MPs, a contrast indeed to the
present governing class in both London and Washington.

One of the dwindling band of patrician Liberals, Agar-Robartes
had an uneventful political career except for one moment: in June
1912 he was the author of the Agar-Robartes amendment to the
Home Rule Bill. This would have offered a way out of the escalating
Ulster crisis by excluding the easternmost and predominantly Protestant four counties of Ulster from Home Rule. The amendment
was defeated by no more than 61 votes, against the 101-vote majority for the Bill on Second Reading a month earlier, but then the
amendment had been dismissed by the Asquith government.

If Agar-Robartes's name and his amendment have been forgotten, so has Asquith's strong antipathy to the idea of partitioning Ireland. Were that remembered, it would serve as a caution against a

curious myth that has caught on, about willful or malevolent partition. Certain such concepts become fashionable from time to time, not so much with either the large public or real scholars, but among the "lumpenintelligentsia," readers who lack an informed critical understanding and are susceptible to intellectual trends that the learned view with more skepticism. Several examples come to mind (did someone say "Orientalism"?), not least this myth of malicious partition, which has been assiduously propagated, notably by Christopher Hitchens.

Writing recently about Iraq, he was quite unchastened by his passionate earlier enthusiasm for the invasion, which he had insisted would be greeted with open arms by Iraqis eager to welcome their great liberator, Ahmed Chalabi. He now expresses reservations about Peter Galbraith's proposals for something like an effective division of that country into its Shiite, Sunni, and Kurdish segments, "because I think that partition is always and everywhere a defeat and often leads to more wars and more partitions."[1] The same writer has energetically asserted the idea that not only is "partition" a form of crime, but also that, as retreating empires unwillingly or resentfully leave territories, they partition them with malice aforethought, and he flourishes the title of Sir Penderel Moon's book about India, *Divide and Quit.* That case of partition is then linked with the two other classic cases, Ireland and Palestine. And so the unproven assumption that partition must always be bad is linked with the claim that imperial rulers consciously wanted to divide before quitting.

In answer to which, one could borrow A. J. P. Taylor's words about another amateur historical thesis (Disraeli's notion of the "Venetian oligarchy" that supposedly ruled England under the Hanoverians): "This myth has no glimmer of truth."[2] All contemporary documentary evidence shows, in copious and formidable detail, just the opposite: that the British governments of the day, so far from being determined to partition these various countries, were reluctant or even desperate to avoid partition, and used every expedient to avoid it until it became the only possible recourse.

Proponents of this idea of malicious partition are usually partisans in disguise, taking the side of the Irish nationalists against Ulster Unionists, Congress nationalism in India against the Muslim League and the creators of Pakistan, and it might be worth making a broader initial point. Conquest, persecution, and exploitation are all wrong, morally wrong, ethnic cleansing, slavery, and mass murder all the more so. But once you have made that somewhat obvious statement, the language of morality simply does not apply to communal or national conflicts. Between Greek and Turk, between Ibo and Yoruba, between Singhalese and Tamil, between Jew and Arab, between Serb and Croat, between Irish Green and Ulster Orange, there *is* no right or wrong. It depends who you are. There is a case for a sovereign Bosnia and there is a case for a Greater Serbia; there is a case for a state of Israel and there is a case for a binational Palestine; there is a case for a United Ireland and there is a case for a United Kingdom of Great Britain and Northern Ireland. Neither is inherently more virtuous than the other. It depends who you are.

The malicious partition thesis invokes a series of begged questions, the first that "all partitions lead to another partition." But where do you start? If the partition of Bosnia is wrong, wasn't the partition of Yugoslavia to create Bosnia the prior wrong, or before that the partition of the Habsburg and Ottoman empires to make Yugoslavia? Logically, to condemn "all partitions" means that we should deplore the original partition, early in the last century, of the British Isles, which indeed led to the partition of Ireland. And of course the very phrase "united Ireland" is a begged question all its own. For some reason, those who use it as a slogan never seem to intend what might be logical enough: the unification of Ireland by reincorporating the twenty-six counties of the Republic into the United Kingdom, to which, after all, they did once belong; instead, they always intend the incorporation of the six counties of Northern Ireland into an Irish Republic to which, by definition, they have never belonged, since the elementary political facts about Irish history are that no independent Irish state ever existed before 1922 and that Ireland has never been politically united since the beginning of time except under English rule.

No one has made this point more nicely than Fred Halliday, professor of international relations at the London School of Economics, authority on the Arab world and Iran, and, as it happens, Irish by birth and upbringing. Some years ago he gave a brilliant lecture on Ireland and Ulster in which he said that if Irish republicans wanted a great national hero to venerate, they should perhaps choose him who first created a united Ireland—King Henry VIII. The English partitioned Ireland in the early twentieth century, just as the English had united Ireland in the early sixteenth century. And so the very idea of an independent, united Irish Republic is a fine example of invented tradition, describing something that has never existed. Or it might be a case of what Oliver St. John Gogarty, the Dublin surgeon and wit who was the model for Buck Mulligan in *Ulysses,* called the Royal Hibernian Academy, a triple contradiction in terms.

One more of Hitchens's assertions, that "Unionist" means "someone who favors the 'union' of the Six Counties of Northern Ireland

with the United Kingdom—in other words, someone who favors
the disunion of Ireland," is historically ignorant and simply false.[3]
A hundred years ago the Irish Unionists had no wish at all to partition Ireland; they wanted all Ireland to remain united, in the Union
with Great Britain. Although Lord Randolph Churchill's playing
"the Orange card" was consciously cynical, his phrase was also an
apt metaphor. At the bridge table, one card wins a trick of four,
and it was Churchill's intention, like that of other Unionists at the
time, to use the card of Ulster to keep the other three provinces
of Ireland in the Union. In practice, of course, this tactical gam-
bit went awry. Democracy and self-determination argued inexorably
for Home Rule—in Catholic-nationalist Ireland. As Gladstone came
to see, holding the country in the United Kingdom against its will
would only poison the whole body politic. But then where did that
leave the idea of forcing Protestant-Unionist Ulster into an autonomous Ireland? The nationalists wanted to be "a nation once again"
in reality less than they wanted not to be ruled from Westminster;
the Unionists didn't want to divide the British Isles, and they didn't
want to want to divide Ireland: they wanted not to be ruled by a
nationalist parliament in Dublin. They then found that the logic of
this desire led inexorably toward partition.

What is nevertheless so striking when one looks back is the
dogged and almost dogmatic hostility of all sides to partition. The
nationalists, committed to a united Ireland as an article of faith, repeatedly brushed aside Ulster sentiment as exaggerated or factitious
or all got up by the English. It is worth remembering that all the
great leaders of the Irish cause had very little personal knowledge
of Ulster. O'Connell was a Catholic gentleman from Kerry, in the
southwest; Redmond, a hundred years later, was a Catholic gentlemen from Wexford, in the southeast; and de Valera was a Cuban by
way of New York and Limerick. Between O'Connell and Redmond
came Parnell, a Protestant gentleman from Wicklow, and even more
ignorant than they of popular feeling in Ulster.

Only in such ignorance could he have assured Gladstone in 1886
that in Ulster "the Protestants, other than the owners of land, are
not really opposed to such concession," that is, to Irish autonomy.[4]
Decades later, de Valera was still saying much the same, that the
reciprocal animosities of Orange and Green in Ulster were purely a
product of English rule and would disappear when that rule ended.
This is still a view held on the sectarian Left: the Protestant working class and the Catholic working class are brothers under the skin
who should unite against their common oppressor. As Conor Cruise
O'Brien drily observed at the time the renewed, awful conflict was
boiling over in the early 1970s, this notion has always been more

popular in intellectual *marxisant* circles in south Dublin than in the republican Falls Road, although not all Marxists are so foolish: more recently, E. J. Hobsbawm said that the experience of these past decades has, if nothing else, finally made clear that the roots of Irish disunity do not lie in London.

As the Ulster crisis intensified in 1912-14, Asquith remained as strongly opposed to partition as Redmond himself: his rebuff to the Agar-Robartes amendment proved that. He responded to Ulster resistance, and to the Tories' disgraceful fomenting of something nearer mutiny than civil disobedience, by becoming ever more obdurate. He insisted that "the claim of Ulster . . . is not a claim that due regard be had to the interests of a minority . . . but a claim on behalf of a minority, and a comparatively small minority of the population of Ireland, to veto the wishes and frustrate the aspirations of a great mass of the Irish people."[5]

But then the Unionists were scarcely readier than their foes to see partition as the remedy. Their leader by now was Carson, a Dubliner, who was deeply attached to the interests of his fellow southern Unionists. Speaking for the Tories at Westminster, Balfour reiterated a stand of outright opposition to Home Rule, with or without "exclusion" of Ulster. At the same time, the crisis began to divide Asquith's Cabinet. Less obdurate than he, three ministers—Sir Edward Grey, Foreign Secretary; David Lloyd George, Chancellor of the Exchequer; and Winston Churchill, First Lord of the Admiralty—had already begun to see that Home Rule could not be imposed on Ulster by force, and it is baffling that anyone can now doubt that they were right.

Still, the resistance to dividing Ireland continued. In the summer of 1916, following the Easter Rising, when Asquith was still Prime Minister, just about, the Cabinet discussed the Irish situation and reviewed the options; the minutes of that Cabinet include the words "The permanent partition of Ireland has no friends." De Valera was now emerging as the dominant voice of republican or intransigent nationalism. In the summer of 1917, he said with commendable bluntness that "if Ulster stood in the way of Irish freedom, Ulster would have to be coerced," and no nonsense about democratic consent.[6] The official London position was restated after the war, when a Cabinet committee in 1919 said that the government should do "everything possible to promote Irish unity," and as late as the summer of 1920, Lloyd George was still leaning as hard as he could on the Ulster Unionists to push them toward unity.[7]

Behind the idea that partition is always wrong is one more begged question or unexamined assumption: that territories exist by some divine right or prescriptive tradition and should never be divided.

If one blinks, it takes only a moment to ask the simple question: Why *should* Ireland—or any other land—be united? After all, states all across Europe were being partitioned at just this time, after the Great War, and on what were meant to be the virtuous principles of national justice and self-determination. Ireland was finally partitioned by the Government of Ireland Act (which also made ample constitutional provision for subsequent reunification), in 1920; that was also the year of the Treaty of Trianon. That partition dealt much more harshly with Hungary than "the slave treaty of Versailles" did with Germany, removing two-thirds of the territory of the thousand-year-old, historic, not to say "apostolic," kingdom of Hungary—"a united Hungary."

If that was proper there, why not in the case of Ireland? And those who supported the partition of Hungary or any other lands in Europe on Wilsonian grounds of self-determination were hoist with their own petard when they contradictorily argued for enforced Irish unity. The population of eastern Ulster was "as hostile to Irish rule as the rest of Ireland is to British rule, yea, and as ready to rebel against it as the rest of Ireland is against British rule," Lloyd George pointed out in Parliament in March 1917. "To place them under national rule against their will would be as glaring an outrage on the principles of liberty and self-government as the denial of self-government would be for the rest of Ireland."[8] And some quicker-witted Tory Unionists spotted the same catch. "No one can think that Ulster ought to join the South and West who thinks that the Jugo Slavs should be separated from Austria," Balfour said in 1919; "No one can think that Ulster should be divorced from Britain who believes in self-determination."[9]

To THIS DAY THAT REMAINS A CONUNDRUM for "anti-partitionists." Do they support the multinational empires of the old regime, British or Ottoman or Habsburg as it might be? If not, and if Ireland and India are properly to be severed—or partitioned—from the British Empire, Yugoslavia and Czechoslovakia from the Habsburg monarchy, all in the name of national freedom, why should that right be denied to those who find themselves inside these new states against their will, Croats and then Serbs in Yugoslavia, Sudeten Germans and then Slovaks in Czechoslovakia? As Hobsbawm has observed, the supposedly national states that were born in the nineteenth and early twentieth centuries turned out in practice to be as much "prison houses of nations" as the empires they succeeded. The partisans of one nationalism have to resort to sundry specious arguments to explain away the fact that humankind does not live in neatly parceled groups like the squares on a chessboard. Failing any way round that difficulty, by pretending that the Macedonians are no more than "Slavonic Greeks" or that the Ulster community is really no more than Protestant Irishmen who fail in their blindness to see their real identity, there is always the ultima ratio of nationalism: "transfer of population," which de Valera did indeed later recommend in the case of Ulster.

However ingenious they may think themselves, critics of partition sometimes give the game away, and almost amusingly. One such is Professor J. J. Lee, sometime of Cork University, and indeed sometime of the Irish Senate, where I have heard him speak. In his book *Ireland, 1912–1985,* a huge and learned work written from a strongly nationalist perspective, he deplores partition in principle and in practice, and in the process makes a most revealing mistake. The line drawn by the 1920 act was unfair to the southern Free State, he claims, which is in itself disputable: it is true that there were solidly Catholic areas on the "wrong" side of the line, in South Down, South Armagh, and Tyrone, though the same thing was true on the other side, in the three counties of historic Ulster that went to the Free State, Donegal, Cavan, and Monaghan. These had large Catholic majorities but also substantial and, in places, compact Protestant communities, which were ruthlessly abandoned by their fellow Unionists, and have since vanished almost without trace. And yet since partition boiled down to separating Catholic-nationalist southern Ireland from the Protestant-Unionist northeast, the division of territory, 82 to 18 percent, was pretty much fair concerning population, which makes an interesting contrast with the later partition of Palestine.

In Lee's view, the boundary as drawn flew against the rule prevailing at the time, or so he believes, when "borders were revised in central and eastern Europe in favour of smaller states."[10] But that was not at all the case. What happened in Europe after the Great War was what a cursory study of history—or merely a knowledge of human nature—might have suggested: contentious borders were everywhere decided in favor of the victors and at the expense of the losers. Diminished little Austria lost the South Tyrol, with its German community, to far larger Italy; diminished little Hungary lost the Banat and Transylvania, with their Hungarians and Germans, to much larger Rumania; and not for honorable reasons of self-determination, but because Italy and Rumania had been lucky enough to back the winning side. Since one might say that in 1916 the Easter rebels backed the losing side and the 36th Ulster Division the winning (as Carson regularly reminded his colleagues in London), the same thing might have been true in Ireland.

But then Lee says something still more revealing. As he correctly observes, "the most explosive problems subverting new states" were communal conflicts in the form of language, race, or religion. His book was published in 1989, and it scarcely needs noting that the point has been given much more force since then: two of those new states with which autonomous Ireland was coeval were called Czechoslovakia and Yugoslavia, and neither exists any more. In the end, those problems proved so explosive that before the twentieth century had ended, they had destroyed both countries. As Lee goes on to say very truly, partition saved the Irish Free State from those problems "by the simple device of exporting them to the North."[11] That is a good phrase; what Lee, like any Irish nationalist, cannot quite bring himself to say is that from the point of view of southern Ireland, partition was the best thing that could have happened. It was the essential factor that made possible the creation of an orderly and, in the end, prosperous Irish state. Might not this be the true explanation, in Ireland and elsewhere, for the inevitability of partition?

THE DISPARITIES AMONG THE THREE CASES, notably between Ireland and India, in history and culture and sheer scale are clear, but there are enough similarities to confute the idea of malicious partition, quite apart from the copious evidence that the British never wanted to divide these territories. There is the fact that neither Ireland nor India—the Indian Raj until August 1947—had ever in history been a political territory except when ruled by someone else. And then there is the ingenious ruse of "exporting the problem to the north"—of India as of Ireland. However much Indian politicians may lament partition and the creation of Pakistan, itself later partitioned to create Bangladesh, they must be more than dimly aware of demography. Today the Muslims of India are 175 million, or about 16 percent of the population, and are more numerous than the population of either Pakistan or Bangladesh.

Imagine a "united India" today comprising the three countries. Apart from being much the most populous country on earth, whose more than 1.4 billion inhabitants would easily outnumber China's, very nearly 500 million of them, or 35 percent, would be Muslim. Historians and political analysts have juggled such figures and generalized from them, and it does seem to be the case that at a certain size a minority becomes a grave political problem: below 10 or even 20 percent, the group can be emancipated and assimilated; 30 to 40 percent spells trouble. As it happens, 35 percent was much the size of the Catholic-nationalist minority in Northern Ireland at the time of partition, an ominous precedent.

In India as in Ireland, no objective historian can attribute blame to one side only—or say that the apprehensions of the minority were imaginary, even if the partisans have tried to do so. After representative local government was introduced in Ireland in the late nineteenth century, the Protestant Unionists of the southern three provinces found that they had far fewer county councillors than their numbers—more than 12 percent, though Protestants have since fallen to less than 2 percent in the Republic—should have given them; just so, when representative provincial government was introduced by the 1935 India Act, Muslims likewise found that everywhere they were a minority, even a large one, they were squeezed out.

In one version, or heroic narrative, the virtuous Congress nationalists were thwarted by the obstinate or malevolent villains of the Muslim League as well as, of course, by the dastardly British, with their dark schemes for partition. To say that "Many Indian Muslims refused their support to Mohammed Ali Jinnah, but once Britain became bent on partition, it automatically conferred authority on his Muslim League as being the 'realistic' expression of the community, "[12] is plain wrong, as may be seen from Narendra Singh Sarila's fascinating recent book *The Shadow of the Great Game: The Untold Story of India's Partition*.

As a senior Indian civil servant who acted as an aide to Mountbatten during his final viceroyalty, Sarila knew many of the chief players, notably the Congress leaders, about whose arrogance, inconsistency, and "poor political judgement" he is sharply critical. Like the Irish republicans a generation before—not to say like de Valera during that same 1939–45 war—they were so fired up with their own sense of virtue that it did not seem to occur to them that the ruling power might take it amiss if the nationalists actively damaged the war effort during a desperate conflict.

Although Sarila describes Jinnah as vain and sybaritic, he sees that the Muslim League leader was also single-minded—as one might say Carson and Craig had been in Ulster—and describes more damagingly the sheer folly of the Congress leaders, especially Nehru, in their dealings with the British. If Nehru had given even conditional support for the war from the beginning, he might have done what poor Redmond tried but failed to do, and won a political victory of his own. Instead he petulantly struck attitudes. In 1942 he refused an offer of self-government after the war, the "post-dated cheque" of Gandhi's derisive phrase, as though any government would have offered full and immediate payment in the circumstances, with the Japanese army on the borders of Assam. A. J. P. Taylor characteristically says that "the British insisted on defending India, against the will of her political leaders, and paid for the privilege of doing so," to which one might add that those leaders paid the higher price of Indian unity through their own obstinacy.[13]

From the mid-nineteenth century to the mid-twentieth, every step taken by Irish nationalism away from Crown and Union—from O'Connell's demand for Repeal, to Home Rule, to Free State, to Republic—deepened the division between the nationalist south and the Unionist north. With the Congress leaders, as Jad Adams puts it, "every retreat they made from conciliating the British was an advance for Jinnah and the Muslim League," who could barely claim to represent a quarter of Muslim voters at the beginning of the war but who by its end were successfully demanding partition.[14] Which was the more important factor in bringing about that partition, British imperial deviousness or Indian-nationalist blindness?

Well before Sir Penderel, George Orwell was using the phrase "divide and quit," in 1944. He acknowledged the "absurdity" of asking for independence during the war, which would have meant "simply to hand India over to the Japanese." And he saw that dividing and quitting, or granting India independence once Pakistan was established, "might help to avert civil war after the British power is withdrawn."[15] There was, of course, terrible bloodshed at the time of partition, and in Ireland there had already been a civil war, between nationalist factions, but an attempt to create an independent united state in either case would very likely have led to bloodier civil war still.

As Roger Louis has shown, the British were painfully aware of analogies between India and Palestine, and sometimes between Ireland and Palestine as well. Field Marshal Sir Henry Wilson lived to compare Ireland to Palestine, in each case two peoples living in close quarters and hating each others' guts, as he put it, before his observation about violent national passions was made still more emphatically by his assassination at the hands of the IRA in 1922. Whether the Jews, by analogy, were the Irish or (as Shaw saw it) the Ulstermen is a dinner-table game that is maybe more entertaining than fruitful.

OF THE THREE CASES, THE MOST COMPLEX for a number of reasons is the Holy Land. I use that old-fashioned name since it is very convenient both geographically and politically. It intends the territory of British Mandatory Palestine after Trans-Jordan had been carved off as a separate territory in 1921 to make what is now the kingdom of Jordan; which is to say, the territory ruled today by Israel, pre- and post-1967. And "Holy Land" also neatly avoids any tendentious implications of other terms, whether "Ertez Israel" or "Filistin."

When Herzl published *The Jewish State* in 1896, no one doubted that the Jews existed, but many proud and pious Jews vehemently rejected the idea that they were a nation. And almost none of them then lived in the Holy Land. Its population at the time seems to have been about half a million—has any other such territory on earth seen its population increase nearly twentyfold in the past hundred years?—of whom barely 5 percent were Jewish.

As a general rule, the proponents of partition are the minority community and the opponents are the majority, for entirely obvious reasons. The Holy Land was different, not least because during the crucial period of the Mandate, the Zionists were an expanding minority that wanted to become a majority, even if this ambition was not always loudly proclaimed. As early as 1920, Churchill envisaged "in our lifetime by the banks of the Jordan a Jewish State under the protection of the British Crown, which might comprise three or four millions of Jews," but this was at a time when there were fewer than 100,000 Jews in the new territory of British Mandatory Palestine, and when few Zionists cared to speak openly of a state or of "millions" of citizens.[16]

Nor were the Zionists quite clear about the shape and size or their envisaged homeland, or state. If "partition is always and everywhere a defeat and often leads to more wars and more partitions," does that apply to the partition of the original Mandatory territory into Palestine and Trans-Jordan? Since the latter had an almost entirely Arab population, that might seem to be a clear and unexceptionable case of self-determination, even to anti-partitionists. But the plot thickens. In the early 1920s, Vladimir Jabotinsky founded the Revisionist branch of Zionism and the Betar organization, usually, even if not quite accurately, characterized as a right-wing, militaristic, ultra-nationalist movement. Its program demanded a Jewish state with a Jewish majority on both banks of the Jordan: "The Jordan has two banks and they are both ours," went the Betar marching song. Needless to say, Jabotinsky opposed the first partition, which created Trans-Jordan, but then so did Chaim Weizmann, the leader of the General Zionists.

Just as neither community in Ireland wanted partition, so did neither side in Palestine, or at least not publicly and not at first. That became clear at the time of the Peel Commission, in 1937. The Arabs had flatly rejected partition and the creation of a Jewish state in any part of the Holy Land, with unflagging zeal turning to violence: Lord Peel's mission with his colleagues was prompted by the Arab revolt that had broken out in April 1936. But the idea of partition was not originally received with any enthusiasm by the Zionists either. Once the idea of partition was broached in January 1937, however, Weizmann found himself in a very difficult position. On the one hand, it meant renouncing the hope of a state embracing the whole country; on the other, it seemed to offer the hugely enticing prospect of a Jewish state in the near future. By comparison with the Irish nationalists, the Zionists could not easily make a public demand of "a united Palestine," and yet the Zionists were also better than some other national movements—or than their own foes—at grasping the principle that *le mieux est l'ennemi du bien,* and that a bird in the hand should not be rejected.

If there was a willful partitioner, it might have been Reginald Coupland, Beit Professor of Colonial History at Oxford and a former editor of the *Round Table,* who was the most effective member of the Peel Commission and the first to raise the possibility of partition as a solution. But so far from being doctrinaire about this in all cases, he was a man who had said that "the unification of Ireland, however long it may take, does seem the right and natural thing in the end." [17]

Before long the Peel Report was overtaken by events, after the London government had rejected, be it remembered, its recommendation for partition and an exchange of populations, and the story of the European Jews was overtaken far more horribly. As the war ended, Arab violence was succeeded by Jewish violence. The British received little sympathy for their role in Palestine, and they deserved none: their troubles had begun, as everyone knows, when they made mutually exclusive promises to Arabs and Zionists during the First World War, and they thereafter found that the problem became more intractable and insoluble with every year until they finally gave up. Lieutenant General William Odom, formerly of the U.S. Army, has been writing about our present difficulties in Iraq (a country that, far from being malevolently partitioned, was in the first place perversely unified out of disparate elements). If Odom writes his own headlines, then he missed his metier in journalism: one of these recent essays is entitled "Victory Is Not an Option," and another, "Cut and Run? You Bet," and that pretty well described British policy in Palestine during the ignominious last phase.

At least some effort was made to find a solution before cutting and running, and the solution that London did not want was partition. As Roger Louis has also shown, "the goal [of the Attlee government] was to avoid partition in both India and Palestine," just as it had been in Ireland until the very end. [18] That was particularly true in the case of Palestine and of Ernest Bevin, Attlee's Foreign Secretary, and it is ironic that one strand of *bien-pensant* opinion damns the British for their eager acceptance of partition while at the same time poor Bevin is damned from another quarter as a mortal enemy of the Jewish people because he resisted what he thought would be a grossly unjust partition.

As long as he could, Bevin favored a binational state as the outcome: that is to say, not a country divided into Jewish and Arab polities—the outcome toward which the international community is now at last supposed to be moving, or perhaps edging—but one state in which Jews and Arabs would live side by side, each expressing their own national identity. Far from invoking the example of partitioned Ireland, Bevin thought in terms of Canada and South Africa, where two peoples, British and French in the one case, British and Boer in the other, were supposedly brought together in harmonious political brotherhood. This chimera of a binational state in the Holy Land has never vanished, and was floated again not long ago by the historian Tony Judt, who was bitterly reviled for his pains. And yet however beguiling it might seem, the problem was clear enough during that cruel last phase of the Mandate, when Coupland's conclusion that the conflict was intractable seemed truer than ever.

Here is the problem. The notion that partition is always wrong rests on an abstract sense of national identity, an assumption—one more begged question—that an all-Irish or all-Indian identity is more virtuous than the loyalties those concerned actually feel. When asked what he thought of Western civilization, Gandhi is supposed to have replied, "It would be a nice idea." So would the "common name of Irishman," embracing Protestant, Catholic, and Dissenter, on which a united Ireland was meant to be founded, or the common name of "Indian," embracing Hindu, Muslim, and Sikh. In the third case, the idea of Muslims, Jews, and Christians shedding their identities for a common name as yet to be decided was even more far-fetched: not many Jews actually wanted a binational state, and almost no Arabs did. Hannah Arendt got it right more than sixty years ago when she said that however attractive to some liberals it might be, a binational state was "no solution, since it could be realised as a result of a solution." That too applies to Ireland and India, and that is why in each case partition was the outcome that forced itself against all resistance.

So far from their having relentlessly and maliciously partitioned territories at every opportunity, the British, one might well argue, made many of their worst errors in the past century by perversely attempting to unite disparate areas, from Iraq onward. Late-imperial history, from the 1950s to the 1970s, is littered with the relics of aborted federations, from East Africa to Malaysia, from the West

Indies to Central Africa, all of which in the end partitioned themselves with no intervention from London.

There is in fact no basis at all for the idea that the British malevolently partitioned these countries, or that partition was inherently deplorable. This whole notion collapses when an elementary point is grasped: "united" Ireland and India alike were the creation of English rule, and partition is not a consequence of imperialism but of nationalism. Over and again partition has been the entirely inevitable solution; not a good remedy, but the least bad remedy in the objective circumstances—and least bad remedies are the meaning of democracy. Over and again partition has averted civil war and made possible the establishment of orderly states.

It is not a debating trick to say that Ireland, India, and Palestine might each be united today if only they had remained under British rule. As it is, if their often sad stories illustrate anything at all, it is Evelyn Waugh's more profound observation: "The foundations of Empire are often occasions of woe; their dismemberment, always."[19]

Spring Semester 2007

1. Christopher Hitchens, "Mesopotamia Split?" *Slate*, 26 Mar. 2007.
2. A. J. P. Taylor, "Dizzy," in *Essays in English History* (New York, 1976), p. 120.
3. Christopher Hitchens, "The Perils of Partition," *Atlantic Monthly*, Mar. 2003.
4. Quoted in R. C. K. Ensor, *England, 1870–1914*, (Oxford, 1936), p. 451 n.; their meeting was on 6 January 1886.
5. Quoted in Michael Sheehy, *Divided We Stand: A Study of Partition* (London, 1955), p. 44.
6. *Irish Times*, 13 July 1917.
7. T. G. Fraser, *Partition in Ireland, India and Palestine: Theory and Practice* (London, 1984), p. 28.
8. House of Commons Debates, 7 Mar. 1917.
9. A. J. Balfour, "The Irish Question," 25 Nov. 1919, PRO CAB 24/93.
10. J. J. Lee, *Ireland, 1912–1985* (London, 1989), p. 46.
11. Ibid., p. 77.
12. Hitchens, "Perils."
13. A. J. P. Taylor, *England, 1914–1945* (Oxford, 1965), p. 545.
14. Jad Adams, "The ill-fated battle for Indian independence," *Sunday Telegraph*, 28 Aug. 2006.
15. George Orwell, review of Beverley Nichols, *Verdict on India* (*Observer*, 29 Oct. 1944), in Peter Davison, ed., *The Complete Works of George Orwell*, Vol. XVI: *I Have Tried to Tell the Truth, 1943–44* (London, 1988), pp. 446–48.
16. Winston Churchill, "Zionism versus Bolshevism," *Illustrated Sunday Herald*, 8 Feb. 1920, in Michael Wolff, ed., *The Collected Essays of Sir Winston Churchill*, Vol. IV, *Churchill at Large* (London, 1976), p. 29.
17. Reginald Coupland, *The Empire in These Days* (London, 1935), p. 70.
18. Wm. Roger Louis, *Ends of British Imperialism: The Scramble for Empire, Suez, and Decolonization* (London, 2006), p. 403.
19. Evelyn Waugh, *A Tourist in Africa* (London, 1960), p. 164.

13

Edward Evan Evans-Pritchard:
A Great Englishman Nonetheless

JOHN DAVIS

Evans-Pritchard's father was Thomas John Pritchard from Caernarvon, who, after a university education at Oxford, was ordained in the Anglican Church and became a curate in Liverpool. He married Dorothy Edwards, the granddaughter of a Liverpool notable, but they moved for health reasons to Sussex, where he became curate in the towns of Lewes and Eastbourne. About this time, the family moved into a large house called Lea, in Crowborough, and changed their name to Evans-Pritchard, presumably in recognition of Dorothy's inheritance from Eyre Dixon Evans, JP, of Liverpool. Their first child, Thomas, was born in 1900; Edward followed on 21 September 1902. In 1913 the father of the family became rector of Waterperry, a small rural parish between Thame and Oxford with a pleasant church and a grand manor house. In 1916, Evans-Pritchard went away to an expensive boarding school, Winchester College. While there, he later said, he gained a sense of "loyalty, honour, duty, and disinterestedness." He then moved to Exeter College to read history, graduated in 1924, and moved to the London School of Economics (LSE) to read anthropology.[1]

At this time, Oxford anthropologists (who numbered four or five, depending on who is doing the counting) were of the library kind; they read widely and enthusiastically and created theories of primordial society: where religion came from, where arts and culture originated, and so on, without stirring from their armchairs. None had done fieldwork as it is understood today, and indeed none of them had done anthropological work overseas.[2] At the LSE, C. G. Seligman and his wife were active survey anthropologists, using administrative records and interpreters to create basic descriptions of territories overseas, listing the main physical and social traits of the inhabitants. Seligman, a distinguished man in his time, had been a medical member of the Torres Strait and Borneo expeditions, and was engaged by the British government to do the work that would eventually be published as *The Pagan Tribes of the Nilotic Sudan* (London, 1932) and *The Races of Africa* (London, 1930). It seems that when Evans-Pritchard arrived, in 1924, Seligman (age fifty-three) was tiring of arduous survey work, and he arranged for Evans-Pritchard to complete the Seligmans' survey of the tribes of the Nile basin in the Sudan. He was introduced to Sir Harold MacMichael, Civil Secretary to the government of Anglo-Egyptian Sudan in Khartoum.[3]

MacMichael, like the Seligmans, became a firm supporter of the young anthropologist and, as head of the administration in Khartoum, protected him from the bureaucratic maneuvers of subordinate officials who resented his arrival in their territories. Although Evans-Pritchard later advised his students to make friends with colonial administrators, and in fact found some of them congenial and their work useful, he was contemptuous of the time-servers and bigots among them, who saw him as a protector of the natives.

Evans-Pritchard, quickly attracted by the new method of participant observation, began his fieldwork with the Azande in southwestern Sudan, near the watershed between the Congo River and the White Nile.[4] He spent a total of twenty months with them, and a further year or so in discontinuous visits with the Nuer, a people who lived to the north of Zandeland at the confluence of the White Nile and the Bahr el-Ghazal. In 1932 he joined the staff of the University of Egypt in Cairo, and in 1934 (with the support of R. R. Marett, rector of his old college, and of Reginald Coupland, Professor of Imperial History) became research lecturer in African sociology at Oxford.

He married Ioma, a graduate student from South Africa, in 1939. He then tried to enlist in the Welsh Guards, but Oxford refused him permission. He went to the Sudan, ostensibly to do fieldwork, but signed on to the Sudan Civil Service, which allowed him to enlist in the Auxiliary Defence Force as an officer (*bimbashi*). He recruited and led an irregular force of fifteen to twenty men, mainly Anuak, that fought behind Italian lines. The army seconded him to various other military units, and he ended the war as tribal affairs officer in Libya, based in Benghazi.[5] He was received into the Roman Catholic Church in Benghazi Cathedral in 1944. In 1946 he was elected as the second incumbent of the chair of social anthropology in Oxford, at which time he virtually ceased fieldwork. He devoted his time to the Institute of Social Anthropology, to his family, and to writing, mostly ethnographic work, and also to some surveys of social and anthropological theorists. His wife died in 1959, following an overdose of prescribed medicines.[6]

Evans-Pritchard served his country with distinction as a scholar and an ethnographer. The government of Anglo-Egyptian Sudan substantially modified its policies in the Upper Nile as a result of his advocacy and of the understanding he created. In war he achieved no great victories, but acted with courage and intelligence in campaigns of some tactical importance. Again in Libya, his patient acquisition of understanding undoubtedly shaped and improved military and civilian administration of the Bedouin of Cyrenaica. But in the military, as in the Sudan, he was regarded as eccentric, resistant to authority, too individualistic, and inclined to trust his own judgment. These were perhaps also qualities he had acquired at school: in the army he was regarded as a rogue Wykehamist—a man with the manners and social class of an old boy of Winchester College, but without the restraint and conformity. We may admire his actions and qualities, but they do not perhaps earn him the accolade of greatness. Rather, it is his ideas that matter.

AZANDE WERE PREOCCUPIED BY WITCHCRAFT. It was a constant threat to their well-being—to their wealth, to the placid collaborations of their domestic lives, to the success of their enterprises, ventures, schemes, and plans. Witchcraft was an effect of unwitting malice in other people (nobody *chose* to be a witch): their resentment, envy, and adulterous intentions could cause you to experience accidents, to suffer betrayal, to be confronted by opposition to your most promising and harmless adventures. Witchcraft was thus a kind of explanation of events. Here is Evans-Pritchard:

> A boy knocked his foot against a small stump of wood in the centre of a bush path . . . and suffered pain and inconvenience in consequence . . . it began to fester. He declared that witchcraft had made him knock his foot against the stump . . . I told the boy that he had knocked his foot . . . because he had been careless and that witchcraft had not placed [the stump] in the path, for it had grown there naturally. He [argued] that he had kept his eyes open for stumps, as indeed every Zande does most carefully, and that if

he had not been bewitched he would have seen the stump . . .
He remarked that all cuts do not take days to heal but, on the contrary, close quickly, for that is the nature of cuts. Why, then, had his sore festered if there were no witchcraft behind it?[7]

Englishmen, Americans too, explain misfortune by carelessness, or coincidence, occasionally by conspiracy. Azande did not accept coincidence (the random intersection of separate chains of cause and effect) as an explanation. In the summer, they sometimes sat in their grain stores, which were shady and relatively cool. Azande knew that termites ate the beams supporting the stores and that consequently their constructions sometimes fell down. Sometimes the grain store collapsed when people were sitting inside it. For Westerners, that would be a matter of chance—occasionally perhaps of accident proneness. But Azande wanted to know why those particular people were sitting in the grain store when it fell down. The answer had to be witchcraft. As Evans-Pritchard memorably says, it is in the nature of fire to burn; it is not in the nature of fire to burn *me*.

Witchcraft was an everyday explanation. It did not frighten Azande, as contact with the supernatural or mysterious might frighten others. On the contrary, it made Azande angry: some person, a witch, had caused misfortune. Azande were indeed skeptical in some cases. If a very old man fell ill, he and his family would invoke witchcraft, but more distant neighbors might say he was old and liable to get ill anyway. A bad potter would blame witchcraft when his pots cracked in the fire; others might say he was a bad potter. But on the whole, people accepted witchcraft as the intervening cause to explain why granaries injured people, wounds festered, pots broke, spouses committed adultery, and healthy people fell sick and died. It was a human agent who had caused the misfortune, and Azande consulted an oracle to find out who the witch was.

Once Azande knew who the witch was, they would approach him, then ask him to stop and to show his goodwill. No Zande thought he or she was a witch, and they easily denied evil intent in ceremoniously conditional form: "If I am responsible, I disavow any evil intent and withdraw any inadvertent witchcraft." Sometimes the sick person recovered or the wound healed, and all was well as health and goodwill were re-established. And sometimes the patient continued to be ill in spite of the disavowal. In that case, Azande began again with a new oracle, explaining the failure of the first by saying they had not met the exact ceremonial procedures for consulting the oracle. The words had to be precise; the consulter had to abstain from particular foodstuffs—and to abstain from sex in the more momentous consultations. A weakness in the procedure would explain this particular patent failure of the oracle. These subsidiary explanations are what Evans-Pritchard called "secondary elaborations of belief." Azande frequently invoked them and regarded them as entirely satisfactory.

When a man died in spite of all the efforts to identify and placate the witch, his closest family would resort to vengeance magic. It was vindictive but generalized: "Go out, find the witch, kill him." Thenceforth, at each local death, the family consulted an oracle— was that man's death the result of our vengeance magic? When they got the answer yes, they did two things. First, they consulted the oracle of their prince. Especially powerful, hedged around with the most carefully observed restrictions, the prince's oracle could definitely confirm the success of the vengeance magic. The consultation was secret, a reassurance given as part of a prince's services to his people. If the prince's oracle failed to confirm that their vengeance magic was the cause of that particular death, they resumed their deathwatch. But if it confirmed their success, then they hung out a sign to show they had achieved vengeance and to demonstrate that they were proper, caringly vengeful kinsmen who had done their duty. Azande considered it extremely impolite, however, to inquire who it was who had bewitched the person avenged.

It was an elaborate and coherent set of practices with an internally consistent rationale. And it brought comfort, or at any rate satisfaction, to Azande who had been confronted with otherwise inexplicable misfortune. It was of course false and untrue, unscientific. The world simply does not work like that and never did, not even in the twentieth century. It is part of Evans-Pritchard's claim to greatness that he explains how it was sustained. First, he demonstrated that witchcraft, oracles, and magic formed a system of action, a set of practical procedures, rather than a set of beliefs or systematic knowledge; Azande externalized and examined the system for consistency. Every component was rigorously checked and controlled, which distracted attention from the inadequacies of the whole. Second, it was supported by secondary elaborations of belief: when actions failed, conventionally accepted explanations could be found for that as well. Third, etiquette, politeness, the need for good relations among neighbors, and perhaps deference to princes prevented people from asking questions that might have led them to examine what their neighbors were doing. For instance, if you saw a "vengeance magic successful" sign and inquired who had been killed by it (and got an answer), you would soon discover that every Zande death was explained twice: once as a result of witchcraft, and then as a result of magic. Every man who died was a victim of witchcraft in some Azande eyes, while other people had oracular proof he was a witch and murderer. But it was severely disruptive and insulting to ask that question.

In other words, the information needed to make one a skeptical Zande was so scattered among the population that no one person or group was ever in possession of sufficient knowledge to put two and two together and indulge in empiricist skepticism. The only exceptions were perhaps the princes, who used their oracles to confirm the success of vengeance magic. They could have known that each death was explained twice—when a man died, one set of kinsfolk would ask if he had been killed by their vengeance magic, and then a few months later the deceased's family would turn up to ask if their magic on his behalf had been responsible for the death of another man. Perhaps people went to different princes; perhaps the prince knew, but kept silent for political or other reasons.

This account is a crude violation of a subtle and extensive book. Nevertheless, its significance is clear. As can be imagined, it has stimulated philosophers to ask questions about Zande reasoning. Is it logic? Is it something else? Historians have asked new questions about witches, witch hunts, and inquisitions in early modern Britain, France, and the United States. Sociologists of knowledge have generalized the questions to ask about the social distribution of knowledge in Western nations, with their rational, science-based technologies. Is it possible that the European social order might also depend on distributed knowledge, etiquette, or other "imperfections"? How might that affect the social order? Evans-Pritchard's work relates to a central issue in René Descartes's philosophy of knowledge. Imagine a purely rational being, who takes as "knowledge" only those truths that have been established by logic and experiment. Such a person could create an austere, parsimonious, and perhaps rather limited world in which he was sure of the truth of everything he knew. Even so, he could never be sure of not being deceived: all the data, all the tests, might be the creation of a malign higher power who made a world that was illusory, all its certainties a bespoke deception. Evans-Pritchard's achievement, then, was not only to stimulate a wide range of inquiry by historians, sociologists, and philosophers, but also to describe in detail how sensible, skeptical, experimenting people such as the Azande could live an illusion. If all human kind is rational, if that is a defining quality of our nature, *Witchcraft, Oracles and Magic* leads us to set limits, to qualify that assumption—and to raise doubts whether our own certainties, knowledge, and practical explanations may be as flawed as Zande ones.

EVANS-PRITCHARD'S SECOND MAJOR CONTRIBUTION concerned another common assumption about human nature. People need the state (governments, lawgivers, enforcers) to enable them to live in peace, and the state has a claim on our resources to finance its activities on our behalf. Evans-Pritchard was the first to provide a serious and convincing account of how people could organize themselves to live more or less at peace without a Leviathan. This was principally in his book *The Nuer*.[8] Nuer numbered about 100,000 pastoralists who cultivated gardens but moved in the dry season to follow the water they needed for their cattle. They spoke a common language, recognized each other as Nuer, claimed a shared Nuer way of doing things, but lacked a sovereign power to make law or to extract surplus from them. Nuer had no head, not even a committee of important local men. Nuer were literally anarchic—no -*archy* at all—but managed to lead orderly lives. People did fight, and were injured or killed, but probably no more often than in governed nations. They had law and order but no laws, and no one gave orders. Evans-Pritchard referred to this as "the order in the anarchy," and identified a system of contingent alliances: villagers (at basis, those who cultivated gardens in the same area) expected to live peacefully together and had rules about how to settle disputes. A very angry Nuer would in effect say, "If no one holds me back, I'm going to kill that adulterer (or cheat or thief)," and people would then rush to hold him back. If people did fight, the convention was that they should use only non-lethal weapons—clubs rather than spears.

Villagers lived cheek by jowl, they were in daily contact, and most actual conflicts were within those small groups whose members had an interest in minimizing violence. The problems came during conflicts with more distant groups. As Ernest Gellner pointed out, a shepherd is extremely vulnerable: a raider can capture all the victim's capital and take it away to a safe place.[9] The raider doubles his wealth in one night's enterprise and has a good chance of taking it away to a place of safekeeping. On the other hand, a conqueror of territory, who certainly has to have nerve and cunning and force, cannot take his booty with him. He has to settle down to defend it against reprisals by reinforced victims.

So Nuer villagers made a series of contingent alliances: "If you are raided by a larger force, we will come to your aid, if you will come to our aid when we are attacked by a superior force." It was a deterrent system in which people could—in theory—amass force to meet a threat. The result was that villagers generally lived in peace and maintained their herds without continual warfare. Evans-Pritchard was concerned with active aggression, but it seems more probable that the general practice was for Nuer to unite defensively. Their reputation as prototypical warriors given to spontaneous aggression was the product of climate change together with British military campaigns (native troops recruited largely from the Dinka).[10]

The idea that underlay this pattern of contingent alliances was that a man owed loyalty to those with whom he shared descent in the male line, and that he shared responsibility for them. He belonged to a group recruited from the male line and was, at birth, endowed with brothers, cousins, second cousins, and remoter cousins. All Nuer said they were descended from one aboriginal ancestor, and all Nuer—at a pinch, in an extremity—had a shared loyalty and thus membership in an enormous descent group. It was a theoretical potentiality that, as far as is known, they never realized. For most of the time, Nuer lived in small villages—the descendants of a grandfather or great-grandfather, along with their wives and children and a few others. Conflict was normally restricted to the social groups that came most often into contact with each other. I against my brothers; I and my brothers against our cousins; I and our cousins against remoter cousins.

Some banal but important points. First, everyone necessarily has a father, so a patrilineal method for determining where loyalties lie necessarily includes everyone; the method is exhaustive and allows no escape. The second point is that each person has only one father: patrilineal descent provides everyone with only one descent group, so, in theory, Nuer did not have divided loyalties. And the third is that people do not choose their fathers. Belonging to a descent group is not like belonging to a political party because it is not a matter of shared opinion or agreed goals. It is not like a group of friends: one does not have to like or approve of the people to whom the highest loyalty is owed and who in turn owe one their lives.

This summary simplifies Evans-Pritchard's model. Nuer were occasionally disloyal, for instance. Hot-blooded young warriors could behave irresponsibly, involve their brothers and cousins in aggression or in resisting reprisals rather too often. In these cases, Nuer could question a person's true membership in the group and expel men who made their lives interminably troublesome. Also, the deterrent of matching opposition of sections relies on rough equality of numbers, but not all families produced the required proportion of boys. If one section could muster only five fighters, and another had fifteen or fifty, the theoretical equality of terror in fact deterred no one. What Nuer did then was to manipulate their genealogies: a stronger group would absorb the weaker one, and a father or grandfather substitute would be invented to explain the new configuration of loyalty and kinship. Genealogical fictions maintained the principle that people owed loyalty from birth, that political solidarity was a natural rather than social obligation. Nuer were egalitarian in the sense that if one lacked the strength of numbers to be equal, he went to the wall: expelled, absorbed, exterminated.

The model has to be qualified in other ways. Nuer settlements or tribal sections had leopard-skin "chiefs," who could impose ritual sanctions to force fellow section members to make peace. Leopard-skin chiefs had strictly ritual power, of uncertain territorial extent. They did not meet in conclaves or synods to plan a common policy.[11] On the very few occasions when Nuer were said to mass in large numbers, they seem to have been inspired by individuals known as prophets. And, finally, Nuer kinship groups were exogamous: men and women had to find marriage partners from outside their usual circle of daily cooperation. So, while they were firmly patrilineal in their loyalties, each Nuer had maternal or affinal kin outside the patrilineal descent group: mother's fathers, fathers-in-law, and brothers-in-law, who might easily belong to a group that was patrilineally opposed to their own group. Nuer did have divided loyalties on this account, and these could lead them to mediate disputes and to mitigate the supposedly unremitting hostility they owed to members of other groups.

Nuer social organization was not particularly attractive. It was probably not capable of assimilating more than 100,000 people. It was not fitted, for example, to run schools or hospitals. It was intolerant of weakness. Evans-Pritchard printed numerous photographs from Nuerland, and only two of them show a Nuer with a smile, and (in contrast to his books on Zandeland) Evans-Pritchard has no examples of Nuer jokes or irony.[12] That said, the Nuer had no government, no system of offices, and no laws, and yet they lived relatively peaceful lives. They were egalitarian, with no class system and no privileged accumulations of wealth.

J.-J. Rousseau's state of nature was an idyllic imagining of humankind living in relative affluence, without hierarchy or disputes, noble savages eventually corrupted by civilization and authorities. On the whole, Rousseau's vision is discounted nowadays in the West, having been superseded by political and biological orthodoxies claiming that the state of nature was brutal and merciless. It was a state of war and of the survival of the fittest. People became civilized only by subjecting themselves to a sovereign and his entourage of savage nobles. The importance of Nuer, and of Evans-Pritchard's ethnography, is not, therefore, as a guide to policy making or as a blueprint for a truly egalitarian social order in the modern world. It is, rather, of imaginative importance. When people are told that states are necessary to protect them from the consequences of human nature, they can point to this counter-example (which is by no means unique): some peoples have succeeded in living without the state. It was not nice; it was not caring; it was demanding on the individuals. But it was egalitarian, relatively peaceful, and stateless.

EVANS-PRITCHARD'S WAY WITH THEORY was nearly always inexplicit. He scarcely ever "wrote theory," but allowed his organizing ideas to transpire from his text. He did write and publish on the history of anthropological or sociological ideas, but as a part of history rather than in any attempt to produce a refined composite framework for the analysis of social order.[13] Clifford Geertz has attacked him for this—his reticence taken as a symptom of upper-class Englishness, seductive and perniciously imperialistic.[14] It is true that anthropological theory (like all social theory) is generally short-lived and subject to fashions that rise and fall rather than accumulate into an edifice of agreed-upon principles. An anthropologist who wants the next generation to read his works would be well advised to keep his theory inexplicit. Easily imitated, not without certain period charms, sharing some traits with the high literature of the times, Evans-Pritchard's works can leave the reader bewitched or repelled— or both bewitched and repelled, as Geertz was. The real point for criticism is that Evans-Pritchard insinuates his ideas through the form his writing took.

It seems fairly clear that Evans-Pritchard thought he was concerned, like Durkheim, with things he called "societies," which he thought of as possessing "structures" that to some extent and in certain ways controlled the lives of those who lived them. By writing as he did, he discouraged his readers from inquiring further. Here is an example:

> Each village acts independently in arranging for its boys to be initiated. After the operation the boys live in partial seclusion and are subject to various taboos . . . Only age-mates of the father of the initiate in whose homestead the feasting takes place attend it: others keep at a distance lest they see the nakedness of their kinswomen and mothers-in-law.[15]

The point can be made more clearly by offering in contrast an account by Raymond Firth of a similar event:

> At the time of an incision ceremony in Rofaea, Pa Niukapu made a double journey to Matafana and back after dark in pouring rain

to see how his children were. He knew they were sleeping with their grandmother, in no discomfort, but he wished to be assured of their well-being. As he was a mother's brother of one of the initiates he had to return again to Rofaea to sleep.[16]

What is most notable about Firth's account is its vividness. It is located in time and space and weather, conveying the contingency of action and the intersection of motives and proscription. It gives a sense that the father had a motive—he wanted to reassure himself that all was well; and he had to return home because he was an uncle of the initiands, and uncles were excluded from the ceremony. He weighed his need to check on his son's well-being against the unpleasantness of the weather, took a decision, and then returned home because ritual good manners demanded he should. If subjects are treated like individuals, as in Firth's account, they can be shown acting from a sense of duty or sentiment, weighing desires against the weather.

Evans-Pritchard, in contrast, writes in the present tense: readers are immediately distanced from any actual time; they have no place. There are indeed no men or women doing things: the actors in this account are villages and age-mates and so on. Evans-Pritchard gives us no sense that people did things joyfully or reluctantly, had conflicting desires or obligations.

This seems related to Evans-Pritchard's ideas about social structure. He thought that the purpose of anthropology was to uncover the structures of societies, and that individuals matter less because they are in some sense constrained by structure. The normal state of Nuer social life was a kind of equilibrium between fission (reducing all to village units) and fusion (amalgamating tribal sections into larger units), and the structure was a series of institutions (age sets, kinship, descent, feud, leopard-skin chiefs, typical responses to ecological constraints) that maintained them in balance.

These remarks are intended to qualify Evans-Pritchard's greatness. Whereas Clifford Geertz sees Evans-Pritchard's language as giving away his intrinsic imperialism, in fact it identifies notions of structure as if they had, in fact, been abstracted from the actions he observed and noted so thoroughly and (in many instances) affectionately. But Evans-Pritchard makes a leap of imagination rather than a careful abstraction. He assumes the existence of a structure rather than demonstrating it or constructing it out of its component parts. This is rather un-English, at any rate for a social anthropologist, because it is essentially mystical. One cannot see or touch Evans-Pritchard's structures, nor can one see how they were made; nor can one see how structures relate to the experience of life of one or another Nuer. Anthropology that does not base itself on the varieties of human experience and is unconcerned with intentions and their results is seriously flawed. The contrast with Firth, and with Malinowski—who taught them both—is marked. In this sense, the New Zealander Firth and the Polish Malinowski are both more down-to-earth, more concerned with re-creating peoples' experiences, more interested in peoples' dilemmas and the plans they make to resolve them, than Evans-Pritchard was. In short, and in this regard, the Kiwi and the Pole are more English than the Welshman. I should say that the structural Evans-Pritchard is evident in *The Nuer*, rather less so in *Witchcraft, Oracles and Magic*, which benefits from the skeptical empiricism of the Azande themselves.

EVANS-PRITCHARD WAS INTENSELY LOYAL to those who were loyal to him, and that was a warm and heartening relationship to be in: academic support and encouragement as well as good fellowship in social matters, especially drinking. He was inclusive and solidary with such people, none of them unworthy of respect as anthropologists or teachers. But it was a rather small band, which he encouraged to become an Evans-Pritchard–centered coterie. He was ungenerous to those who disagreed with him, and could be vindictive to those who, having been admitted to the circle, asserted their independence or, in his view, deserted him. The shrift he gave them was so short as to appear contemptuous, and his word—pithy, bluff, abrupt—passed as witty and wise inside the circle, as wayward, partial, and dismissive outside it.

He inspired great affection, even filial love, in most of his colleagues and in many of his students, but the price was to have to share in the belief that the Oxford Institute had an exclusive monopoly on sensitive intelligence and understanding—sensitivity enhanced, if possible, by a shared membership of the Church of Rome. In his view, every other department of social anthropology lacked the sensitivity and dedication to pure anthropology that characterized the Oxford Institute.

These are all matters that detract from his greatness and that justify the "nonetheless" in the title of this essay. They are insufficient to undermine the value of his two great ethnographic works or of his contributions to the understanding of politics and rationality. It is immensely important not to accept hook, line, and sinker the notion that the state is necessary for peace and order. Some economists (such as Friedrich Hayek) have argued that an economy can grow spontaneously, that state regulation is superfluous. But without Evans-Pritchard's work on Nuer, there is no empirical counter to the self-justifying ideologies of state's men. Armed with *The Nuer,* libertarians can claim that people have in fact created and maintained social order without a state. Nuer life was not attractive—people are unlikely to choose to live as Nuer—but it has been done: it is established as part of our human repertoire. It was not part of a state of nature, utopian or otherwise, but something that known people made and maintained.

The point is that Nuer devised institutions that resisted both internal and external hierarchy and that maintained their egalitarian statelessness. Besides Nuer, a number of peoples devised rules to maintain anarchic or nearly anarchic regimes. But it was Evans-Pritchard, emissary of an encroaching government, who discovered and explained the distant anchor point of a spectrum that has modern bureaucratic government more or less at the other end.[17] Without his work, neither statelessness nor contemporary society would be comprehensible.

Witchcraft, Oracles and Magic has had an equally eye- and mind-opening role. The ancient claim that the core of human nature is rationality has always had to confront the obvious fact that human beings display so little of it. A survey of the universe, an allocation of human actions among the categories "stupid," "feckless," and "rational," might lead to the conclusion that human rationality is at best a hypothesis. Azande were inquisitive—they wanted to know the causes of things, even beyond the usual Western limits at which we give up and invoke chance, coincidence, and probability. And they were empirical: they introduced checks and tests to cover known areas of error and deception. Evans-Pritchard showed they could live with untruth nonetheless because they did not systematize their practice into any kind of theory: they did not create intellectual systems that they could then examine for coherence and consistency. Their knowledge was distributed among them in such a way that at any given moment no one person possessed the relevant facts that might encourage him or her to rethink the foundations of conventional explanation.

It was mainly British anthropologists and philosophers who asserted the universality of human rationality. In doing so, they confronted James Frazer's evolutionary scheme, by which mankind progressed from a religious to a magical to a scientific mentality—as Evans-Pritchard put it, "From the monkey-house to the Senior Common Room of Trinity College, Cambridge." The objection being, briefly, that this schema corresponded to no known historical changes. They also confronted the French philosophical-anthropological tendency exemplified by Lucien Lévy-Bruhl, according to which some peoples had pre-logical mentalities and therefore "thought differently." Evans-Pritchard's greatness in this respect was to show how error could be built into social organization, incorporated in the everyday practice of people who were sensible, logical, rational: not "other," but like us.

Spring Semester 2006

1. This outline of Evans-Pritchard's life draws chiefly on John A. Barnes, "Edward Evans-Pritchard," *Proceedings of the British Academy* (1987), pp. 447–90; Godfrey Lienhardt, "E-P: A Personal View," *Man*, (NS) 9, (1974), pp. 229–304; Wendy James, "Evans-Pritchard, Sir Edward E. (1902–73)," *International Encyclopedia of the Social and Behavioral Sciences* (Amsterdam, 2001), pp. 4937–41. Evans-Pritchard's own notes, "Fragment of an Autobiography," *New Blackfriars* (1973), pp. 35–37, is the source for some of the details in the other works and includes an account of how he became a Roman Catholic.

2. Marett visited archaeological sites, excavated a prehistoric cave in his native Jersey, and briefly visited an Aboriginal tribe when in Australia at the beginning of the First World War.

3. MacMichael joined the Sudan Political Service in 1905; he became civil secretary in 1926, then Governor and High Commissioner of Tanganyika, 1933–37, and served as well in Palestine and Trans-Jordan, 1938–44. His works include *The Tribes of Northern and Central Kordofan* (London, 1912), and *A History of the Arabs in the Sudan* (London, 1922).

4. Participant observation is a method of anthropological fieldwork pioneered by Bronislaw Malinowski; it is characterized by living with a people, learning their language, and coming to a more detailed and coherent understanding than possible from a survey.

5. His army work in Libya, chiefly concerned with the tribesmen of Cyrenaica and their support of the religious order headed by the Sanusi family, resulted in another notable work, *The Sanusi of Cyrenaica* (Oxford, 1949).

6. A report is in the *Oxford Times*, 3 Sept. 1959.

7. E. E. Evans-Pritchard, *Witchcraft, Oracles and Magic among the Azande* (Oxford, 1937), pp. 65–66.

8. *The Nuer: A Description of the Modes of Livelihood and Political Institutions of a Nilotic People* (Oxford, 1940). Other major and relevant works are *Kinship and Marriage among the Nuer* (Oxford, 1951) and *Nuer Religion* (Oxford, 1956).

9. Ernest Gellner was a sheep man; Nuer and Evans-Pritchard were cattle men; the principles apply to camel and goat herders equally well.

10. Evans-Pritchard did his fieldwork at a time when the government of Anglo-Egyptian Sudan, using Dinka troops, was attempting to pacify and to tax the Nuer; an armed incursion by the government interrupted one of his field trips. It is a complex history, and not an edifying one. Douglas Johnson, "Political Ecology in the Upper Nile: The Twentieth Century Expansion of the Pastoral 'Common Economy,'" *Journal of African History*, 30, 3 (1989), pp. 463–86, deals with, among other things, extraordinary climatic variation and the expansion of colonial control. His "The Fighting Nuer: Primary Sources and the Origin of a Stereotype," *Journal of the International African Institute*, 51, 1 (1981), pp. 508–27, discusses the characterization of the Nuer as natural warriors, in spite of evidence to the contrary, in the reports of colonial officers. His "Evans-Pritchard, the Nuer and the Sudan Political Service," *African Affairs*, 81, 323 (1982), pp. 231–46, uses correspondence from the archives at Khartoum to outline Evans-Pritchard's relations with governmental officers in Anglo-Egyptian Sudan. These sources were mostly not available to Evans-Pritchard, and Johnson shows that Evans-Pritchard was constrained to take a rather short-term view. Wendy James points out the irony, given Evans-Pritchard's lifelong concern with the relation of history and anthropology (James, "Evans-Pritchard"). Douglas Johnson, *Nuer Prophets: A History of Prophecy from the Upper Nile in the Nineteenth and Twentieth Centuries* (Oxford, 1994), shows what can be done by someone practiced in both disciplines.

11. See, for instance, Peter J. Greuel, "The Leopard-skin Chief: An Examination of Political Power among the Nuer," *American Anthropology*, (NS) 73, 5 (1971), pp. 1115–20.

12. The exceptions are Plate I and XXIV and perhaps also Plate XV(b).

13. His principal published books are *Theories of Primitive Religion* (Oxford, 1965), *The Sociology of Auguste Comte: An Appreciation* (Oxford, 1970), and *A History of Anthropological Thought*, edited by André Singer with an introduction by Ernest Gellner, (New York, 1981).

14. Clifford Geertz, *Works and Lives: The Anthropologist as Author* (Stanford, 1988).

15. Evans-Pritchard, *Nuer*.

16. Raymond Firth, *We, the Tikopia* (Boston, 1936).

17. Evans-Pritchard had his precursors, though none of them achieved the economy and precision of his account of segmentary systems. The most notable was W. Robertson Smith, especially in *Kinship and Marriage in Early Arabia* (Cambridge, 1885) and *Lectures on the Religion of the Semites: First Series; The Fundamental Institutions* (Edinburgh, 1889). Meyer Fortes claimed to have been present when Radcliffe-Brown told Evans-Pritchard that E. W. Gifford had described a (Tongan) segmentary system and that it might help him organize his Nuer material; see John W. Burton, "The Ghost of Malinowski in the Southern Sudan: Evans-Pritchard and Ethnographic Fieldwork," *Proceedings of the American Philosophical Society*, 127, 4 (1983), pp. 278–89.

14

No-Man's-Land:
C. Wright Mills in England

JOHN SUMMERS

C. Wright Mills had a little to say about a great many subjects and a lot to say about a few subjects of great importance.
The New Men of Power (1948), *White Collar* (1951), and *The
Power Elite* (1956), his trilogy, marked a fault line in Anglo-American
cultural history, not only between the Left old and new, but also
between the modern and the "post-modern epoch," as he wrote
in 1959.

Modern ideologies marshaled the Enlightenment against the
myth, fraud, and superstition of the medieval epoch. Liberalism and
Marxism developed theories of human beings as secular, rational,
peaceable creatures, then transformed these theories into collective
projects. But the social structure of advanced industrial capitalism
defeated the ideologies of progress. The failures, betrayals, and ambiguities of liberalism and Marxism disinherited modern man, according to Mills, who wrote as a defender of humanist aspiration as
well as a witness to its eclipse.

No biography of Mills worth reading has appeared in the forty-
five years since his death.[1] This is surprising, since he was a spiritual descendant of Stendhal's Julien Sorel, Turgenev's Bazarov, and
Jack London's Martin Eden, one in a long line of "new men" born
into mass society. Sons without fathers, nonparty revolutionists,
they were intellectuals as well as actors, roles between which they

acknowledged no need to choose. They stole into the imagination of Europe and America in the nineteenth century, and played havoc ever after.

Mills, too, was an outlander. Born in Waco, Texas, in 1916, he endured a year in military school before enrolling in the University of Texas in 1935. In Austin, he studied sociology and philosophy with a group of professors trained in the Chicago School of pragmatism. At the University of Wisconsin, where he went for his doctorate in sociology and anthropology, he met German social thought in the person of Hans Gerth, the refugee scholar. Following an interlude at the University of Maryland, he joined Columbia College in 1945 and taught there until his death, in 1962.

A Texan by birth, an anarchist by temperament, a pragmatist by training, Mills made himself into a "Hemingway Man." An autobiographical note in 1953 envisioned his breakout from Morningside Heights: "The Hemingway Man is a spectator and an experiencer; he is also a world traveller, usually alone or with changing companions. When I have travelled and camped out west, when I have thought about Europe, always when I have thought about Europe, I have tried in somewhat feeble ways perhaps even ridiculous ways, to be a Hemingway Man."[2]

Mills grew into the role he set for himself as if expanding in concentric circles, first focusing on the American Midwest, then widening to encompass the cities of the East, then radiating outward to Europe, where he went for the first time in 1956. Late though he was in going abroad, he was not long in making up the time. He arrived as the Cold War system in international politics was suffering shocks from which it was never fully to recover. Writing in 1957, after spending a weekend with the Students' Union of the London School of Economics, Mills saw a possible renaissance in humanist values: "I've the vague feeling that 'we' may be coming into our own in the next five or ten years."[3]

If 1948 was the last year of the 1930s in the United States, then let 1956 stand as the first year of the 1960s in England. Khrushchev's speech against Stalin collided with the rebellions in Poland and Hungary later that year to burn away the final residue of faith. Belief in the need for a revolutionary Left now coincided with disbelief in the Communist Party as its organizing agent and moral tutor. E. P. Thompson and John Saville, two of 7,000 who resigned their Party memberships after the events of 1956, founded the *New Reasoner* to educate the disappointed and savage the culpable. Thompson assailed Stalinism as "militant philistinism" and demanded a confrontation with its crimes.

Mills learned about the personalities and politics of the changing English Left from a Belgian Jewish émigré named Ralph Miliband, who had invited him to the LSE. Miliband was a perfect host. A member of the editorial board of the *New Reasoner,* he had joined forces with a second group of dissenters, headquartered at Oxford University. There it was the Suez affair, rather than the crisis of communism, that quickened pulses. Awareness that a post-ideological epoch had already dawned was the theme of the Oxford group's magazine, *Universities and Left Review.*

An early contribution by Stuart Hall, "A Sense of Classlessness" (1958), located the significance of the Suez affair at home. A "sense of class confusion" befogged liberal and Marxist efforts to describe post-war English society and its resource-grabbing foreign policy. Urban housing complexes were replacing brick homes in working-class neighborhoods, where attitudes were changing in favor of automobiles, kitchen appliances, and televisions. Corporations were conquering small enterprises with the aid of bureaucracies that were reaching deeper into private life. "A number of interpenetrating elites or narrow oligarchies," Hall wrote, now superintended "a permanently exploited, permanently alienated 'mass' of consumers—consuming goods and culture equally. The true class picture which so skillfully conceals itself behind the bland face of contemporary capitalism is broadly speaking that which C. Wright Mills describes in *The Power Elite.*"[4]

Mills visited his new friends in England as often as he could. He appeared on *We Dissent,* a television documentary produced by Kenneth Tynan. He headlined a speaker series in Soho at the Partisan Cafe, a forum run by *Universities and Left Review.* He went with Miliband to Warsaw, where he met Zygmunt Bauman, Julian Hochfeld, and Leszek Kolakowski, leaders of Poland's 1956. In the best-selling pamphlet that grew out of the trip, *The Causes of World War Three* (1958), Mills asked readers to imagine "a world without passports" and argued forcefully for the political independence of Europe.

Around his academic colleagues at Columbia, Mills's manner was guarded. Around his friends in England, he let out his gregarious side. "He had this enormous intellectual curiosity, a real willingness to learn," Norman Birnbaum has said.[5] John Saville has "very warm memories" of him: "He was an extremely lively, very intelligent, bloody interesting intellectual."[6] Stuart Hall, Charles Taylor, and Peter Worsley held similar impressions.

Mills arrived in London on Saturday, 10 January 1959, for a week's visit. The next day, he appeared on a television program. On

Monday, Tuesday, and Thursday, he delivered the University Lectures in Sociology at the LSE. He found time to attend Miliband's
seminar on political theory, fielding questions from the students,
and to attend a meeting of the editorial board of the *New Reasoner*
at Doris Lessing's flat. Dorothy Thompson, watching him on television, thought he looked like most American professors. Then she
met him at Lessing's, "and this great cowboy heaved into sight." In
Mills she perceived an example of left-wing integrity, a man of commitment in an age of collapsing faiths: "He was a good listener, and
intellectually very curious and open. I was completely swept away."[7]

The BBC recorded Mills's LSE lectures and broadcast them for
three weeks. *The Times* described him as "6 ft tall, with a chest like a
grizzly-bear's and a face as tanned and craggy as a cowboy's." According to the *Times Literary Supplement:* "Mr. Wright Mills bursts among
the pundits' discussion of the American situation with the explosive
force of James Cagney at a tea party of the Daughters of the American Revolution." Michael Foot, editor of the weekly *London Tribune,* announced: "HERE, AT LAST, IS THE TRUE VOICE OF AMERICAN
RADICALISM." Mills was "radical, adventurous, free of jingoism and
militarism, open to exciting thought and effective popular action."
Many English intellectuals believed the Cold War had snuffed out
America's revolutionary heritage, "but it is not dead. And it speaks
through Wright Mills."[8]

Mills's "Letter to the New Left" summoned these special relations
to a consummatory moment. Published in September 1960 in the
New Left Review (the project of a merger between the *New Reasoner*
and *Universities and Left Review*), the letter implored English intellectuals to transform the absence of ideology into new theories of
history and human nature, to take what they needed from the warring dogmas of the Cold War and leave the rest behind. Mills wrote
in slangy prose and memorable wisecracks, but it was the first paragraph that endeared him to his comrades abroad: "When I settle
down to you, I feel somehow 'freer' than usual. The reason, I suppose, is that most of the time I am writing for people whose ambiguities and values I imagine to be rather different from mine; but
with you, I feel enough in common to allow us to 'get on with it' in
more positive ways."[9]

Getting on with it meant going to Cuba. In August 1960, Mills
took two Nikon cameras and an audio recorder out of his suitcase,
dropped into a jeep waiting outside the Havana Riviera, and toured
the island. Everywhere he looked, he saw a society expanding under
a morning sun of success. A revolution had convulsed a despotism.
The military stage of the revolution was giving way to social recon-

struction. The transition was carried along by a spirit of voluntary self-education. Standing in a downpour at the edge of a former cattle ranch, Mills listened to Fidel Castro and a cadre of military officers debate the best species of tree to plant in the fields. "So the real ideological conflict under discussion is pine trees versus eucalyptus!" he exclaimed into his recorder.[10]

"We are new men," proclaimed *Listen, Yankee* (1960). "That is why we are so original and so spontaneous and so unafraid to do what must be done in Cuba."[11] Mills's pamphlet, part explanation, part evocation, met with unified acrimony in the United States. The *New Republic* compared him to "a merger of Judas Iscariot, Benedict Arnold, and Vidkun Quisling, retaining the worst features of each." The *Washington Post* compared him to Wilhelm Reich, a genius gone mad. Syndicated columnists assailed him in towns and small cities from coast to coast. "Don't Let Prof. Mills Fool You on Cuba" ran one headline; "Author of Book on Cuba Thinks He Fools You" ran another. The Federal Bureau of Investigation deployed agents near his home in West Nyack, New York. The strain was too much. The night before Mills was to debate the revolution on NBC television, he suffered a heart attack that put him into a coma and nearly killed him. Pushed by hostility at home, pulled by the offer of a chair in sociology at the University of Sussex, he returned to England in April 1961. He took a flat in London, enrolled his daughter in school, and thought about settling.

Shortly after this, the *New Left Review* confronted its first crisis. The magazine's ambitious publishing arm had issued a series of pamphlets, but organizational bickering and financial difficulties had impeded progress. E. P. Thompson, broke and demoralized, arrived at editorial meetings with holes in his shoes. Both John Saville, chairman of the magazine, and Stuart Hall, editor from its inception, quit the board late in 1961. Other resignations followed.

The disarray enhanced Mills's value as a mentor. Perry Anderson and Robin Blackburn, part of the second generation of student radicals to rattle through Oxford, met with him often in these months. "We were pumping him for information and advice," recalls Blackburn, who also remembers looking on, guiltily, as Mills strained to climb the stairs to the fifth-floor flat where they held their tutorials.[12] Cuban politics and classical social theory occupied the sessions. Mills's *The Sociological Imagination* (1959) struck Anderson and Blackburn as a text at once exotic and relevant. Sociology had gained a toehold at the LSE, and the British Sociological Association (BSA) had opened in 1951. But most of the founders of the BSA did not identify themselves as sociologists. Membership still counted in the low hundreds, and only two universities had departments, neither of them located at Oxford or Cambridge. "We live in a society that is essentially opaque," wrote Anderson and Blackburn in *New University,* a campus extension of the *New Left Review:* "The origin and sense of the events in it systematically escape us. This obscurity is also a separation: it prevents us seeing one another and our common situations as they really are, and so divides us from each other." [13]

Along came Mills, promising that sociology, classically conceived, could uncover orienting points and organizing principles, could spur "a transvaluation of values." [14] His radically sociological approach to power offered methodological aid as well. In 1957, a group of researchers for *Universities and Left Review* compiled the income, benefits, training, and social connections of the men who staffed the top posts in industry. The group titled its report *The Insiders* (1957) after determining that a few hundred corporations controlled the economy, and that wherever the state intervened, it became a partner in monopoly enterprise rather than its critic. "Public ownership," the slogan of state socialism, hid oligarchy. *Universities and Left Review* published *The Insiders* as a special pamphlet, which sold out quickly.

No record remains of Mills's impressions of Anderson and Blackburn, but they must have impressed him strongly. One of the last things he did in January 1962, when he went home to die, was to nominate a new editor for the *New Left Review.* Anderson assumed control and Blackburn joined the editorial board in March, the month Mills succumbed to a heart attack. He was forty-five.

E. P. THOMPSON COMPARED HIM TO WILLIAM MORRIS. "We had come to assume his presence—definitions, provocations, exhortations—as a fixed point in the intellectual night-sky," Thompson wrote in a two-part essay on Mills in *Peace News:* "His star stood above the ideological no-man's land between the orthodox emplacements of West and East, flashing urgent humanist messages. If we couldn't always follow it, we always stopped to take bearings." [15] Ralph Miliband mourned his death "bitterly and personally" in the *New Left Review:* "In a trapped and inhumane world, he taught what it means to be a free and humane intellect." [16] Miliband named his newborn son after him in 1965. "I got to feel closer to Mills than I have ever felt to any man, or shall ever feel again, I should think," Miliband wrote to Thompson. [17]

The editorial reconstitution of *New Left Review* instilled in veterans of *Universities and Left Review* and the *New Reasoner* "a sense of isolation," Thompson later wrote. [18] Those who had come to political

awareness in the 1930s and 1940s, for whom 1956 had been a pivotal
year, lost the initiative to a generation that came to awareness in
the late 1950s. When a Labour government assumed power in 1964
and supported the American war in Vietnam, it was Anderson and
Blackburn who directed the New Left in England.

Mills's influence continued accordingly. Blackburn's long essay
"Prologue to the Cuban Revolution" (1963) offered a sociological
history of the "power structure" in Cuba and a political alternative to
the liberal portrait of a middle-class revolution betrayed. According
to Blackburn, Cuba's belated independence from Spain, the shocks
delivered to its economic and political institutions in the decades
thereafter, plus foreign manipulation of its markets: these peculiarities of Cuban history had inhibited social cohesion on the island.
The middle-class had not developed any collective interests, had not
grown conscious of itself as an ideological opponent of Fulgencio
Batista's dictatorship. Rather than standing for any popular goals or
social programs, Batista had ruled through a patchwork of strategic
alliances, the hollowness of which was revealed by its inability to sustain a fight against the outnumbered, outgunned guerrillas. These
weaknesses of ideology and social structure explained why the dictatorship had collapsed so speedily, leaving behind a vacuum. Castro's
guerrillas, once in power, expanded into it with a comprehensive
program of practical assistance.

Anderson's "Origins of the Present Crisis" (1965) and "Components of the National Culture" (1968) worked the theoretical side
of his inheritance into a paradox. England, the cradle of capitalism,
had produced neither first-class Marxist theoreticians nor bourgeois sociologists equivalent to French and German exemplars. In
Anderson's struggle to see through this background of parochial
complacency, in his effort to gain a total view of social structure by
means of a sociological analysis that was at once historical and comparative, the hidden hand of Mills showed through.

Mills lived on as political ally, as sociological tutor, and as the
author of aphorisms, epigrams, and slogans that lingered and expanded in the mind of his English readers. Labour MP Anthony
Crosland complained to the BBC about the diffusion of his ideas:
"Many people on the left see America as the arch-capitalist country
dominated by a power elite of big industrialists, Wall Street bankers, military men and all the rest of it. And so, since they are anti-
capitalist, they are inevitably anti-American. Personally, I think that
this picture of America is terribly exaggerated. I do not think America is run in this crude way by a capitalistic power elite."[19] An essay
by Denis Brogan in the *Times Literary Supplement,* titled "Spooks of

the Power Elite," also complained about his influence. Mills "appeals to the same conspiratorial tastes on the left as do the theories of the John Birch Society on the right. His diagnosis is fundamentally passive and pessimistic."[20] But his admirers did not fail to recognize the intentions behind his post-1956 work, his effort to forge from the homelessness of radical values a new beginning. They remembered indeed what he had said of those values in his LSE lectures in 1959: "It is time for us to try to realize them ourselves—in our own lives, in our own direct action, in the immediate context of our own work. Now, we ought to repossess *our* cultural apparatus and use it for our own purposes."[21]

In October 1966, the Socialist Society at the LSE published a pamphlet challenging the selection of Walter Adams as the school's new director. The pamphlet argued that Adams, recently the Principal of University College in Rhodesia, had not proved himself liberal enough on the matter of race to enjoy the privilege of leading a student body riddled with questions about colonialism. The pamphlet struck up a furor. The leader of the LSE Students' Union sought answers about the appointment from the official selection committee. He received none. Instead, he was arraigned by a disciplinary court for criticizing school authorities: an offense against regulations. Very soon, protest over the new director grew into the first major student strike in English history.

The rebellion at the LSE introduced sit-ins, boycotts, and marches that lasted for the remainder of the academic year. Here as elsewhere, not only the decisions of the authorities, but the authority to make the decisions in the first place, stimulated the indignation of students. Officials punished them for defying the rituals of dissent. The punishments spurred bolder acts of defiance. Most English universities endured such conflicts, but none rivaled the LSE for scale. More than 40 percent of the student population took part in at least one of the protests in 1966 and 1967; more than 60 percent of sociology students did so. And here as elsewhere, the confrontation escalated in 1968. Thousands of protesters were expected to come to London at the end of October to voice their displeasure over the war in Vietnam. Would the LSE allow some of them to stay on campus? Walter Adams answered no. Eight hundred students seized a building for themselves.

Robin Blackburn, recently appointed lecturer in sociology at the LSE, co-edited a volume of essays on the occupation: *Student Power* (1969). The essays connected the state of production and consumption in advanced capitalism to the misshapen condition of higher education, and challenged the image of universities as island communities, innocent of the violence of foreign policy. As Perry Anderson wrote in his contribution: "This is a direct attack on the reactionary and mystifying culture inculcated in universities and colleges, and which it is one of the fundamental purposes of British higher education to instil in students."[22]

References to Mills appeared throughout *Student Power*, but the essays, ironically, bore the greater influence of French, German, and Italian Marxists. The irony lay in the ideology. Mills had made his appeal in England as a critic of left-wing cant and dogma. Alone among American intellectuals, he brought none of the moral liabilities of a communist past and at the same time exemplified unbroken radical commitment. This effort to stand in no-man's-land, taking fire from both sides, made his work uniquely available to dissenters on all sides of the Cold War. His greatest achievement was his independence. "There is now no substantial reason to believe that Marxist revolutions will come about in any foreseeable future in any major advanced capitalist country," he wrote in 1962, completing the end-of-ideology thesis in his trilogy.[23]

The movement for an independent Left in England, thus encouraged, had been born in its refusal to be misled by the false rivalry of communist and bourgeois. It had withdrawn from the bankrupted ideologies of the modern period so as to begin the task of rehabilitating the moral culture of humanism. And yet when the most important student strike in English history presented itself, the New Left imported its model of thinking from a knock-off edition of the same old texts.

Anderson's paradox, bemoaning the apparent fact that England had given birth to the social system of capitalism without producing any corresponding Marxist thinkers, was an actual paradox only from the perspective of the Marxist theory of history. "The starting-point here," Anderson wrote, "will be any observed irregularities in the contours of British culture, viewed internationally. That is, any basic phenomena which are not a matter of course, but contradict elementary expectation from comparative experience and hence seem to demand a special explanation. Such irregularities may provide a privileged point of entry into the culture as a whole, and thereby furnish a key to the system."[24] Or in other words: Anderson slipped on X-ray glasses, which afforded him metaphysical confidence that "the system" could be rendered transparent, then, looking through his "privileged points of entry into the system," he identified the very asymmetries, irregularities, and disjunctions that Marxism had keyed him to find in the first place. The bourgeois opposition he buried in overlapping contexts. His own model he floated above time and place: "Marx's thought was so far in advance of its time and its society that it was unassimilable in the nineteenth century."[25]

Mills named such reasoning by fiat "Sophisticated Marxism" and likened its obfuscating function to Grand Theory in liberal social thought. In both cases, he wrote, a "sophisticated" conceptual knowledge and elaboration of radical theory coincided with a radically arrant political intelligence, for what appeared to be a bid for greater rationalism concealed a note of mysticism. Anderson wrote accordingly: "Events that fail to happen are often more important than those which do; but they are always infinitely more difficult to see."[26]

If Anderson was right about "the complete mutism of the past" and the "objective vacuum at the centre of the culture," did it not mean that there was nothing in society to defend?[27] Blackburn's contribution to *Student Power* gave a clear answer. "A Brief Guide to Bourgeois Ideology" indicated that Anglo-American social theory amounted to nothing more than the functions it fulfilled in "the system," the wheels and levers, pulleys and pumps, hooks and handles of the capitalist machine. Ideas? No more than myths by which the "power elite" ruled.[28] Blackburn hooted at "bourgeois analysts," "the bourgeois political theorist," "bourgeois social theory," "bourgeois economists," "bourgeois sociologists," "the myths of bourgeois pluralism," "most bourgeois theorists," "the customary refuge of the bourgeois sociologist," "the weak stomach of the modern bourgeois social theorist," "the amnesia of modern bourgeois epigones," and on and on. Subtracting the word "bourgeois" from the essay would have exposed it as a mix of phrase-mongering and finger-pointing.

The New Left gained something more decisive than polemical firepower from its turn toward Marxism. Anderson made much of the fact that both Marxism and bourgeois sociology had produced a "theory of society as a totality," arguing that without such a concept of totality, then "the era of revolutions is, necessarily, unthinkable."[29] It was this longing for a concept of totality, needed for the purposes of clarification and available in Marx's metaphysics, that struck Anderson and Blackburn blind when they went to judge the political significance of the occupation of the LSE.

The manifesto of the Revolutionary Socialist Students' Federation told the tale. Adopted in November 1968 and subsequently published in the *New Left Review,* the manifesto shunted aside political parties, trade unions, and student reform organizations. "Mass democracy," it said, needed "red bases in our colleges and universities" on the model pioneered by Mao Tse-tung's Cultural Revolution. Here was a concept of totality, armed and dangerous. Begun in 1966 under the banner "Combat Bourgeois Ideas," Mao's program was in the hands of Chinese students, who were burning books, closing parks, destroying paintings, and torturing their teachers. "It should not be thought that the call to make the creation of Red Bases a strategic goal of our struggle is merely a flight of rhetoric," Blackburn explained, in the same issue of the magazine that carried the RSSF's manifesto: "Capitalist power cannot just be drowned in a rising tide of consciousness. It must be smashed and broken up by the hard blows of popular force."[30]

Communications from Mao appeared in the *New Left Review* alongside enthusiastic reports from the Cultural Revolution. When Anderson wrote an introduction to Marshall Mikhail Tukhachevsky, it was not difficult to share his preference for Mao.[31] But it ought to have been difficult to credit the comparison in the first place, morally thin as the choices were. Observe that Anderson believed Mao's theory of revolutionary practice was driving war and politics into a new unity. Recall how the Chinese students were treating their teachers. Now listen to Anderson on the occupation of the LSE: "A revolutionary culture is not for tomorrow. But a revolutionary practice within culture is possible and necessary today. The student struggle is its initial form."[32]

On the evening of 24 January 1969, Blackburn was presenting a paper to a conference of the British Sociological Association. Gathered on the fourth floor of the St. Clement's Building at the LSE, the conferees heard shouting through the window. A young man bounded into the room and interrupted Blackburn's presentation. While you are *talking* about the revolution, said the young man, it is *happening* outside. LSE officials had installed iron gates to guard against breaches of security. An emergency meeting of the Students' Union had threatened to rip them down. Now a crowd of students tugged and whacked at the gates with a sledgehammer, crowbars, and pickaxes. They went at it for about an hour.

Later that night, in a previously scheduled speech, Blackburn celebrated the attack on the gates. Had he fallen silent then, rather than repeating his remarks on BBC television on 30 January, he might have evaded punishment. Instead, he was instructed to appear before a disciplinary tribunal, which was empowered to reconsider his future at the school. His letter of reply jeered at "the entire clique of self-appointed capitalist manipulators."[33]

The "capitalist manipulators" acknowledged that Blackburn had neither committed any direct actions nor incited any. He had made his remarks after the gates had fallen. They fired him anyway and

closed the LSE for twenty-five days. The Maoists responded by occupying a building at the University of London and setting up an LSE-
in-Exile. They greeted the reopening of the LSE a month later by
boycotting classes, interrupting lectures, tossing stink bombs into
meetings, and pulling fire alarms.

   The LSE-in-Exile closed one day after it opened. The Revolutionary Socialist Students' Federation folded. By the end of the summer
of 1969, scarcely a year after Anderson articulated his revolutionary
prophecy, the rebellion at the LSE stammered and wheezed to a
halt. Thereafter, student interest in sociology fell, while the "capitalist manipulators" moved on to other enemies: inflation, shrinking
support from the state, and dwindling morale. The American war
in Asia went on and on.

WHAT WOULD MILLS HAVE THOUGHT? In 1959 at the LSE, he recommended "direct action." The next year, his "Letter to the New
Left" exhorted the uncorrupted to consider that "the cultural apparatus, the intellectuals" might be best positioned to initiate a new
beginning. He lectured on the subject in Austria, Brazil, Canada,
Cuba, Denmark, Mexico, Poland, West Germany, and the Soviet
Union. By and by, he spread his message all over the world. In September 1968, the Central Intelligence Agency concluded a classified
report, "Restless Youth," which identified Herbert Marcuse, Mills,
and Frantz Fanon as the three leaders of the international Left. Between Marcuse's abstract Marxism and Fanon's revolutionary violence, there was his ghost, chasing both action and ideas without
acknowledging the need to choose.

   The New Man's dream of creating new values out of the dialec-
tic of thought and action must always know the difference between
thinking too long and acting too soon. Mills's American followers,
no better at telling this vital difference than their English counterparts, met the same end. With the LSE strike about to break out,
Columbia University students took over Hamilton Hall, the building where Mills had once had his office. Four additional buildings
fell in quick succession. *Who Rules Columbia?* a pamphlet written by
his former students on the model of *The Insiders*, justified the occupation, after which a Strike Education Committee opened a "Liberation School" that lasted not much longer than the LSE-in-Exile.
Tom Hayden, an ardent admirer of Mills, presided for four days in
Mathematics Hall, where he showed teams of militants how to slick
the steps with soap in preparation for the police. "Columbia opened
a new tactical stage in the resistance movement which began last
fall," Hayden wrote after the bust, sounding like Perry Anderson.

"What is certain is that we are moving toward power—the power to stop the machine if it cannot be made to serve humane ends," he wrote, in the same vein of misbegotten prophecy.[34]

As Mills's students carried his writings from 1956 into the maelstrom of 1968, the meaning of his biography changed in response to events he could not have been expected to anticipate. He may have accepted his portion of responsibility for the psychodynamics of the international Left before it reorganized into terrorist cells. Had he lived long enough to choose sides in 1968, however, his experimentalism would have seen him through many unknown contingencies, which would have altered and improved his perspective many times by then. All along, his pragmatism would have tempered his exhortations. The "Letter to the New Left" reminded readers to be "realistic in our utopianism" and asked: "Is anything more certain than that in 1970 our situation will be quite different?" Most likely, the choice of sides would not have been his to make. In his independence, he had refused to narrow the idea of radical commitment to a choice between confrontation and withdrawal. Yet these were the only terms on offer from his enemies and epigones at the end of the decade. His legacy torn apart by the very forces he unleashed, he would have been marooned on no-man's-land.

The full story of Mills's life and thought, cast across three generations of intellectuals on four continents, stands uniquely at the intersection of history and biography, illuminating the incidents, sentiments, and personalities of the international Left in all its heroism and foolishness. If that sounds trite, think of the upcoming anniversary of '68; of the leftward surge in Latin America; or of the unpopular war in Iraq, waged by American elites with the support of a Labour government—and linger on the news that David Wright Miliband is Foreign Secretary. Set against the possibilities for *another beginning*, the untold tales of Mills's life and thought may yet reveal how the New Men turned into Hemingway Men, how Hemingway Men became Castro's Men, and how Castro's Men became Mao's Men before the rest of us became . . . Academic Men.

Fall Semester 2006

1. On Mills's posthumous career, see John H. Summers, "The Epigone's Embrace," *Minnesota Review*, n.s. 68 (Spring 2007), pp. 107–124.

2. C. Wright Mills, "For Ought," 19 Sept. 1953, Box 4B390, CWM Papers, Center for American History, University of Texas at Austin.

3. C. Wright Mills to Harvey and Bette Swados, 12 Mar. 1957; Harvey Swados Papers, W. E. B. DuBois Library, University of Massachusetts at Amherst.

4. Stuart Hall, "A Sense of Classlessness," *Universities and Left Review*, 1, 5 (Autumn 1958), pp. 26–31.

5. Telephone interview with Norman Birnbaum, 10 Oct. 2003.

6. Telephone interview with John Saville, 11 May 2004.

7. Personal interview with Dorothy Thompson, 9 May 2004.

8. *London Tribune*, 16 Jan. 1959.

9. C. Wright Mills, "Letter to the New Left," *New Left Review*, no. 5 (Sept.–Oct. 1960), p. 18.

10. Audio recording, in author's possession.

11. Mills, *Listen, Yankee* (New York, 1960), p. 43.

12. Personal interview with Robin Blackburn, London, 11 May 2004.

13. Perry Anderson and Robin Blackburn, "Cuba, Free Territory of America," *New University*, no. 4 (5 Dec. 1960), p. 22.

14. Mills, *The Sociological Imagination* (New York, 1959), p. 8.

15. E. P. Thompson, "Remembering C. Wright Mills," in Thompson, *The Heavy Dancers* (London, 1985), p. 261; and E. P. Thompson, "C. Wright Mills: The Responsible Craftsman," *Peace News*, no. 1431 (29 Nov. 1963), p. 8.

16. Ralph Miliband, "C. Wright Mills," *New Left Review*, no. 15, (May–June 1962), p. 15.

17. As quoted in Michael Newman, *Ralph Miliband and the Politics of the New Left* (London, 2002), p. 67.

18. E. P. Thompson, foreword to *The Poverty of Theory and Other Essays* (New York, 1978), p. ii.

19. "Anti-American Attitudes: A Symposium," *Listener*, 67 (19 Apr. 1962), pp. 667–68.

20. Dennis Brogan, "Spooks of the Power Elite," *Times Literary Supplement*, 17 Aug. 1967, p. 736.

21. C. Wright Mills, "The Decline of the Left," *Listener*, 61 (2 Apr. 1959).

22. Perry Anderson "Components of the National Culture" (1968), in Alexander Cockburn and Robin Blackburn, eds., *Student Power: Problems, Diagnosis, Action* (London, 1969), p. 218.

23. C. Wright Mills, *The Marxists* (New York, 1962), p. 468.

24. Anderson, "Components of the National Culture," p. 218.

25. Ibid., p. 222.

26. Ibid., p. 219.

27. Ibid., p. 268.

28. Robin Blackburn, "Brief Guide to Bourgeois Ideology," in Cockburn and Blackburn, eds., *Student Power*, p. 164.

29. Anderson "Components of the National Culture," p. 277.

30. James Wilcox (pseudonym of Robin Blackburn), "Two Tactics," *New Left Review*, no. 53 (Jan.–Feb. 1969), pp. 23, 24. The attribution of this article to Blackburn is in Gregory Elliott, *Perry Anderson: The Merciless Laboratory of History* (Minneapolis, 1998).

31. See Anderson's (unsigned) "Introduction to Tukhachevsky," *New Left Review*, no. 55 (May–June 1969), pp. 85–86; attribution in Elliott, *Perry Anderson*, p. 59.

32. Anderson "Components of the National Culture," p. 277.

33. Robin Blackburn, quoted in Ralf Dahrendorf, *LSE: A History of the London School of Economics and Political Science, 1895–1995* (London, 1995), p. 470.

34. Tom Hayden, "Two, Three, Many Columbias," *Ramparts*, 6 (15 June 1968), p. 40.

15

"Decline" as a Weapon
in Cultural Politics

GUY ORTOLANO

In 1963 the satirical magazine *Private Eye* published an "All Purpose 'What's-Wrong-With-Britain' Graph." It consisted of five lines steadily descending between 1900 and 1962, the implication being that whatever it was that might want measuring, it had surely been getting worse. The headline at the top of the page posed the question "How, Now, Does Britain Stay At the Top?" a problem made all the more pressing by laments about everything from athletics ("the Olympic Games has not been held in Britain since 1948!") to the weather ("Britain's weather in 1963 has already been worse than AT ANY TIME SINCE 1754"). These and other findings were supported by evidence of undeniable power, including statistics ("45% of our State schools have pianos but no music teachers, 32% have music teachers but no pianos, while 27% have NO TEACHERS AT ALL!") and xenophobia ("WHO WERE FAHRENHEIT, REAUMUR AND CENTIGRADE IF THEY WERE NOT ALL FOREIGNERS!").[1] In 1963, as the winds of change were blowing through what remained of the Empire and the Profumo scandal was blowing apart the credibility of the government, *Private Eye* appeared to be marking Britain's ignominious decline with its trademark brand of gallows humor.

Yet the actual target of *Private Eye*'s ridicule was less the sorry state of Britain's international position than the apologetic state of its national punditry. What was being skewered, that is, was not a state of affairs but a mode of discussion, as betrayed by the disclaimer that preceded the laments above: "What the Cassandras Say." Hence the mockery of a graph that would offer pessimistic interpretations regardless of the facts, as well as the ironic tone couching those supposedly dire complaints about athletics and the weather. Overblown anxieties about the state of the nation were clearly ripe for satire in 1963, as were the kinds of arguments typically mustered on their behalf: misleading statistics that failed to add up and appeals to national chauvinism that were strained at best. In short, this snapshot from *Private Eye* makes clear that discussions about national decline were prevalent in British culture in the early 1960s, but its skepticism toward the form and content of those discussions suggests that something more was at work than merely the unproblematic reflection of obvious realities.

This lecture suggests another way of thinking about Britain's "decline" in the early 1960s. The focus falls on another document published the same year as that special edition of *Private Eye*, the "Suicide of a Nation?" number of *Encounter* magazine, in July 1963.[2] That issue, edited by Arthur Koestler and featuring some of Britain's most well-known intellectuals, advanced a powerful critique of British society and politics, one that has since enjoyed influence through multiple reincarnations: first as a stand-alone volume published in 1963, and most recently as a Vintage paperback published in 1994.[3] Moreover, because of its historical significance as part of the national political culture, "Suicide of a Nation?" has also come to figure as a touchstone in historiographical debates about Britain's decline.[4] A re-reading of this central text in the literature of decline will show that the discourse of decline in this period consisted of a malleable set of assumptions and anxieties that could be harnessed to competing—indeed, contradictory—ends. In this light, decline appears neither an obvious fact nor a shared experience, and it may be better understood as a rhetorical weapon deployed by advocates of rival positions in the cultural politics of postwar Britain.[5]

NATIONAL "DECLINE" HAS LONG FIGURED AT THE CENTER of historical accounts of twentieth-century Britain. A slippery concept, it has been invoked to refer to everything from a loss of influence in global politics to the dismal fate of the English gentleman.[6] Most commonly, however, Britain's decline refers to the diminution of national economic performance, the sense stated most clearly in the opening sentence of Martin Wiener's influential *English Culture and the Decline of the Industrial Spirit* (1981): "The leading problem of modern British history is the explanation of economic decline."[7]

In the past two decades, however, historians have challenged the concept of economic decline on a number of fronts. These challenges may be divided into two broad groups, the atheistic and the agnostic: the former denies the fact of economic decline, whereas the latter attempts to direct attention toward alternative developments.[8] The atheistic critique stands at the opposite pole from Wiener in its denial of the existence of economic decline, a denial that derives from the distinction between relative economic decline (which may have happened) and absolute economic decline (which did not).[9] Once that distinction is made, and the British economy is not thought of as having declined straightforwardly, then discussions of decline cannot be explained as merely the cultural articulation of an economic fact. Jim Tomlinson has thus shown that the invocation of decline emerged in response not to economic trends but out of political debate, and David Edgerton has recently published a "post-declinist" history of twentieth-century Britain that treats decline as a cultural myth rather than an economic reality.[10] The agnostic critique, by contrast, reserves judgment on the question of the reality of economic decline, aiming instead to displace that narrative from its central position in the historiography. Harold Perkin's social history, for instance, resists a characterization of the twentieth century that would de-emphasize the fact of rising living standards enjoyed by the majority of the population, while Lawrence Black and Hugh Pemberton have recently (and reasonably) suggested that the focus on decline be set aside in favor of alternative—and less muddled—terms of analysis.[11]

Whatever the verdict of even the most polarized historians on the factual matter of economic decline, it is difficult to dispute the agnostic contention that decline is merely one concept among many that might be selected to structure accounts of recent British history. Given the availability of competing developments, the question becomes why the historian should adopt a narrative of decline over any other. One justification might be the claim that it was the perceived experience of the historical subjects—that despite whatever numbers revisionist historians might cobble together, Britons believed themselves to be living through a period of decline, and so an experience central to twentieth-century history should retain a position central in twentieth-century historiography. Wiener, for instance, has responded to skeptics on the reality of decline by arguing, "It is as if all of the people who have talked about decline in twentieth-century Britain are suffering from false consciousness, a kind of mass delusion. As in anything else, one should generally look for a more straightforward explanation."[12] That more straightforward explanation, Wiener was suggesting, would be the shared recognition of real economic problems. Yet upon closer examination, the evidence testifying to the experience of decline is no more coherent than that attesting to the fact of the matter.

It will come as no surprise that as the world wars receded and the Cold War got heated, Britain struggled to find its feet internationally. The outlines of this story are familiar: after the war, the United States terminated lend-lease and begrudgingly granted Britain an emergency loan, and shortly thereafter the Americans assumed the burdens of communist containment and European development through the Truman Doctrine and the Marshall Plan. Clement Attlee's Labour government, meanwhile, took the decision to develop an atomic bomb while withdrawing from India, abandoning Palestine, nationalizing industry, and extending the welfare state. The trajectory of this story continues into the 1950s with Winston Churchill's disappointed efforts to play the honest broker among equals vis-à-vis the United States and the Soviet Union, Anthony Eden's disastrous intervention at Suez, and Harold Macmillan's acceptance of the transformation of the Empire into the Commonwealth.

Despite these developments, however, evidence at both the popular and elite levels resists falling into a simple narrative of steady decline. In 1951 the planners of the Festival of Britain promoted a modern, optimistic, and scientific vision of Britain, and in 1953 the coronation of Queen Elizabeth II provided an occasion for celebrating continuing—indeed, renewed—national greatness.[13] Even after Suez, many Britons remained proud of their country's international stature, particularly its position as first among equals in Europe. Kenneth Morgan points out that Moscow continued to behave publicly as though Britain remained a military and industrial power, and even the humiliation of Suez did not prevent the Conservative Party from cruising to re-election less than three years later. Tory Britain was affluent Britain, as memorialized in Macmillan's famous remark on the stump, "You've never had it so good."[14] In short, while developments overseas helped create a context in which discussions of decline would eventually flourish, they did not automatically generate those discussions in and of themselves.

If not the direct result of economic or international experience, how did decline become so prominent in public discourse by the dawn of the 1960s? It is necessary here to distinguish between three concepts: declinism, economic decline, and national decline. "Declinism" refers to the articulation of cultural anxieties related to Britain's shifting economic and international status—it is an historian's word for a cultural phenomenon, and another way of referring to the same idea would be to put *decline* in quotation marks ("decline"). "National decline" predated the post-war decades and surfaced in any number of debates and discussions, making it at once a more tenacious and amorphous concept. But "economic decline" has a more discrete history: born after the war, it did not figure prominently in political discussion until the end of the 1950s.

Ironically, the same decade that saw the pleasures of affluence supplant the experience of austerity also saw economic decline emerge as a topic of concern. Tomlinson has shown that this emergence was made possible by a combination of factors, including the availability of statistics for comparing the economic performance of nations as well as a shift in the assessment of economic performance from the rate of unemployment to the rate of growth.[15] While these developments rendered economic decline thinkable in ways that it had not been before, what initially pressed the issue to the fore was the political leverage it offered to the out-of-power Labour Party. Labour embraced the rhetoric of declinism after its defeat at the polls in 1959, finally finding its feet by lambasting the Tories for their hidebound policies and by promising to reverse Britain's decline through technological modernization. The governing Conservatives were understandably more reluctant to adopt a narrative of decline, but when they embraced the pursuit of accelerated growth, they implicitly agreed that it had thus far been insufficient. By 1961, then, and for very different reasons, both parties had embraced the politics of decline, as testified to by the government's establishment of the National Economic Development Office and the opposition's policy document *Signposts for the Sixties*. In the general election of 1964, Labour and the Conservatives fought over the mantle of modernization, which promised to offset economic decline.[16]

To prove politically useful, however, decline had to be plausible as well as thinkable. Its plausibility resulted from the grafting of these new concerns about economic decline onto existing anxieties about national prestige. Relative economic decline was thus presented as evidence of more profound problems, and the two concepts became conflated into a single phenomenon: national decline. Between the disastrous intervention at Suez in 1956 and Labour's victory in 1964, laments of this malaise flourished among analysts and commentators, in Penguin's "What's Wrong with Britain?" series, Andrew Shonfield's *British Economic Policy since the War* (1958), Michael Shanks's *Stagnant Society* (1961), Bryan Magee's *New Radicalism* (1962), Anthony Sampson's *Anatomy of Britain* (1962), and Perry Anderson's "Origins of the Present Crisis" (1964).[17] These writers had no doubt that Britain faced a grave crisis, but they ranged so widely in their diagnoses and prescriptions that they can hardly be said to have been discussing the same thing at all. The idea of decline proved compelling in part because it could be yoked to a range of positions, from Shonfield's critique of international economic overstretch to Shanks's critique of Shonfield. The common ground in each case was that *something* was wrong with Britain, a lament so hackneyed that it came in for ridicule from *Private Eye* in 1963.[18] The declinist craze peaked by the mid-1960s, but not before it had made an indelible mark on public debate.[19]

The prescriptions that emerged to combat this newfound decline frequently entailed a liberal dose of technocratic modernization. Critics of Tory Britain presented national decline as the result of hidebound institutions and practices, so reversing it would require that existing institutions, such as universities and industries, be brought into line with the latest scientific developments. A widespread commitment to science and technology was characteristic of the period, surfacing in discussions of university education, economic practices, scholarly methodologies, and national politics. These arguments reflected a consensus on the desirability of scientific solutions even as they insisted upon the marginalized status of science in contemporary Britain—a curious spiral of self-flagellation that secured prominent attention for increasingly familiar laments about Britain's lack of esteem for science. In fact, however, that esteem spanned the political spectrum, from Harold Wilson's well-known embrace of the "white heat" of the scientific revolution to Harold Macmillan's less-familiar program of economic modernization. At the same time, initiatives designed to harness science and technology flourished, from the opening of Churchill College, Cambridge (inspired by the Massachusetts Institute of Technology), in 1960, to the enthusiastic support of science education in the Robbins Report of 1963.[20] In short, as anxieties about decline gained prominence in the early 1960s, politicians and commentators rushed forward with proposals to reverse its course by embracing science and technology.[21] That program, and the assumptions that underlay it, were most clearly on display in a special number of *Encounter* in July 1963.

AMID THESE ONGOING DISCUSSIONS ABOUT THE CRISIS of decline and the need for modernization, the Hungarian-émigré-turned-British-man-of-letters Arthur Koestler proposed an issue of *Encounter* devoted to the subject of the state of England. *Encounter,* the well-heeled monthly of politics and culture (still several years from the revelation that it was secretly funded by the CIA), promised to be the ideal forum to address the issue, and its editors, Stephen Spender and Melvin Lasky, invited Koestler to edit the issue himself.[22] He asked some of Britain's most prominent commentators to discuss the state of England, and those taking him up on the offer included Cyril Connolly, Malcolm Muggeridge, Michael Shanks, Andrew Shonfield, and John Vaizey. They were joined by an array of writers, journalists, dons, and members of both houses of Parliament. These prestigious contributors combined to produce an influential polemic against British society, one that offers an ideal point of entry through which to analyze the historical phenomenon—and the historiographical legacy—of the declinism that was coursing through British culture and politics in the early 1960s.[23]

"Suicide of a Nation?" advanced a searing critique of contemporary Britain. Koestler divided the essays into three main parts: "Cold Class War," "Island & Mainland," and "Towards a New Society?" The question marks at the end of the volume title and the third section were significant: Britain's "suicide" may have been imminent, but it was not inevitable; and the "new society" might be elusive, but it was still within reach. As the volume unfolded, it quickly became clear that the responsibility for the crisis lay on both Right and Left: the Right because the political establishment remained staffed by antiquated gentleman, and the Left because Britain's economy was hobbled by work-averse, communist-infested trade unions. Instead of a meritocracy, Britain was a "mediocracy," and rather than being run by professionals and experts, it was being run into the ground by amateurs and class warriors.[24] The result was that Britain's share of world trade had plummeted since 1951, and its volume of exports and industrial production were not rising as quickly as those of select European peers.[25] The essays demanded that education, industry, and government be modernized by purging them of the dilettantes who bore responsibility for these failures and replacing them with experts equipped with training and instincts more appropriate to the modern world.[26] The British educational system, riddled with problems of caste and class, was subjected to particularly harsh criticism, but therein also lay hope for a new society that would turn its back on the amateurism and class warfare of the present in order to foster a new elite of entrepreneurial professionals in the future.[27] "Suicide of a Nation?" amounted to a liberal critique of both Left and Right in contemporary Britain, and it endorsed instead a more modern, scientific, technological, and professional society.

In his introductory and concluding essays, Koestler articulated these arguments with particular zeal. Defining the terms of analysis

from the outset, he insisted that Britain's decline was economic, not
imperial, and that its causes were cultural, not structural. He had
chosen the term "suicide" because, far from succumbing to the inevitable adjustments of a former imperial power, Britain was dying
by its own hand: "What ails Britain is not the loss of Empire, but the
loss of incentive."[28] Britain's elites had sat idly by as the nation's economic productivity came to be surpassed by America in the 1880s,
Canada before the First World War, and much of Western Europe after 1945. Where other observers might have acknowledged Britain's
increasing economic output and material abundance, Koestler saw
only dire straits: "We fail to realize the full extent of the country's
economic decline in the long-term perspective over the last century,
and its alarming acceleration in the course of the last few years."[29]
The trends, the culprits, and the prescriptions were all plain, and
the only remaining question was whether Britain would prove willing to take the necessary steps to arrest its own ongoing decline.
The polemical intention behind "Suicide of a Nation?" was to send
Britain down that path willy-nilly.

Muggeridge expressed his arguments every bit as forcefully as
Koestler. He began by painting a grim portrait of a country in decay: "Each time I return to England from abroad the country seems
a little more run down than when I went away; its streets a little
shabbier, its railway carriages and restaurants a little dingier; the
editorial pretensions of its newspapers a little emptier, and the
vainglorious rhetoric of its politicians a little more fatuous."[30] The
gentlemanly Prime Minister, Harold Macmillan, was an absurdity, a
"decomposing" figure of the "flavour of moth balls," who "conveyed
the impression of an ageing and eccentric clergyman who had been
induced to play the part of a Prime Minister . . . by a village amateur
dramatic society."[31] Yet Macmillan was the leader mid-twentieth-
century Britain deserved, "antique," "meandering," and "aimless."[32]
He resembled that most inept of leaders, Don Quixote, his manners
and instincts out of place in the world in which he found himself:
"As in Cervantes' masterpiece," Muggeridge explained, "one feels
today that things are out of sync."[33] A nation in decay, shoddy next
to its international peers, incompetently run by outmoded amateurs—small wonder that the historian Dominic Sandbrook, in his
recent history of the 1960s, brackets Muggeridge and Koestler as
representatives of the "withering attack" unleashed by "Suicide of a
Nation?" on the backwardness of contemporary Britain.[34]

Despite their similarities of tone and structure, however, Koestler
and Muggeridge were actually discussing very different things. The
structures of their critiques were broadly similar: the nation's politi-

cal leaders were outmoded incompetents who were not up to the job of running a great country, with the result that Britain was forced to endure a humiliating fall in its world position. Yet their actual assessments of Britain's decline—when it began, what it entailed, and what could correct it—stood completely in opposition to each other. Where Koestler saw a nation that had frittered away the esteem and position it had enjoyed as recently as 1945, Muggeridge saw a nation that had become poorer and weaker under every government since 1916.[35] Where Koestler saw an economy in a state of paralysis, Muggeridge saw a nation spiritually impoverished by material affluence.[36] Where Koestler prioritized educational reform to ensure equal opportunity, Muggeridge recoiled against the prospect of comprehensive schools.[37] And where Koestler endorsed a program of scientific and technological modernization, Muggeridge reserved his sharpest barbs for New Towns, television aerials, and the mindless worship of mathematics and science.[38] To Koestler, national decline was a recent economic crisis that modern technology could reverse; to Muggeridge, however, national decline was an ongoing moral crisis that those very measures would only exacerbate.

Koestler certainly recognized the gulf separating Muggeridge from himself, and he was not about to allow his party to be spoiled by this unruly guest. He branded Muggeridge's contribution an "antribution," an unhelpful distraction from the matter at hand, and bracketed it apart from the rest of the issue in a "Prelude" (subtitled "Blind Man's Buff").[39] He dismissed Muggeridge's analysis as "a lashing-out at all and sundry with impartial gusto," and explained that he included it only to illustrate the misguided thinking that was itself part of the problem in contemporary Britain.[40] Koestler's severe treatment of Muggeridge makes clear that he intended "Suicide of a Nation?" to be something other than a dispassionate rumination on the state of England, and that its ostensible analysis of a nation in decline actually advanced a more substantive program of technocratic modernization. Since Muggeridge disagreed fundamentally with the desirability of that program, his acceptance of a broad narrative of decline counted for little in Koestler's eyes—and he was dealt with accordingly.

The relative dispensability of decline, especially when compared to the much more important commitment to technocratic modernization, becomes even plainer in Koestler's treatment of Henry Fairlie's contribution. The only other dissenting voice in the issue, Fairlie rejected calls for using managerial expertise to combat economic decline. Instead of experts and management, he valued individualism and liberty—both of which he viewed as threatened by programs that traveled under seemingly benign labels such as "dyna-mism," "efficiency," and "greatness."[41] In the guise of attacks upon amateurs, Fairlie detected the politics of managers—and he knew another word for these managers: "The voice of the *manager* then, now the voice of the *technocrat*, proclaiming, as does every opponent of free institutions, that freed from the necessity to consult ordi-nary people, he could run their lives for them far more efficiently and beneficently than they can themselves. It is time that, against their evil doctrine, we re-asserted our right to be inefficient."[42] An unlikely rallying cry at any time, the "right to be inefficient" struck an especially discordant note at the height of the technocratic mo-ment, one not echoed elsewhere in the volume.

Fairlie differed from Muggeridge by rejecting the very concept of decline, but this fundamental difference regarding the state of England did not derail Koestler's parallel treatment of them both. As with Muggeridge, Koestler branded Fairlie's contribution an "an-tribution," and he consigned it to the same ignominious "Prelude." Koestler's decision to group both dissenters together, and to place them at the beginning of the issue, represented an effort to depict their perspectives as typical of the views finally being left behind by more realistic critiques.[43] Koestler cast Fairlie's rejection of declinist hysteria as "a proud, sulky retreat from the crowd's ignoble strife," and he explained that Fairlie and Muggeridge signified "the oppo-site poles in between which we must try to wend our way."[44] In his concluding postscript, Koestler seemed almost driven to distraction by Fairlie's dissonant essay: he cited Fairlie no less than four times, nearly apologizing the last time ("I hate picking again at Mr. Fair-lie, but . . .").[45] Fairlie disputed so many of Koestler's fundamental premises—about the need for modernization, the example of the French, the significance of social class—that his argument emerged as the antithesis to that of the volume itself. Yet despite those fun-damental differences, Koestler presented Fairlie as the counterpart to Muggeridge: one depicted a nation in decline, the other rejected a narrative of decline, and together they figured as extremes to be avoided on the path being beaten toward Britain's shiny new future.

THE EMERGENCE OF DECLINE AS A POLITICAL ISSUE rendered the concept available to Malcolm Muggeridge and his critique of utili-tarian materialism no less than to Koestler and his celebration of technocratic modernization. While at first glance the prominence of decline in both accounts might be thought to point to a shared experience of a real phenomenon, the range of experiences co-existing within that category suggests that decline is better understood less as a shared *experience* than as a shared *resource*.

This lecture began with an agnostic reluctance to prioritize narratives of economic decline, but it has worked its way toward a position more like the atheistic denial of the existence of any phenomenon answering to decline at all. That is, while some defenders of decline have answered challenges to the fact of economic decline by pointing to the persistence of discussions about it, the slippery case for decline in "Suicide of a Nation?" has rendered the content of those discussions similarly difficult to pin down. Explaining and analyzing those discussions—that is, explaining and analyzing declinism—thus emerges as a historical problem in its own right, and the distinction between the economic phenomenon (which may or may not have happened) and the cultural discussion (which undeniably did happen) is significant because it demands that the latter be explained without being reduced to the inevitable expression of the former. One ironic result of this analysis is that the agnostic ambition to direct attention away from decline has led to the need to pay continuing attention to the phenomenon of declinism.

How, then, has declinism—that is, how have discussions and arguments about decline—functioned in British history, politics, and culture? This essay has suggested one answer to that important question. In their arguments about British society and culture in "Suicide of a Nation?" both Arthur Koestler and Malcolm Muggeridge articulated and harnessed broader anxieties about national decline. The fact that two such very different critiques may both be understood to fall under the rubric of "decline" testifies not to their derivation from shared experiences, but rather to the problems inherent in a concept stretched so thin as to include them both. Historians looking back should not attempt to shoehorn those arguments into a single category, but rather to rummage around inside that capacious category itself. In this analysis, "decline" functions not as a common response to a real economic development, but as a common label available to be applied to diverse experiences, arguments, and agendas. It functions, that is, as a powerful weapon, one put to diverse—even competing—ends in the cultural politics of modern Britain.

Fall Semester 2005

I am grateful to Wm. Roger Louis, and to Christine Johnson, Steven Miles, Nancy Reynolds, Corinna Treitel, Lori Watt, and Matt Wisnioski, for their comments on an earlier draft of this lecture.

1. Christopher Booker et al., *Private Eye's Romantic England: The Last Days of Macmilian* [*sic*] (London, 1963), p. 31.

2. Arthur Koestler et al., "Suicide of a Nation?" *Encounter*, July 1963.

3. Koestler, ed., *Suicide of a Nation? An Enquiry into the State of Britain Today* (London, 1963; Vintage, 1994).

4. Martin Wiener, *English Culture and the Decline of the Industrial Spirit, 1850–1980* (1981; Cambridge, 2004), p. xiii; Jim Tomlinson, *The Politics of Decline: Understanding Post-War Britain* (Harlow, 2001), pp. 23–25; David Edgerton, *Warfare State: Britain, 1920–1970* (Cambridge, 2005), pp. 191–92, 203.

5. My thinking about decline (as well as my title) follows David Hollinger's analysis of science in "Science as a Weapon in Kulturkämpfe in the United States during and after World War II," *Isis*, 86 (1995), pp. 440–54; my focus on cultural politics builds on the analysis of Ian Budge, "Relative Decline as a Political Issue: Ideological Motivations of the Politico-Economic Debate in Post-War Britain," *Contemporary Record*, 7 (Summer 1993), pp. 1–23, and Tomlinson, *Politics of Decline*.

6. See A. N. Wilson, *After the Victorians: The Decline of Britain in the World* (New York, 2005); Marcus Collins, "The Fall of the English Gentleman: The National Character in Decline, c. 1918–1970," *Historical Research*, 75 (Feb. 2002), pp. 90–111. On the history, meanings, and realities of the concept, see Peter Clarke and Clive Trebilcock, eds., *Understanding Decline: Perceptions and Realities of British Economic Performance* (Cambridge, 1997).

7. Wiener, *English Culture and Decline*, p. 3.

8. For a survey of the debate, see Richard English and Michael Kenny, eds., *Rethinking British Decline* (London, 2000), especially the introductory chapter by Andrew Gamble and the concluding assessment by English and Kenny.

9. Barry Supple makes the distinction between relative and absolute decline clear: "Relative decline and absolute growth can and do co-exist. British national income has certainly grown; but over the last quarter century or so that of other leading economies has grown faster" (Supple, "Fear of Failing: Economic History and the Decline of Britain," in Clarke and Trebilcock, eds., *Understanding Decline*, p. 10).

10. Tomlinson, *Politics of Decline*; Edgerton, *Warfare State*.

11. Harold Perkin, *The Rise of Professional Society: England since 1880* (London, 1989); Lawrence Black and Hugh Pemberton, eds., *An Affluent Society? Britain's Post-War "Golden Age" Revisited* (Aldershot, 2004), especially Black and Pemberton, "Introduction: The Uses (and Abuses) of Affluence," pp. 1–13.

12. Interview with Wiener in English and Kenny, eds., *Rethinking British Decline*, pp. 25–36, quotation on p. 31.

13. Becky Conekin, *"The Autobiography of a Nation": The 1951 Festival of Britain* (New York, 2003). Ross McKibbin links the festival and the coronation in *Classes and Cultures: England, 1918–1951* (New York, 1998), p. 535.

14. Kenneth Morgan, *The People's Peace: British History, 1945–1989* (New York, 1990). Macmillan is popularly believed to have uttered this phrase in response to a heckler, but Morgan points out that he was actually issuing a warning about inflation (p. 176).

15. This paragraph paraphrases the arguments of Jim Tomlinson, "Inventing 'Decline': The Falling Behind of the British Economy in the Post-War Years," *Economic History Review*, 49 (1996), pp. 731–57.

16. See also Jim Tomlinson, "Conservative Modernization, 1960–64: Too Little, Too Late?" *Contemporary British History*, 11 (Autumn 1997), pp. 18–38.

17. Andrew Shonfield, *British Economic Policy since the War* (Baltimore, 1958); Michael Shanks, *The Stagnant Society: A Warning* (Baltimore, 1961); Bryan Magee, *The New Radicalism* (New York, 1962); Anthony Sampson, *Anatomy of Britain* (London, 1962); Perry Anderson, "Origins of the Present Crisis," *New Left Review*, no. 23 (Jan.–Feb. 1964), pp. 26–53. Tomlinson discusses the "culture of decline" in *Politics of Decline*, pp. 21–26.

18. Booker et al., *Private Eye's Romantic England*, p. 31. The vogue of decline is evident even in the book's subtitle, *The Last Days of Macmilian*, which evokes a comparison between Britain and the Roman Empire.

19. Tomlinson, *Politics of Decline*, p. 21.

20. Tomlinson, "Conservative Modernization, 1960–64."

21. On the "technocratic moment" of 1959–64, see Edgerton, *Warfare State*, chap. 5.

22. On *Encounter*, see Frances Stonor Saunders, *The Cultural Cold War: The CIA and the World of Arts and Letters* (New York, 2000); Hugh Wilford, "'Unwitting Assets?' British Intellectuals and the Congress for Cultural Freedom," *Twentieth-Century British History*, 11 (2000), pp. 42–60.

23. Wiener, *English Culture and Decline*, p. xiii.

24. Goronwy Rees, "Amateurs and Gentleman, or The Cult of Incompetence," pp. 20–25; Michael Shanks, "The Comforts of Stagnation," pp. 30–38; Andrew Shonfield, "The Plaintive Treble," pp. 39–44; Austen Albu, "Taboo on Expertise," pp. 45–50; Aidan Crawley, "'A Red Under Every Bed?'" pp. 50–55; John Cole, "The Price of Obstinacy: Crises in the Trade Unions," pp. 56–64.

25. These trends were illustrated by a series of charts, pp. 26–29. My intent here is to present, rather than critique, the case for economic decline, but it must be said that these charts are highly selective—and often misleading—indicators of economic performance. For instance, there seems little reason for alarm in the fact that Britain's *share* of world trade decreased as the economies of its competitors developed between 1899 and 1962 (a period when its *volume* of trade continued to increase); a second chart shows that Britain's volume of exports increased significantly between 1954 and 1962, and while those numbers are dwarfed by those of its competitors, those competitors are made to consist not of comparable European states but rather of the conglomerations of the EEC and EFTA; and the more rapidly rising indices of industrial production of select European rivals neglects to take into account the fact that when the index was pegged in 1953, the recovering post-war economies of continental Europe were beginning from a point considerably behind that of Britain. What these charts do not reveal, for instance, is the not insignificant fact that in 1963 absolute standards of living in Britain remained the highest in Europe (Tomlinson, "Inventing 'Decline,'" p. 753). The economic case against decline is presented in more detail, and with far greater dexterity than I can manage, in Tomlinson, "Inventing 'Decline'"; Clarke and Trebilcock, eds., *Understanding Decline*; and David Edgerton, *Science, Technology, and the British Industrial "Decline," 1870–1970* (Cambridge, 1996).

26. These points are especially prominent in the two contributions by Koestler: "Introduction: The Lion and the Ostrich," pp. 5–8, and "Postscript: The Manager and the Muses," pp. 113–17.

27. Elizabeth Young, "Against the Stream," pp. 105–07; John Vaizey, "The Tragedy of Being Clever," pp. 107–10.

28. Koestler, "Introduction," p. 8.

29. Ibid., p. 7.

30. Malcolm Muggeridge, "England, Whose England?" p. 14.
31. Ibid.
32. Ibid.
33. Ibid., p. 15.
34. Dominic Sandbrook, *Never Had It So Good: A History of Britain from Suez to the Beatles* (London, 2005), p. 509.
35. Koestler, "Introduction," p. 6; Muggeridge, "England, Whose England?" p. 14.
36. Koestler, "Introduction," p. 7 (and passim); Muggeridge, "England, Whose England?" p. 17.
37. Koestler, "Postscript," p. 117; Muggeridge, "England, Whose England?" p. 17.
38. Koestler, "Postscript," p. 115; Muggeridge, "England, Whose England?" p. 17.
39. Koestler, "Prelude," p. 9.
40. Ibid.
41. Henry Fairlie, "On the Comforts of Anger," p. 10.
42. Ibid., p. 11; emphasis added.
43. I am grateful to Nancy Reynolds for bringing this point to my attention.
44. Koestler, "Prelude," p. 9.
45. Koestler, "Postscript," pp. 113, 114, 116 (quotation on p. 116).

16

A Glance Back at Fifty Years in the British Book Trade

GRAHAM GREENE

R eaders of *Adventures with Britannia* may be interested to know that I have an odd connection with Texas. My uncle Graham Greene founded the Anglo-Texan Society in 1953. He and a friend were on a train journey, and in their compartment there were a couple of pretty Texan girls. Not knowing how to approach them, they wrote a letter to *The Times*, suggesting the need for Anglo-Texan relations to be strengthened by the formation of a society. This jape got out of hand, and the first function, a barbeque, was attended by 1,500 guests. The society flourished, and arranged for a brass plaque to be erected at the corner of 3 St. James Place in London to mark the location of the Texas Legation in Great Britain during the final years of the Republic of Texas, 1842–45. The plaque, unveiled by Governor Price Daniel, Sr., is now the only monument to the existence of the Anglo-Texan Society.

In this lecture I will give some impressions of my fifty years in the book business through the books with which I have been involved— and also of national and international book-trade politics.

I left Oxford at twenty-one, and within a few weeks found myself flying to Dublin to take up a trainee post as a banker with Guinness and Mahon. My grandfather was Chairman of the holding company in London. This was a privileged start, but I still can't remember how I came to accept this destiny, since throughout my childhood I had

said banking was not for me. During the flight I found myself reading the small ads in the left-wing *New Statesman* (of which I became
Chairman many years later) to see whether I could find a job in
publishing. In due course I returned to London and was called to a
number of interviews. I was almost invariably turned down for being unlikely to want to stay at the lowly rungs of the ladder, where I
thought it proper to start. Though I protested my lack of ambition, I
was not believed. In desperation I consulted my mother (who was a
literary agent) and my stepmother (who was also one). My stepmother
got me an interview with Fredric Warburg of Secker and Warburg.
He agreed to see me in order to tell me that I should stick to banking. He himself came from the Warburg banking family, so this was
not very convincing. My mother suggested that I ask Mr. Warburg a
question about how he had done with a book on the Dead Sea Scrolls
that he had published, perhaps uniquely at that time, in paperback
and hardback simultaneously. This I did, and so he did most of the
talking. This taught me my first lesson about publishers.

Publishers are very vain people who can be irritating to authors,
who feel, rightly in my view, that their publishers should seek the
limelight for them rather than for themselves. Warburg, as far as I
can remember, put me to only one test. He dropped his fountain
pen on the floor and I picked it up. He could see I might be useful, so offered me a job at £5 a week—even in those days a pretty
small salary. However, my wife-to-be was earning £9 a week, and I
had a private income of the princely sum of £4 a week, so we had
£18 a week between us—an income on which one could live fairly
comfortably. Warburg's offer was contingent upon my taking up a
pre-arranged job in New York with the Chemical Corn Exchange
Bank (as it was then called), since he said it would help make me
numerate, which so few publishers are. To this day I list banking in
Ireland, the UK, and the United States as part of my career, so there
is a myth in publishing that I know about business. Later I even became, for nearly twenty years, a non-executive director of Guinness
and Mahon—more to do with my family background than my banking abilities, but it certainly provided me with useful contacts and
some knowledge not shared by my publishing colleagues.

I spent three months at the Chemical Corn Exchange Bank,
mainly in the United Nations branch, where I served Dag Hammarskjöld with foreign currency when he went off to solve the Turkish-
Syrian border crisis. I returned to London to get married in the
Crypt Chapel of the House of Commons, a telegram from Clem
and Vi (Clement Attlee and his wife) in my pocket, and to take up in
January 1958 my job at Secker and Warburg. After six months I got

a raise of 10 shillings a week, and soon thereafter I overheard the directors saying that they might as well make me temporary sales manager (the sales director had resigned on some question of principle) until they could get "someone who was any good." I held the job for four years, until I resigned.

A thumbnail sketch of the firm might be useful because it was a characteristic one of the period. Apart from Fred Warburg there were three other directors, all bachelors: Roger Senhouse, a very great friend of Lytton Strachey and all the Bloomsbury group; B. D. Farrer, formerly Private Secretary to Lord Beaverbrook, the newspaper owner and great friend of Winston Churchill; and John Pattison, a meek man, who came into his own by introducing Angus Wilson, a now mainly forgotten novelist—undeservedly, I believe—to the firm. One must remember we were living in a time when homosexual relations were still a criminal offense, and generally lovers remained in the closet. However, on one occasion Angus Wilson wanted for some reason to take Tony Garrett, who was his companion until his death and whom I still occasionally see, with him to Manchester. I was instructed to make the necessary booking for Angus, and I didn't know whether I should book two single rooms or a double one. I expect I ordered two.

I have often thought that most of my publishing career has been carried out in an atmosphere more akin to that of the nineteenth century and the 1920s and 1930s than to the current period of high tech and conglomerates. At Secker and Warburg, as elsewhere in publishing, we started at around ten and finished at five or five thirty. Lunches were long, preceded by gin and followed by wine and, for some, brandies afterward. David Farrer, for example, would play bridge at the Garrick Club after lunch and return to the office between three and three thirty. Then as now, most senior publishers were Garrick members, and I have no doubt that it was in the Garrick bar that all senior appointments were made. Just before my arrival at Secker and Warburg, Jomo Kenyatta, later the Mau Mau leader—or so the British believed—and the first President of Kenya, came into the office with the typescript of *Facing Mount Kenya*, the first work of anthropology written by an African. Do I rightly recall that he deposited his spear in the umbrella stand?

I was really only the office boy, but I was occasionally given manuscripts to read. I nearly lost my job when I recommended *Lolita* for publication as one of the funniest books I had read. Warburg called me in to castigate me for not pointing out the legal problems that almost certainly would arise from its publication. He had been seared by his experience of criminal prosecution for publishing *The*

Philanderer by Stanley Kauffmann in 1953. It had been seized by the police from Boots the Chemist (a drugstore chain) in the Isle of Man. He had had to endure a long trial. Though he had been allowed by the judge to sit with his counsel rather than in the dock, except when he was taken to the cells while the jury was considering its verdict, he had not, despite his acquittal, got over the experience. Secker and Warburg was a nonetheless brave and adventurous house and published much foreign literature in translation—Thomas Mann, Kafka, and the more controversial Andre Gide and Colette.

I enjoyed my time with Secker but felt my career was not progressing with much speed. I was pleased to be approached by Tom Maschler, who had recently joined Jonathan Cape and was looking for a younger colleague. He demonstrated his renowned negotiating skills and persuaded me to join Cape as a director without any pay increase. I was given lunch—a gentlemanly form of interview—by G. Wren Howard, Jonathan Cape's founding partner. We talked of roses, about which I know little, and he watched to see how I ate my peas. I persuaded them that I needed a two-month interval to make a journey by Land Rover with my wife through Europe, Turkey, Persia, Afghanistan, and India to Kathmandu in Nepal. It was an exciting journey, and in 1962 it was before the hippies spoiled the traditional welcome of the local inhabitants. I remember, as I left Kathmandu, the arrival of the first contingent of the Peace Corps. I knew that the good times had ended. In Kathmandu I met an American writer who was keen to write a biography of Raymond Chandler. My mother, as a literary agent, had represented him and indeed had intended to marry him. It never happened, owing to his death.

I flew back to London to take up my post on a September Friday in Bedford Square, an elegant square in Bloomsbury over which I still look. There I found a handwritten note from Michael Howard, the son of G. Wren Howard, welcoming me to the board and pointing out that it was not customary at Cape for directors to work on a Friday, as they needed reading time. I was introduced to my secretary and shown the engraved writing paper that directors were entitled to use. This showed how seldom directors left the firm, since it would have been expensive to change the paper. I was given a key to the directors' lavatory, which in true revolutionary style I refused to use, and caused much consternation by using the ladies' lavatory, since it was nearer my office than any non-directorial men's. I caused equal trouble by refusing the China tea supplied for directors. Only later did I discover this, when the tea lady confided in me that there was cursing about my Indian tea, since it caused more work when the directors met over afternoon tea. I really preferred

China tea, and later drank thousands of mugs of it when I became much involved in Chinese affairs and the campaign to get China to accede to one of the copyright conventions.

The atmosphere, despite Tom Maschler's and my thrusting personalities, still remained very old fashioned. We did not have to put in individual expense claims, since no gentleman should have to justify himself. We were given round-sum allowances, which some years later were stopped by the unconvinced Inland Revenue. I had no special work allocated to me, though I did get involved in general oversight of sales. An old pro held that staff job at Cape, and he certainly knew more about the nuts and bolts of the trade throughout the British Commonwealth and Empire than I did. I suggested some experiments, and naturally only remember the successes. We were publishing a volume of poetry by Archibald MacLeish, and I thought it ridiculous to be satisfied with the usual printing of 1,000 copies and a sale of around 600, so we printed 2,000. I wrote to every bookseller with any serious literary pretensions.

We sold out, and the experience taught me two lessons. First, attention to the promotion of an individual title was absolutely necessary to any success; and second, the cost of such an exercise was out of all proportion to what could be achieved. Not very comforting for an author. My second experiment was to say that we should print 50,000 copies of Ian Fleming's *On Her Majesty's Secret Service* in 1963 and tell the world that we had done so. This was a great departure for Cape, which was very secretive about print numbers and sales, believing that such figures were confidential to the author and indeed might give an indication of his income and earnings; revealing them might be as much a breach of confidence as revealing his bank balance. The announcement worked, and sales for all James Bond books were immensely greater in future years. Ian Fleming himself took a great interest in promotion and once said to me that he thought his sales turnover was equivalent to that of a small factory. Every new book was sent to President Kennedy with a personal note. The President's love of the Bond books was widely publicized. Even now I have a golden head of Ian Fleming in my house to remind me and my family that the earnings from publishing usually come from popular books rather than the more literary ones that appeal to us.

With nothing specific to do, I came up with a few new ideas. I wrote a series of phrase books, which were primarily mini-dictionaries. I felt like Dr. Johnson, and it amused my friends that my lack of knowledge about popular culture and music was demonstrated by my including in the dictionaries the waltz rather than the jive, which was then the fashionable dance. I put some of our more famous works of history—by authors such as J. E. Neale, C. V. Wedgwood, and Duff Cooper, all of whom I had read at school and Oxford—into inexpensive paperbacks. I had no idea how to implement my ideas because no one had told me how things worked. It was soon clear to me that a director could order almost anything. Indeed, he was given special yellow paper on which to issue internal instructions—known to the staff as "yellow perils." Directors met every morning around ten thirty to open the post and exchange views. This turned out to be a form of decision taking. The Company Secretary would come in, but was not asked to sit until I pointed out that he had heart trouble and should probably be asked to do so. A few weeks after my arrival I got a note from Michael Howard suggesting that I visit a number of our overseas customers (40 percent of our trade was export). He said that his father was too old to do so anymore, he was disinclined to go, and Tom Maschler was unsuitable, for reasons not explained.

I hadn't the foggiest idea how to start planning such a trip but was jogged into action by the Chairman's saying he would like to discuss my itinerary, since he probably knew most of the places I was planning to visit. I had no plans but hastily importuned the sales manager into telling me where I should go. I planned a ten-week tour that took in Toronto, Ottawa, Vancouver, Delhi, Bombay, Calcutta, virtually the whole of New Zealand, and all the capitals of Australia, which the Chairman thought was rather overdoing it. He told me he had enjoyed his publishing journeys best in the time of flying boats and, in particular, landing in Rangoon for tea.

In Singapore I had lunch with Han Suyin, the author of *A Many Splendored Thing*, and she complained by letter to the Chairman that I was seen with a man who had libeled her in a novel. Since the novel was by our agent, my association was hardly surprising. My friendship with Han Suyin has survived, and now nearly ninety, she has made me Chairman of the Han Suyin Foundation and the controller of her copyrights.

While on this journey, I received a letter asking me about the prospects for a few lines of verse. I replied that they would make a best-selling book if written by the Duke of Edinburgh or a Beatle. When I returned, I found that the author was John Lennon, and *In His Own Write* became an enormous seller. We had a party for the Beatles in Bedford Square and had not been able to make up our minds whether it would be good to inform the police about it. We feared the police would not resist telling their teenage children. At a Foyles Literary Luncheon for John Lennon, I found that a waiter had cut out the piece of tablecloth under his plate.

My travels became regular. I was once accused justifiably by an English bookseller that I probably knew the streets of Adelaide better than those of Manchester. Miss King of the Book Nook in a small town in New Zealand, where the turnover was about as big in eggs as in books, once said I was a more satisfactory regular visitor than Sir Stanley Unwin, who was famed in publishing for his frequent journeys because he always used a card index as a crib. I blushed: I had taken my own index card out of my pocket before entering the bookshop.

In 1968, I paid my first visit to Japan, as part of a delegation of publishers. I learned the truth of the Bernard Shaw saying that England and America are two countries separated by a common language. (Incidentally, I am now an executor of Shaw's estate.) When Andre Deutsch was asked by a distinguished Japanese publisher where the English would like to go after dinner, he said "a gay bar." We were dropped off by our chauffeur-driven cars in a sleazy part of Tokyo. I asked our host whether we were going to his favorite bar. He went pale, and just at that moment we were told to descend into a cellar. I was the first to go, and realized at once that we were being greeted by men dressed in Madam Butterfly costumes. Soon my colleagues, with much embarrassment, also realized where we were. After one drink, we made our excuses and left. "Gay" had not yet reached Britain as a word for "homosexual." I am now a Trustee of the Sainsbury Institute for the Study of Japanese Arts and Culture—one thing leads to another.

From 1973 onward I wrote each year to the Chinese Ambassador, suggesting that a delegation of British publishers should be asked to visit his country. I do not recollect getting an answer to these letters, but in 1978 a telephone call came from the Embassy, asking me to call on the following day. By then I was the President of the Publishers Association, but that did not appear to be the reason. The official who received me immediately asked me to bring a delegation to visit his country under the auspices of the Society for Anglo-Chinese Understanding. This caused a dilemma for me, since the society was a mildly fellow-traveling organization under the chairmanship of my cousin, Felix Greene, who was well known in China. As a resident of the United States, though a British citizen, he had been able, to the horror of many members of Congress, to visit China a number of times when such visits were forbidden to American citizens. He had written a number of books published by Jonathan Cape. I said

I thought the Publishers Association was of sufficient status for the delegation to go under its own auspices. This was unconvincing, since, as I well knew, the Chinese always demanded Chinese sponsors. I stuck to my guns, though, and saw my longed-for visit slipping away. I said to the seemingly intransigent diplomat that they might consider consulting my cousin. This brought a wide smile to his face as he admitted that they had seen Felix Greene earlier that morning. He had said I might make a fuss and that ultimately a publishers' visit was more important than the sponsoring organization. The visit was on. I gathered together a distinguished group.

We did all the things delegates should do. I laid a wreath on Chairman Mao's tomb, but on the wreath was not allowed to use my own wording about his being a great writer rather than the great communist leader. We gave talks to authors and even found some publishers to whom to tell about copyright, of which they had not heard. That led to many exchange visits over the next twenty years and in 1992 to Chinese accession to international copyright. This was a triumph for quiet professional British diplomacy, though undoubtedly the last push came from America and American power.

In 1998, though I had visited China many times—often as Chairman of the Great Britain–China Centre, sponsored by the British Foreign Office—I was invited to lead a publishers' delegation to mark the twentieth anniversary of our first visit. We talked much about piracy, including internal piracy by publishers of other Chinese publishers' rights. One publisher told me the problem was that the penalties for infringement were too light. Foolishly, I used this remark in a speech at another publishing house the next day. The chairman said that during the last year a publisher had been executed for copyright infringement: "Is this a sufficient penalty for you, Mr. Greene?"

It is said that I was the first President of the Publishers Association, since its foundation in 1896, to have a baby while in office. This may have been because I was the youngest President or because I was the only one to acknowledge a child's birth. My son, Alexander, became an important instrument of diplomacy. The early Chinese delegations liked to come to my house in the country. I have a photograph of Alexander in Chinese arms. On our walks, they were astonished that I would join them in picking blackberries myself, and they would ask questions about agriculture that I, as a mere publisher, could not answer.

As a small child, Alexander once came into my study at home to say good night while I was having a meeting with the redoubtable Carmen Callil of Virago—the great feminist publisher—and on

meeting her he immediately burst into tears. Grown men are said
to have done the same. Alexander is now in publishing with Time
Warner.

ONE OF THE MOST DIFFICULT BUT REWARDING AUTHORS to work
with was Patrick White, the Nobel Prize winner. He left his previous
publisher, quite unfairly I thought, because it had submitted a book
for a prize. I was told by his agent that he was choosing a new publisher and that we were on the list. I was informed that he wanted a
publisher with a proper Australian publishing house. We had an old
distribution company of which I was chairman. It published only a
very few books, so I set up a Jonathan Cape Australia company in
the hope that it would be sufficient for Patrick White. It certainly
wasn't what he wanted. He was interested only in a distinguished
London name.

On a visit to Sydney, I was invited to dinner at White's home
and was unaware that many people traveled "interstate," as out of
state was known, in order to avoid his dinners, cooked with much
acrimony with his friend Manoly Lascaris. My first faux pas on arrival was to say that I had been dropped off by Lady Drysdale, the
widow of the great painter Russell Drysdale. Patrick hated her, as
he did most people. But then I was lucky. I saw a woman in a corner
whom I had not seen for ten years but fortunately recognized as a
bookseller—Patrick's favorite, I discovered. We fell into each other's
arms. This seemed to demonstrate a knowledge of the Australian
scene and perhaps wiped out the silly idea, inspired by his London
agent, of an Australian publishing house.

The dinner proceeded with endless quarrels between Patrick
and Manoly and numerous attacks on Australian literary figures of
whom I generally had not heard. The next day I sent a telegram
back to the office to say we certainly had not won the competition to
get White on our list. Within minutes of dispatching the telegram, I
heard from White's agent, who had not been invited to the dinner,
that he had heard what a success it had been. Later I was told that
White had decided to join us. I never felt entirely comfortable with
him, but I admired his books and sometimes enjoyed his company.

On one visit I saw Patrick on my first day, and he told me that he
had finished a novel but that I should not be excited, since he had
put it into his bank, as he always did. He liked to mull it over for
many years. On my last day in Sydney, I suddenly thought I would
look a real fool if I could not get hold of this typescript. I rang Patrick and said it occurred to me that it might save him the cost of
postage if I collected the typescript on the way to the airport and

carried it to London for him. He thought this was a good idea, and he did not appear to realize how much more than any postage my taxi had cost as a result of this deviation from the road to the airport. During the flight I read the novel with great admiration, but some of my joy was reduced by its being typed single space on both sides of the page. On my return to Bedford Square, I bravely wrote to say how much I liked the book but really felt that now he was a Nobel Prize winner he could be more considerate to the eyes of his publishers. I can't remember any comment from him.

I remember one notable dinner with Patrick. He was in London, and I believed he was so interested in cooking that I invited him to dinner with Elizabeth David, the woman who almost single-handedly turned Britain into a food-loving nation in the 1950s and 1960s. They had, I think, just known each other in Cairo during the war. The other guests were David and Deborah Owen. David was later to be Foreign Secretary and leader of the Social Democratic Party. The dinner was held in the Albany, the home of many writers and politicians over the last two hundred years and where I still live, and have lived on and off, having been banished for some years for having children, which is strictly prohibited by its trustees. On that evening the power failed, and we ate in darkness. I can't remember about the food—the point of the dinner—but the evening was a great success. Adversity brings out the best in the British.

Do those at the head of publishing houses read? I sometimes doubt it. Jonathan Cape, according to Dame Veronica Wedgwood, the distinguished historian, "loved books but in a curious way that it is difficult to analyze: those he had on his own shelves looked as though they had never been used. He had a great respect for literature rather than a familiarity and feeling for it. He thought he knew about books, but he knew about them from a point of view of the traveler on the road, not that of the bookman. He liked the outside of books, he was interested in the standards of production, but I don't think he cared for the inside very much. He had a marvelous contempt for a badly produced book. He would take a shoddily bound volume and with three vicious jerks shake it clean out of its case. He liked knowing the pecking order of authors, and had acquired a considerable surface knowledge of literature, knowing the titles of 'what sold.'"

Sir Arthur Bryant, the popular historian and a neighbor of mine in the country, used to come to dinner with his mistress, and always started the evening by saying, "Greene, do you know why you will never be a great publisher? It is because you read. My publisher [Sir William Collins] doesn't read and spends all the time on the telephone selling my books."

In the late 1960s, I became increasingly aware that the bigger publishers had an advantage over a small house like Cape. There were economies of scale in distribution and back-office costs, so I cast around for a novel form of establishing a group without destroying editorial independence. I held discussions with Heinemann, owner of Secker and Warburg, about bringing it into a partnership; at the same time I was continuing long-running talks with Chatto and Windus. Heinemann eventually decided that Secker and Warburg, albeit loss making, was too distinguished to let go. Chatto joined us in 1969. Some could not see the point financially of a union that placed the emphasis on editorial independence, but the authors appreciated it. Jennifer Couroucli wrote some verses that began:

> Chatto's merging with Jonathan Cape—
> Better to marry than burn,
> Better to wed than to give in to rape
> By a tempting Big Business concern.
> For richer, not poorer, for better, not worse,
> Till death do us part; may you publish our verse.

The Bodley Head and Virago later joined the group on the same unusual basis, maintaining their editorial independence at least as far as authors and the public were concerned. My father, having retired from the Director-Generalship of the BBC, was non-executive Chairman of the Bodley Head, so I was able to say he had followed in my footsteps. On his deathbed I discovered that he had recommended Jeffrey Archer's first book, *Not a Penny More, Not a Penny Less,* to the Bodley Head but had not got his way. This I was, as Chairman of the group that included Bodley Head, able to verify from the files. Later I was to buy the rights, after fifteen publishers had turned it down, for such a modest advance (£3,500) that Jeffrey Archer walks the other way when he sees me. Benefactors are never popular. He behaved as badly to us as he has done everywhere since. While I was lunching with Archer one day in his London penthouse, he showed me a bookcase and asked me what all the books had in common. I recognized them as all being by Nobel Prize winners. "One day my books will join them," Archer said.

Freedom to publish was one of my special causes, and I spent much time advising my colleagues on libel, which is a far greater problem in Britain than in America. Damages could be large, and the cost in sales of having to withdraw a book, if a complaint was made, was enormous. I built up a lot of experience and gained the reputation of being brave. I am not a lawyer but somehow got a useful feel for who would and who would not sue. Judgments about what is in good taste are even harder to gauge and, of course, change with the times. I tried unsuccessfully to persuade Baron Philippe de Rothschild to take out of his memoirs a story about King George VI, when Duke of York, being sent to Paris to learn about sex and being called by the prostitute *"Mon petit jambon d'York,"* but he would not do so, despite his great friendship with the Queen Mother. I said it would be mentioned by every reviewer and cause great pain to the King's widow. No one mentioned it. I was quite wrong.

I did cause pain when lunching one day at Buckingham Palace by treading on the Queen's corgis, which were much the same color as the carpet. She looked furious but did discuss with me a book Chatto was publishing on her horses. I then realized that the extensive corrections made to the proofs were in her handwriting and demonstrated real expertise, which was not available in Chatto's offices.

My biggest legal case arose out of the publication of Richard Crossman's diaries. It caused me many months of anxiety. Hugo Young wrote in *The Crossman Affair:*

> For twenty years Crossman had been keeping diaries, recording in copious detail the life and thoughts of a man who was variously a journalist, political theorist, politician, editor and cabinet minister. He regarded these diaries as his monument, and for two years before the diagnosis (of cancer) he had devoted his life to preparing the first part for publication. This he intended to be not a revisitation of the 1950s when they began but a chronicling of his own arrival at the centre of power in 1964, when he became Minister of Housing and Local Government in Harold Wilson's first Cabinet. This choice was made for a simple purpose; to blow apart the tradition of secrecy in British government and destroy the conventions which had rendered innocuous or misleading, or both, the writings of most former cabinet ministers about their time in office.

When Crossman died, it was my responsibility as publisher and one of the literary executors to ensure that the diaries were published. I sent the first volume to the Cabinet Secretary, and in due course heard that he did not see how the diaries could possibly be published within the "closed period" for Cabinet records, which was usually thirty years. There was thus deadlock, and a period of fascinating and worrying negotiations ensued. During sleepless nights, I felt that I alone was ruining our traditional form of Cabinet government, which relied on collective responsibility.

The upshot was that Crossman's representatives refused to withhold the diaries from publication and intended to allow them to be serialized in the *Sunday Times*. The Attorney General took action, and the case was tried by the Lord Chief Justice, who ultimately found in favor of the defendants. Despite some weaknesses and lack of clarity in the judgment, it can with certainty be concluded that the *Crossman Diaries* opened up the proceedings of government in an unprecedented way.

I do not come to many important conclusions about the course of book publishing over these fifty years. The Chatto, Bodley Head, and Cape formula began to falter, and it was clear by 1988 that many of the shareholders were uneasy and did not see a future unless considerable more capital became available—so a sale to a conglomerate was made. The personal style has gone. My son, working for an international conglomerate such as Time Warner, would not recognize my publishing lifestyle, which, as I have mentioned, was nearer to that of the nineteenth-century and prewar days than that of today—except that some of the copyright problems with the Internet seem painfully similar to those I wrestled with. More books are published. I felt British publishers were overproducing when they issued 40,000 titles a year. They now issue 160,000 titles. The best sellers hog the scene, and this is mirrored by the cult of celebrity, which we all find so distasteful. There is one thing I am optimistic about, and that is the survival of the book in its present form. It still seems to be the most convenient way of disseminating learning and entertainment.

The trade I have practiced is still best, as Dean Inge said, "when it is half a trade and half an art." It may have swung too far to the former.

Spring Semester 2006

Feliks Topolski, portrait of George Bernard Shaw, 1943. Oil on canvas, 213.4 × 104.1 cm (84 × 41 in.). Harry Ransom Humanities Research Center, University of Texas, Austin. Courtesy of HRHRC.

Topolski's portrait gave Shaw "a new reason for living" (p. 235).

Feliks Topolski, portrait of Edith Sitwell, 1959. Oil on canvas, 180.3 × 120.0 cm (71 × 47.2 in). Harry Ransom Humanities Research Center, University of Texas, Austin. Courtesy of HRHRC.

Sitwell believed the portrait to be a cruel depiction, while Topolski himself intended it as a perceptive and sympathetic study (p. 241).

Feliks Topolski, portrait of C. P. Snow, 1962. Oil on canvas, 127.3 × 96.5 cm (50 × 38 in). Harry Ransom Humanities Research Center, University of Texas, Austin. Courtesy of HRHRC.

Snow commented that he had many vices, but physical vanity was not among them (p. 238).

Feliks Topolski, portrait of T. S. Eliot, 1961. Oil on canvas, 96.5 ×
64.8 cm (38 × 25.5 in). Harry Ransom Humanities Research Center, University of Texas, Austin. Courtesy of HRHRC.

Eliot "indicated his displeasure" with the portrait (p. 238).

17

The Controversial Portraits
of Feliks Topolski

LARRY CARVER

I chanced on him in the fifties on an underground train and began to sketch at a distance even before realizing who was this uncharming haughty, black-homburged, black-coated city gent, attracted by his obvious rush-hour contrast with the subordinate and indifferent secretarial breed round him. This resulted in a largish painting-invention of a ceremonially red-robed Eliot in an honour-giving scene.

Topolski, *Fourteen Letters: An Autobiography*

The man doing the sketch is Feliks Topolski; the Eliot is T. S.; and the portrait, a gorgeous riot of color, is one of the "Twenty Greats," a collection of Topolski's playful, psychologically acute portraits of twenty great English writers. The portraits, in their reception, have proved controversial; the story of how the Harry Ransom Humanities Research Center (HRHRC) at the University of Texas commissioned them, the finest institutional collection of Topolski portraits, is fascinating.[1]

THE ARTIST

The airless studios grow stifling. Kick the door open—the hum of life turns into a roar . . . We need an art of synthesis, painting fed on reality, the reality of today, which is that of awareness of multitudes on the move, of global oneness, torn by conflicts, and

achieved, not by retrogression into "realism," but through the formal freedom won by modern art.
                                Topolski, "Realist Art," *Listener,* 17 October 1946

I feel I must make it clear that my work is neither "academic" nor
caricaturing on the basis of photographs—it is done "from life."
                                Topolksi to the director of the National
                                Portrait Gallery, 25 June 1976[2]

Feliks Topolski was born in Warsaw in 1907, his father an actor
and his parents both political activists at a time of rising Polish nationalism. Trained as an artist at the Academy of Warsaw, he came
to London in 1935 to record the Silver Jubilee of King George V
and Queen Mary. In carrying out this commission, he found a new
home, settling in London and some years later, in 1947, becoming
a British citizen. He was quickly accepted into a talented group
that included, among others, Graham Greene, Evelyn Waugh, J. B.
Priestley, Anthony Powell, and William Empson. And he went to
work, publishing *The London Spectacle 1935,* humorous, clever impressions of English life, a work Wyndham Lewis found "full of wit and
keen observation, and, though devoid of any hint of malice, agree-
ably sub-acid."[3] For the next fifty-four years, Topolski, in Graham
Greene's felicitous assessment, would serve as "a talented anthropologist . . . conducting a little regular field-work in these islands and
[laying] bare, as with a scalpel, the essential whatever-it-is of Britain's most cherished institutions."[4] Chronicler, illustrator, portrait
painter, caricaturist, and, in G. B. Shaw's judgment, "amazingly talented draughtsman" (postcard to Roy Gilbert, 11 November 1938),
Topolski, as Christopher Lloyd points out, "was not an artist who
liked to be pigeon-holed . . . he remained unfettered. Essentially
his work in whatever medium—chalk, pencil, brush and ink—was
wholly dependent on line. Rhapsodic and agile, his line leaps across
the paper like a bird in flight. Often lines are redrawn at speed,
for this is kinetic art, always energetic, volatile, highly charged, and
often explosive."[5] According to Topolski, "In the late thirties this
fable went about, smuggled out of a secret Tate Gallery meeting:
somebody opposed the purchase of my three mere wash drawings
with: 'We must draw the line somewhere,' to which Augustus [John]
retorted: 'But can you draw the line like Topolski?'"[6]
       An artist-reporter with the interests and powers of observation of
a sociologist and an historian, Topolski traveled the globe, he and
his art restlessly engaged in recording the human condition. The
war years consolidated Topolski's reputation as a draftsman. An official war artist, he made drawings of the Blitz, which he experienced
firsthand. The day before a bomb hit his studio, sending him to the

hospital for four weeks, he "entertained Mr. and Mrs. Bernard Shaw to lunch" there during an air raid, an episode he amusingly captured in an article he wrote for *Lilliput*.[7] He followed Allied armies into France and Germany, witnessed the liberating of the Bergen-Belsen concentration camp, and attended the Nuremberg trials. After the war he continued his travels, recording what Bernard Denvir calls his "passionately personal angle"[8] on contemporary events: Indian independence, the Chinese and Cuban revolutions, civil war in the Congo, the building of the Berlin Wall, the Chicago Democratic Convention in 1968, the rebuilding of Japan, the Vietnam War, the "New wild West gold-rush" in Brazil, and "Ulster's Belfast battlefield."[9] Topolski published his work in magazines—*Night and Day, Punch, Horizon,* and *Lilliput*—and in some thirty illustrated books, including three mined from his wartime experiences: *Britain in Peace and War, Russia in War,* and *Three Continents.*

From 1953 to 1979 he published *Topolski's Chronicle,* twice-monthly broadsheets on brown wrapping paper, recording in Topolski's distinctive style the events of the day, a work that actress Joyce Carey described as "the most brilliant record we have of the contemporary scene as seized by a contemporary mind."[10] Topolski began publishing *Topolski's Chronicle,* perhaps his greatest work, because:

> Today's newspapers forget the uses of draughtsmen, books and exhibitions are too "precious" and too selective—my *Chronicle,* its rough-and-ready character, its immediacy and flexible format had to be invented—indeed, invented, because even the last century's broadsheet was not quite a precedent . . . the creative gap had to be filled in a major way, and my toyed-with idea of *Topolski's Chronicle* became a fact . . . In 1953, *Topolski's Chronicle,* No. 1, Vol. 1 (the first of a great many) came into existence—printed on an old pedal machine by a young Polish couple in a gatehouse to the grounds of the Polish mental hospital at Mabledon, where the husband worked as a gardener.[11]

He goes on:

> The *Chronicle*'s motivation: my mania for drawing "in action" (never redrawing)—drawings accumulating in vast numbers, but denied a proper "stage": books and exhibitions too precious and selective for their numerosity-impact; the contemporary periodicals jealous of their spaces. Hence the natural conclusion: a paper/broadsheet of my own, showing the best of them and accumulating into a singular record of our time.

Topolski's Chronicle, the "very essence of a makeshift anti-periodical," runs to 348 issues and contains 3,000 drawings, "a large slice of global history, every line drawn 'on the spot' and never touched up."[12]

Topolski's ceaseless efforts to chronicle his times led in 1949 to a large mural, done at the invitation of Jawaharlal Nehru, entitled *The East,* which celebrated the independence of India. For the Festival of Britain in 1951, he was commissioned to paint *Cavalcade of the Commonwealth,* a work sixty feet by twenty feet, which was mounted under one of the arches of Hungerford Bridge. In 1959 the Duke of Edinburgh, drawing upon Topolski's talents as a narrative artist, commissioned his artist friend to paint a mural commemorating the coronation of Elizabeth II. This panoramic composition, ninety-five feet in length, hangs at Buckingham Palace. In 2003, Topolski's *Coronation Frieze* was taken from the palace's Lower Corridor and hung in the Queen's Gallery, becoming a centerpiece for the celebration of Queen Elizabeth II's Golden Jubilee.[13]

Topolski was fascinated by the 1960s, and his art, in its energies and experimentations, its "devotion to the impermanent, the makeshift," and an "awareness of multitudes on the move, of global oneness," was a perfect fit for the turbulent decade.[14] He was not, however, an "activist." When Bertrand Russell invited him to join a group protesting nuclear war, Topolski replied:

> I am a side-liner; a pictorial recorder of history made by others. My instinctive need, supported by life-long practice, to watch and DRAW has withered away my action-urge potential. Being in the thick of "it" would force me to drop the pencil to free my hands for weapons or banners—this, I must not do. I am a professional by vocation, by which I mean that there is no citizen or revolutionary reformer above my artist self, and that I have no leisure. I assure you that I find no smug satisfaction in this confinement. I hope you will not file my refusal amongst the mental dodgers and physical cowards.[15]

In his last years Topolski worked on his massive *Memoir of the Century,* a huge mural installed in the spaces under two arches of Hungerford Bridge. Describing the *Memoir,* Bernard Denvir writes:

> Huge structures, twelve to twenty feet high, inhabit this great cavernous space, protruding into it, covering the walls, stretching up to the distant arched roofs. The spectator is conducted by the arrangement in a clockwise direction around a seething mass of imagery, each section of which is dominated by some major theme, some event, some attitude, which Topolski has seen as central to the history of his, and our, time. Unlike the Coronation murals, there is no chronological sequence, scales and planes vary, the rules of visual logic are constantly violated. It is a total experience, the techniques employed ranging from the savage to the lyrical, the sense of actuality, of emotion heightened by the impetuous

bravura of the brushwork, every accident of application surviving
to perpetuate the moment when eye, feeling and medium meet in
a creative act.[16]

The *Memoir*, as Topolski explains in his autobiography:

> Evolves naturally out of accumulated and overflowing testimony.
> Its raw material: experiences understood or enigmatic/on-the-spot
> drawings/to-and-fro associations/dreams—never documentation
> of events unwitnessed. It is a painting, not a potted history—thus
> its chronology is skeletal, as it oscillates between images and ab-
> straction of memories. The work is open ended, in constant prog-
> ress . . . The facts of my life, spread over the globe and woven into
> the history of this century, were pinned down by me in drawing
> on the spot from very early days. These drawings, masses of them,
> are the main fodder of this *Memoir*. But the *Memoir*, being a paint-
> ing, develops its own form, the image and story-telling, merging
> with the unifying movement of colour. . . .
>
> And one more point: I don't work consecutively, but move
> about, returning to add passages and balance abstract against fig-
> urative elements . . . There is no ending. The *Memoir* reaches the
> present, becomes the Diary and continues from day to day to be
> cut short only by nature's will.[17]

Topolski died in 1989, the funeral service taking place at St.
Martin-in-the-Fields on 10 November, with a "Representative of
HRH the Duke of Edinburgh" in attendance. Sir Hugh Casson, Simon Callow, and Lord Birkett gave addresses.[18] The map to his grave
in Highgate Cemetery tells us that Topolski was "a controversial artist." In the "Twenty Greats," the artist lived up to his reputation.

THE COMMISSION AND ACQUISITION

> My manner of working is this. A few hours spent with you, with-
> out holding you to any firm position, preferably in conversation or
> anyway at ease would result in my making several drawings. These
> would serve me to start the "oil on canvas" on my own at my stu-
> dio—and possibly complete it on my own. It may, however, prove
> that my materials are insufficient and in that case I would beg
> from you another sitting, but I am almost sure no more. I do hope
> that this letter will make it more possible to gain your accord.
>   Topolski to T. S. Eliot, 1960 (TA)

A man of great charm, Topolski made friends easily, one of his
most important friendships being that with George Bernard Shaw.
And it is by way of Shaw that the Ransom Center and Feliks Topolski

will be forever linked. In 1938, Shaw "summoned" the young artist to his rooms in Whitehall: "I went in the spirit of a pilgrimage to a godhead." [19] Soon Shaw was asking his "Dear Filipovsky" to illustrate his plays. Though obviously holding the son in great affection, father Shaw was not averse to giving him the occasional thump on the head. When Topolski sent Shaw his preliminary drawings for *St. Joan,* Shaw replied in a postcard: "I am shocked. St. Joan is sacred. She must not be burlesqued. You of all men must not touch her" (4 September 1946). In a later note on the same subject, Shaw wrote: "Do you know the lithographs of Delacroix, illustrating Faust and Hamlet? Some day you may persuade a publisher to issue a *folio* St. Joan illustrated by your monstrosities in the same fashion. That would be a magnificent work of art, especially if you had outgrown your damned scriggles and could be gravely monstrous throughout, like Delacroix" (16 April 1946).

When it came to a portrait of Shaw himself, the sage told "Dear Feliks": "If I were not married I might let you debunk me for the fun of it. But my wife, who admires everything you draw *except your pictures of me,* would object. So I think that project must be abandoned unless you repent and beautify me, which would be very dull and fatal to your reputation" (22 April 1940). When Topolski proposed to illustrate *Pygmalion* with a drawing of the author, Shaw shot back in a postcard:

> Absolutely, positively and finally I will not have any portrait or caricature or impression of me as you know me connected with Pygmalion, which I wrote when I was 55, thirty years ago.
>
> Your attempt to go back to me as I was then is even more repulsive than the present truth. I was perhaps not quite as good looking as the Hermes of Praxitales [*sic*]; but I was at least presentably clean and decent.
>
> I enclose authentic evidence. (2 June 1941)

The gruff playwright was clearly taken, however, with Topolski's "damned scriggles." Hugh Burnett, who worked with Topolski on the television program *Face to Face,* tells the story that as a boy he went to interview Bernard Shaw for his school magazine. [20] Shaw, who was reading a current copy of *Lilliput,* "got rid of me by saying that he had work to do . . . When I got home I checked on that magazine. Far from working, Shaw had been studying a set of portraits of himself drawn by Feliks Topolski." [21] Shaw, relenting, allowed Topolski to draw "endless likenesses." The result was three full-length portraits and the publication in 1946 of the book *Portrait of G.B.S.* Shaw accompanied Topolski at an exhibition of one of his portraits at the

Leicester Gallery in 1944, commenting to a reporter: "It's a wonderful Topolski; but it makes me look 20 years older. This gives me a new reason for living until I'm as old as that."[22]

It was this full-length portrait, once owned by film director Alexander Korda, that the HRHRC, with the book dealer Lew David Feldman acting as a middleman, acquired in 1960. The deal also included Topolski's original illustrations of Shaw's plays *Geneva, In Good King Charles's Golden Days,* and *Pygmalion.* In a letter dated 8 September 1960, Feldman told university president Harry Ransom: "Dear Harry, We have just come from the restorer's and we are engaging to send down the Topolski GBS—it is breathtaking! It will dominate any room you place it in—if we charged 10,000.00 for it—it wouldn't be too much" (Ransom Papers). From these acquisitions and Feldman's enthusiasm for a commission from the university sprang the "Twenty Greats." On 4 June 1960, Feldman wrote to Ransom: "We think this a stroke of genius! Let us commission him to do *20* portraits of our 20th Century *best* all from life—he [Topolski] balks at doing these any other way. His usual charge for portraits is 4-500 guineas (12-1500 dollars) but with the challenge of this group we can work him down to a more reasonable figure" (Ransom Papers). Ransom was not sure, and he asked F. Warren Roberts, director of what was then the Humanities Research Center, to investigate. In a memorandum dated 19 August 1960 on the subject of "Feliks Topolski and Feldman's Portrait Plan," Roberts told his president: "Topolski seems to be a competent and well known painter, although his work tends to the caricature." He questioned "Mr. Feldman's original list," arguing, "I don't think we should commission portraits of persons who are deceased. . . My list includes 14 American names and 13 British names. If the plan is carried out, we would be lucky to make arrangements with ten of each, hence we would allow some room for failure" (Ransom Papers). In an undated, quite candid follow-up memo on "Feldman's Topolski scheme," Roberts advised Ransom:

> Although we have agreed that Mr. Feldman's project for twenty portraits of contemporary writers by Topolski does not fit in with our plans or collections, he is apparently determined to go ahead with this project on his own account whether or not we participate. For this reason, I have the following suggestion to make. Mr. Feldman has chosen for Topolski's first subjects the writers E. M. Forster, T. S. Eliot and Ezra Pound. In as much as Topolski is a competent and well-known artist, I suggest that we should reserve judgment for the present on the matter of Topolski portraits

> in general with a view of obtaining two or three representative
> portraits . . . I feel we should not close the door definitely on
> Mr. Feldman's Topolski activities. (Ransom Papers)

Negotiations would go on for the next two years, Feldman making the case to Ransom that the "Twenty Greats" would "prove to be an extraordinarily interesting and important achievement, in fact we are so convinced that we have drawn a letter of agreement with Mr. Topolski, and we have authorized him to proceed in this matter, *completely upon our own responsibility*" (18 November 1960, Ransom Papers). Feldman accurately described Ransom's reaction, however, as "rather mixed." Nevertheless he pressed on: "We have already written to T. S. Eliot and E. M. Forester requesting their co-operation in lending themselves to Mr. Topolski's portraiture. The other two that we have authorized him to proceed with are Edith Sitwell and Evelyn Waugh." Feldman also played the money card: "From the viewpoint of simple economics, we must say to you that in our considered opinion this will prove to be (if completed) a $50,000 property, and was proposed to you at the modest figure of $20,000" (18 November 1960).

Topolski continued to work, but the list of sitters and the terms of any agreement remained in flux. Feldman wrote to the restless and questioning artist in August 1961: "We note that you apparently still do not believe that we do not have a client for the project. We have told you a number of times now that the project in its original form was refused . . . There is always a possibility . . . that the people we approached originally may change their minds but certainly at this moment we have no commitment from any one. Our plans for your coming over in 1962 are still undecided, particularly now with the demise of Ernest Hemingway" (Ransom Papers). In February 1962, Topolski, seeking publicity, leaked the story, much to the chagrin of Feldman and the university, to the *Sunday Telegraph*. The article (25 February 1962), with three photographs of Toposki at work on the portraits in his studio, began: "Feliks Topolski has been commissioned by an American organization to paint 20 distinguished writers. By which American organization? 'There,' says Topolski, 'is the "drama." I just don't know.' The commission reached him through a man who had come over here to buy manuscripts." The article continued: "Topolski's Top Twenty aren't actually Topolski's choice. The list of selected authors comes to him in installments from across the Atlantic."

As late as May 1962, Ransom and Roberts had their doubts. A letter from Topolski to Feldman on 11 May contained an updated list of sitters and assurances that the project would be finished by the end of the month. It went on to suggest that Sir Herbert Read, who had seen the portraits and expressed admiration for them, should write the introduction to a proposed catalogue of the exhibition. The letter was forwarded to Roberts, and it is not clear whether it was the updated list, the projected time of completion, the quality of the work, or the proposed exhibition that bothered him. But he wrote to Ransom: "Do you suppose it might be possible to get an independent appraisal of the Topolski project? We might be able to write confidentially either to J. B. Priestley or Stephen Spender" (21 May 1962, Ransom Papers).

Artist and book dealer were to prevail. In what a university press release at the time described as "PORTRAITS A GALAXY OF BRITAIN'S TWENTIETH CENTURY GREATS" arrived on 31 August 1962.[23] The cost of shipping, Feldman wrote to Roberts, was $381.45, "making for a grand total of $20,381.45." Ten thousand dollars to the artist, $10,000 to the book dealer, and, in Feldman's judgment, every penny well spent: "We honestly feel that this is now, and time will prove the fact, certainly our most original contribution to the collections at Austin and perhaps ultimately it will prove to be among the most rewarding" (27 August 1962, Ransom Papers). Topolski— "Delighted with the news of the inevitable and predictable!"—laid out plans to visit the university to give "one, two, or set of three talks" that "should cover the contemporary art scene and my 'stand' within it; my own development; and the theme of these portraits, both as a stage in my own art and as a tale of the subjects" (Topolski to Feldman, 5 October 1962, Ransom Papers). Feldman wrote to the happy artist that were also plans "to use the J. B. Priestley portrait as a frontispiece to a descriptive catalogue of an intended exhibition" and to publish the portraits in the *Texas Quarterly,* Sir Herbert Read writing an introduction. In the same letter, Feldman assured Topolski, "Dr. H. H. Ransom, who is the dynamic genius responsible for the acquisition of the paintings . . . is very favorably inclined" to both trip and publication (25 October 1962, Ransom Papers). Neither was to take place.

The reason was twofold. To the end, Ransom remained bemused by what Topolski had wrought and what he had bought. He turned to Donald Goodall, Chairman of the Art Department, whose judgment—praise with telling qualifications—must have given him pause: "This is the least pious, and I must say most witty sequence of pictures on the contemporary great with which I am familiar. The caricatures would never pass the relatives-test, but communicate more of the genuine and less of the superficially apparent than is usual to this genre. I am not well enough acquainted with the phyz [*sic*] of the sitter in each case to comment on the matter of likeness." Goodall went on to observe: "The pictorial qualities range from the near-miss to attractive painting, and . . . should induce viewers to look again," only to close with a note of irony: "Also, one may be encouraged to think again with interest and compassion on the subjects" (3 October 1962, Ransom Papers). "Witty" and "genuine" but "caricatures" that would not pass a "relatives test" with subjects who should be looked upon with compassion. Hardly reassured, Ransom sought the reaction of the sitters. Warren Roberts wrote to each: "Some time ago, the Library of The University of Texas obtained a series of caricature portraits of contemporary British writers painted by Feliks Topolski, and the editorial staff of the *Texas Quarterly* is considering an article by Sir Herbert Read on the work of Feliks Topolski . . . A photograph of your portrait by Mr. Topolski is enclosed . . . We will appreciate very much having your reaction to this proposed use of the portrait (6 March 1963, "Letter Sent to All of the Sitters," Ransom Papers).

The responses put the project to rest. Three of the twenty never replied; six refused outright; one, Louis MacNeice, never got his letter; only nine consented—one, Stephen Spender, with reluctance. Sir Herbert Read, moreover, declined to write an essay on the portraits, explaining in a letter to Roberts: "While I do not wish to adopt the instransigeant [*sic*] attitude of Mr. Eliot and Mr. Priestley, I feel that as one of the 'victims' of Mr. Topolski's satirical portraiture, I am hardly the right person to comment on the series" (27 May 1963, Ransom Papers). Roberts wrote to Topolski that he could not share the sitters' actual replies, but he did go on to summarize:

> T. S. Eliot definitely indicated his displeasure at the thought of the paintings being reproduced . . . C. Day Lewis assured us he was not "so corpse-like as the portrait suggests." E. M. Forster said that he did not think it a "successful caricature." C. P. Snow prefaced his permission . . . with the statement that he has "many vices, but physical vanity is not among them." Evelyn Waugh noted that he ordinarily discourages photographs because of the risk of being recognized in public, but that "this danger does not arise in connexion with Toplski's drawing." Graham Greene "would rather that you did not use the caricature" . . . Herbert Read was non-committal insofar as permission to use the portrait was concerned, but the tone of this letter indicated that he would prefer not to have it used. Bertrand Russell wrote, "I should prefer *not* to have a photograph of this portrait by Feliks Topolski used." (13 August 1964, Ransom Papers)

The reactions of J. B. Priestley, Rebecca West, and Aldous Huxley were perhaps the most damning. Priestley sent a cablegram: "All my family loudly protest against Topolski for both personal and aesthetic reasons." In a follow-up letter, Priestley elaborated:

> I have often been portrayed as a bit of a monster, but I have to be shown as my own kind of monster, just as an elephant must not be made to look like a rhinoceros. This caricature sketch-portrait is really quite a shocking job. He has given me concavities in place of convexities, a kind of broken Roman nose instead of my own modest snub, and the drawing is so bad that the head could not possibly go into the hat. As a piece of work it really is a shocking mess, with no real attempt to build up and highlight the essential form but in place of this a number of meaningless devices to attract attention. (17 November 1962, Ransom Papers)

Rebecca West wrote:

> I must explain that it was more or less by accident that I was painted by Mr Topolski. I consented only because a temporary secretary of mine had in my absence answered a letter from him with some rudeness, and I felt obliged to make amends by consenting to sit for him. I felt that in this situation I should be prepared to accept what Mr Topolski did without question, since I had let myself in for it. But I really feel that as I am a small woman, weighing under 130 pounds, of inconspicuous appearance, it is rather much to accept a caricature, which, granted that it is a caricature, can only be a caricature of a woman who is both enormously tall and grossly obese, a sort of Gilray duchess. (6 May 1963, Ransom Papers)

"As it happens," Aldous Huxley acidly observed, "I find Topolski's mannerisms aesthetically distasteful and wholly incompatible with portraiture or even with [word crossed out] caricature of a psychologically significant kind" (20 May 1963, Ransom Papers). Five months after sending this letter, on November 22, 1963, Huxley died. According to Topolski: "At some gathering, Lady Huxley, the wife of Julian his brother, rushed at me distressed and almost accusing: that ill-informing black-and-white photograph of my painting of him sent routinely by Texas University had shaken him terribly, and—she insisted—had contributed to his demise." [24]

If any consolation was to be found, it was in the response of William Empson, who "gladly" gave his permission, adding, "I wish to take the opportunity of congratulating Texas University on carrying out this generous-minded plan" (20 April 1963, Ransom Papers). Topolski had his own explanation:

The University of Texas planned a book of my portraits, and presumably following some code of academic publishing chivalry,
sent out smallish black-and-white photographs (entirely false as
visual information) to each of the "subjects." A few reacted quite
violently: but only from amongst the oldest (similarly to GBS some
years earlier); a reaction caused, plainly, not by vanity, but by a
preserved/treasured mirror-view of themselves, still existing with
the help of grimaces and wishful memory—challenged by what
to me was a living face, but to them the kept-at-bay face of disaster—in short, the feared evocation of death.[25]

Five years after the acquisition, William Robinson, a research associate, wrote Topolski that "we are planning a rather intimate but
distinguished showing of your twenty portraits of literary figures in
the Museum Gallery of the Art Department here at the University"
(14 September 1967, Ransom Papers). The exhibition opened on
13 October of that year and ran for a week. In 1991 another exhibition of the portraits, again a low-key affair, took place in the Leeds
Gallery on the fourth floor of the Flawn Academic Center. Finally,
in an exhibition that would have brought joy to the artist, the portraits, handsomely reframed, were shown in the new gallery of the
HRHRC in an exhibition from 5 September to 31 December 2006,
the artist's son and daughter, Daniel and Teresa Topolski, giving the
talk their father no longer could.

The portraits remain as controversial as ever. In their talk, Daniel
and Teresa Topolski defended their father's work from the charge
of being mere "caricature." It was an old charge. Though Warren
Roberts came to admire Topolski's work and thought the artist possessed "a unique ability to extract submerged character traits and
present them graphically" (Roberts to Topolski, 17 August 1971,
Ransom Papers), he always described the "Twenty Greats" as "caricatures." Similarly, when Topolski, who was never admitted to the
Royal Academy, offered some of his work to the National Portrait
Gallery in London in 1976, the trustees, judging Topolski to be a
journalist, thought it not "worth pursuing the possibility of acquisitions at this stage" (Richard Ormond to Topolski, 15 November
1976, NPG). Even someone as sympathetic to Topolski's work as William Epsom advised that if there were to be an exhibition of the
"Twenty Greats," "the University [should] make an offer for at least
one of the preliminary sketches for each painting. The sketches are
full of witty comment and of energy of Topolski's line, and I expect
some people will always think, as I do, that they are better than he
paintings" (Empson to Warren Roberts, 20 April 1963, Ransom Papers). Caricaturist, chronicler, and draftsman, but not artist.

Topolski, of course, was aware of these criticisms; they had dogged him all his life. And he passionately rejected them, his most moving statement about his art and about the art of these portraits coming in a letter he wrote to Edith Sitwell. She disliked the portrait of her as shown in the photograph that Warren Roberts had sent, the hunchback reminding her of the orthopedic device her parents made her wear for "a slight curvature of the spine," "a sort of Bastille of iron, from my shoulders to the soles of my feet."[26] Topolski, upset that he had hurt "a person I admire and would hate to distress," wrote to Sitwell: "As an artist, I am utterly SERIOUS in my work. My intentions are never those of a satirist, caricaturist or even a gentle mocker; and they can be clumsily summed up thus:

> I yield to my instinctive "bent" and I "let go" towards an *unpremeditated* completion, which signals itself rather cajolingly and hesitantly, appealing to my often puzzled consciousness from "below", as it were; I paint (and draw) with tentative guidance of something undefined, which may be crudely called the theme's character; and I cut my exploratory path (I repeat without any derogatory or idealizing preconceptions) until my instinct tells me that I arrived (or failed).
>
> I do not need to tell you about this: how contemporary art has left the "portrait" behind and how common "academic" flatteries, or painting of "pattern and colour", embarrassed by the presence of a face within it, cannot claim the term. In my work, whether a composition or a portrait, I try, in contemporary terms and in utter gravity of purpose, to reinstate the human shape. And not because I persuaded myself this as a private or fashionable "ideology", but because this is my "VOCATION" impossible to resist.
>
> One more point. I draw many drawings from a model and paint my "portraits" out of these and of my memory of the person, *on my own*. Thus I can work on *paintings* as such, free from the bounds of overpowering reality.[27]

Topolski devoted his life to seeking and exploring the limits of a new realism.[28] The "Twenty Greats" are one magnificent result of the artist's quest.

Fall Semester 2006

1. In addition to the Eliot, the collection includes portraits of W. H. Auden, John Betjeman, Ivy Compton-Burnett, Cyril Connolly, C. Day Lewis, William Empson, E. M. Forster, Graham Greene, Aldous Huxley, Louis MacNeice, John Osborne, J. B. Priestley, Herbert Read, Bertrand Russell, C. P. Snow, Stephen Spender, Edith Sitwell, Evelyn Waugh, and Rebecca West.

2. All unpublished correspondence will be cited parenthetically and is from one of four sources: Offers File, Heinz Archive and Library, National Portrait Gallery, London (NPG); George Bernard Shaw, Letters, 1939–46, Box 45, HRHRC (all Shaw correspondence cited); Ransom File, HRHRC (Ransom Papers); and the family archive of Daniel and Teresa Topolski, London (TA).

3. Feliks Topolski, *The London Spectacle 1935*, intro. D. B. Wyndham Lewis (London, 1935); the quotation is from the preface.

4. Graham Greene, "How To Read This Magazine," *Night and Day*, 1 July 1937, p. 5.

5. Christopher Lloyd and Hugh Roberts, *Ceremony and Celebration: Coronation Day, 1953* (London, 2003), pp. 41–42.

6. Feliks Topolski, *Fourteen Letters: An Autobiography* (London, 1988), no pagination.

7. Feliks Topolski, "My September Memory," *Lilliput*, Sept. 1941, p. 189.

8. Bernard Denvir, "The Eye of History: The Art of Feliks Topolski," in *Feliks Topolski's Panoramas* (London, 1977), p. 5.

9. Topolski, *Fourteen Letters*.

10. Quoted in Denvir, "Eye of History," p. 5.

11. Topolski, *Fourteen Letters*.

12. Ibid.

13. See Lloyd and Roberts, *Ceremony and Celebration*, for an account of this event.

14. Topolski, *Fourteen Letters*.

15. Ibid.

16. Denvir, "Eye of History," pp. 8–9.

17. Topolski, *Fourteen Letters*.

18. "Feliks Topolski, 1907–1989, St Martin-in-the-Fields, Trafalgar Square, Friday, 10th November 1989" (program for the funeral service).

19. Topolski, *Fourteen Letters*.

20. *Face to Face*, first broadcast in 1959, began each episode with a Topolski drawing of the personality to be interviewed by John Freeman. From these drawings, Topolski published the book *Face to Face*. Three of the portraits of the "Twenty Greats," those of Bertrand Russell, Edith Sitwell, and Evelyn Waugh, began as drawings for this program.

21. Feliks Topolski, *Face to Face*, ed. Hugh Burnett (London, 1964), p. 3.

22. "Topolski Draws Bernard Shaw," *Picture Post*, 12 Feb. 1944, p. 23.

23. The "Twenty Greats" turned out to be more. "I persuaded Texas," Topolski writes in *Fourteen Letters*, "to give the twentieth painting to a group of younger writers of my choice: John Osborne, John Whiting, Arnold Wesker, Shelagh Delaney." In the same painting, barely detectable, Topolski also sketched in playwrights Christopher Fry and Harold Pinter, writing "Fry" under one and "Pinter" over the other. Recently Daniel and Teresa Topolski identified one of the two obscure figures in the Stephen Spender portrait as the poet Christopher Logue. The "Twenty Greats" are really twenty-six in number—and counting.

24. Topolski, *Fourteen Letters*.

25. Ibid.

26.   Sitwell to Topolski, 7 Sept. 1963, in Topolski, *Fourteen Letters*.
27.   Topolski to Sitwell, 29 Aug. 1963, in Topolski, *Fourteen Letters*.
28.   No one has yet provided a good analysis of Topolski's style, his mingling of abstract art with expressionism and near cubism, let alone of his use of color. Those who admire the portraits, which vary greatly in style and color, tend to do so by drawing upon psychology. Perhaps the best impressionistic account of Topolski's portraiture is that of Bernard Denvir: "The faces emerge, thoughtful, haggard, noble, querulous, pompous, anguished, apoplectic even, from an incandescent mass of colour, reaching out to the spectator as though to engage in a wordless dialogue. There are no barriers, no distracting incidentals. Never is one's attention diverted away from the central fact of the face, the map of a life, the signal which a solitary human being emits in his hunger for communication with others" ("Eye of History," p. 7). In a review of the HRHRC exhibition, critic Debra Broz makes the case that "Topolski's portraits, his essence, his worldview and his affinity for expressionism often seem to have outweighed the objective of physical likeness. Topolski's paintings evolved from sketched caricatures into commentary about vanity, age, and the fear of death informed by his experience witnessing the atrocities of war, the ravaged and precarious state of postwar Europe, the beginnings of social upheaval in the 1960s and the changing state of modern art" ("The Painting That Killed Aldous Huxley," *Cantanker*, 4 Dec. 2006).

18

All Souls and Suez

WM. ROGER LOUIS

On the evening of 3 November 1956, when television was still a novelty, Sir Anthony Eden addressed Britain on the crisis in the Middle East. Of all his speeches over a long career, this one proved the best in his political life and became ingrained in public memory. He described himself as a man of peace, working throughout his life as a League of Nations man, as a United Nations man. His voice rang with sincerity when he expressed his deepest feelings that the decision to invade Egypt would stand the test of history as the right course at the right time: "There are times for courage, times for action and this is one of them." The Egyptian dictator had to be stopped.

Eden's speech produced radically different reactions. In London, the chairman of Reuters, Sir Christopher Chancellor, hurled his whisky glass at the television screen.[1] At All Souls, at least in one group, the response was subdued and reflective. In 1956 there was only one television set in the college. It happened to be in the Warden's lodgings. A group of four or so watched the broadcast together. They included the Warden himself, John Sparrow; a young Prize Fellow, Keith Thomas; the publisher Geoffrey Faber; and the Chancellor of the University, Lord Halifax. At the end of the speech, the Warden turned off the television set. There was silence. Finally Halifax said: "The trouble about Anthony is that he's always had a thing about dictators."

Halifax is far more significant in the history of All Souls than in the history of the Suez crisis, and he gives point to the argument of this lecture. In 1956 the college more closely resembled the All Souls of 1936 rather than of 1976, or for that matter of the critical year 1966. There was, however, one major difference. By 1956 there were far fewer grandees at All Souls than there had been in 1936, at least those with influence in national affairs. Grandees there certainly were: Halifax above all, but also Lord Brand, Lord Bridges, and Lord Salter. Yet by the time of Suez, the mystique of the college had begun to crack. It no longer seemed to be a nexus of power and intellect. From the 1930s onward, there were widespread suspicions that All Souls in one way or another had been responsible for the policy of appeasement. No one, so far as I know, has ever held All Souls accountable for Suez.

The purpose of this lecture will be to establish the meaning of the Suez crisis for All Souls, and for Oxford more generally, by commenting on Suez as a moment in the history of the British people, part of Our Island Story—I hesitate to use the word "our," but I have lived with the story for so long that I feel a part of it. I was in Cairo in 1956 during the initial phases of the crisis.

I shall pursue the direct involvement of three members of the college: Roger Makins, Patrick Reilly, and Quinton Hailsham. They were of the same generation, Makins elected to All Souls in 1925, Hailsham in 1931, and Reilly in 1932. Makins was Ambassador in Washington when Gamal Abdel Nasser nationalized the Canal Company on 26 July 1956—the salient point being that it was the nationalization of a company, not the canal, which lay within Egyptian sovereign territory. Reilly was working in the embassy in Paris. He returned to the Foreign Office to become Deputy Under-Secretary at a critical stage of the crisis. Hailsham was First Lord of the Admiralty. All three were critical of Eden and believed his handling of the crisis to be disastrous, though Hailsham came closer than the others to sympathizing with the purpose of British intervention. In broad strokes, Makins and Reilly were anti-Suez while Hailsham was pro-Suez, though he objected, violently, to the Prime Minister's methods and behavior.

Reflect for a moment on the year 1956 as a point in time. It was still the world of the bowler hat, a symbol of stability and status. Hailsham, a formidable cyclist throughout his life, even in old age, always wore a bowler while cycling. One member of the Foreign Office recalls going to lunch in St. James's Park with sandwiches and hard-boiled eggs. Since there were no litter bins, he put the eggshells under his bowler until he got back to the Foreign Office. The challenge to such decorous and quaint behavior, the challenge to the bowler itself, came in May 1956 with the production of John Osborne's play *Look Back in Anger* and what one critic of All Souls has described as "the rude entry of Jimmy Porter."[2] The anger and the iconoclasm of the play represented attitudes that erupted subsequently at the peak of the Suez crisis. Michael Howard, who later played a significant part in the history of All Souls, remembers going to Trafalgar Square to join the crowd of 30,000 people protesting against the invasion of Egypt. He felt alienated from fellow demonstrators: "The crowd consisted mainly of people who could have worn demonstration campaign medals . . . who were really to come into their own a few years later with the foundation of the Campaign for Nuclear Disarmament."[3] Comparable protest did not exist at All Souls. But by 1956, almost invisibly, social and political attitudes had altered during the previous decade. The change was most apparent, perhaps, in the attitude of the post-1945 generation toward the British Empire and Commonwealth. In the interwar years, whatever one thought about the Empire, there could be no doubt that it played an important part in college affairs. L. S. Amery and Lionel Curtis, stalwarts of the Empire in different ways, both died in 1955. Their deaths can be seen as closing the chapter on empire at All Souls.

Reflect on Oxford in 1956. In April, in the spirit of the post-Stalin era, Khrushchev and Bulganin visited London and Oxford. Students chanted "Poor Old Joe" to the tune of the "Volga Boat Song." Oxford, in the view of the public, made up part of the Establishment, but students themselves wanted to tweak the Establishment and keep it on the hop as much as be a part of it. In the sense that the word caught on in the 1950s, the Establishment consisted of people with power and influence who ran the country. In the first edition of Anthony Sampson's *Anatomy of Britain* (1962), Oxford and Cambridge occupy an entire section, but his comments focus on All Souls, by then having lost its national influence and possessing no particular academic function other than to elect two or so new fellows each year.[4] This view of the college coincided with the outlook of both A. J. P. Taylor and Hugh Trevor-Roper, the two prominent Oxford historians in the 1950s who disagreed on almost everything but the ossified nature of All Souls. In the context of Suez, Taylor and Trevor-Roper provide a perspective that runs parallel with the divide within the college. Taylor denounced the Suez operation and held views similar to those of A. L. Rowse, while Trevor-Roper detested the Prime Minister but was pro-Suez in the same way that Hailsham was pro-Suez. All Souls revealed the same fault lines that ran through Oxford itself.

Within the college, Isaiah Berlin is a figure of particular interest, not only because, as will be seen, he changed his mind about Suez, but also because of his connections. He remained on good terms with both Taylor and Trevor-Roper, for example, though he shared gossip much more freely with the latter. But one is also struck by the missing voices, and it is important to remember that in late 1956 there was a dual emergency. The crises of Suez and the Hungarian revolution coincided. I had hoped to be able to report on the view of All Souls' historian of Hungary, C. A. Macartney, but, alas, his papers at the Bodleian are mute on these questions. (Macartney is of interest in college lore because he thought Hitler was not such a bad chap after all.) Nor can I say much about his friend Geoffrey Hudson, whose potential for a great book that was never written rivals anyone else's at All Souls. (Among those who never wrote their great book, he ranks right up there with Trevor-Roper.) By 1956, Hudson was already director of the Far Eastern Centre at St. Antony's, but he still moved within college circles and was as much a hawk then as he was later on Vietnam. Alas, there are no Geoffrey Hudson papers. Nor on the other side of the divide is there any written evidence about the views of the Professor of Social Anthropology, E. E. Evans-Pritchard, though in college lore he ranks among the most vehement critics of the Suez operation. I mention these silent voices—silent because of the lack of documentary evidence—because I think it important to be clear that much of what I have been able to piece together about the response to Suez at All Souls is based on oral testimony and is by no means a complete record. But it is possible to detect changes of mood. In 1957, Max Beloff arrived as the Gladstone Professor of Public Administration. As David Butler has pointed out, no cause was truly lost until Max espoused it. Perhaps this helps explain why the balance of college sentiment finally became anti-Suez.

Nothing succeeds like success, and in the case of Suez, nothing failed like failure. It is also possible that the college mood shifted in the aftermath of the crisis not because of personal influences but because of the forbidding reality of a botched operation that had divided the nation and jeopardized Britain's relations with both the United States and the United Nations. The Suez operation might have succeeded, at least in a limited sense, if the Canal Zone had been reoccupied and then the issue of withdrawal used as a weapon to extract concessions from Nasser on the management of the canal. The stopping of the troops midway down the canal carried great symbolic importance. Britain could no longer conduct a major military operation independently of the United States. The outcome of the Suez crisis thus came as a revelation: Britain no longer ranked with the Soviet Union and the United States as a world power. In the early 1950s, Goronwy Rees, when he was Estates Bursar at All Souls, represented the view that Britain was in decline and that the Establishment concealed the truth.[5] From the time of the Suez invasion onward, the issue of "collusion" raised doubts—profound doubts—about the integrity of the British government. It was not until the opening of the archives, in the 1980s, that evidence revealed conclusively the details of the secret arrangements among Britain, France, and Israel to invade Egypt. But to many at the time, not least to the All Souls figures directly involved, it was clear what had happened. To Makins, Reilly, and Hailsham, England's honor had been tarnished.

THE CHRONOLOGY OF THE SUEZ CRISIS, for purposes of this lecture, can be described as the beginning, or Roger Makins, phase; the middle, or Patrick Reilly; phase; and the end, or Quintin Hailsham, phase. The first part of the crisis occupied the last weeks of Makins's ambassadorship in Washington. The Eden government agreed to a maritime conference and to the creation of a Suez Canal Users Association. Sir Robert Menzies of Australia went to Cairo to try to reason with Nasser. He reported that Nasser remained impervious to common sense and would roll his eyes upward in response to practical suggestions. In September 1956, Harold Macmillan, then Chancellor of the Exchequer, visited Washington and met with President Eisenhower. Makins was present at the meeting. As is obvious from his papers in the Bodleian, the Suez affair greatly preoccupied him then and forever after.

The second phase, Patrick Reilly's, lasted from late September to the beginning of military operations, in late October. During this time, negotiations at the United Nations nearly succeeded in reaching a peaceful solution, but in the meantime the Prime Minister made commitments to the French and Israelis. The treaty of Sèvres coordinated military action for the invasion of Egypt—in effect, collusion. Reilly indirectly witnessed these events; his analysis of the complex interplay of personalities, written later, is preserved in his papers in the Bodleian. Like Makins, Reilly regarded Suez as an event that had burned itself into his soul.

In the last phase, Israel invaded Egypt on 29 October. The British and French attacked Egyptian airfields and dropped paratroops in the Canal Zone. These events coincided with the revolt in Hungary. At the United Nations, the General Assembly on 2 November voted 65–5 for an immediate cease-fire and the withdrawal of troops from

Egypt; of the five, three of course were Britain, France, and Israel.
Only Australia and New Zealand sided with them against the resolu-
tion. In the Canal Zone, military operations suddenly came to an
end when Eden, under unprecedented and extreme pressure from
Eisenhower, halted the advance of the troops. Hailsham had become First Lord of the Admiralty in early September, but he was not
allowed access to the secret plans for the invasion until late in the
day. He bitterly resented his exclusion. In his memoirs, he describes
his part in the Suez operation as "absolute agony." [6]

When Roger Makins was elected a Fellow of All Souls in 1925,
at the age of twenty-one, he stated that he had never known "such
perfect satisfaction." The son of a brigadier general who later became a Conservative MP, he was educated at Winchester and Christ
Church. He arrived at All Souls in the same year as A. L. Rowse. In
his own words, "the College gulped heavily before electing Rowse,
and then, having done that, they looked for the most conventional
candidate in sight." [7] The word "conventional" is not quite right,
though it reflects his sense of modesty. Makins was among the most
able of his generation. He spent much of his career in the United
States, beginning in 1931 in the embassy in Washington. He married an American, Alice Davis, the daughter of Dwight Davis, who
was a former governor of the Philippines and who is best known
for endowing the great prize in American tennis, the Davis Cup.
Makins later believed that one of the problems underlying the Suez
crisis was that neither Anthony Eden nor Sir Ivone Kirkpatrick, the
Permanent Under-Secretary at the Foreign Office, had much understanding of the United States. Eden had a genteel anti-Americanism
characteristic of his generation. Kirkpatrick had devoted most of
his career to Germany and never visited America. Makins himself
strengthened his familiarity with certain leading American personalities, including Eisenhower, while working on Harold Macmillan's
staff in Algiers during the Second World War. Macmillan became
one of Makins's patrons, a point of interest in view of later trends
in historical interpretation. In the 1990s, perhaps to the present,
it became fashionable to denounce Macmillan for having plotted
or schemed to bring about the downfall of Eden so that Macmillan
himself could become Prime Minister. Imagine my astonishment
last spring when I found in the Makins Papers a memorandum entitled "Note of Conversation with Professor Roger Louis." [8] The reason for the memorandum was that we both agreed that there had
been no conspiracy. I stand by that judgment. Macmillan became
Prime Minister through a combination of luck, skill, and opportun-
ism, which is not the same thing as active scheming.

After 1945, Makins rose through the ranks of the Foreign Office. His involvement in the Persian oil crisis of the early 1950s gave him a knowledge of economic issues that later served him well at the Treasury. His tenure as Ambassador in Washington, 1952–56, is remarkable for many things, but two will serve the purposes of this lecture. First, he took an interest in Eden's health. It was Makins who made the arrangements in Boston in 1954 for a famous American surgeon, Dr. Richard Cattell, to repair damage from a previous operation on Eden's bile duct, when the scalpel had slipped and Eden had nearly died. Makins believed that Eden was never the same person, and that his later swings in mood, which sometimes approached hysteria, could be traced to these medical misfortunes. Whatever the truth of that, Makins got firsthand accounts of Eden's health during the crisis of 1956. He had no doubt that the Prime Minister was frequently doped—his eyes dilated, his mood plunging from excitement and emotional instability to a Dunkirk attitude of quiet and fatalistic determination. This was Makins's firm and considered verdict.

The other point is Makins's clear and consistent judgment on Eisenhower and Dulles and their attitude toward the possible use of force. Makins got on well with John Foster Dulles, apart from his ponderous and tedious moralism. Makins found him willing to engage in argument and to be a good companion who enjoyed his bourbon. But Makins was emphatic that it was Eisenhower who controlled matters of importance. Dulles always took care to square things with Eisenhower before making important pronouncements: "It was Eisenhower, not Dulles, who made the decisions."[9] Makins thought that Eden had allowed himself to become obsessed with Dulles while failing to see the identity of outlook between the President and the Secretary of State on the point of transcendent importance: the United States would not condone the use of force. In Makins's view, this point was so clear and so vital that he would have jumped on the first airplane to London if he believed anyone held otherwise. He thought no one could have failed to get it.

Yet when Makins returned to London, he became the equivalent of a political leper. No one wanted to see him; no one would discuss with him the crisis in Egypt. He finally learned from Sir Ivone Kirkpatrick about the plans for invasion. "I was astounded," he wrote in his unpublished memoir. "It had never occurred to me that we would go to war without full American support, and I at once realised that there would be a disaster, for which I began mentally to prepare myself."[10] Why had his advice been ignored? Why did his sharp and cogent view of Eisenhower and Dulles fail to impress?

The answer is to be found in the perceptive biography of Eden by D. R. Thorpe: Eden believed that Makins had gone native.[11]

One of Makins's last acts in Washington had been to accompany Macmillan on his visit to Eisenhower. They entered through a side door to the White House so as not to attract attention. The President and the Chancellor greeted each other as old comrades-in-arms. They enjoyed each other's company. They talked, so it seemed to Makins, about everything under the Anglo-American sun but avoided, to his astonishment, discussing Suez. Eisenhower believed he had made his view so clear that the subject was a closed book. Macmillan thought that Eisenhower, by skirting the topic, had implicitly endorsed the British plan to topple Nasser by force if necessary. In Macmillan's phrase, which became infamous, Ike would "lie doggo" (lie low). Makins thus witnessed one of the great misunderstandings of the twentieth century. Nor was it any easier to follow the pattern of Macmillan's thought after Makins returned to London. Makins was now at the Treasury, an appointment made at the initiative of Macmillan, though he now seemed to give Makins the cold shoulder. Perhaps sensing opposition, Macmillan refused to see him until the troops disembarked. He then sent an "urgent summons" for Makins and said, "Now that the expedition has sailed, I can talk to you." Makins immediately raised the issue of how the Americans would respond; Macmillan "reacted like a man coming out of a trance."[12] This is an extraordinarily revealing line about Macmillan, and entirely consistent with Makins's overall interpretation of his intricate personality. A few days later, just as Britain and France announced conditions for a cease-fire on 3 November, Makins was elected a Distinguished Fellow at All Souls. The circumstances of Suez made his satisfaction with life a little less than complete.

Patrick Reilly's career in the diplomatic service was the mirror image of Makins's, but with a French reflection. While Makins was associated forever with the United States, Reilly served three times in France, the last as Ambassador in the 1960s. He was born in India, in a family that had served the British Raj for four generations. After a lonely childhood, he attended Winchester and New College before being elected to All Souls in 1932—the same year as Isaiah Berlin and Richard Wilberforce. A. J. Ayer commented that Reilly's election "astounded Oxford," a remark referring to his modesty and low-key personality. Reilly was a man of complete and unassuming integrity. He was self-deprecating. He once told me how Lionel Curtis had wounded him by remarking that he talked so little that he contributed nothing to the college. Most people would have disregarded such a comment or would have viewed it as ironic in view of

Curtis's own volubility. I was interested to see in Reilly's papers how
he morosely mulled this over. He was an extraordinarily sensitive
man. His part in the Suez crisis is of interest because he was in Paris
at the time of Nasser's nationalization of the Suez Canal Company
but returned to the Foreign Office when the crisis reached its cli-
max. He was thus able to assess the French origins of the Suez crisis
as well as the dynamics within Whitehall.

To Reilly and others at the time, the plan for an Anglo-French
strike force had a "made in Paris" imprint to it. The French held
Nasser responsible for the troubles in Algeria. In their view, Nasser
was an octopus whose tentacles extended throughout the Middle
East and North Africa: lop off the head and the tentacles would
wither. But the French needed British military assistance as well
as use of the airfields and harbors in Cyprus to be able to attack.
The question was, to change the metaphor and to use Aneurin
Bevan's earthy language, would Marianne be able to seduce John
Bull? Reilly, though he became Deputy Under-Secretary when he
returned to the Foreign Office in late August 1956, heard only rumors about British conversations with the French. He believed that
the Prime Minister would seek a peaceful solution. But one day in
late August or early September (the exact date is not clear) the veil
was lifted from his eyes. It happened by mistake. Kirkpatrick placed
a telegram in Reilly's box that should not have been there: "One
morning I was astounded to find . . . a telegram on which was written in pencil in the Prime Minister's unmistakable handwriting:
'Foreign Secretary, perhaps this will give us the pretext for which we
are looking' . . . I sat and looked at the telegram for a long time." It
came as a revelation: "Eden was deeply committed to military intervention."[13] Marianne may have seduced John Bull, but it was Reilly's
view that Eden wanted to be seduced.

Reilly became aware of the extraordinary lengths the Prime Minister would go to keep plans for the military operation as secret as
any of the secret operations of the Second World War. Eden's wartime experience gave him both the inspiration and the knowledge
of how to manipulate the government machine. Only a handful of
officials in the Foreign Office knew of the plans. The key figure
was Kirkpatrick. Here I am grateful to Patrick Reilly for putting me
right, some fifteen years ago, on an important issue. I had believed
Kirkpatrick to be the guiding genius behind the operation. He was
intelligent, deft, and bellicose—wholly convinced of the danger of
Nasser. He said at one point: "The PM was the only man in England
who wanted the nation to survive; that all the rest of us have lost
the will to live; that in two years' time Nasser will have deprived us

of our oil, the sterling area fallen apart, no European defence possible, unemployment and unrest in the UK and our standard of living reduced to that of the Yugoslavs or Egyptians."[14] But Kirkpatrick had his doubts about the Suez operation. He continued to perform his duties out of loyalty to Eden and because he was a scrupulous civil servant, not because he believed it to be a good plan. He paced the corridors of the Foreign Office, wringing his hands and exclaiming to himself that it was a daft idea. It was Eden himself, according to Reilly, who must bear the responsibility for the consequences—and they were catastrophic. Conspiracy had involved British ministers "in deceit and lies." Dishonesty had penetrated into the heart of the British government and could be summed up in the word "collusion": "It undermined the moral basis for our military intervention."[15] In Reilly's judgment—his words are inscribed in my memory and he used phrases carefully—Britain's reputation for ethical conduct had been irrevocably damaged.

Hailsham's part in the Suez crisis can be related more briefly because more of it is already in the public record. Like Makins and Reilly, Hailsham believed the Suez expedition to be a shambles, but for quite different reasons. Reflect for a moment on Hailsham's defiant toughness and pugnacious courage. A photograph from the 1950s shows him wading into a freezing sea in a baggy old swimsuit, perfectly capturing an uncompromising Tory determination. Much later, when the IRA bombed the Old Bailey in 1973, Hailsham decided immediately to visit the site. Since his official car would cause further problems for the security forces, he arrived on his bicycle (wearing, of course, his bowler). He became the longest-serving Lord Chancellor in the twentieth century. By the time of the Suez crisis, he had long established a reputation for bold, even if not always original, legal judgment—which was often spiced with a trace of brilliance for its own sake, something not unexpected from an All Souls Prize Fellow. In the case of Nasser's nationalization of the Suez Canal Company, Eden's most tenacious legal critic, Sir Gerald Fitzmaurice of the Foreign Office (who later became a judge of the International Court at the Hague), held that Egypt possessed sovereign rights over the canal and that Nasser had merely taken over a company. The shareholders in the company could expect reasonable compensation but little more. Hailsham would have nothing to do with this argument. In his view, unoriginal but reflecting popular sentiment at the time, Nasser had behaved recklessly and violated international law. Hailsham became one of Eden's more effective defenders. Within the government, he was among the most belligerent, though in a particular sense. He was appalled by the plans for invasion, but once in, he wanted to fight on to the end.

Hailsham had served during the Second World War in a tour of duty that took him, briefly, to Egypt, Syria, and Palestine. He became familiar with the deadly force that naval bombardments could have on civilian populations even if the targets were exclusively military. As First Lord of the Admiralty in the Suez crisis, he was acutely aware that he would be held publicly responsible for civilian deaths in Egypt. He also faced unprecedented internal revolt. Lord Mountbatten, the head of the professional navy, threatened to resign. Hailsham met this challenge head on: he told him that as First Lord he himself was responsible for the good name of the Royal Navy and gave Mountbatten a written order to stay on duty. Hailsham acquitted himself very well.

A note of disclosure: I never especially liked Hailsham or warmed to him. One evening at dinner when I was sitting next to him, he looked at me quizzically and said in a clear and rather loud voice, "Play it short, play it up, play it noisy." I was mystified, but Tony Honoré came to the rescue by explaining that this was one of Hailsham's campaign slogans in the 1950s. I remain flummoxed as to why he said it to me, though I am glad to have collected a Hailsham aphorism. I have come rather to like him as an historical figure, and I find his position on Suez significant. Hailsham had been anti-Zionist, believing the creation of the state of Israel to be a mistake. But once Israel had taken its place in international society, then it was morally incumbent on Britain, the United States, and all other law-abiding nations to protect Israel from Arab aggression. He had no doubt that Nasser aimed to bring the Arab states into an alliance to destroy Israel. Hailsham believed that Israel could strike first in self-defense under Article 51 of the United Nations Charter. He despised what he considered Eisenhower and John Foster Dulles's pusillanimous attitude: "Their behavior throughout this unhappy affair seems to me to be both misguided and quite incomprehensible."[16] As for Eden, Hailsham had no use at all for the "hypocrisy" of the secret operations. Keith Thomas remembers him in the Common Room declaiming—playing it loud and certainly not short—his resentment at being misled and deceived. This is the only instance during the Suez crisis that I can find that bears resemblance to the debates on appeasement at All Souls in the 1930s.

IN ASSESSING THE MEANING OF SUEZ FOR ALL SOULS, and for Oxford, it helps to think briefly about the Warden, John Sparrow, who later became, to critics of the college, the personification of reaction. But not in 1956. Elected in 1952, Sparrow was still a popular Warden. He had been elected in part because he would have, it was hoped, a healing effect after a period of bitterly divisive college politics. At the time of Suez, he was still in his early period of popularity. It is useful to bear in mind that he was of the same generation as Maurice Bowra, Cyril Connolly, Anthony Powell, and Evelyn Waugh. Like them, he had an interest in human foible. At All Souls, he could be charming, witty, and kind when he wanted to, though he was devastating on sloppy thinking and academic pretension. He held strong views about Nasser and considered the Suez expedition a jolly colonial war to stop the rot. He had aesthetic objections to Nasser. He kept a photograph of the Egyptian dictator on his desk and would summon visitors to his office to gaze at it and contemplate Nasser's ugliness. His views on Nasser's grotesque physical appearance, his own impression at least, perhaps anticipated the John Sparrow of the 1960s and the attacks on the bearded and unkempt student generation that he detested—"filthy young things." Or, in his delicious phrase, "revolting students." In any event, his reaction to the Suez crisis indicated, as Robin Briggs has written in his wonderful essay on Sparrow in the new *DNB*, how he failed, totally, to perceive the immense changes that would overtake All Souls, Oxford, and the country itself in the next decades. Nevertheless, at the time of the Suez crisis, Sparrow himself probably best summed up the mood at All Souls by saying that the College was a hotbed of cold feet.

In Oxford generally, the Suez crisis caused the same divisions as in All Souls, though probably at a higher pitch. Sparrow's sentiments resembled those of the famous scholar and classicist Gilbert Murray, who led the pro-Suez group at Oxford. Despite championing the League of Nations, Murray believed that the United Nations consisted of a horde of barbarous nations, one of which had broken an international agreement. Murray took a public stand in support of Eden against Nasser.[17] He led the Oxford pro-Suez petition, which was signed by 8 Heads of House, 2 former Heads, 15 Professors and Readers, and 75 Fellows of Colleges—and supported by the men of Brasenose singing "Rule, Britannia."[18] The protest against the Suez venture was led by Alan Bullock, whose views were identical with those of A. L. Rowse and David Astor. I mention David Astor as part of the national background because he penned in the *Observer* the most famous of all anti-Suez declarations: "We had not realised that our government was capable of such folly and crookedness."[19] Emotions ran as high as on any other issue in living memory. Alan Bullock's anti-Suez petition was signed by 10 Heads of House, 20 Professors and Readers, and 235 Fellows of Colleges. The total was thus 265 anti-Suez versus a pro-Suez count of 100. The same proportion would have held true for All Souls, perhaps with a slightly higher figure for the pro-Suez cohort. But there are no solid figures, because people altered their views. Isaiah Berlin, for example, wrote to Clarissa Eden after Nasser's nationalization of the Suez Canal Company that Egypt should be punished. But he changed his mind after he pondered the consequences for Britain of another prolonged occupation of Egypt and the possibility of an expansionist Israel. In a highly complex play of emotions, his anti-colonialist convictions clashed with his pro-Zionist sentiments.[20]

I began this lecture by calling for reflection on Suez and the year 1956 as a point in time, and for a comparison of the college then with the All Souls of 1936. To recapitulate: the college in 1956 more closely resembled the college of twenty years earlier rather than that of twenty years later. The key year was 1966. The anti-Suez demonstration at Trafalgar Square had become institutionalized in the Campaign for Nuclear Disarmament. The hippies whom John Sparrow detested were in the ascendancy. All Souls was under siege, challenged by a University Commission for infirmity of purpose. Yet the college survived—and in fact entered into a period of renewed purpose. There is great irony that this change took place under John Sparrow, whose aim in life had become to keep the college in exactly the same state, if not where it had been when he was a Prize Fellow in the 1920s, then at least in its condition from the day before yesterday. Sparrow rose to the challenge of the University Commission by acquiescing in the plan for Visiting Fellows. For him, it was merely the best among bad alternatives, one of which, amalgamation with St. Antony's, would have created, according to Geoffrey Hudson, a new Oxford institution called St. Antony's and Other Souls. The Visiting Fellowship program was viewed by some at the time as Sparrow's double-cross, a way of keeping the College the same but camouflaging it with visitors. It proved otherwise. At one stroke All Souls was transformed from an Oxford college that had ceased to have a public function, and was becoming academically insignificant, into an international intellectual institution that began again to flourish by attracting distinguished academic talent from throughout the world. In 1966, ten years after Suez, the British were beating a retreat from the southern Arabian Peninsula at Aden and were about to wind down the Empire once and forever more. At Oxford, All Souls was still more than a decade away from Warden Sparrow's retirement, in 1979, and still some fifteen years away from an event perhaps as significant as the creation of the Visiting Fellows program. In 1981, All Souls elected a female Fellow, exactly twenty-five years after the Suez crisis and what now seems a remote era.

Spring Semester 2007

This lecture was given originally as a Chichele Lecture at All Souls College, November 2006.

1. Keith Kyle, *Suez* (London, 1991), p. 432.

2. David Caute, "Crisis in All Souls," *Encounter*, 36, 3 (Mar. 1966), p. 15.

3. Michael Howard, *Captain Professor: The Memoirs of Sir Michael Howard* (London, 2006), p. 155.

4. Anthony Sampson, *Anatomy of Britain* (London, 1962), pp. 214–15.

5. Noel Annan, *Our Age* (London, 1990), p. 228.

6. Lord Hailsham, *A Sparrow's Flight* (London, 1990), p. 292.

7. Memorial service addresses by Sir Peter Ramsbotham, Sir Jeremy Morse, and Lord Carrington (All Souls College, 1997).

8. Dated June 1993, Makins Papers MS Sherfield, Box 957, Bodleian Library.

9. Makins to Sir Donald Logan, 2 Aug. 1978, Makins Papers, Box 957.

10. Makins, "Sidelights on Suez."

11. D. R. Thorpe, *Eden: The Life and Times of Anthony Eden* (London, 2003), p. 496; William Clark Papers, Box 160.

12. Makins, "Sidelights on Suez."

13. Unpublished memoir by Reilly, Reilly Papers MS. Eng., Box 9621, Bodleian Library.

14. Quoted in W. R. Louis, *Ends of British Imperialism* (London, 2006), pp. 637–38.

15. Unpublished memoir by Reilly.

16. Hailsham, *Sparrow's Flight*, p. 285.

17. Frances West, *Gilbert Murray: A Life* (London, 1984), p. 244.

18. Brian Harrison, ed., *The History of the University of Oxford*: Vol. VIII: *The Twentieth Century* (Oxford 1994), p. 408.

19. Quoted in Louis, *Ends of British Imperialism*, p. 23.

20. Michael Ignatieff, *Isaiah Berlin: A Life* (London, 1998), p. 237.

Britannia's Mau Mau

JOHN LONSDALE

Kenya was always Britain's most troublesome African colony because it was neither one thing nor the other. It was not on the Atlantic west coast, with a wholly African population, nor in the south, where white settlers dominated. It was betwixt and between. British policy vacillated accordingly. Kenya's historiography has been similarly stormy. Its controversies are important, not only for what they reveal about Kenya, but also for the light they shed on wider debates about imperialism and colonialism, especially settler colonialism, and the nature of African interaction with it. As to the last, historians used to frame their arguments in simple terms of resistance and collaboration. They have long conceived of a more complex dialogue. That historiographical transition informs the present argument, in which three controversies are examined in the light of colonial Kenya's seven ages of ambiguity.

ANY ANALYSIS OF COLONIAL KENYA'S HISTORY excites disagreement. Its three main controversies concern large simple concepts for organizing an historical narrative. The first focuses on European imperialism generally: was it a civilizing or a brutalizing mission? The second concerns, specifically, the political economy of settler colonialism: did it destroy indigenous peasant forms of production, or did it, instead, bring them into a productive relationship with the state? Finally, what was the relationship between race and class in colonial capitalism: did racial difference straightforwardly separate

white capitalists from black workers, and did that racial-class correlation determine their political behavior? All these simple questions
are owed complex, that is, historical, answers.

The first controversy, about the nature of imperialism, has in
Kenya's historiography centered on the Mau Mau movement that
dominated the local politics of decolonization. At the time, in the
1950s, almost all British observers saw Mau Mau—a rising that mobilized many of Kenya's largest ethnic group, the Kikuyu, who were
themselves about 20 percent of the total population—as irrational,
tinged with religious reaction, and lacking legitimate grievance.
Most officials, missionaries, and settlers thought it to be the convulsion of a bewildered people, disoriented by colonial development,
literacy, exposure to modern markets, and the subversion of former
social hierarchy. Such people were too easily led by self-seeking agi-
tators, of whom Jomo Kenyatta was the chief. This explanation presumed that British rule was either too progressive to be assimilated
by the native Kikuyu mind or that civilization had not yet penetrated
far enough. There was room in the British view for deep disagreement over the counterinsurgent relationship, therefore, between
repression and reform, each with an eye to fostering a rational, racially and ethnically inclusive Kenyan political culture within which
power might safely be shared and to which, eventually, it could be
devolved.[1]

Against that British analysis, rejected and then ignored these last
forty years, historians now argue that most Kikuyu, especially the
young and the poor, had a burning sense of grievance in their fear
of impending social extinction. This pitted them not only against
the British but also against their own elders and betters. They felt
they were about to lose the opportunity to achieve civilized, fully
adult Kikuyu status. The scarcity of land, employment, and education meant that there was no way for them to gather the material
means with which to marry, bring up children, build the future of
their society, and so become respected ancestors. Social extinction
was eternal.

But what caused this apprehension? This leads to the second layer
of controversy, about the nature of settler colonialism in Kenya and
how far it did, or did not, destroy African agriculture. The radical
supporters of Mau Mau, of whom Caroline Elkins is the latest, argue that white settlement rested on the "stolen lands" that Kikuyu
and others lost early in the twentieth century, before the First World
War. That loss caused a general sense of poverty and oppression, and
all for the benefit of worthless settlers up to all sorts of white mis-
chief with other men's wives—"parasites in paradise," as Ngugi wa

Thiong'o, a Kenyan novelist, has called them. On this analysis, Mau
Mau was a nationalist vanguard, crushed, as Elkins argues, with
horrific savagery because of the total opposition, within a generally brutal imperialism, between whites who exploited the land, and
Africans who had been pushed off it. The repression of the revolt
could therefore be almost genocidal in scale with, in her estimation,
between 136,000 and 300,000 dead among a Kikuyu population
of around 1,600,000. The main actors were the British, local and
metropolitan, desperate to regain supremacy by restoring a racial
balance of terror. Their African auxiliaries were not so much allies
as quislings. There was no civilizing impulse visible in counterinsurgency thought and practice, despite propaganda claims to the
contrary.[2]

Like the original British view, this radical analysis of Mau Mau
and British counterinsurgency is too simple in its assumptions about
Kenya's political economy. In reality, the colonial era saw a great expansion of African peasant farming, largely at the expense of cattle
keepers, the Maasai and Kalenjin peoples. While Kenya is a large
country, a little larger than France, with nearly a quarter of a million square miles, useful Kenya is small. Most of the country is desert and semi-desert. There are about 30,000 square miles of what
agriculturalists call high- and medium-potential land, fertile and
well watered. Eighty percent of this land was in the "native reserves";
about 20 percent was in white hands. Much of the White Highlands
(mostly over 5,000 feet) was less well watered, used mostly for ranch-
ing. The important point for this analysis is that the large area of
good rain-fed land available to Africans allowed peasant agriculture
to grow and differentiate. It was, moreover, at times encouraged to
do so. The colonial government repeatedly called on smallholders
to repair the weaknesses of large-farm agriculture, first to boost government revenues in the depressions of the early 1920s and 1930s,
and then in the 1950s as part of the "second prong," the civilian
arm, of counterinsurgency, to give Africans the incomes, and hopes,
that settler farming had failed to offer. Whenever the British did
try to enlarge peasant export production, however, they generally
did so under rigorously conservationist land- and cattle-husbandry
regimes that imposed real and immediate costs in labor, land, and
livestock, but offered only long-term, rather speculative benefits not
open to all.

The other crucial point to make is that African agriculture developed not only on this premium "native" land, but also on much
of the White Highlands, previously uncultivated, where the Maasai had herded. Like the Cherokee seventy years before them, the

Maasai were forced to embark on a trail of tears in 1911. They had
to vacate half their land for the benefit of British settlers and their
largely Kikuyu clients, the so-called squatters, tenant-workers. These
colonized the former lands of the Maasai to often greater productive effect than their white patrons had done. Other pastoral people
lost land too. The cultivating Kikuyu, the people of Mau Mau, lost
about 6 percent of their land. Those most involved in the militant,
violent wing of Mau Mau were in northern Kikuyuland, where the
least land was lost. Those in the southern Kikuyu lands, who lost the
most, were the least involved in Mau Mau warfare, a paradox yet to
be explained.

Land loss and the consequent poverty, therefore, are too simple as
explanations for Mau Mau. Similarly, extermination of a rebel tribe
is too simple to be a plausible aim of British counterinsurgency. The
Mau Mau war was unquestionably barbaric, on both sides; guerilla
wars are. But from the outset of the Emergency, the British envisaged the need for a second prong to offset the political costs of military repression. It was also unavoidable in a political economy that
had long needed to bring the peasant in. The British instituted land
reforms, bringing what they saw as economic and legal reason to the
social intricacies of African inheritance; and they fostered African
coffee and tea culture, even while fighting Mau Mau rebels, detain-
ing suspects in vast wired-in camps, and herding women and children
into strategic hamlets. Counterinsurgency would make no imperial
sense without the growth and stability that might, with luck, restore
Kenya to a governability that made politically thinkable a decolonization that was, in any case and in the long run, inevitable. Again, one
has to pursue a more complex argument to grasp the experience
and thoughts of both insurgents and rulers.

The third controversy raises questions about the relationship
of race and class, and the nature of political community. Among
Kenya's first professional historians, in the 1960s and '70s, when a
vulgar neo-Marxism was in vogue, one finds two parallel arguments.
According to the first, the settlers, whose leaders were drawn from
the British officer class, saw Africans as a working class—a seemingly natural correlation. Fitting Africans into a known class system, it used to be argued, dictated Kenya's unequal race relations.
The second argument mirrored the first by analyzing Mau Mau as a
worker-and-peasant revolt that drew on class rather than ethnic solidarity. This had the added advantage of making Mau Mau a class-
conscious nationalism rather than an ethnically sectarian outburst.

Both theses can be questioned on their own neo-Marxist terms.
As to the supposed class character of Mau Mau, the racial appor-

tionment of Kenya's best farmland, together with the settlers' economic weakness before 1940, allowed African social differentiation to grow. Not all were flattened economically into workers and small peasants, especially not in Kikuyuland, situated as it is in the center of Kenya. Well watered, cool at night, above the malaria line, it was not only good for peasant farmers but also attractive to missionaries, who there established more schools than in other, less climatically favored regions. Kikuyu made the money to pay their school fees by trading beans, maize, and charcoal in the capital city, Nairobi, their local market town, and by generally making themselves useful to their white employers and rulers. Partly as a result, the Mau Mau movement lacked solidarity and fell apart from within even as it was attacked by the British from without. Kikuyu squatters were also the foundation of white farming. That is why it is also vital to understand how settlers saw Africans.

There is certainly truth in the idea that middle-class Britons thought of Africans as a natural working class, but, again, that is too simple. One can discern at least three British attitudes toward race and class in Kenya, changing through time. The first was aristocratic. Early colonists invested in Kenya because, in the words of one, "you could feel the future of it *under your feet.*"[3] Similarly, Violet Carnegie, married to a ninth earl's third son, called her Somali headman Omar "the best type of old family retainer," since he was "perfectly frank, but never familiar."[4] Initially, whites imagined a hierarchy of individual patrons and their personal African clients, not two opposed classes. Moreover, since there were few telephones or police before the 1940s, and most white farmhouses were miles from a neighbor, "self-help" promised more safety than any rule of law. This aristocratic attitude was transmuted over time as settlers came to realize that Africans were also political animals, and that they themselves were no longer superior colonists but, rather, a cultural minority, and one unable to rely on the unconditional support of the metropolitan government. Insecurity made them defensive, unwilling to concede to Africans, increasingly threatening as a majority race, the rights of an organized working class. Finally, after the Second World War, some urban employers with managerial rather than pioneering instincts were increasingly willing to see Africans as workers and, with Colonial Office persuasion, allowed them to bargain as organized trade unions.

There is a nice irony here, of the sort historians enjoy. Organized workers were the least likely to join Mau Mau—contrary to the neo-Marxist thesis. Their leader, Tom Mboya, became the man the British most trusted in negotiating the politics of decolonization.

An easy identification of race and class, and of class and Mau Mau rebellion, therefore, is entirely misleading. The more complex truth is that socially differentiated class formation occurred within African peasantries sufficiently prosperous to sustain such division. Those who have studied African class politics have tended to look for the evidence in towns. People certainly act as workers there, but what made them workers? Who drove them off their land? To answer that question, one has to look within rural families, within landholding lineage corporations. Intimate rivalries and jealousies are the ones to engender violence; Mau Mau's origins are here. Kikuyu were the richest peasantry in Kenya, which is to say they were the most divided: there were those who exploited their kin seniority in the markets for power, land, and labor, and there were the weaker kin and clients whom they excluded from opportunity. It was the insecurities of incipient class division, under the constrictions required by white supremacy, that made Mau Mau, not class solidarity.

IN SUMMARY, THEN, KENYA'S SETTLER COLONIALISM was no simple tyranny but a maze of contradictions. These complexities were played out in seven stages. The colony's origins, first, rested on a complementarity between an imperial geopolitics focused on India and an entirely African politics of British conquest. Settlers could make trouble here but could scarcely take command. The First World War, next, reinforced the global British dependence on India. Settlers could try to counter this only by creating something they could scarcely foresee and would certainly not have welcomed, the possibility of a modern, educated African politics. In the third stage, between the wars, the failures of settler agriculture allowed African peasant expansion on the misnamed White Highlands and forced the government to encourage farming in the "reserves" so that Africans could continue to pay tax. This relationship between settler and African economy, next, led to disaster only as the profitability of production in the Second World War allowed settlers to repudiate their African squatter clients while refusing them the rights of workers. But the consequent intimacy of conflict between returning squatters and their more secure kin in the reserves was almost entirely confined to the Kikuyu people, who almost alone entered the ranks of Mau Mau. Kenya's penultimate example of ambiguity was in the Mau Mau war itself, degrading and dirty on both sides and yet also providing a final opportunity for the colonial government to bring black peasants into a political economy that would once again be safe for settlers. In a final irony, colonial reform made Kenya safe for Kenyatta, the man the British blamed above all for the misery of

Mau Mau. History is not a linear process. Neither a Whiggish story of imperial enlightenment nor a "subaltern" tale of oppression and resistance does justice to Kenya's past and the lives of those who made it move.

As IMPORTANT TO AN UNDERSTANDING of colonial Kenya as the small number of British settlers was the comparatively large number of Indian immigrants, which rose from 25,000 in 1921 to 180,000 at independence, in 1963. By contrast, Indians were of negligible importance in Rhodesia (Zimbabwe) and South Africa, other than in Natal. British Kenya was initially an African province of India, part of India's African line of defense. Kenya's railway, without which there could be no settlement, was designed by Indian engineers and built by Indian labor. The Indian rupee was Kenya's currency until 1921. Indian law held sway in the courts. Indians controlled most local trade. They occupied all those subordinate positions, on the railway or in government, requiring technical or clerical skills. The Viceroy of India and, after 1947, Prime Minister Nehru were more central to British diplomacy and security than any colonial governor. This meant that London could not approve any policy that too blatantly favored settlers over Indians. The Colonial Office increasingly tried to stay above such quarrels by declaring that Kenya belonged to neither.

Representative outpost of a multiracial empire, Kenya was an African and Indian rather than a white-settler colony. It was conquered with the help of Indian troops before the first settlers arrived, in 1903. The British had already made peace with Africans by practicing what Ronald Robinson, my mentor, called "the politics of collaboration."[5] All colonial governments tried to generate legitimacy by enlarging, leaning on, and rewarding the authority of those whom they thought already possessed it in indigenous society. So it was in Kenya. Settler politics, far from exercising a racial tyranny, are better seen as an ultimately failed effort to supplant the multiracial props of empire that they found in place: the global Indian prop, the local African one. This failure too was a fatal cause of Mau Mau, as settlers tried to segregate themselves from multiracial patronage and retreat into something like a British Home County on the Equator.

The twin foundations of British rule, Indian and African, were closely joined in Kenya. Indian traders imported consumer goods—bicycles and cottons—and bought African produce, everything from maize to hides and skins, in exchange. The politics of collaboration was made fruitful by Indian commerce long before whites produced anything. Better-connected Africans could pay their tax and mission-school fees without working for whites. Indian trade was a major promoter of African agriculture and education.

Early settler politics, in consequence, were often outrageous. Whites went to histrionic lengths to make themselves more visible, useful, and troublesome than Africans and Indians. Utility demanded investment, and that often brought ruin. Trouble was cheaper and attracted more attention. Settlers often beat their employees, who lacked recourse to the courts—indeed, once beat them in front of the courts—and threatened to suppress imagined native revolt if the colonial government did not demand more labor or impose higher taxes or take more land. Yet for all these efforts to assert control over Kenya's imperial narrative of progress, the colony's politics never escaped the complexities of its hybrid, Indo-African origins.

During the First World War, the second episode in this brief history, the East African campaign cost tens of thousands of African lives. What is now Tanzania was then German East Africa (Deutsch-Ostafrika), where Paul Erich von Lettow-Vorbeck, a tenacious general, led the British a miserable dance for all the four years of war, at African expense. The consequences were as ambiguous as Kenya's origins. War appeared to strengthen the settlers' hand. They officered African troops in defense of the Empire and saw off the Hun. They obtained local executive responsibility. They were promised the vote as reward. Locally, they were essential imperial allies; globally, the story was different. Indian troops and taxpayers were strategically vital. Two thousand settlers of military age were not. This contrast between pygmy settlers and militarily mighty India was the root of the post-war political crisis, the "Indian question." As settlers pressed for their promised electoral power, the Viceroy in India, responding to Indian National Congress alarm, vetoed such gains unless Indians were also brought into the political arena. The Colonial Office resolved the dilemma by reiterating for Kenya the "west coast" doctrine of British trusteeship for African interests, in which neither settlers nor Indians could expect to share.

The least noticed yet most important effect of this crisis was the settlers' realization that to receive imperial recognition, they must portray themselves as co-trustees of the African future and deny that role to Indians. They allied in this with the otherwise mistrusted Christian missionaries, who feared lest African opinion be led by Indians, many of them Muslims. In the 1920s, with some minor financial help from settlers, Protestant missionaries started the first African secondary school, the Alliance High School, still the Eton of Kenya. By the 1940s, Alliance did better than white schools in public examinations, and in 1963 supplied half the cabinet ministers of Jomo Kenyatta's first independent government. Settlers had scarcely bargained for this when calling in the African cause to trump the Indian claims. Probably by the 1940s, and certainly by the 1950s, the Alliance school choir was singing the folk song "In an English Country Garden." It was to a segregated country garden on the Equator that, by the 1940s, the settlers were trying to retreat. To many whites it was intolerable that the Alliance High School boys should presume to get there too.

The unacceptability of a modern African elite owed something to the fact that a mass of poor Africans, a fifth column, had already got inside the White Highlands fence, or under it, as farm squatters. In this third aspect of Kenya's story, whites could recruit labor and pay it the meager wages the first farmers could afford only by offering cultivating and grazing rights to African, largely Kikuyu, peasant families in return for the obligation to labor. Both parties benefited from this arrangement until at least the late 1930s, partly because settlers found it hard to make a profit. They were 500 miles from Mombasa's docks. Shipping lines did not offer freight rates competitive with those at Durban or Bombay. Whites with the least capital grew maize in competition with Africans, a hopeless proposition in the 1930s. Ranchers faced the risks of rinderpest plagues and tick-borne East Coast fever and could not compete with Argentine beef. Squatter cultivation and livestock did at least keep farmland clear of bush and grasses sweet. At the same time, the government, as deep in debt as any white farmer, encouraged cash-crop cultivation in the reserves in order to maintain its African tax base. African farming therefore prospered on two fronts. But squatters seem to have had the best of it; a survey in the 1940s found that squatter householders had more wives than their counterparts in the reserves.

Disaster came to first black and then white when settler farmers started to mechanize in the Second World War, the fourth episode in Kenya's history, and as ambiguous in its results as the Great War had been twenty years before. White farming at last flourished. The overseas market that had been so difficult to enter now came to Kenya instead. An army of South African and West African troops arrived to help the King's African Rifles, the local regiment, throw Mussolini out of Ethiopia, across Kenya's northern frontier. Italian prisoners of war flooded in, more than doubling the white population. Not far away, Montgomery's Eighth Army was keeping Rommel from Suez. Soldiers and prisoners had to be fed. The Indian Ocean was less risky for shipping than the Atlantic or Mediterranean. Even in overseas markets, therefore, Kenya gained a comparative advantage.

Settlers paid off their debts. They became the state's economic managers. Kenya became a settler colony.

Settlers were also imperially visible, but as ambiguously as before. They again led African troops, of whom some 90,000 volunteered from Kenya. Farmers' sons died, along with peasants' sons, to put Haile Selassie back on his Ethiopian throne. East Africans then helped drive the Japanese out of Burma (Myanmar). Settlers' sons leading African platoons—senior officers were from Britain—thus helped make it possible for the British to decolonize India and for Nehru to become white Kenya's weightiest critic.

Most significant for the settler future, however, was the war's effect on African social differentiation. Black cultivators prospered along with whites. Their maize, East Africa's staple, fed not only armies but also the enlarged urban workforces that in Mombasa and Nairobi helped supply the war. Economic growth did not, in general, create the degree of differentiation that might have split African politics into moderate and militant camps. Kikuyuland was the exception, close to both the railway and Nairobi, the hub of Kenya. Kikuyu landowners continued to do well after the war, as did settlers, so long as primary products commanded high prices in a half-starved world.

Three sorts of Kikuyu, however, did particularly badly. Few were so marginalized among other ethnic groups. Those who fared worst were the squatters who had colonized the White Highlands under white patronage. During the war, settlers not only put more land under the plow, but also became nervous about how a future British Labour government might regard their squatters' rights. They turned the screws on their squatter dependents, accordingly, reducing their rights to cultivate and herd. Many squatters left the White Highlands and tried, often unsuccessfully, to find a home back in the reserves. This second theft of land was more grievous than the first. Most of the white farmland they had enjoyed was not theirs historically but had been made their own by a generation of sweat. Here, in squatter dispossession by their former patrons, lay the proximate cause of Mau Mau.

Moreover, settlers could not accept the one alternative the government proposed. Officials argued that if farmers no longer wanted squatter tenants, if they wished to reduce them to landless laborers, then an English remedy would be to settle them in villages between white farms, with property rights as cottagers and able to sell their labor to whomever they chose. Settlers rejected this class-divided solution. They saw squatters not so much as a class but as a race. It was as a race that whites enjoyed their exclusive Highland property.

They could not share it; in an uncertain world it was their one insurance. Refusal to allow Africans working-class status was one of the chief stimuli to Mau Mau. Displaced squatters were prominent in the rebellion, joined by poor peasants from the reserves, squeezed off their land by successful Kikuyu farmers, and by townspeople caught in the scissors between raging wartime inflation and an end to wartime employment.

In all three categories men and women feared social extinction, exclusion from all hope of founding a family, all hope of honor and esteem. Mau Mau was in part an intergenerational conflict. Younger men were first inspired by moderate nationalists like Jomo Kenyatta, but then—disillusioned by his failure to deliver what they most needed, land and self-mastery—outran him in the violence of their political action.

CONTROVERSY RAGES AT PRESENT about casualties in the Mau Mau war, the sixth episode of this history. The historiography of the Emergency has changed radically over the years. The first studies, in the 1960s and 1970s, were by Frank Corfield and Anthony Clayton. Corfield, a retired civil servant from the Sudan and Palestine, wrote the one official report on Mau Mau's supposed origins, and Clayton was a Kenyan official who has since become a distinguished military historian. While Corfield said little about the counterinsurgency that Clayton detailed, both took the view that the British had fought a war, principally in the forests where Mau Mau militants took refuge. Their statistics, therefore, were military. Of those killed in action, Mau Mau numbered over 11,000; the security forces, 164. In these accounts, the civilians killed by Mau Mau numbered 32 whites, 26 Asians, and nearly 2,000 Africans. Clayton and Corfield agreed on the figures. Clayton also noted, however, as Corfield did not, that the British hanged over 1,000 Mau Mau convicts, an unprecedented use of the gallows. Neither, however, saw counterinsurgency as a social trauma for the Kikuyu, but rather as a war in which casualties were confined, broadly, to those on either side who were murdered or killed in action.[6]

Only recently have two historians, David Anderson of Oxford and Caroline Elkins of Harvard, examined the total nature of the war and asked other than military questions. In his *Histories of the Hanged,* Anderson analyzed, principally, the degradation of British judicial norms and procedures protective of suspects. From official files and court records, he found that the colonial government, largely for fear of white vigilantism, reclassified many offenses as capital crimes: the possession of arms, consorting with or giving aid to guerrillas, and so on. To judge by its collusive cover-ups, the British establishment was properly ashamed of the rough justice it meted out in its panic to get justice done, although of 1,500 capital convictions, 400 were either commuted to imprisonment or were successfully appealed. Many Kikuyu—Anderson thinks probably 150,000 in all, about 71,000 at the peak, in late 1954—were also detained, on suspicion rather than on evidence, in a "pipeline" of wired-in work camps. Almost all were released by late 1958, after between three and five years of detention and after confessing their Mau Mau oaths.

Elkins, whose *Britain's Gulag* (or *Imperial Reckoning*) was also published in 2005, was interested in a still wider aspect of the Emergency: the Kikuyu experience of the physical and mental rigors, tortures even, of a counterinsurgency war waged more often behind barbed wire than in the dripping forests of Mount Kenya. While Elkins calls this an untold story, most of it was known at the time, was subject to parliamentary inquiry, greatly embarrassed the government of Harold Macmillan, and has been analyzed by more than one historian since. She argues that no less than 95 percent of the Kikuyu population was detained, since she includes villagization, largely of women and children, as a form of detention, along with the generally male work camps. In this she is justified, since Kikuyu had not previously lived in close village communities. The agricultural upheaval, forced labor, and new proximity of living brought malnutrition and disease in its wake. From the census reports of 1948 and 1962, either side of the Emergency years, Elkins calculated that up to 300,000 Kikuyu died or were not born in the 1950s, largely due to the hardships of villagization. She could propose what seems to be an unbelievable level of mortality because of her general interpretation of colonial rule in Kenya as settler tyranny, a political economy that needed Africans only as the cheap labor that, by the 1950s, was available in larger numbers than could be employed. British rule in Kenya had no prudential disincentive, therefore, against genocide. Having little need of Kikuyu, the British had little reason not to kill them. The more complicated story I have outlined suggests that the British had every need of Kikuyu, not just as labor but also, and increasingly, as independent market-minded cultivators.

More detailed census findings are in an article in *African Affairs* by John Blacker, an official in the East African Statistical Department in the 1950s and 1960s and a consultant for two Kenyan censuses after independence.[7] He has used not two censuses but four, and calculated back-projections of family formation. He believes up to 50,000 Kikuyu went missing during the Emergency years, one-sixth of Elkins's higher estimate. How many of these were unreported killings by Mau Mau, he does not speculate. Of the 50,000, some 17,000 were men—and the British admitted to killing over 11,000. Probably 7,000 women died, chiefly of malnutrition. Half of all apparent deaths—26,000—were of children under ten. Blacker finds this tragedy unsurprising. A raised mortality rate for under-fives, 20 percent higher than normal in the Kikuyu case, is to be expected at time of war. In the 1990s, after the first Gulf War, Blacker was chief demographer for the United Nations in Iraq, where he found that child mortality had doubled. He cannot say how many of these Kikuyu children died and how many were yet to be born. There was a baby boom, as after all wars, in Kikuyuland after the Emergency.

Death rates matter, not because they tell us much about the relative brutality of insurgent and counterinsurgent war—which was harsh enough no matter how many died—but because of what they say about the historical structures of settler colonialism within which the Mau Mau war was fought. Blacker has found that young Kikuyu women of secondary-school age in the 1950s had a year or two of education more than their sisters in other ethnic groups. This Kikuyu advantage lasted through the Mau Mau years. While many children undoubtedly perished, many were also apparently missing because of the later age of female Kikuyu marriage, which was due both to the horrors of war and, more prosaically, to the fact that many teenage young women were still in school.[8] The second prong of social and economic reform was not all propaganda. The British had experienced too many years of educated African pressure to get away with that. Peasant ambition had acquired its own momentum. The missionary interest was too strongly entrenched.

The final complication in the Kenya story is that settler property, stolen land, became the foundation of postcolonial stability. Unlike most other African colonies at the time, Kenya was well surveyed, a precondition for orderly resettlement. It was also relatively well provided with agricultural services, roads, irrigation, and veterinary controls. Once it was decided to buy out the settlers at the time of independence, it was quickly done. The state-supervised peasant settlement of the former White Highlands in the early 1960s was the chief source of popular support for Jomo Kenyatta and, since then, an important reason for Kenya's comparative post-colonial peace.

Peasants were once again central to the political economy. They had been there from the start as the basis of the politics of collaboration. Their production had founded many an Indian fortune. They had invaded the White Highlands as squatters, and there prospered until the 1940s. Their dispossession thereafter, officials knew, was a major cause of Mau Mau. It was this knowledge that had stirred the government to embark on an agricultural revolution during the Emergency—which was, together with trade-union recognition, the second prong of counterinsurgency—to force peasants to consolidate their patches of land into smallholdings, with freehold title, on which to grow coffee and tea. These reforms were intended to draw the sting of African landlessness, to make Kenya safe for the white minority under any future "multiracial" government. In a final irony of history, they helped Africans, instead, finance their anti-colonial politics and then brought stability to a Kenya ruled not multiracially but by Jomo Kenyatta, the man whom the British had so recently hated and feared.

Neither imperialism nor settler colonialism were total impositions. They were not civilizing or brutalizing missions, but dialogues. The British had to weigh profit against peace. Africans adopted changing combinations of acceptance, opportunity, and resistance. And for much of Kenya's colonial history, Indians held the ring between them.

Fall Semester 2006

1. John Lonsdale, "Mau Maus of the Mind: Making Mau Mau and Remaking Kenya," *Journal of African History*, 31 (1990), pp. 393–421. The present paper owes much to critical reaction from Professor Patricia Romero's seminar at Towson University, Md.; to the "Year of Kenya" audience at Kennesaw State University, Atlanta; to the British Studies seminar at Austin; and to the Rev. Ben Knighton at the Oxford Centre for Mission Studies.

2. Caroline Elkins, *Britain's Gulag: The Brutal End of Empire in Kenya* (London, 2005 [published in the United States as *Imperial Reckoning: The Untold Story of Britain's Gulag in Africa*]), pp. 366, 429; Ngugi wa Thiong'o quoted in David Anderson, *Histories of the Hanged: The Dirty War in Kenya and the End of Empire* (London, 2005), p. 79. For the figures later quoted, see his appendices.

3. Beryl Markham, *West with the Night* (1942; London, 1984 edn.), p. 67; emphasis added.

4. V. M. Carnegie, *A Kenyan Farm Diary* (Edinburgh, 1930), p. 25.

5. Ronald Robinson, "Non-European Foundations of European Imperialism: Sketch for a Theory of Collaboration," in Roger Owen and Bob Sutcliffe, eds., *Studies in the Theory of Imperialism* (London, 1972), pp. 117–40.

6. F. D. Corfield, *Historical Survey of the Origins and Growth of Mau Mau*, Cmnd. 1030 (London, 1960); Anthony Clayton, *Counter-Insurgency in Kenya, 1952–60* (Nairobi, 1976).

7. John Blacker, "The Demography of Mau Mau: Fertility and Mortality in Kenya in the 1950s—A Demographer's Viewpoint," *African Affairs*, 106 (Apr. 2007), pp. 205–27.

8. For a firsthand account, see Jocelyn Murray, "Kenya, 1954," in Patricia W. Romero, ed., *Women's Voices on Africa: A Century of Travel Writings* (Princeton, 1992), pp. 269–78.

20

Empire in the Twenty-First-Century English Imagination

STEPHEN HOWE

The early spring of 2007 marked a coincidence of four anniversaries in Britain, all widely celebrated, and all in some ambiguous and contested sense "imperial." These were the 200th anniversary of Britain's abolition of the Atlantic slave trade, the 50th of Ghana's independence, the 25th of the war with Argentina over the Falkland Islands, and the 4th of the invasion of Iraq. A little later in 2007, the 300th anniversary of the Union of England and Scotland would be marked, although seemingly more people than at any time in the intervening centuries either desired or expected that Union's imminent end.[1] So too would be the 150th anniversary of India's 1857 revolt and the 60th of its (and Pakistan's) independence, plus the 400th of English colonial settlement in Jamestown, Virginia.[2]

These multiple commemorations intervened in what seemed to be a crescendo of debate over the legacies and significance of empire for British history and identity, which in its turn interacted or worked in parallel with a heightened and transformed climate of attention to colonial questions in academic circles. Argument over what kind of British history, in what kind of association with citizenship education in British national identity and values (if any), should be taught in schools had a probably unprecedented vigor.

And central to such argument were clashing perceptions of Britain's global role in the past—and the present.

In March 2005 and again in January 2006, Chancellor—and Prime Minister-in-waiting—Gordon Brown sparked heated exchanges with his call to "celebrate Britishness" and stop apologizing for empire (to which some critics inevitably responded: "When did we start?").[3] David Cameron, about to become the new leader of the Conservative Party, echoed this view. "We need to re-assert faith in our shared British values which help guarantee stability, tolerance and civility," Cameron said in August 2005, urging that school history teaching, especially in relation to empire, should encourage all children to be proud of Britain's history and values.[4]

All four early-spring anniversaries had their own, often sharply contested, politics of commemoration, though these were relatively absent in relation to Ghanaian independence, which was celebrated in almost unalloyedly positive terms. The most widely marked of these commemorations, by some margin, was that of slave-trade abolition. How should England "remember" slavery, its abolition, and aftermath? Should there be formal apologies, reparations, or compensation? If so, from and to whom should they be made? Are there distinct, even antagonistic, "black" and "white" memories of slavery?[5] What were the implications for the rethinking of Britishness and its history? Officialdom walked a tightrope between celebration of Britain's role in destroying slavery, and a far more somber, even anguished or shame-filled, commemoration of the preceding centuries. The Prime Minister's posture on the tightrope was to say: "Personally I believe the bicentenary offers us a chance not just to say how profoundly shameful the slave trade was—how we condemn its existence utterly and praise those who fought for its abolition—but also to express our deep sorrow that it ever happened, that it ever could have happened and to rejoice at the different and better times we live in today."[6] There were some sharp criticisms that such statements did not amount to a full apology: it was reported that Whitehall advisers had warned that such apology could open the door to claims for reparations from the descendants of slaves.

More pointedly still, critics argued not only that commemoration unduly highlighted the roles of particular white abolitionists, especially William Wilberforce, but also that its celebratory aspects masked or even covertly furthered a notion of "liberal Empire," of Britain's global role as a crusade for freedom, which had disconcerting resonances for the twenty-first-century present.[7] There reemerged, in such critics' eyes, an "abolitionist syndrome," whereby the ending of slavery was credited only to its moral condemnation by some within Britain, and both the protests and revolts by slaves themselves, and the economic and strategic interests in play, were ignored.

The coincident anniversaries of the Falklands War and of intervention in Iraq were considerably more difficult still to consign to history than was 1807. The Falklands War has for some while been seen as a crucial, transformative moment in Britain's recent past. There is little surprise that in 2007 it was rhetorically linked to the conflict in Iraq, but to sharply opposed ends. Tony Blair made the connection on the eve of the Falklands' twenty-fifth anniversary. There may have been an intention to suggest enhancement of his own standing in the way that, to her admirers, Margaret Thatcher had done by leading the country in a victorious war—just as his own ten-year premiership was coming to its end. If so, hostile observers suggested, it was bound to backfire: the parallel only highlighted the stark contrast between a quick, decisive triumph in the South Atlantic and the unended Iraqi embroilment.

In a post-war victory speech at Cheltenham on 3 July 1982, Thatcher had been explicit, indeed triumphalist, about the "imperial" nature of the Falklands and its lessons. She proclaimed:

> When we started out, there were the waverers and the fainthearts.... Those who believed our decline was irreversible—that we could never again be what we once were . . . People who in their heart of hearts had their secret fears that Britain was no longer the nation that had built an Empire and ruled a quarter of the world.
>
> Well they were wrong. The lesson of the Falklands is that Britain has not changed . . .
>
> Britain has found herself again in the South Atlantic and will not look back from the victory she has won.[8]

A quarter-century later, on the deck of HMS *Albion* on 12 January 2007, Blair's linking of past, present, and future was far more somber in tone, but no less resolute in advocating a global British military and political role. He argued that the country must not allow its former imperial strength to slip away. Despite all the divisions in the country and in his own party, Blair made it clear that the Islamist threat—"every bit as pervasive . . . as revolutionary communism in its early and most militant phase"—must be met primarily by the "hard" power of military force, in whose exercise Britain should continue to have a leading role. He criticized those who saw Britain's role as only one of leading "the fight against climate change, against global poverty, for peace and reconciliation." He expressed passionate disagreement with that case; instead, Britain must maintain a world position, not least through willingness to employ military force:

> The frontiers of our security no longer stop at the Channel. What happens in the Middle East affects us. What happens in Pakistan; or Indonesia; or in the attenuated struggles for territory and supremacy in Africa . . . The new frontiers for our security are global. Our armed forces will be deployed in the lands of other nations . . . in environments and ways unfamiliar to them.[9]

IF THE EXTERNAL FACE OF EMPIRE'S IMAGINATIVE, and very material, legacies to the twenty-first century lies in this continued, indeed enhanced, geostrategic role, it is widely and surely rightly felt that its internal, domestic aspect is present above all in thinking about national identity and its relation to race.[10]

However difficult these things may be to measure, it seems accurate to think that after 1945 there was more open and intense racism in Britain's public culture than in those, say, of France or the Netherlands. And although parties of the extreme right have, since the 1940s, been a very marginal presence in British politics, racially motivated violence has been a feature of British history since the anti-Jewish and anti-Chinese provocations a century ago, or anti-Irish ones even longer ago. Reading almost any day's issue of some British newspapers, perhaps especially the "middle market" tabloids the *Daily Mail* and *Daily Express,* immediately reminds one of how bitter the hostility to refugees and asylum seekers is in some quarters.

There are, however, important features of Britain's historical experience that may help account for the more positive trends in its race relations today. Most obviously and most recently, there are the distinctive patterns of non-European migration to Britain since 1945 and of citizenship policies toward immigrants. Lying behind that, there is an older history of the United Kingdom and of Britishness as multinational phenomena: these have become interrelated with contemporary ideas about multiculturalism in ways that are still too little explored. Then there are the legacies within Britain itself of the Empire—and especially at the efforts now being made to investigate how the colonial experience shaped the cultures not only of the colonies but of Britain and Britishness too. Related to this last point is the manner in which colonial and postcolonial intellectuals have contributed to rethinking Britishness.

Certainly, major aspects of Britain's race-relations record have been heavily shaped by the legacies of overseas empire, but it may be that an even older historical experience is also highly relevant, especially to the ways in which Britishness has been conceived and reworked. Multiculturalism in modern Britain has had at least two faces: a centuries-old one concerned with multiple national identities within a compound state, and a newer one relating to migrants and their children. The two are closely connected, particularly through the experience and legacies of empire. Almost all European states have emerged from processes of secession or amalgamation, and almost all of these have involved experiences both of peaceful integration and of coerced, even extremely violent, incorporation of minorities.

England created Britain and Britishness through the conquest and integration of Wales, Scotland, and Ireland. The process was intertwined with the creation of a centralized, increasingly powerful monarchical state and, later, of an overseas empire. But it did not follow a single, unifying logic: the extent to which local and national distinctiveness was crushed, overridden, or incorporated varied hugely among Wales, Scotland, and Ireland, among regions within each, and within England too. The British state combined a strong, unitary structure of rule with a decentralized, even chaotically diverse, set of social and cultural institutions. Acceptance of diversity, indirect rule through local preconquest elites, and tolerance of cultural and institutional variation minimized political conflict—though of course this worked far less well in Ireland than in Wales or Scotland. The central state concerned itself mainly with issues such as foreign policy and defense. Most other functions of government were exercised locally. London dominance would inevitably become more of an issue as the central government's scope of activities greatly expanded across the twentieth century. Culturally, the notion of Britishness overlay rather than replaced the distinct national and sectional identities of the Union's component parts. So far as there was a British *Leitkultur,* it included substantial, continuing, distinctive English, Scottish, Welsh, and Irish elements.

The process became intertwined with another, slightly later one: the attempt to create a global Britishness, a sense of collective identity that expanded the imagined national community right across the Empire. Whether such a conception ever became universal, hegemonic, or even dominant may be questioned: but it connected distant communities of British descent and others too. Empire building in its turn helped cement Britishness: Scots, especially, could retain national pride within the Union, in conjunction with a sense of political Britishness, through their role in imperial expansion.

Tendencies of decentralization were also characteristic of Britain's imperial system—perhaps more so than in any other major modern colonial empire. The colonies of white settlement, with Canada in the lead, quite rapidly achieved a high degree of self-government. And British colonial rulers across much of Africa and Asia opted for indirect rule. Local precolonial authorities were not swept away but sustained, with British officials ruling through them and acting as the half-hidden powers behind the throne.

The management of race relations within Britain after 1945 fitted into or copied that structure of decentralization and indirect rule. There was a strong tendency on the part of local, state, and other public agencies to identify, co-opt, and work with—or through—the leaders of minority communities. They were invariably unelected, usually male, usually middle-aged or elderly, religiously or culturally conservative. A pseudo-colonialist structure of patronage and clientage thus congealed in areas where members of minority groups were most numerous. Local politicians became ethnic entrepreneurs, bargaining the bloc votes or party affiliations they claimed to control in return for favors. Even where the result was not direct financial corruption, it undermined local democracy and equality of access and set up ethnic groups as rivals for scarce resources.

This whole set of structures, of rule and of compound identity, came under extreme strain beginning in the 1980s. Wales, Scotland, and northern England suffered disproportionately from economic restructuring and depression under Thatcher. Nationalism and demands for devolution, even independence, revived in Scotland. In Wales, the revival of nationalist feeling tended to be linked to use of the Welsh language, but demands for greater self-determination intensified there too. In Northern Ireland, nationalist assertion also increased, but only among Catholics; in the Protestant majority, pro-British Unionism consolidated its strength. Indeed, this is the only section of the United Kingdom where the self-description "British" has grown more popular in the past few decades. Just a little later, the indirect-rule model of multiculturalism too came under fire, from black and Asian spokespeople as well as white ones, for failing sufficiently to value social cohesion or a strong sense of nationally shared values.[11] Alarms and revelations about the appeal of militant Islamism among some young British-born Muslims sharply increased such concerns, especially after the London suicide bombings of July 2005.

The new institutions established in 1998 seem so far to have fed the desire for more devolved powers in Scotland and Wales, not satisfied it, while the power-sharing assembly and executive in Northern Ireland has been in a state of near-permanent crisis despite the partial ending of paramilitary violence.[12] In their national identity, as measured by self-description, the English, Scottish, and Welsh appear to be growing further apart. In Scotland, a huge majority now identifies itself as more Scottish than British; only among people over sixty-five is there still strong allegiance to "being British."

There appeared also to be a growing divergence between English and Scots perceptions of the United Kingdom's international role and its relation to imperial pasts. Certainly there was more widespread opposition to the Iraq War in Scotland than in England, and the Scottish National Party articulated a more forthright anti-war stance than did any of the "pan-British" opposition parties. Such feelings focused strongly around the role of Scottish army regiments like the Black Watch in Iraq, and the relatively heavy casualties they suffered there. Traditions of Scottish radicalism and militarism thus entered a complex, unstable new relationship.[13] Some Scottish nationalists had long viewed Scots soldiers as a kind of mercenary, mindlessly fighting and dying in England's wars. It was probably the historian John Prebble who first popularized the idea of Scottish regiments in British uniform being "colonial auxiliaries," easily disposable cannon fodder for the wars of empire.

As writers like Tom Nairn and Neal Ascherson document, the Scots' political and cultural ethos was dramatically renewed in the drive for self-government from the 1970s onward. And this included, so some argued, hostility to the legacies of empire, well encapsulated in Hamish Henderson's song "Freedom Come All Ye," which was adopted as an anthem by many nationalists.

> Nae muir will the bonnie callants [young men]
> Mairch tae war when oor braggarts crousely [joyously] craw,
> Nor wee weans [children] frae pit-heid and clachan [farm]
> Mourn the ships sailing doon the Broomielaw;
> Broken families, in lands we've herriet [harried],
> Will curse Scotland the Brave nae mair, nae mair.[14]

As Ascherson notes in his great book *Stone Voices,* its words "declare that Scottish soldiers are not glorious, but have drenched the world with innocent blood for the sake of a racialist Empire." Those feelings, even in their conservative and uniform-loving parts, threatened to redound with great force against the Iraq War.

As Britishness appears to be in retreat, debate over the meanings of Englishness comes ever more to the fore. Indeed, the "English question" is increasingly going to demand attention in the next few years. With or without a surviving British identity, how will the English—whose separate identity was in so many ways submerged by an expansionist, globalized Britishness—define themselves? Who, today, are the English anyway? There has already been a small flood of polemical or journalistic accounts, ranging from Simon Heffer's, Peter Hitchens's, and Roger Scruton's sorrow and rage at what they perceive to be the decline of Englishness, to Jeremy Paxman's more relaxed and liberal-minded stroll round the oddities of English character.[15]

The English question is crucially important to debates over migration, integration, and multi-ethnicity because the vast majority of migrants and members of ethnic minorities live in England, not in Scotland, Wales, or Northern Ireland. For members of these groups, the idea of Englishness poses sharper, more difficult identity dilemmas than does Britishness. And there are serious fears that English identity may, as it re-emerges into greater political and cultural prominence with the decline of Britishness, prove to be a narrower, more exclusionary—perhaps more belligerent, xenophobic, and racist—discourse than Britishness.

Members of minority groups in Britain identify themselves in various ways: by their or their families' country of origin, by color, often by religion. But survey evidence shows that for the vast majority, such identifications are not necessarily felt to conflict or compete with a sense of Britishness. Most respondents from all the main minority groups describe themselves as British, and these figures rise, as expected, among young people and among those born in Britain. Even those who do not think of themselves as being British do not so much reject the label as feel that the majority of white people do not accept that they belong to it.

Establishing some sort of multicultural Englishness, however, is far more difficult from this point of view. Few minority respondents to identity surveys spontaneously describe themselves as English. "Englishness" is seen as a closed ethnic label. Many blacks and Asians have come to think of themselves as British, but few think of themselves as English. At the same time, many commentators—including senior government ministers, the authors of the most influential recent report on Britain's race relations, and left-wing historians—have argued that English identity is peculiarly vulnerable to appropriation by the xenophobic right. At worst, it seems as though the nightmare image of the football hooligan rampaging across the streets and bars of Europe has become the dominant representative of Englishness.

Some on the political Left and Center argue that this has arisen simply because Englishness has been neglected except by far-right Europhobes, racists, and perhaps football fans. Welshness, Scottishness, and Irishness have been the subjects both of intense debate about conceptions of nationhood and of popular celebration.

For Englishness, neither has happened: almost nobody marks St. George's Day, while Saints David, Andrew, and, above all, Patrick are hallowed around the world wherever the Welsh, Scots, or Irish can be found. Official culture ignored Englishness, which had become almost swallowed up by imperial, global Greater Britishness. The Left, embarrassed, tried to distance itself from Englishness. The Right, even the racist extreme Right, could thus control the agenda by portraying racism as a natural outgrowth of English patriotism. The only way out is "to grasp the thorny rose of our English identity and start drawing inspiration from contemporary, multicultural England." So argues the rock singer—and very serious political thinker—Billy Bragg.[16]

YET A SLIGHTLY MORE RECENT WAVE of historical and political writing has begun to suggest that it was a mistake to see the Empire as "coming home" or "striking back" only in the post-1945 era of mass immigration. This omission has been corrected—and perhaps in some cases overcorrected. Even if some proponents of a "new imperial history" take it as an article of faith that colonialism's domestic influences were all-pervasive—that the very ideas of Englishness and Britishness were products of imperialism—the new emphasis on how colonial expansion affected national histories, cultures, and identities in the colony-owning countries has important implications for the present and future.[17]

Colonial and postcolonial migrants to Britain were in this view not people from outside British national history who were now inserting themselves into British life as an unwelcome, alien wedge. They had been part of that history, part of what shaped Britishness, for generations and often for centuries. Caribbean migrants, especially, thus expected to be perceived not as inferior aliens, but as part of the national family, as people who were also British. Trinidad-born C. L. R. James proclaimed that when he first left his home island for London, "The British intellectual was going to Britain."[18] Being British and being colonial were not mutually exclusive identities. Nor was the relation of latter to former simply one of physical transplantation or imitation.

Colonial subjects' affirmations of Britishness have often been seen as mere illusions, dreams that encountered a harsh and disenchanting reality in Britain itself: the vast majority of the white British did not recognize immigrants' claims to be "one of us." Yet there was another side to the story. Claims to Britishness were frequently utilized by the colonized, in both colony and metropole, in pursuit of racial justice, political representation, and social equality.[19]

They were not necessarily incompatible with local patriotism or even
with some forms of political nationalism—though such a combination became more difficult with time, in both colony and metropole. One could at least for a time think of oneself as Trinidadian or
Antiguan, and as West Indian, and as British.

Something further, something just as crucial for thinking about
multi-ethnic futures in Britain and their relation to national pasts,
follows from this: that "it was through the encounter with the formerly colonial peoples of the Caribbean that native white Britons
were first able to see themselves in their true historical light."[20] We
can sketch part of this through the ideas of C. L. R. James: "The
populations in the British West Indies have no native civilisation
at all. These populations are essentially Westernised and they have
been Westernised for centuries."[21] But it was precisely in this absence that their potential lay. For James, what made the West Indians distinctive was their thoroughgoing modernity—created by
history in a more complete way than any other people, they were
consequently unable to delude themselves that they had been products of tradition, of the soil, of racial inheritance.

The distinctive modernity of Caribbean peoples, their formation
through a very special kind of historical process, was for James just
one of three crucial features, all of which together might account
for the kind of impact that he—and West Indians in general—had
on the world. They also, together, enabled the kind of perceptions
about Britain that its Caribbean-originating minorities could bring
to bear. The other two features were internationalism—West Indians, James believed, "are essentially an international people . . .
therefore we are particularly open"—and smallness of scale.[22] The
scale of the island societies contrasted sharply with that of Britain
and enabled West Indians' special perspective on the latter. In the
West Indies, it was possible for the observer or intellectual to know
the whole society, whereas "the average English worker" knew only
his or her own area and class. In that way, the Caribbean was, in
James's view, "more developed" than Britain: "We brought that [to
Britain]—at least I brought that with me, Padmore had it too—we
kept on seeing the whole thing as a whole."[23] Coming from a small-
scale society produced also a particular kind of dynamism in both
the arts and politics.

The whole question of the ways in which British and imperial
cultures and identities each constituted the other is thus placed at
the center of debate on national futures. The key questions revolve
around how far or in what ways the former colonizers' and colo-
nizeds' notions of themselves as "being imperial" have entered into,

or even become in some strong sense constitutive of, their collective identities. Historians have been debating such questions for some time, but a wider public sphere has increasingly engaged with them too. Both the recent dramatic changes in Britain's international position and the transformed relations between nationalities and communities within Britain are feeding into and reshaping those debates. The sense of what it means to be British and, perhaps yet more sharply, what it might mean to be *English* are both being re-created by, and are themselves transfiguring, views of empire and its afterlives.

Spring Semester 2007

1. In the Scottish Parliament elections in May 2007, the Scottish National Party emerged as the largest single group, with its central campaign platform being the holding of a referendum on independence.

2. Some liberal British writers pointed to the founding of the United States as the most "positive" aspect of Britain's imperial legacies: Martin Kettle, "The story of empire is not one of unalloyed shame," *Guardian*, 31 Mar. 2007.

3. Philip Webster, "Brown calls for an end to guilt over the Empire," *The Times*, 15 Mar. 2005; Gordon Brown, speech to Fabian Society, 14 Jan. 2006.

4. David Cameron (then Shadow Education Minister), speech to the Foreign Policy Centre, 24 Aug. 2005.

5. Some writers suggested that a direct continuity of memory and resistance among black British citizens could be traced from anti-slavery revolts to present-day discontents. For a recent example, see Matt Clement, "Bristol: 'Civilising' the Inner City," *Race and Class*, 48, 4 (2007).

6. David Smith, "Blair: Britain's 'sorrow' for shame of slave trade," *Observer*, 26 Nov. 2006.

7. For instance, Richard Gott, "Britain's vote to end its slave trade was a precursor to today's liberal imperialism," *Guardian*, 17 Jan. 2007

8. Margaret Thatcher, speech at Cheltenham racecourse, 3 July 1982.

9. Tony Blair, speech on the deck of HMS *Albion*, Devonport, 12 Jan. 2007.

10. The following paragraphs draw on my "C. L. R. James: Visions of History, Visions of Britain," in Bill Schwarz, ed., *West Indian Intellectuals* (Manchester, 2003) and "Britishness and Multiculturalism," in Rene Cuperus, Karl Duffek, and Johannes Kandel, eds., *The Challenge of Diversity: European Social Democracy Facing Migration, Integration and Multiculturalism* (Berlin, Amsterdam, and Vienna, 2004).

11. See, for example, David Goodhart, "Too diverse?" *Prospect*, Feb. 2004, and *Progressive Nationalism: Citizenship and the Left* (London, 2006).

12. Though just as I write, in May 2007, there seems renewed grounds for optimism as the formerly extremist parties, Sinn Fein and Ian Paisley's Democratic Unionists, formed a new executive together.

13. Overviews of Scotland's role in empire include John Mackenzie, "On Scotland and the Empire," *International History Review*, 15, 4 (1993); Michael Fry, *The Scottish Empire* (Edinburgh, 2001); and T. M. Devine, *Scotland's Empire, 1600–1815* (London, 2003).

14. Neal Ascherson, *Stone Voices: The Search for Scotland* (London, 2002), pp. 167–68.

15. Simon Heffer, *Nor Shall My Sword: The Reinvention of England* (London, 1999); Peter Hitchens, *The Abolition of Britain* (London, 1999); Roger Scruton, *England: An Elegy* (London, 2000); Jeremy Paxman, *The English: A Portrait of a People* (London, 1998). For more substantial, scholarly treatments, see Robert Colls, *Identity of England* (Oxford, 2002); Krishan Kumar, *The Making of English National Identity* (Cambridge, 2003); Richard Weight, *Patriots: National Identity in Britain, 1940–2000* (London, 2002).

16. Billy Bragg, "Looking for a New England," *New Statesman*, 17 Mar. 1995. The argument is made more fully in his book *The Progressive Patriot* (London, 2006).

17. See, for example, Antoinette Burton, "Rules of Thumb: British History and 'Imperial Culture' in Nineteenth- and Twentieth-century Britain," *Women's History Review*, 3, 4 (1994); and "Who Needs the Nation? Interrogating 'British' History," *Journal of Historical Sociology*, 10, 3 (1997). Catherine Hall, *Civilising Subjects: Metropole and Colony in the English Imagination, 1830–1867* (Cambridge, 2002) is among the most detailed and effective attempts to flesh out this kind of argument. The

strongest statement for the relatively insignificant place of empire in British life is Bernard Porter, *The Absent-Minded Imperialists: The Empire in English Society and Culture, c. 1800–1940* (Oxford, 2004).

18. C. L. R. James, *Beyond a Boundary* (London, 1963), p. 114.

19. See, for instance, Anne Spry Rush, "Imperial Identity in Colonial Minds: Harold Moody and the League of Coloured Peoples, 1931–50," *20th Century British History,* 13, 4 (2002); and Laura Tabili, *"We Ask for British Justice": Workers and Racial Difference in Late Imperial Britain* (Ithaca, N.Y., 1994).

20. "Crossing the Seas," in Schwarz, ed. *West Indian Intellectuals,* p. 2.

21. C. L. R. James, "On Federation" (1958), republished in James, *At the Rendezvous of Victory* (London, 1984), p. 97.

22. C. L. R. James, "A National Purpose for Caribbean Peoples," (1964), in ibid., p. 143.

23. Stuart Hall, "A Conversation with C. L. R. James," in Grant Farred, ed., *Rethinking C. L. R. James* (Oxford, 1996), p. 22. The reference is to another prominent Trinidadian writer and anticolonial activist, James's friend George Padmore.

21

The Break-Up of Britain?
Scotland and the End of Empire

T. M. DEVINE

Most of the great territorial empires in world history have broken up slowly over several generations of decline and decay. This was not so in the case of Britain. As late as 1945 its empire was still virtually intact, as British rule extended across the oceans of the globe and encompassed a population of around 700 million people. A mere two decades later this figure had fallen to 5 million, of which 3 million were concentrated in Hong Kong. In June 1997, even that last major outpost of the Empire was relinquished, handed back to the Chinese while the Black Watch played "Auld Lang Syne" and the Union Jack was lowered over the territory for the last time.

The end of empire was not only rapid; it was also remarkably peaceful. True, there were outbreaks of nationalist hostility in Cyprus, Aden, and Kenya during the imperial retreat. But in Britain itself, all was calm. Indeed, as several scholars have noted, the British seem to have accepted the collapse of their empire with an equanimity bordering on indifference. Here, contrasts are often drawn with the experience of France and Portugal. In Africa, Asia, and Indo-China, both had much smaller empires than the British. Yet in their cases, decolonization was followed by social trauma and political convulsion at home.[1]

In one important sense the relative silence in Britain, outside the right wing of the Conservative Party, is intriguing. As the break-up of empire loomed, some commentators predicted that imperial decline would place considerable strain on the Anglo-Scottish Union. As early as 1937, Andrew Dewar Gibb, professor of constitutional law in the University of Glasgow and a prominent nationalist with deep imperial sympathies, noted in his *Scottish Empire:* "The existence of the Empire has been the most important factor in securing the relationship of Scotland and England in the last three centuries."[2] He implied that without the Empire this ancient political connection might not stand the test of time. Similarly, in his last work, Sir Reginald Coupland, a distinguished imperial historian of the old school, considered the potential rise of Scottish and Welsh nationalism in the aftermath of decolonization and gloomily concluded that Ireland might not be the last of the nations of the British Isles to leave the United Kingdom.[3]

This theme was taken up even more vigorously in the 1960s and 1970s as the Scottish National Party (SNP) began to achieve its first spectacular electoral successes. H. J. Hanham observed in 1969: "Now that the Empire is dead many Scots feel cramped and restricted at home. They chafe at the provincialism of much of Scottish life and at the slowness of Scottish economic growth, which is related to that provincialism. To give themselves an opening to a wider world the Scots need some sort of outlet, and the choice appears at the moment to be between emigration and re-creating the Scottish nation at home."[4] For Jan Morris, an author who had written extensively about the British Empire, the acceleration of decolonization meant that there was no longer much scope for a shared pride among the nations of the United Kingdom. All that remained in the Union, she remarked memorably, was "this grubby wreck of old glories" in which few could take any satisfaction. Hence, the time was ripe for a new constitutional beginning.[5] It was then left to the Marxist writer Tom Nairn to provide, in 1977, a full-scale analysis of those issues. For him, the breakup of Britain was not only inevitable but also necessary as a constructive response to the crisis in the Union triggered by the end of empire.[6]

These observers had, on the face of it, a plausible case. The British Empire was seen traditionally as a vital economic cement of union. For upper- and middle-class Scots from the later eighteenth century onward, the Empire provided a remarkable set of opportunities in trade, the professions, military service, and administration, while the entire production structure of Scottish industry from the age of cotton to the era of heavy industry was built around imperial markets. The Empire supplied a powerful material rationale for Union; it therefore seemed attractive to argue that with its disappearance, the economic ties that had for so long bound Scotland to England could easily be cut as well.

With decolonization, nationalist aspirations could come to the fore. As John Mackenzie has put it: "With the end of Empire the Scots could at last escape from their self-interested complicity and reunite nation with state after the dramatic rupture of that particular Union. With the loss of the colonies, the imperial cataracts can be removed from the eyes of the imperial collaborators and a new democratic dispensation can be discerned emerging from which the national ophthalmologist can free the Scots as much as the subordinate peoples of the white settler territories, India and the dependant empire." [7] Thus far, however, more than fifty years after the independence of India, the dire predictions of the disintegration of the Union have proved to be false.

Of course, the Union was itself transformed by the devolution of important powers to Edinburgh in 1999. But any direct or convincing link between the end of empire and the new constitutional settlement has yet to be demonstrated. Political scientists and modern Scottish historians have tended to look elsewhere for the root causes of devolution and have found them in the disenchantment felt in Scotland in the 1960s and 1970s, when neither Tory nor Labour, the two "unionist" parties, proved capable of delivering long-term economic and social benefit as UK governments struggled against recurrent currency crises and the menace of rising inflation. [8] However, these pressures were not enough to trigger general hostility to the terms of the constitutional relationship with England, as the failed referendum on a Scottish Assembly in 1979 made clear. Only in the 1990s did such a consensus emerge. It was fashioned not by any nostalgia for lost imperial glory, but by the profound economic crises of the 1980s, the "democratic deficit" caused by the cleavage between Scottish and English voting patterns, and perhaps, above all, by growing opposition to the social policies of a succession of Conservative governments. Mrs. Thatcher has an infinitely greater claim to be the midwife of Scottish devolution than does the factor of imperial decline.

Indeed, historically, Scottish Home Rule and empire were not incompatible. The first search for some form of devolution for Scotland took place in the late nineteenth century, at the high noon of the British Empire, and was seen by its protagonists as a means of ensuring that the governance of the Empire might be improved. This was not just a theoretical discussion. A series of Home Rule

Acts were promulgated between the 1880s and 1914. In 1913 the policy had secured widespread agreement and was merely awaiting parliamentary time and the solution of the Irish question. The outbreak of the First World War, however, put paid to this aspiration.

There is also the problem of chronology in associating the rise of Scottish political nationalism with imperial decline in the 1940s and 1950s. The Scots mainly identified with the colonies of white settlement, Canada, South Africa, Australia, and New Zealand. These were the countries that had experienced mass Scottish immigration since the eighteenth century. But these Dominions had enjoyed autonomy since the Statute of Westminster in 1931 while at the same time retaining a symbolic and sentimental form of attachment to the mother country through the British Commonwealth of Nations. The process of decolonization in Asia and Africa after 1945, which was chronologically closer to the rise of the SNP, evoked little protest or opposition in Scotland. On the contrary, the Church of Scotland vigorously supported the cause of black nationalism in Africa and, through its annual General Assembly, criticized the government for not conceding independence more quickly.

A CONUNDRUM, THEREFORE, REMAINS. Historians claim that Scotland was heavily involved with the imperial project, yet the passing of empire seems to have had little perceptible consequence for the nation. Certainly, the anticipated causal relationship between the end of empire and the dissolution of the Union has proved thus far to be fallacious. One possible way of resolving the puzzle is to question the very premise that the British Empire was of central significance to the British people. This view has a long pedigree. Some time ago, for instance, the novelist H. G. Wells famously remarked that nineteen Englishmen out of twenty knew as much about the British Empire as they did about the Italian Renaissance. Historians as different as Max Beloff and A. J. P. Taylor also insisted that imperialism was on the whole an irrelevant factor in the lives of most Britons.

More recently, however, the most powerful and detailed exploration of this thesis has come from the pen of Bernard Porter in *The Absent-Minded Imperialists: Empire, Society and Culture in Britain* (2004). Despite its subtitle, Porter's focus is almost entirely Anglocentric. In 108 pages of endnotes and 30 pages of bibliography, there is only one article with a Scottish emphasis. Essentially, therefore, it is for historians of England to judge the overall validity of his argument. But Porter's general thesis hardly convinces when put into a specifically Scottish context. Far from being a marginal factor in the nation's domestic history, empire was crucial to the Scottish experience during the eighteenth and nineteenth centuries. Indeed, one author has recently claimed that so fundamental to the molding of the modern nation was the British Empire that it should rank alongside the Reformation, the Union of 1707, and the Enlightenment as one of the truly seminal developments in Scottish history.[9]

In the eighteenth century, the colonial tobacco and sugar trades were two of the key drivers of Scottish industrialization, while during the Victorian and Edwardian eras, Scottish heavy industry was strongly biased toward export markets, and the principal outlets for ships, locomotives, and engineering products were the British colonies. Dundee, one of Scotland's four principal cities, became "Juteopolis," its booming textile industry founded on the importation of raw jute from India. Gordon Stewart, who later wrote an important study of jute, recalled the imperial connections of his native city:

> I grew up in Dundee and I thought that the Scottish city was the centre of the world jute trade. This impression was dinned into me by my geography lessons at school and by a host of childhood encounters with jute. When I felt depressed by the drabness of life amidst the row of identical, rain-stained buildings on the housing scheme where I lived, I would pedal my bike down to the docks and watch hundreds of bales of jute being unloaded from the holds of great cargo steamers which had sailed half-way round the world from Chittagong and Calcutta. . . . Because of the names on the sterns of the cargo ships and the faces of the crewmen, I understood there was an Indian dimension to jute. I also learned of this connection by listening to family stories about relatives and friends of my parents who had spent time in India.[10]

In Glasgow, the economic connections were equally deep. It arrogated to itself the description "Second City of the Empire" (a term first used as early as 1824), while the broader west of Scotland region was celebrated as the "Workshop of the British Empire." Scottish society more generally had strong ties to the Empire. As one author has put it, the Scots professional and middle classes claimed "not merely a reasonable but a quite indecent share of the [imperial] spoils."[11] Throughout the eighteenth and for much of the nineteenth centuries, Scottish educators, physicians, soldiers, administrators, missionaries, engineers, scientists, and merchants relentlessly penetrated every corner of the Empire and beyond, so that when the statistical record for virtually any area of professional employment is examined, Scots are seen to be over-represented.

This elite emigration was but one element in a greater diaspora from Scotland. Between 1825 and 1938, over 2.3 million Scots left

their homeland for overseas destinations. This ranked the country
with Ireland and Norway as one of the three European countries
with the highest levels of net emigration throughout that period.
The emigrants had three main destinations: the United States (after 1783), British North America (which became the Dominion
of Canada in 1867), and Australia. After around 1840, the United
States was the choice of most who left, but Canada predominated
in the early twentieth century. Also, for a period in the 1850s, Australia was taking more Scots than either of the two North American
countries.[12] These huge levels of emigration generated a vast network of family and individual connections with the colonies and Dominions, ties that were consolidated by return migration (in one
estimate averaging more than 40 percent of the total exodus in the
1890s), chain migration, letter correspondence, and widespread coverage of the emigrant experience in the Scottish popular press and
periodical literature.

The British Empire also had a potent influence on Scottish national consciousness and identity. Several recent analyses have em-
phasized that for the Scots elite in the years before 1914, nationalism
was not in conflict with the Union but rather was integrated closely
with it. The Empire was the means by which the Scots asserted their
equal partnership with England after 1707. By the Victorian era,
it was commonplace to assert that substantial imperial expansion
occurred only after the Union and hence was a joint endeavor in
which the Scots had played a full part. This was no empty boast.
Works such as John Hill Burton's *The Scots Abroad* (2 vols., 1864)
and W. J. Rattray's monumental four-volume *The Scot in British North
America* (1880) were easily able to demonstrate the mark that Scottish education (especially at the college and university level), Pres-
byterianism, medicine, trading networks, and philosophical inquiry
had made on the colonies. Pride in the Scottish achievement was
taken even further by those who saw the Scottish people as a race of
natural empire builders. Thus the nationalist Andrew Dewar Gibb
argued in 1930:

> The position of Scotland as a Mother nation of the Empire is at
> all costs to be preserved to her. England and Scotland occupy a
> unique position as the begetters and defenders of the Empire.
> They alone of all the Aryan peoples in it have never been other-
> wise than sovereign and independent. Ireland and Wales, mere
> satrapies of England, can claim no comparable place. Scotsmen
> today are occupying places both eminent and humble throughout
> the Empire, and Scottish interests are bound up with every colony
> in it.[13]

Nonetheless, it might be objected that the argument thus far ignores the important factor of differences in the attitudes of social class to empire. Bernard Porter in *The Absent-Minded Imperialists* focuses especially on this aspect. He sees the upper and middle classes as most committed to the imperial project, while the working classes were "either apathetic towards the empire or superficial in their attitude to it." Porter also claims a deep ignorance about the Empire on the part of the majority of the British people.[14]

Again, this interpretation hardly fits the Scottish case. While it is impossible, of course, in the current state of knowledge to determine precisely what the ordinary Scot thought about the Empire, it is nevertheless unlikely that the words "apathy" and "ignorance" would be appropriate terms for describing public opinion. Exposure to imperial themes started early in Scotland. In 1907 the Scottish Education Department directed that the history curriculum should develop from the study of Scotland to British and international themes but throughout stressing the nation's role in the Empire.

But this was not all. The 1900s also saw the celebration of Empire Day in schools, when flags were exchanged between Scottish schools and those elsewhere in the Empire. The stories of such imperial heroes as General Gordon, Sir Colin Campbell (of Indian Mutiny fame), the missionary Mary Slessor, and, above all, David Livingstone, would have been very well known to Scottish schoolchildren. Biographies of Livingstone, the "Protestant Saint" and the most famous and venerated Scotsman of the nineteenth century, were widely read and also awarded as prizes in schools and Sunday Schools, a practice that continued unabated to the 1960s. Of course it was not simply children who were taught to respond to these imperial heroes. They were also celebrated by the trade union movement, workingmen's clubs, and Labour politicians such as Keir Hardie as models of Scottish virtue and exemplars for the nation. Knowledge of and loyalty to the Empire was also communicated by such organizations as the Junior Empire League, with around 20,000 members, and the Boy's Brigade.

Among the mass of the population, however, perhaps the main symbols of empire were the Scottish regiments. Recognized as the spearheads of imperial expansion, and widely celebrated in music, story, painting, and statue as the tartan-clad icons of the Scottish nation, they enjoyed "unchallenged prominence in Scottish society as symbols of national self-image."[15] Ironically, despite the fame of the Highland soldier, the kilted battalions were mainly recruited during the Victorian age from the working class of the Scottish cities. Their exploits were widely recorded not simply in the popular press, but also in such famous paintings as *The Thin Red Line*. The

---

regiments made a remarkable impact on Scottish consciousness. Seen as the heirs of a national martial tradition that went back for centuries, they also acted as important agents for the wide diffusion of the military ethic throughout the country.

THERE THEREFORE SEEMS, ON THE FACE OF IT, to be a huge gap between the imperial enthusiasms of the nineteenth century and the apparent equanimity with which Scotland accepted decolonization in the middle decades of the twentieth century. The crucial period for understanding this transformation in attitude to empire occurred between the 1920s and 1950s, despite the fact that imperial sentiment did not entirely fade away during these decades.

There is, after all, plenty of evidence of continuity in the years after 1918. The massive war losses suffered by Scotland, officially counted at 74,000 but unofficially reckoned to be over 110,000, were commemorated in the Scottish National War Memorial, completed in Edinburgh Castle in 1927. The Roll of Honour included all those who had served in Scottish regiments and in those of the Dominions overseas, eloquent affirmation of the continuing importance of the imperial bond. The link between empire and the national church also seemed intact. The cult of David Livingstone reached its apotheosis in the 1920s, when many small donations by ordinary Scots financed the creation of the Livingstone Memorial Centre in Blantyre, Lanarkshire, in the cotton mill complex where the legendary explorer and missionary had worked as a boy. The center remained a place of pilgrimage for schools and Sunday Schools until the 1950s. The public face of imperial Scotland seemed also to change little. A great imperial exhibition was held in Glasgow in 1938, the fourth in a series that since the 1890s had attracted millions of visitors. As late as 1951, a colonial week was held in the same city. Empire was also still very much on the political agenda. In the inter-war years, factional arguments raged in the Scottish nationalist movement over the nature of the relationship that a self-governing Scotland would have with the Empire. Even the Labour Party temporarily diluted its earlier hostility, and some of its leading intellectuals in Scotland, including John Wheatley, argued that through the Empire could come not only economic regeneration but also the hope of protecting a socialist Britain from the menace of international capitalism.

In some ways, however, all this was a mirage, a false image of continuity after the trauma of the First World War. Andrew Dewar Gibb in 1937 recognized the change. With the granting of dominion status to the colonies of white settlement, he observed, "the hegemony of Britain in the Empire is steadily becoming more formal and more ornamental."[16] Popular imperialism also waned. Scholars now regard the Glasgow Empire Exhibition of 1938 not so much as a catalyst for regenerating imperial enthusiasms as an event of mere nostalgic significance. Iain Hutchison has also noted that Scottish Tory and Labour candidates in the 1945 election referred even less frequently to imperial themes than did their English counterparts.[17] This was a symbolic and ominous prelude to the results of that election, when the Unionists, par excellence the party of empire, were roundly defeated by Labour, which had a quite different set of political and social priorities for the future governance of Scotland.

The traditional career route of middle-class Scots into imperial administration was crumbling. In this respect, the Indian Civil Service (ICS) had long enjoyed pre-eminence in the rank order of colonial administrations. By 1939, Scots accounted for 13 percent of the Europeans on the ICS books, a significantly lower ratio than in the eighteenth century and for much of the nineteenth. Indeed, Anthony Kirk-Greene suggests that demoralization was rampant in the ICS after 1918 because of a perceived decline in the career prospects it offered as Indian self-government became a likely prospect.[18]

Scottish elite families were still exporting their male progeny, but were no longer constrained to the same extent by opportunities within the formal Empire. The great Scottish business syndicates had become global rather than simply imperial corporations. The United States, Latin America, China, and Japan all provided rich pickings for ambitious and educated Scots. They no longer felt themselves restricted by imperial frontiers, if they ever had. Above all, career goals were still more easily satisfied in London than in faraway places. The modern "Scottish Raj" in the UK cabinet and the high-profile Scottish presence in the British media are simply the latest variants in a trend that goes back for many generations.

NO SINGLE CAUSE CONSPIRED TO ERODE Scotland's emotional attachment to empire. But the profound crisis that overwhelmed the nation in the period between the world wars was a major factor. To understand this fully, however, it is necessary to describe the context of the long-term relationship between the Scottish economy and empire in the Victorian and Edwardian eras. Such a perspective strongly suggests that the disastrous inter-war experience was the culmination of structural weaknesses reaching much further back in time.

Certainly the close connections with imperial markets helped boost productive capacity enormously in Scotland. One significant consequence was a marked increase in Scottish population as the economy created more employment opportunities for the new generation. In 1701, Scotland had a population of around 1.1 million. By 1831, the figure stood at 2.3 million, and in 1911 reached 4.7 million. Further confirmation of the dynamic nature of the economic system was the large increase in immigration in the Victorian era, most notably from Ireland, but also including significant numbers of Italians, Jews, and Lithuanians. This level of immigration over such a short period, something quite new in Scottish history, was testimony to the economy's strength.

Again, trading with the Empire made some Scots very rich indeed. A handful of families amassed colossal fortunes. Sir Charles Tenant of the chemical empire; William Baird, the ironmaster; Sir James and Peter Coats of the thread-making dynasty; and William Weir, colliery owner and iron manufacturer, were among the forty individuals in Britain reckoned to be worth £2 million or more in the nineteenth century. Recent research has shown that the super-rich were as well represented in Scotland as in any other part of the United Kingdom.[19] In addition to these tycoons, there were the solid ranks of the prosperous middle classes, who ranged in occupational status from highly paid professionals, such as lawyers, to small businessmen and senior clerks. In his analysis of national income, published in 1867, the Victorian economist R. Dudley Baxter reckoned that the 267,300 people who were in this group in Scotland had an annual income of between £100 and £1000 and represented nearly one-fifth of the total number of what he termed "productive persons" in the country. The impact of the spending of this middle class could be seen in the elegant suburbs that blossomed around the major cities in the nineteenth century: Broughty Ferry, near Dundee, the graceful terraces of the West End of Glasgow, and the substantial villas of Newington and Corstorphine in Edinburgh.

The increase in the outflow of capital from Scotland after 1870 was also in part a reflection of the increase in savings among the Scottish middle classes. Most of this came through Scottish solicitors and chartered accountants, who raised funds on behalf of overseas clients from professional and business families at home. It was said that Edinburgh in the 1880s was "honeycombed" with agents of these companies, who were the main channel for this substantial mobilization of middle-class capital.[20] This level of overseas investment was one of the most telling manifestations of the new wealth. It grew from an estimated £60 million in 1870 to £500 million by 1914. Not all of this went to the imperial territories—land, mining, and railway developments in the United States were also major beneficiaries—but much did. In the 1880s it was reckoned that three-quarters of the British companies established for overseas investment were of Scottish origin. Nearly half of all Australian borrowing in the late nineteenth century came from Scotland. Tea planting in Ceylon, jute production in India, and railways in the Canadian West also benefited. One estimate for 1914 suggested that the value of overseas investment was equivalent to £110 for every Scot, compared to the per capita average of £90 for the United Kingdom as a whole.[21] Here was unambiguous confirmation that Scotland's imperial economy had indeed generated huge increases in capital. The social elites and many in the business and professional classes had done rather well out of empire.

The picture is, however, somewhat gloomier for the rest of the population. Scotland was a grossly unequal society in the heyday of its imperial success. R. D. Baxter's calculations for 1867 suggest that around 70 percent of "productive persons" in Scotland, almost a million people, belonged to his two bottom categories of "lower skilled" and "unskilled," which consisted of male workers who earned on average less than £50 a year.[22] For many at this level, short-term unemployment was always a threat. In the four major cities there were large pools of seasonal and casual labor, reckoned in the early 1900s at around 25 percent of the workforce, which were engaged in jobs such as portering, catering, and street selling, in which earnings were both paltry and unpredictable. For most of the period between 1830 and 1914, Scottish industrial wage rates were lower than the English average. Living costs, on the other hand, were higher. Recent work by Richard Rodger has shown that Glaswegians paid on average over 5 percent more for their food and rent (which accounted for four-fifths of the weekly working-class budget) than did the population of Manchester, Leeds, Salford, or Nottingham—and this against a background of low wages and volatile levels of employment on Clydeside.[23]

That Victorian industry was not a source of general prosperity is confirmed by the examples of Scottish migration and housing in this period. Precisely when manufacturing was achieving remarkable success in overseas markets, the Scots, as noted above, were leaving their native land in large numbers for the United States, Canada, and Australasia. Over 2 million people emigrated from Scotland overseas between 1815 and 1939, a rate of outward movement that, per capita, was around one and a half times that for England and Wales. This figure did not include another 600,000 who moved south of the border. Scotland was therefore almost alone among European countries in having experienced both large-scale industrialization and a great outward movement of population. Most other societies prone to high levels of emigration suffered from poor rural economies. It seemed that many Scots were voting with their feet in the search for better prospects than those easily available at home.

The conclusion must be that despite high levels of emigration, Scotland suffered from a chronic oversupply of labor in the heyday of empire.[24] Low pay, underemployment, casual work, and broken time were all consistent with that pattern. Some Scots had grown wealthy, but the majority, despite modest gains in the later nineteenth century, remained mired in poverty and endured a hard daily struggle to make ends meet. The imperial economy was also building up potential problems for the future. The dependency on low wages and semiskilled or unskilled labor placed the nation at a strategic disadvantage in the twentieth century, when home demand propelled the new consumer economy, with its focus on household goods, motor vehicles, bicycles, furniture, and electrical products. Scotland missed out on most of this "Second Industrial Revolution." Even before 1914, the economic structure seemed precarious. The heavy industries were all interconnected, geared to overseas markets, especially in the Empire, and at risk from such mighty competitors as the United States and Germany. The threat was especially real because the Scots excelled at making simple capital goods such as iron, steel, locomotives, bridges, and the like, which could be easily and rapidly imitated by emerging competitors. Imperial markets had therefore left a flawed legacy, with serious consequences for Scotland by 1914, when international trade collapsed during several years between the world wars.

The manifestations of crisis were everywhere. Unemployment soared to unprecedented levels in the early 1930s. In the industrial heartland of the western lowlands, the "Workshop of the British Empire," over a quarter of the entire labor force, nearly 200,000 people, was out of work in 1932. New industries failed to develop, and poor housing and slum conditions remained as bad as ever: in 1935, the rate of overcrowding in Scotland was six times greater than that south of the Border. As several failing firms were bought up by financial interests from England, fears were expressed in the business community of long-term economic decline and the erosion of indigenous Scottish control. The unprecedented scale of emigration in the 1930s intensified these anxieties. So great was the exodus that the Scottish population actually fell by nearly 40,000 in that decade, the only period since record keeping began when absolute decline between censuses occurred.

Now, rather than being seen as evidence of the virility of an imperial race, emigration was viewed as a scourge and a confirmation of a terminal national crisis. The novelist and poet Edwin Muir saw it as a "silent clearance" in which "the surroundings of industrialisation remain, but industry itself is vanishing like a dream." His apocalyptic vision was of a country "being emptied of its population, its spirit, its wealth, industry, art, intellect, and innate character." As his fellow intellectual George Malcolm Thomson put it: "The first fact about the Scot is that he is a man eclipsed. The Scots are a dying race."[25]

The most arresting illustration of the economic irrelevance of empire was the experience between the wars of the Dundee jute industry. By the 1890s, Bengal had already overtaken its Scottish parent to become the world's dominant center for the production of the jute sacks and hessian cloth that carried the world's foodstuffs and raw materials. Not surprisingly, in the depressed market conditions in the 1930s, Dundee jute interests pleaded on numerous occasions for tariffs to be imposed on cheap imports from Calcutta. But their pleas were in vain. Now it was Dundee that looked more like the colony, and Bengal the metropole: "Jute presents an unusual example of a powerful industry emerging in a colonial setting which almost destroyed the rival industry back in Britain while the empire was still flourishing."[26]

All this shattered faith in Scotland as the powerhouse of the Empire. Long before decolonization took place, imperial markets were no longer seen to be of much benefit. Though the economy recovered during the Second World War and the immediate post-war period, the fully enfranchised masses now had other social priorities, which could be delivered through the ballot box. It was therefore hardly surprising that the majority of the Scottish people reacted to the end of empire with indifference, despite Scotland's historic role in imperial expansion. After 1945, state intervention in industry, political commitment to full employment, and, above all, the welfare state slowly delivered security and material improvement to the mass of Scots. These were the issues that now had widespread popular appeal, especially in light of Scotland's social history over the previous century. The age of empire may have passed, but, ironically, the Union was now even more important than before. As one of the poorer parts of the United Kingdom, Scotland was likely to gain more than other regions from the introduction of an interventionist social and economic policy, which was being implemented in the very decade that decolonization accelerated through the independence of India. State support from cradle to grave became the new anchor of the union state.

Summer 2007

302 T. M. Devine

A version of this lecture was read before the Royal Historical Society on 6 July 2005 as the Prothero Lecture, and was printed in society's *Transactions* in 2006.

1. John Darwin, *The End of the British Empire: The Historical Debate* (Oxford, 1991), pp. 1–4, 34–35; *Britain and Decolonisation* (London, 1988), pp. 324, 328; *The Oxford History of the British Empire: The Twentieth Century*, ed. Judith M. Brown and W. R. Lewis (Oxford, 1999), pp. 330, 706.
2. Andrew Dewar Gibb, *Scottish Empire* (London, 1937), p. 311.
3. Reginald Coupland, *Welsh and Scottish Nationalism* (London, 1954), pp. xv, 12, 13.
4. H. J. Hanham, *Scottish Nationalism* (London, 1969), p. 212.
5. *Daily Telegraph*, 24 February 1979, cited in Keith Robbins, "'This Grubby Wreck of Old Glories': The United Kingdom and the End of the British Empire," *Journal of Contemporary History*, 15 (1980), p. 84.
6. Tom Nairn, *The Break-Up of Britain* (London, 1977), pp. 118–20.
7. John M. Mackenzie, "A Scottish Empire? The Scottish Diaspora and Interactive Identities" in T. Brooking and J. Coleman, eds., *The Heather and the Fern: Scottish Migration and New Zealand Settlement* (Otago, N.Z., 2003), p. 19.
8. I. G. C. Hutchison, *Scottish Politics in the Twentieth Century* (Basingstoke, 2001), pp. 121–22; Keith Webb, *The Growth of Nationalism in Scotland* (Glasgow, 1977), pp. 85–90.
9. Michael Fry, *The Scottish Empire* (Edinburgh, 2001), p. 498.
10. Gordon Stewart, *Jute and Empire* (Manchester, 1998), p. ix.
11. D. Allan, *Scotland in the Eighteenth Century* (Harlow, 2002), p. 185.
12. M. Gray, "The Course of Scottish Emigration, 1750–1914: Enduring Influences and Changing Circumstances," in T. M. Devine, ed., *Scottish Emigration and Scottish Society* (Edinburgh, 1992), pp. 16–36.
13. A. D. Gibb, *Scotland in Eclipse* (London, 1930), p. 187.
14. Bernard Porter, *The Absent-Minded Imperialists: Empire, Society and Culture in Britain* (Oxford, 2004), pp. 115–33.
15. Stuart Allan and Allan Carswell, *The Thin Red Line: War, Empire and Visions of Scotland* (Edinburgh, 2004), p. 40.
16. Gibb, *Scotland in Eclipse*, 187.
17. Hutchison, *Scottish Politics in the Twentieth Century*, pp. 121–22.
18. A. Kirk-Greene, *Britain's Imperial Administrators, 1858–1966*, p. 17.
19. W. D. Rubenstein, "The Victorian Middle Classes: Wealth, Occupation and Geography," *Economic History Review*, 2nd series, 30 (1977), pp. 609–11, 614.
20. Quoted in A. S. J. Bastier, *The Imperial Banks* (1929).
21. C. H. Lee, "Economic Progress: Wealth and Poverty" in T. M. Devine, C. H. Lee, and G. C. Peden, eds., *The Transformation of Scotland: The Economy since 1700* (Edinburgh, 2005), pp. 138–41.
22. T. C. Smout, *A Century of the Scottish People, 1830–1950* (Glasgow, 1986), pp. 109, 111.
23. R. Rodger, "The Labour Force," in W. H. Fraser and I. Maver, eds., *Glasgow*, Vol. II: *1830 to 1912* (Manchester, 1966), pp. 16–85.
24. The following two paragraphs are based on T. M. Devine, *The Scottish Nation: 1700–2000* (London, 1999), pp. 201–66, 268–72, and C. H. Lee, "Unbalanced Growth: Prosperity and Deprivation," in Devine, Lee, and Peden, *Transformation of Scotland*, pp. 209–24.
25. Edwin Muir, *Scottish Journey* (Edinburgh, 1935), p. 110; G. M. Thomson, *Caledonia, or the Future of the Scots* (Edinburgh, 1932), pp. 18–19.
26. Stewart, *Jute and Empire*, pp. 2–4.

22

Placing American Empire
in a British Imperial Perspective

DANE KENNEDY

Discussions of America as an empire have until recently been noteworthy for their rarity. For decades, only a handful of historians and leftist critics of American foreign policy dared to take up the topic. Now pundits of all political stripes are openly talking about an American empire, periodicals are devoting special issues to the subject, professional societies are organizing conferences on it, and publishers are issuing a veritable flood of books that detail its workings. Spurred largely by the military interventions in Afghanistan and Iraq, a vigorous public debate has arisen over what it means for the United States to be an empire.[1]

This debate has given rise to a number of fruitful questions. Is an American empire the inevitable outcome of the United States' unrivalled global presence and power, or is it the opportunistic consequence of decisions taken by particular groups pursuing particular ends? Is it the necessary guardian of international order and prosperity, or is it the inexorable engine of global inequality and conflict? Is it sui generis, or does it resemble past empires? Does its imperial reign represent the end of history, or does it portend the United States' own end? These are questions about the political purposes and moral consequences of power. They speak to the ambitions, anxieties, and antagonisms that the United States' present engagement with the world arouses. Yet they hinge on the use of the term "empire," a semantic and conceptual issue that historians have long grappled with, and require an understanding of causation, chronology, and comparison, modes of analysis that are the stock-in-trade of historians. "People in public life reason by historical analogy," observes Wm. Roger Louis.[2] It should be no surprise, then, that historians have figured prominently in the public debate about what it means for the United States to be an empire.

Historians have been among the most vocal proponents of an imperial America, and they have been some of its fiercest critics.[3] Whatever their stance, they have taken an historical perspective on the current controversy about the wars in Iraq and Afghanistan. While America's own history of expansionism has provided one frame of reference, others have come from comparisons to previous empires. The United States' standing in the world has been compared to the empires of Rome, Russia, China, the Ottomans, and various others.[4] At the risk of adding another voice to an already cacophonous chorus, this lecture considers the American imperial experience in relation to its most immediate and obvious predecessor, the British Empire. (Debts owed to other works that have also made this comparison will become apparent in the following pages.) It is important to note how the present approach to the subject clearly differs from the contending stances adopted by Niall Ferguson and Bernard Porter, the two most prominent historians to compare Britain and the United States as empires. The main thrust of Ferguson's work has been a polemical one, lamenting that Americans "lack the imperial cast of mind" that the British proudly possessed.[5] Porter has taken the opposite tack, charging that Americans are far more ruthlessly imperialist in spirit than the British ever were.[6] Rather than argue about which country has or had the stronger will for empire, it would be better to look for more analytically and historically meaningful ways of measuring the two empires against each other. Michael Mann, a historical sociologist whose *Incoherent Empire*, a critique of current U.S. foreign policy, was one of the first and most perceptive of the recent spate of books to view it in terms of empire, suggests that imperial power has several distinct dimensions, which he categorizes as the political, the military, the economic, and the ideological.[7] Although the ideological dimension could be broadened to include cultural power, Mann's categories provide a useful framework for addressing how the American empire does or does not resemble its British predecessor.

THE MOST COMMONLY CITED DIFFERENCE between the British Empire and its American successor has to do with how each has exerted political power. The British Empire was first and foremost an empire of colonies and other dependent territories, famously represented in those maps that colored its far-flung possessions in red. At its height, the British Empire held formal political sway over the entire Indian subcontinent, vast swaths of Africa, large parts of Southeast Asia and the Middle East, as well as Australia, New Zealand, Canada, and countless smaller territories around the globe. Though these disparate lands were ruled in different ways—the ones populated mainly by peoples of British stock enjoyed rights of self-governance that were not extended to the lands inhabited mainly by African, Asian, and other non-Western peoples—all were political dependencies of Britain, acknowledging the Crown as their sovereign.

The United States, by contrast, has shown far less inclination to govern territories as formal colonies. This is not to say that it has not engaged in imperial expansion: on the contrary, from its founding, the nation was constantly seeking to expand its borders, acquiring territory previously claimed by Spain, France, Mexico, and Russia while sweeping aside Native American communities in ruthless campaigns of destruction and displacement. As many historians have noted, this westward march across the continent bore striking similarities to settler expansion in South Africa, Canada, Australia, and New Zealand, not least in the settlers' harsh treatment of indigenous inhabitants.[8] To call this colonialism is standard practice in the British cases, but the term presents problems in the U.S. context. While Native Americans may have been subjected to a form of "internal colonialism," the territories taken from them were not politically subordinated to the conquering state as colonies, but incorporated within it as constituent elements of the nation.[9]

Once the United States reached the limits of continental expansion, it made a sudden bid for the sort of overseas colonial empire that Britain possessed. Starting in 1897, it seized a number of overseas territories, including Hawaii, the Philippines, Puerto Rico, eastern Samoa, Guam, the Panama Canal Zone, and, briefly, Cuba, where the most enduring legacy of its imperial ambitions is the now-notorious Guantanamo. Still, this colonial empire was small by British standards (in part, perhaps, because it came later), and it was marked by greater diffidence: Hawaii, for example, was eventually granted statehood (equivalent in some ways to the unrealized ambitions of British imperial federationists, who sought the political incorporation of colonies like Canada and Australia into a Greater Britain), while the Philippines was granted self-government in 1935 and full independence in 1946. By the Second World War, the United States had become a sharp critic of European colonial rule,

and the main architect of a postwar international order that was
premised on the eventual extension of national sovereignty to all
peoples.

For those who equate imperialism with colonialism, these developments show that the United States, even if it had imperial ambitions in the past, gave them up as it came into its own as a world
power. Some proponents of an American empire make the same
connection, but instead of applauding the fact that most of the U.S.
colonial system was dismantled, they urge its revival on a grander
scale. Their romantic nostalgia for colonial rule is evident in Max
Boot's oft-quoted remark about those "troubled lands" that "cry out
for the sort of enlightened foreign administration once provided by
self-confident Englishmen in jodhpurs and pith helmets." [10]

This preoccupation with colonialism as the main measure of
empire ignores the fact that the British themselves preferred when
possible to exert political power over other peoples through less
intrusive means than direct rule. Historians have long recognized
that Britain extended its reach well beyond the territories colored
red on maps, coercing many formally independent countries to sub-
mit to its will. China saw its political autonomy so severely eroded
in the nineteenth century by "the triple assault" of gunboat diplomacy, predatory capitalism, and missionary zealotry that it became the poster child for what is common referred to as Britain's
informal empire.[11] The Ottoman Empire, Persia, and various Latin
American states came under coercive pressure from Britain as well.
In each of these cases there is some ambiguity, to be sure, about
when and where to draw the line between influence and imperialism. Elsewhere, however, that line was clear—and clearly crossed.
A few examples should suffice. The Persian Gulf protectorates of
Kuwait, Qatar, and the United Arab Emirates (the Trucial States)
were purportedly autonomous polities, but their affairs were actually overseen by British imperial agents. A far more prominent case
was Egypt, where the British maintained the pretense for decades
after their 1882 invasion that they were merely administering the
country on behalf of the Khedive, whose state was still nominally regarded as part of the Ottoman Empire. Across the globe, the British
imposed various forms of indirect rule over putatively independent
states.

The United States has adopted similar strategies in many of its
dealings with other countries. Caribbean and Central American
neighbors have been the frequent targets of American gunboat diplomacy and other instruments of informal imperialism. On various occasions over the past century, the United States has invaded

Cuba, Haiti, the Dominican Republic, Panama, Nicaragua, Hondu-
ras, Grenada, and other countries in the region, impeding revolutions, overthrowing governments, and installing rulers amenable
to its interests. The subservient regimes that resulted from these
actions have been dismissively characterized as banana republics.
Since the Second World War, the United States' efforts to surround
itself with client states have extended across the globe, resulting in
strategies that ranged from financial assistance and military advisers
for friendly governments to economic sanctions and CIA-sponsored
coups against unfriendly ones. The "status of force" agreements that
exempt U.S. personnel stationed in other countries from their laws,
passport and immigration controls, and other powers of national
sovereignty have been compared to the extraterritorial agreements
that Britain imposed on China, the Ottoman Empire, and other
states whose political autonomy it had undermined.

Bernard Porter argues that America prefers informal to formal
empire because its ruling class is capitalist to its core, whereas Britain forged a formal empire because it remained under the thrall of
an atavistic aristocratic elite that liked to lord it over other peoples.[12]
But the contrast in ruling elites' intentions should not be exaggerated: John Gallagher and Ronald Robinson argued long ago that
the British turned to colonial conquest in the nineteenth century
only when they ran out of other options.[13] A more compelling explanation than Porter's for the divergent courses taken by the two empires has to do with the very different global environments within
which they operated. The British faced far less congenial conditions
in which to advance their capitalist interests in various parts of the
world than does the United States, which enjoys the benefit of communication infrastructures, market systems, and cooperative regimes that often came into being as a result of British colonial rule.
And the growing array of competitors that confronted Britain in
the late nineteenth century set off an unseemly and unprecedented
scramble for colonial possessions. The United States, by contrast, as-
cended to global predominance after the Second World War as the
European empires decayed and dissolved, giving it and its rival, the
Soviet Union, an incentive to condemn colonialism and promote
the nation-state as the only political unit worthy of recognition in
international relations.

The U.S. interventions in Afghanistan and Iraq have generated
talk of empire at least in part because they so eerily echo the British
imperial experience in those countries. What makes the likeness all
the more striking is that the British themselves disavowed any desire
to claim them as colonies. Although the British invaded Afghanistan

on three occasions (1839, 1878, and 1919), the outcome they sought
was not direct rule, but the installation of an emir who would be
amenable to their geopolitical concerns. And although the British
occupied Iraq during the First World War and assumed its governance afterwards, they operated under the international sanction
of a League of Nations mandate from 1920 and served a state whose
official ruler from 1921 was King Faisal, the Hashemite wartime ally
whose accession to the throne they had engineered. No one now
questions that these were acts of imperialism, but they were conducted by means that maintained the pretence that Afghans and
Iraqis enjoyed political autonomy. Is it any wonder that the U.S.
presence in these countries has given rise to similar charges?

THE COLOSSAL MILITARY MIGHT THE UNITED STATES EXHIBITED in
its invasions of Iraq and Afghanistan is foremost in the minds of
most of those commentators who refer to the United States as an
empire. For many of them, it is "a new form of empire," one whose
power so far surpasses that of any past empire that it stands in a
class all its own.[14] If power is equated with sheer destructive force,
this is no doubt true, but it is a truth that speaks only to the cu-
mulative advances in military technology. By this measure, it could
be claimed that contemporary Britain, with its nuclear arsenal and
other sophisticated weaponry, is more powerful than its imperial
forebear. Any meaningful assessment of military power must, however, be measured in relative terms, set against the countervailing
forces it confronts. Understood as such, the question that needs to
be asked is how the power the United States has wielded relative to
its rivals compares with the power the British Empire wielded relative to the rivals it faced. Regrettably, there is no agreed-upon way
to measure these power differentials. Historians are deeply divided,
for example, in their views of when and why the British Empire began to decline, an issue made more challenging still by the fact that
military power is inextricably bound up with political and economic
power. This should not preclude, however, the making of some general comparative observations about the military resources available
to the two empires and their use in projecting power.

As the iconic lyrics to "Rule, Britannia" proclaim, it was above all
because the Royal Navy "ruled the waves" that the British were free,
and free to exert their will on other peoples around the globe.[15]
The navy's ability to patrol the seas and to project force along coasts
and navigable rivers made it an intimidating instrument of imperial power in the nineteenth century, able at its peak to safeguard
the smooth operation of the global system of trade that Britain depended upon as well as to coerce those recalcitrant or belligerent

states that interfered with its interests and ambitions. In America's modern arsenal, airpower (understood to include satellites and land- and sea-based missiles) can be viewed as the closest equivalent to the Royal Navy. It clearly carries far greater destructive punch, but only in the aftermath of the Soviet Union's disintegration has it attained the unquestioned superiority over its rivals that the British navy enjoyed through much of the nineteenth century. American airpower does not face the obvious constraints that confronted British sea power in its dealings with land powers like Russia and Germany. Yet it has serious limitations of its own, as the current insurgencies in Iraq and Afghanistan demonstrate, and it requires a similar network of bases around the world from which to supply its forces and stage strikes. America's "empire of bases," which stretches from Guam to Guantanamo, would have been instantly intelligible to Victorian Lords of the Admiralty, whose own strategically important Indian Ocean base of Diego Garcia has become a key air base for American forces.[16]

U.S. land forces seem far more formidable than the British military ever was. Yet the latter's army was well suited to the sort of colonial warfare it was called upon to conduct. Britain's technological superiority over its non-Western foes resulted on occasion in outcomes like the one seen in the Sudan campaign of 1898, a late-Victorian version of "shock and awe." Furthermore, Britain was able to overcome many of its domestic manpower limitations by drawing on Indian and other colonial troops to carry out constabulary functions.

With the collapse of the Soviet Union, American military doctrine has increasingly envisioned a similar policing role for its forces. The influential military theorist Thomas Barnett argues that the United States can expect to fight a lot of wars in the near future, but they will be small wars in "failed" states, where security has broken down and "subversive" elements have gained a foothold.[17] One study counted nearly fifty military interventions by the United States in the decade between 1989 and 1999, compared to just sixteen over the entire course of the Cold War.[18] In recent years the Pentagon has been restructuring its forces into smaller, more mobile units better prepared to meet multiple low-level threats. While these America military initiatives are driven by their own particular dynamics and circumstances, they share at least some of the strategic and structural characteristics of a British military that was designed to maintain an empire.

MILITARY FORCE IS USUALLY REGARDED AS THE MEASURE of last resort in international relations, undertaken when states fail to

achieve their objectives by other means. Among the most important of those objectives for imperial Britain was the advancement
of its global economic interests. The first country to experience an
industrial revolution, Britain became "the workshop of the world"
in the nineteenth century, producing the preponderance of cotton
textiles, iron and steel products, and other manufactured goods
that entered the global marketplace. It also built the ships that
moved these goods from domestic producer to overseas consumer,
and it controlled the shipping lanes along which they traveled. The
profits it accumulated turned the City of London into the world's
financial center and made British sterling the standard measure for
international currency exchange. Although Britain's manufacturing might weakened under growing competition from the United
States, Germany, and other newly industrialized nations from the
late nineteenth century on, its presence in finance, services, and
trade remained strong until the entire international economy collapsed with the onset of the Great Depression. British power waxed
and waned with its international economic standing.

   The classic theories of imperialism advanced by John Hobson
and Vladimir Lenin arose in large measure out of their desire to
explain the workings of this relationship.[19] While various particulars of their interpretations have been discredited, their insistence
that capitalism often acted in tandem with imperialism has not.
A. G. Hopkins and Peter Cain have argued that British imperialism
was intimately associated with the needs of metropolitan capitalist
interests, particularly in the financial and service sectors.[20] While
the precise causal relationship between various parts of the British
economy and manifestations of imperial power remains a matter of
debate, most historians agree that the correspondence between the
two was no accident: the forces that made Britain a capitalist powerhouse were inexorably entangled with those that made it an imperial titan.

   The United States became the engine that drove the global economy after the Second World War. American capital fueled the post-
war revival of international trade, and American factories met the
pent-up demand for consumer goods. Wall Street replaced the City
of London as the world's main money market, and the dollar replaced sterling as its default currency. This economic ascendancy
supplied the United States with a surplus of what has been called
"soft power," the ability to exert its will in indirect and informal ways.
Charles Maier, who refers to the United States as a "post-territorial
empire," attributes its power to the unrivalled capacity it exhibited
after the Second World War for mass production and, recently, for

mass consumption, which it has financed through a feedback loop of credit from countries whose own economic growth is dependent on U.S. consumers' continued demand for their goods.[21]

Although the international economic environment over which the United States holds sway is in many respects very different from the one the British dealt with in the nineteenth and early twentieth centuries, the former has espoused much the same set of liberal economic doctrines as the latter did, stressing the benefits of free trade, safeguards for private property, and so forth. As the dominant partners in their respective systems of trade, both Britain and the United States gained from the expansion of those systems to other countries, leading them to put pressure on weaker states and societies that resisted such practices. In some cases this leverage took the form of gunboat diplomacy, and in others as financial manipulations by the British sterling zone and American dollar diplomacy, but invariably it has advanced the economic interests of these two empires.

Another aspect of the economics of empire that deserves attention is the "military-industrial complex," which President Dwight Eisenhower famously warned against in his farewell address.[22] Though this phrase is inextricably associated with the nexus of forces that arose in the United States after the Second World War, the phenomenon it refers to reared its head in an earlier configuration in imperial Britain. One reason John Hobson's *Imperialism: A Study* remains worth reading today is its incisive analysis of arms merchants, mining magnates, and other interest groups that gained economic advantages out of the imperial wars Britain waged and the colonial territories it won.[23] A similar study needs to be done about the many private firms that benefited from the invasions of Afghanistan and Iraq. This huge and expanding military-industrial complex is one connection between the economic dimension of American policy and its military imperatives. It also points to conspicuous parallels with the British imperial experience.

LASTLY, THERE IS THE IMPORTANCE OF IDEOLOGICAL POWER, to which should be added cultural power. Here too the British experience offers some useful points of comparison to the American one. All empires offer an ideological rationale for their rule over other peoples, invariably condensed into the claim that they are carrying out a civilizing mission. The British saw their mission as a liberal one, freeing their colonial subjects from the shackles of tradition and tyranny through the introduction of good government and legal rights, commerce and Christianity, medicine and

modern education, and other emblems of Western modernity. This
determination to lead the "poor benighted heathen" to the promised land of civilization was famously expressed by Rudyard Kipling
in his poem "The White Man's Burden"—written, of course, for his
American cousins as they set out to acquire an overseas empire at
the end of the nineteenth century. While the British themselves often failed to heed Kipling's call to "fill the mouth of Famine and
bid the sickness cease," this rhetoric cannot be dismissed as merely
empty or hypocritical. Its moral injunctions had a powerful hold on
the political imaginations of the Empire's expatriate agents, and it
influenced the attitudes of local Westernized elites as well. This liberal ideology and its promise of progress gave the British imperial
project a hegemonic strength that it would never have achieved had
it relied merely on brute force.

The United States has crafted its own technocratic version of this
civilizing mission.[24] It honed a rhetoric of development and modernization that held great appeal, especially after the Second World
War, when the American economy dominated the international
scene. According to Harry Harootunian, the Bush administration's
desire to remake the Middle East harks back to this post-war confidence in America's modernizing mission.[25] Its lineage, however,
can be traced to the same liberal roots that informed the British
ration-ale for reforming other societies. Juan Cole notes the parallels between the United States' insistence that its purpose in Iraq
is to bring political and economic liberty to Iraq, and the liberal
rhetoric the British used to justify their invasion and occupation
of Egypt in 1882 (which itself echoed Napoleon's pronouncements
when his army entered Egypt in 1798).[26] The theme trumpeted in
President Bush's inaugural address in 2004 was that America had
an obligation to advance the cause of liberty around the world (the
words "freedom" and "liberty" appear twenty-five times and thirteen
times, respectively, in the speech). Although it seems counterintui-
tive to associate liberty with empire, Edward Rhodes demonstrates
in his penetrating analysis of Bush's "grand strategy" that its crusading ambitions are profoundly imperial in nature.[27]

No such promise arises from imperialism's Janus-faced emphasis
on exclusionism, which insists on the irreducible racial or cultural
otherness of its subjects. Most empires face conflicting pressures to
incorporate and differentiate subject populations, but these tensions have been particularly pronounced in liberal empires. Thomas
Metcalf observes that British India experienced an "enduring tension between two ideals, one of similarity and the other of difference."[28] Although Queen Victoria's proclamation in 1858 establish-

ing crown rule over India famously promised to treat Indians in an "equal and impartial" manner, many of her countrymen in India conspicuously failed to abide by that promise. Racism was perhaps most pronounced in those colonies where white settlers competed with indigenous peoples and non-white immigrants for land, labor, and other resources. There arose what Patrick Wolfe terms the "logic of elimination," a logic made manifest in the fate of American Indians, Australian Aborigines, and others.[29] At the same time, American settlers' demand for African slave labor gave rise to a long-enduring system of institutionalized racism in the United States. Does this heritage make the American empire more racist than its British predecessor? Porter thinks so.[30] But the American empire has never sought to establish the overseas settler colonies that gave impetus to racist strategies of exclusion. To be sure, Americans' overseas ventures have been marked by racist attitudes and actions, as demonstrated by the use of derogatory terms like "gooks" during the Vietnam War and "rag heads" during the first Gulf War. Rarely, however, have these racial doctrines of exclusion posed a serious challenge to liberal principles of incorporation in the American idea and practice of empire.

Perhaps the most striking feature of the ideological and cultural currents shaping America's stance toward the world is the informal alliance of secular neoconservatives and Christian fundamentalists. Porter is one of the few commentators to note this curious convergence of interests, declaring (with undisguised dismay) that the neoconservatives, among whom he detects the "resonances of fascism," and the evangelical right, whose views he considers marked by "madness," have joined forces to give American foreign policy a newly messianic character.[31] Porter treats this development as confirmation that U.S. imperial ambitions are at odds with the pragmatism of Britons. Yet what is striking about this ideological alliance is how much it resembles the one that formed in the early nineteenth century in British India between utilitarians, who were largely rational secularists driven by the desire for radical political change, and evangelicals, who were deeply religious advocates of moral reform. Despite their differences, they found common ground in the determination to bring about the wholesale transformation of Indian society, introducing Western educational and legal institutions, abolishing suttee and other practices deemed morally reprehensible, and much more. Are the neoconservatives' and Christian fundamentalists' designs on the Middle East all that different? In both cases, the ambitions of these improbable partners are deeply idealistic and profoundly ethnocentric.

One further thread of continuity joins the ideological rationale for the British Empire to the arguments many Americans have made to justify the occupation of Afghanistan (though not Iraq). The British believed that the status of women in a society was one of the key indicators of where that society stood on the ladder of civilization. Primitive societies oppressed women; civilized ones privileged them. One of the most compelling moral arguments that the Bush administration made for the invasion of Afghanistan was that it would free Afghani women from the oppressive Taliban regime. (This argument gained far less purchase in Iraq, where the Baathist regime had been one of the most progressive in the regions regarding women's rights.) But even if the U.S. occupation has brought Afghani females greater opportunities for schooling and obstetric care, that achievement cannot be divorced from the exercise of imperial power. The connection was made clear in recent comments by a Marine Corps officer: "You go to Afghanistan, you got guys who slap women around for five years because they didn't wear a veil. You know, guys like that ain't got no manhood left anyway. So it's a hell of a lot of fun to shoot them."[32] Is there a better illustration of the bargains and tensions that underlie the imperial project?

AMERICANS HAVE LONG CLUNG TO THE CONVICTION that their country could wield world power without succumbing to the temptations of empire. Recent developments have done much to erode that exceptionalist stance. The Bush administration's obvious disdain for international law and its aggressive assertion of national interests culminated in an unprovoked war against another sovereign state, followed by a protracted military occupation. Not coincidentally, these actions were accompanied by the ideological embrace of empire by the neoconservative intelligentsia. While the result has been a new willingness across the political spectrum to speak of the United States as an empire, this is often understood in purely contemporary terms. Any meaningful purchase on this analytical category is lost if empire's influence on America's past, and its parallel histories elsewhere, are ignored. There may be no universal template for how an empire should act, but there is a wealth of evidence about how empires have acted. A comparison of America's current engagement with the world with Britain's imperial experience can provide insight into the ways the United States is reproducing its predecessor's experiences as well as the ways it stands apart.

Fall Semester 2006

1. A version of this lecture appeared in *International History Review*, 29, 1 (March 2007), pp. 83–108, where the extended argument and full footnotes can be found.

2. Wm. Roger Louis, "Suez and Decolonization: Scrambling Out of Africa and Asia," in *Ends of British Imperialism: The Scramble for Empire, Suez, and Decolonization* (London, 2006), p. 6.

3. Prominent proponents include Niall Ferguson and Max Boot, while critics include Bernard Porter and Rashid Khalidi.

4. See, for example, Craig Calhoun, Frederick Cooper, and Kevin W. Moore, eds., *Lessons of Empire: Imperial Histories and American Power* (New York, 2006), and special issues of *Daedalus*, 134, 2 (Spring 2005), and the *Wilson Quarterly*, 26, 3 (Summer 2002).

5. Niall Ferguson, *Colossus: The Price of America's Empire* (New York, 2004), p. 29.

6. Bernard Porter, *Empire and Superempire: Britain, America, and the World* (New Haven, 2006), p. 44.

7. Michael Mann, *Incoherent Empire*, (London, 2003), p. 13.

8. Michael Adas, "From Settler Colony to Global Hegemon: Integrating the Exceptionalist Narrative of the American Experience in World History," *American Historical Review*, 106, 5 (Dec. 2001), pp. 1692–1720; Howard Lamar and Leonard Thompson, eds., *The Frontier in History: North America and Southern Africa Compared* (New Haven, 1981).

9. In this respect, the experiences of American Indians may be more directly comparable to Britain's incorporation of the Welsh, Scots, and Irish, as detailed in Michael Hechter, *Internal Colonialism: The Celtic Fringe in British National Development* (London, 1975).

10. Max Boot, "The Case for American Empire," *Weekly Standard* (15 Oct. 2001).

11. Jürgen Osterhammel, "Britain and China, 1842–1914," in Andrew Porter, ed., *Oxford History of the British Empire*, Vol. III: *The Nineteenth Century* (Oxford, 1999), pp. 146-69. The term "triple assault" comes from David B. Abernethy, *The Dynamics of Global Dominance: European Overseas Empires, 1415–1980* (New Haven, 2000).

12. Porter, *Empire and Superempire*, pp. 76–77.

13. John Gallagher and Ronald Robinson, "The Imperialism of Free Trade," *Economic History Review*, second series, 6, 1 (Dec. 1961), pp. 187–208.

14. Chalmers Johnson, *The Sorrows of Empire: Militarism, Secrecy, and the End of the Republic* (New York, 2004), p. 1.

15. Paul M. Kennedy, *The Rise and Fall of British Naval Mastery* (New York, 1976); Barry M. Gough, "The Royal Navy and Empire," in Robin Winks, ed., *Oxford History of the British Empire*, Vol. V: *Historiography* (Oxford, 1999), pp. 327–41.

16. Johnson, *Sorrows of Empire*, p. 23.

17. Thomas Barnett, *The Pentagon's New Map: War and Peace in the Twenty-first Century* (New York, 2004).

18. Ivan Eland, *The Empire Has No Clothes: U.S. Foreign Policy Exposed* (Oakland, Calif., 2004), p. 13.

19. John A. Hobson, *Imperialism: A Study* (1902; Ann Arbor, 1972 edn.); V. I. Lenin, *Imperialism, the Highest Stage of Capitalism* (1916; Moscow, 1970 edn.).

20. Peter J. Cain and Anthony G. Hopkins, *British Imperialism, 1688–2000*, 2nd ed. (Harlow, 2002).

21. Charles S. Maier, *Among Empires: American Ascendancy and Its Predecessors* (Cambridge, Mass., 2006), p. 107.

22. See James Carroll's epic *House of War: The Pentagon and the Disastrous Rise of American Power* (Boston, 2006).

23. Hobson, *Imperialism,* part 2, ch. 1.

24. Michael Adas, *Dominance by Design: Technological Imperatives and America's Civilizing Mission* (Cambridge, Mass., 2006).

25. Harry D. Harootunian, *The Empire's New Clothes: Paradigm Lost, and Regained* (Chicago, 2004).

26. Juan Cole, "Empires of Liberty? Democracy and Conquest in French Egypt, British Egypt, and American Iraq," in Calhoun, Cooper, and Moore, *Lessons of Empire,* pp. 94–115.

27. Edward Rhodes, "Onward, Liberal Soldiers? The Crusading Logic of Bush's Grand Strategy and What Is Wrong with It," in Lloyd C. Gardner and Marilyn B. Young, eds., *The New American Empire* (New York, 2005), pp. 227–52.

28. Thomas R. Metcalf, *Ideologies of the Raj,* New Cambridge History of India, Vol. III, pt. 4 (Cambridge, 1994), p. x.

29. Patrick Wolfe, "Land, Labor, and Difference: Elementary Structures of Race," *American Historical Review,* 106, 3 (June 2001), pp. 866–905.

30. Porter, *Empire and Superempire,* p. 120.

31. Ibid., pp. 109, 112.

32. Ann Scott Tyson, "Marine General Is Told to Speak 'More Carefully,'" *Washington Post* (4 Feb. 2005).

23

An Accidental Criminal

FELIPE FERNÁNDEZ-ARMESTO

"No one truly knows a nation," said Nelson Mandela, "until one has been inside its gaols." On 6 January 2007, after living in the United States for more than a year without understanding the country, I acquired—briefly—a jailbird's authority. I can now share insights you can get only from being assaulted by the police and locked up for hours in the company of some of the most deprived and depraved dregs of the American underclass.

For someone like me—a mild-mannered middle-aged professor of scholarly proclivities, blameless habits, fastidious attire, and frail physique—it was shocking, traumatizing, and deeply educational. It all started on my first morning in Atlanta, Georgia, reputedly the most liberal city in the Deep South, honored as the birthplace of Martin Luther King. I was attending the annual conference of the American Historical Association. Unwittingly, I crossed a street at an unauthorized point. I had seen plenty of pedestrians precede me. There was no traffic in sight, and no danger to me or anyone else. Apparently, as I later learned, a policeman shouted at me to stop, but since I was not aware that I had done anything wrong, I took no notice of the shouting and did not realize that it was directed at me.

As it turns out, "jaywalking" is a criminal offence in the state of Georgia.

A young man in a bomber jacket accosted me, claiming to be a policeman, but with no visible evidence of his status. We got locked in mutual misunderstanding, demanding each other's identification.

I mistook the normal attitude of an Atlanta cop for arrogance, aggression, and menace. He, I suppose, mistook the normal demeanor of an aging and old-fashioned European intellectual for prevarication or provocation.

His behavior baffled me even before he lost patience with me, kicked my legs from under me, knocked my glasses from my nose, wrestled me to the ground, and, with the help of four or five other burly policemen who suddenly appeared on the scene, ripped my coat, scattered my books in the gutter, handcuffed me, and pinioned me painfully on the concrete, leaving a mass of scrapes and bruises.

I am rather flaccid and feeble. It does not take much force to flatten me, or much wit to see that I am physically non-threatening. I had heard of excessive force; I now knew what it meant.

I was bundled into a filthy paddy wagon with some rather unsavory-looking fellow prisoners, and then spent eight hours in the degrading, frightening environment of the downtown detention center, where no humiliation was spared: mug shot, fingerprinting, intrusive search, medical examination, and the frustration of understanding nothing: neither why I was there, nor how I might get out. With no cash for bail, I despaired of ever being released. It was like being kidnapped and held for ransom. Psychological self-torture gnawed while I waited for something to happen. The charge of failing to obey a police officer is really serious. I imagined myself facing deportation or ruin, for my livelihood depends on work in the United States.

Had I made it to my conference, I might have learned about medieval pumpernickel production or seventeenth-century stargazing. Instead, I discovered a lot about contemporary America. First, I learned that the Atlanta police could be barbaric, brutal, and out of control. The violence I experienced was the worst of my sheltered life. Muggers who attacked me once near my home in Oxford were considerably gentler with me than the Atlanta cops. Many fellow historians at the conference, who met me after my release, had witnessed the incident and told me how horrific they found it. The press quoted an onlooker as saying she thought she must be witnessing the arrest of Osama bin Laden.

Once in jail, I discovered another, better side of Atlanta. The detention center was weird—a kind of orderly pandemonium, a bedlam where madness is normal, so that nothing seems mad. It is windowless, filthy, and fetid, but strangely safe, insulated, and unworldly: like Diogenes' barrel, a place of darkness conducive to thought—for there is nothing else to do in the longueurs between interrogations, examinations, and lectures from the sergeant in charge about the necessity of good behavior.

My fellow inmates treated me with gentle curiosity—well, I did look rather out of place. Even in my torn clothes I was conspicuously overdressed for the occasion. I was almost the only man there who was not black. Most of my companions, like me, really didn't belong in jail. They had what Americans call "issues"—mostly involving drink and drugs.

In jail, I saw none of the violence that typifies the streets. On the contrary, the staff treated everyone, including some of the most difficult, desperate, drunk, or drugged-out denizens of Atlanta's demimonde, with impressive courtesy and professionalism. They were especially kind to me—perhaps unfairly so, privileging me as their pet intellectual. They rang my consulate. They allowed me to walk round, which you are not supposed to do, and chat with the other prisoners. I began to suspect that some of the down-and-outs I shared space with had deliberately contrived to get arrested in order to escape from the streets into this peaceable world—swapping the arbitrary, dangerous jurisdiction of the cops for the humane and helpful supervision of the center. Nelson Mandela, I think, was right to say that jail is the best place to make judgments from, because "a nation should be judged not by how it treats its highest citizens, but its lowest." If Atlanta is representative, America, by that standard, comes out commendably well.

I then met the best of America when I appeared in court. Everyone, including the judge himself and the wonderful vice president of the American Historical Association, who accompanied me to lend moral support, told me to get counsel to represent me. A lawyer I had consulted hurriedly that morning advised me to sue the city. But I had no stomach for such a hostile and elaborate strategy. Instead, I watched Judge Jackson at work. He had 117 cases to try that day. He handled them with unfailing compassion, common sense, and good humor.

I noticed that my charge as the judge read it—"failing to obey a police officer and obstructing the police"—did not match the semiliterate scrawl the accusing officer had scribbled on my citation: so I reckoned that, if necessary, I could get the charges dismissed on those grounds alone. Meanwhile, I simply appealed to the wisdom and mercy of the judge.

It took him only a few minutes to realize that I was the victim, not the culprit. The prosecutors withdrew the charges. The judge then proclaimed my freedom with kindly enthusiasm and detained me for nothing more grievous than a few minutes' chat about his reminiscences of the Old Bailey.

I MISSED WHAT HAPPENED NEXT because I had another conference to go, in Arizona. The story of my arrest reverberated around the world. It was front-page news in the UK and Spain. Friends in South Africa heard it on the BBC World Service. People read it in the papers in Chile. It was a subject of half-time chat during the big-league soccer game on the BBC. It provoked editorials and generated scores of thousands of blogs. I got thousands of sympathetic e-mails, including some from Singapore, Australia, and Japan. Colleagues at Leiden University offered me political asylum, pointing to the Netherlands' long record of hospitality to victims of repression. My wife gave interviews about the incident on popular talk shows.

It was pretty baffling to get thugged up by policemen in the first place. The media attention was even more baffling. To me, the appeal of the story was comical. "Man Crosses Road" became headline news. It was a bit like the classic banana-skin gag: dignity humbled, absent-minded professor blunders into trouble. As it happened, I had just published a book, *Pathfinders,* about the history of exploration. So it was funny that I could not find the right path across the street. I will probably never live it down. "Managed to stay out of police custody, have we, sir?" asks the doorman where I live. Instead of being—as I always hoped—the historian who wrote that quite good book or who gave that not bad lecture, I shall probably always be the "Historian Who Crossed the Road." If you don't believe me, try Googling "jaywalking" and "historian."

But the comic aspects were not what interested the world. My misadventure was appealing to the media because it ignited anti-American responses. It confirmed the world's image of the United States as a violent, barbarous place run by thuggery. The Spanish press thought it was all Mr. Bush's fault—which, in a way, I suppose, it was, since government sets the tone that law enforcement agents echo. I became the last and least in a series of victims that included persecuted "illegals" and the inmates of Guantanamo and Abu Ghraib. During my fifteen minutes of Z-list celebrity, I became a minor anti-American icon. People I meet still tell me how angry they feel on my behalf. "Those Americans," they say. "How barbarous! How bizarre!"

In my long-ago boyhood, I was brought up to be anti-American. In my half-English, half-Spanish family, back in the fifties, we blamed the United States for supporting Spain's military dictatorship. Like a lot of intellectual snobs, we thought American cinema, pop music, junk food, and GIs polluting. We acknowledged but resented the free world's dependence on American muscle. The Vietnam years confirmed my anti-American prejudices.

Then I grew up. As an historian, I began to realize that, on balance, the United States had been a pretty magnanimous force in world history for most of the twentieth century—promoting democracy, subverting empires, accommodating refugees, encouraging science, ladling aid. Where you find power you find abuse, but by historical standards, America exercised power with remarkable restraint. To friends who complained about Uncle Sam's overweening might and aberrant foreign policy, "Whom would you prefer," I asked, "as the world's unique superpower? Hitler's Germany? Stalin's Russia? Mao's China? Be grateful for a comparatively benign hegemon."

Then I married a woman who had worked in Boston and loved it. Through a series of visiting professorships, I got to know Americans. I found them, on average, better educated than the English, for more than half of them have some kind of post-secondary or higher education; and once you get used to the cultural differences, they are better mannered. Most of them really want to like you; and they really want you to like them. They are not, on the whole, the greedy ultra-individualists I was taught to expect. On the contrary, social responsibility and civic-mindedness are typical American virtues. Sometimes naively, sometimes superficially, but always sincerely, never sneeringly, Americans believe in democracy, liberty, equality of opportunity, human rights, and the balanced government set out in the Constitution. The actual government subverts, sidelines, or abuses these values, but people continue to revere them and practice them in their town meetings, neighborhood associations, schools, and churches. When I got the chance of a permanent job at a U.S. university, I thought, "At last, after twenty-eight years of marriage, I can do something to please my wife."

Because of my experience, I can speak up for America. I cannot say anything very positive about the police in Atlanta, except that they have a tough job and maybe it is understandable that from time to time a cop goes nuts. But police misbehavior is a common problem all over the world. And parts of the United States are well policed. In Massachusetts, where I work, the cops are pretty civilized, and more likely to help you across the street than batter you for trying to do so mid-block. It is disappointing to find so much cruelty, greed, frustration, anger, neurosis, and psychosis on the streets; but if you are British, you do not have to go as far as America to find them. And what I saw of the judiciary, the detention center staff, and the prosecuting authorities in Atlanta impressed me, especially the compassionate and efficient judge, and public defenders ready to leap in with wise and equitable advice whenever a miscarriage of justice threatened. It all left me convinced that whatever the deficiencies of the legislators and the executive, one branch of the U.S. government can work really well and can help make life better.

The media, however, love the bad news, and almost all the reports of my case focused on the brutality and stupidity of the police. Most papers outside the country used the story to exemplify all that is worst about America. It became—as one American paper complained—a kind of international incident. In the States, in consequence, I have been blamed for stirring up anti-Americanism. I have found myself miscast as another foreign Americanophobe or even as a fellow traveller of America's enemies. I began to get hate mail, which, expletives deleted, said, more or less, "Alien, go home."

I AM NOT GOING TO TAKE THAT ILL-INTENTIONED ADVICE. But I am not sure what to do instead. Suing, as lawyers and others advised, would be a characteristically American response. But I am naturally nonlitigious and cherish naive hopes that reform can happen by persuasion. I certainly do not feel that I can, as Americans say, "move on." For one thing, among the thousands of messages I have had to reply to since my arrest are many from nice, ordinary Atlantans who have also suffered barbarities at the hands of their police without getting any attention or consolation. That makes me feel guilty and anxious to help them. I have identified about forty serious public-interest matters connected with my case, ranging from the location of street crossings to the prevention of police brutality. Those matters need attention. For its own sake, Atlanta needs to scrutinize its policing and reform its practices. I can understand why some officers behave irrationally and unpredictably. Part of the downtown environment in their city is hideous—inoffensive to the eye only when shrouded by the often-prevailing fog. The sidewalks are thronged with beggars, who can turn nasty at night. The crime rate is fearful. The result is that the police are nervy, jumpy, short-fused, and lacking in restraint, patience, or forbearance. Witnesses tell me that up to ten officers took part in the assault on me, though I counted about half a dozen. This is evidence not only of excessive zeal, but also of seriously warped priorities. In cities notorious for rape, murder, and mayhem, the police should have better things to do than persecute jaywalkers.

At the very least, the police need to be told to exercise forbearance with outsiders—especially foreigners—who may not understand the peculiarities of local custom and law.

When the publicity broke over my arrest, and Atlanta's status as a convention destination seemed threatened, the mayor hastily announced an inquiry. Nothing has happened. The police's strategy seems to be to escape reform by temporizing. The promised inquiry is beginning to look like a delaying tactic in a classic cover-up.

My experience in Atlanta is not going to tip me into anti-Americanism. I feel happy and privileged to be able to live and work in the United States. On the whole, in my work as an historian, I have argued consistently that America has had a benign influence on the world. Yet a whole generation of young people, worldwide, is growing up as I did, with the same anti-Americanism I learned in boyhood and struggled to discard. That distresses me. The United States is not going to remain the world superpower for much longer. But while it does, non-Americans need to work with America for a better world. It is no more rational to be anti-American than to be anti-Muslim or anti-Semitic or anti-British. The United States is a big country with far more cultural variety than Europeans generally suppose. It is too big, too diverse to hate uniformly. There is as much liberalism in New England, and as much social democracy in Minnesota, as in most of Europe.

American life, of course, does have some grim features: environmental profligacy, a huge underclass, widespread gun-fetishism, the shame of death row, a frustrating political system in which millions of dollars buy elections and millions of voters abandon them But Americans do some things better than the British: better universities; better provision for culture, art, scholarship, and research; better class mobility; even, in some respects, better health-care provision. In some of these areas, U.S. practice is superior to Europe's generally.

I find the government detestable, but would not blame Americans for Mr. Bush's shortcomings. Few of them voted for him. Of those who voted, half opposed him. Americans accept the role and the cost of being the world's policeman reluctantly, because no one else will do it, not because they want to victimize and exploit everyone else.

But if you like a country, you don't assume it is perfect. You want to make it even better. The difference between patriotism and nationalism is that a patriot wants his country to be the best in the world; the nationalist thinks it already is the best. I am going to continue to do my little bit to help American patriots improve America. I am going to resume the pressure on the mayor. I plan to return to

Atlanta to give a lecture. I want to see more of its beauties and less barbarity. I am hoping to find the city better policed, with the sort of decency, civility, and rational forbearance that make for a better society. I am looking forward to crossing the road and maybe inviting the citizens to cross along with me.

Summer 2007

A version of this lecture appeared in the *Independent*, 13 January 2007; a slightly longer version was given as a talk on BBC Radio 4, 13 March 2007.

24

British Studies at
the University of Texas, 1975–2007

Fall Semester 1975

Paul Scott (Novelist, London), 'The *Raj Quartet*'

Ian Donaldson (Director, Humanities Research Center, Australian National University), 'Humanistic Studies in Australia'

Fritz Fellner (Professor of History, Salzburg University), 'Britain and the Origins of the First World War'

Roger Louis (UT History), 'Churchill, Roosevelt, and the Future of Dependent Peoples during the Second World War'

Michael Holroyd (Biographer, Dublin), 'Two Biographies: Lytton Strachey and Augustus John'

Max Beloff (former Gladstone Professor of Government, Oxford University, present Principal of Buckingham College), 'Imperial Sunset'

Robin Winks (Professor of History, Yale University), 'British Empire-Commonwealth Studies'

Warren Roberts (Director, HRC), and David Farmer (Assistant Director, HRC), 'The D. H. Lawrence Editorial Project'

Harvey C. Webster (Professor of English, University of Louisville), 'C. P. Snow as Novelist and Philosopher'

Anthony Kirk-Greene (Fellow of St. Antony's College, Oxford), 'The Origins and Aftermath of the Nigerian Civil War'

Spring Semester 1976

Joseph Jones (UT Professor of English), 'World English'

William S. Livingston (UT Professor of Government), 'The British Legacy in Contemporary Indian Politics'

John Higley (UT Associate Professor of Sociology), 'The Recent Political Crisis in Australia'

Elspeth Rostow (UT Dean of General and Comparative Studies), Standish Meacham (UT Professor of History), and Alain Blayac (Professor of English, University of Paris), 'Reassessments of Evelyn Waugh'

Jo Grimond (former Leader of the Liberal Party), 'Liberal Democracy in Britain'

Gaines Post (UT Associate Professor of History), Malcolm Macdonald (UT Government), and Roger Louis (UT History), 'The Impact of Hitler on British Politics'

Robert Hardgrave (UT Professor of Government), Gail Minault (UT Assistant Professor of History), and Chihiro Hosoya (Professor of History, University of Tokyo), 'Kipling and India'

Kenneth Kirkwood (Rhodes Professor of Race Relations, Oxford University), 'The Future of Southern Africa'

C. P. Snow, 'Elite Education in England'

Hans-Peter Schwarz (Director of the Political Science Institute, Cologne University, and Visiting Fellow, Woodrow Wilson International Center for Scholars), 'The Impact of Britain on German Politics and Society since the Second World War'

B. K. Nehru (Indian High Commissioner, London, and former Ambassador to the United States), 'The Political Crisis in India'

Robert A. Divine (UT Professor of History), Harry J. Middleton (Director, LBJ Library), and Roger Louis (UT History), 'Declassification of Secret Documents: The British and American Experiences Compared'

Fall Semester 1976

John Farrell (UT Associate Professor of English), 'Revolution and Tragedy in Victorian England'

Anthony Honoré (Regius Professor of Civil Law, Oxford University), 'British Attitudes to Legal Regulation of Sex'

Alan Hill (UT Professor of English), 'Wordsworth and America'

Ian Nish (Professor of Japanese History, London School of Economics), 'Anglo-American Naval Rivalry and the End of the Anglo-Japanese Alliance'

Norman Sherry (Professor of English, University of Lancaster), 'Joseph Conrad and the British Empire'

Peter Edwards (Lecturer, Australian National University), 'Australia through American Eyes: The Second World War and the Rise of Australia as a Regional Power'

David Edwards (UT Professor of Government), Steven Baker (UT Assistant Professor of Government), Malcolm Macdonald (UT Government), Bill Livingston (UT Government), and Roger Louis (UT History), 'Britain and the Future of Europe'

Michael Hurst (Fellow of St. John's College, Oxford), 'The British Empire in Historical Perspective: The Case of Joseph Chamberlain'

Ronald Grierson (English Banker and former Public Official), 'The Evolution of the British Economy since 1945'

Marian Kent (Lecturer in History, University of New South Wales), 'British Oil Policy between the World Wars'

Constance Babington-Smith (Fellow of Churchill College, Cambridge), 'The World of Rose Macaulay'

William Todd (UT Kerr Professor of English History and Culture), Walt Rostow (UT Professor of History and Economics), and James McKie (UT Dean of Social and Behavioral Sciences), 'Adam Smith after 200 Years'

Spring Semester 1977

Carin Green (Novelist), and Elspeth Rostow (UT American Studies), 'The Achievement of Virginia Woolf'

Samuel H. Beer (Professor of Government, Harvard University), 'Reflections on British Politics'

David Fieldhouse (Fellow of Nuffield College, Oxford), 'Decolonization and the Multinational Corporations'

Gordon Craig (Wallace Professor of Humanities, Stanford University), 'England and Europe on the Eve of the Second World War'

John Lehmann (British Publisher and Writer), 'Publishing under the Bombs— The Hogarth Press during World War II'

Philip Jones (Director, University of Texas Press), William S. Livingston (UT Christian Professor of British Studies), Michael Mewshaw (UT Assistant Professor of English), David Farmer (Assistant Director, HRC), Roger Louis (UT History), and William Todd (UT History), 'The Author, His Editor and Publisher'

Dick Taverne (former M.P), 'The Mood of Britain: Misplaced Gloom or Blind Complacency?'

James B. Crowley (Professor of History, Yale University), Lloyd C. Gardner (Professor of History, Rutgers University), Akira Iriye (Professor of History, University of Chicago), and Roger Louis (UT History), 'The Origins of World War II in the Pacific'

Rosemary Murray (Vice-Chancellor of Cambridge University), 'Higher Education in England'

Burke Judd (UT Professor of Zoology), and Robert Wagner (UT Professor of Zoology), 'Sir Cyril Burt and the Controversy over the Heritability of IQ'

Alessandra Lippucci (UT Government), Roger Louis (UT History), Bill Livingston (UT Government), and Walt Rostow (UT Economics), 'The Wartime Reputations of Churchill and Roosevelt: Overrated or Underrated?'

Fall Semester 1977

Donald L. Weismann (UT University Professor in the Arts), 'British Art in the Nineteenth Century: Turner and Constable—Precursors of French Impressionism'

Standish Meacham (UT Professor of History), 'Social Reform in England'

Joseph Jones, 'Recent Commonwealth Literature'

Lewis Hoffacker (former US Ambassador), 'The Katanga Crisis: British and other Connections'

James M. Treece (UT Professor of Law), Roger Louis (UT History), Warren Roberts, and Bill Todd, (UT History) 'The Copyright Law of 1976'

Charles Heimsath (Visiting Professor of Indian History), Bob Hardgrave (UT Government), Thomasson Jannuzi, (Director, UT Center for Asian Studies), C. P. Andrade (UT Professor of Comparative Studies), and Bill Livingston (UT Government), 'Freedom at Midnight: A Reassessment of Britain and the Partition of India Thirty Years After'

Lord Fraser of Kilmorack (Chairman of the Conservative Party Organization), 'The Tory Tradition of British Politics'

Bernth Lindfors (UT Professor of English), 'Charles Dickens and the Hottentots and Zulus'

Albert Hourani (Director, Middle East Centre, Oxford University), 'The Myth of T. E. Lawrence'

Mark Kinkead-Weekes (Professor of English, University of Kent) and Mara Kalnins (British Writer), 'D. H. Lawrence: Censorship and the Expression of Ideas'

J. D. B. Miller (Professor of International Relations, Australian National University), 'The Collapse of the British Empire'

Peter Green (UT Professor of Classics), Robert King (UT Dean of Social and Behavioral Sciences), Bill Livingston (UT Government), Bob Hardgrave (UT Government), Roger Louis (UT History), and Warren Roberts (Director, HRC), 'The Best and Worst Books of 1977'

Spring Semester 1978

Peter Green (UT Classics), Malcolm Macdonald (UT Government), and Robert Crunden (UT Professor of American Studies), 'British Decadence in the Interwar Years'

Terry Quist (UT Undergraduate), Steve Baker (UT Government), and Roger Louis (UT History), 'R. Emmet Tyrrell's *Social Democracy's Failure in Britain*'

Stephen Koss (Professor of History, Columbia University), 'The British Press: Press Lords, Politicians, and Principles'

John House (Professor of Geography, Oxford University), 'The Rhodesian Crisis'

T. S. Dorsch (Professor of English, Durham University), 'Oxford in the 1930s'

Stephen Spender (English Poet and Writer), 'Britain and the Spanish Civil War'

Okot p'Bitek (Ugandan Poet), 'Idi Amin's Uganda'

David C. Goss (Australian Consul General), 'Wombats and Wivveroos'

Leon Epstein (Professor of Political Science, University of Wisconsin), 'Britain and the Suez Crisis of 1956'

David Schoonover (UT School of Library Science), 'British and American Expatriates in Paris in the 1920s'

Peter Stansky (Professor of History, Stanford University), 'George Orwell and the Spanish Civil War'

Alexander Parker (UT Professor of Spanish), 'Reflections on the Spanish Civil War'

Norman Sherry (Professor of English, Lancaster University), 'Graham Greene and Latin America'

Martin Blumenson (Office of the Chief of Military History, Department of the Army), 'The Ultra Secret'

Fall Semester 1978

W. H. Morris-Jones (Director, Commonwealth Studies Institute, University of London), 'Power and Inequality in Southeast Asia'

Hartley Grattan (UT Emeritus Professor of History), Gilbert Chase (UT Professor of American Studies), Bob Crunden (UT Professor of American Studies), and Roger Louis (UT History), 'The British and the Shaping of the American Critical Mind: A Discussion of Edmund Wilson's *Letters on Literature and Politics*'

James Roach (UT Professor of Government), 'The Indian Emergency and its Aftermath'

Bill Todd, (UT History) 'The Lives of Samuel Johnson'

Lord Hatch (British Labour Politician), 'The Labour Party and Africa'

John Kirkpatrick (HRC Bibliographer), 'Max Beerbohm'

Brian Levack (UT Associate Professor of History), 'Witchcraft in England and Scotland'

M. R. Masani (Indian Writer), 'Gandhi and Gandhism'

A. W. Coates (Economics), 'The Professionalization of the British Civil Service'

John Clive (Professor of History and Literature, Harvard University), 'Great Historians of the Nineteenth Century'

Geoffrey Best (University of Sussex), 'Flightpath to Dresden: British Strategic Bombing in the Second World War'

Kurth Sprague (UT Instructor in English), 'T. H. White's *Once and Future King*'

Gilbert Chase, 'The British Musical Invasion of America'

Spring Semester 1979

Peter Green (UT Professor of Classics), Alessandra Lippucci (UT Instructor in Government), and Elspeth Rostow (UT Dean of the LBJ School of Public Affairs), 'P. N. Furbanks's Biography of E. M. Forster'

Roger Louis (UT History), Bob Hardgrave (UT Government), Gail Minault (UT Professor of History), Peter Gran (UT Assistant Professor of History), and Bob King (UT Dean of Liberal Arts), 'E. M. Forster and India'

Paul M. Kennedy (East Anglia University, Visiting Professor of History, Institute of Advanced Study, Princeton), 'The Contradiction between British Strategic Policy and Economic Policy in the Twentieth Century'

Richard Rive (Visiting Fulbright Research Fellow from South Africa), 'Olive Schreiner and the South African Nation'

Charles P. Kindleberger (Professor of Economics, Massachusetts Institute of Technology), 'Lord Zuckerman and the Second World War'

John Press (English Poet), 'English Poets and Postwar Society'

Richard Ellmann (Goldsmiths' Professor of English Literature, Oxford University), 'Writing a Biography of Joyce'

Michael Finlayson (Scottish Dramatist), 'Contemporary British Theater'

Lawrence Stone (Professor of History, Institute of Advanced Study, Princeton), 'Family, Sex, and Marriage in England'

C. P. Snow, 'Reflections on the Two Cultures'

Theodore Zeldin (Oxford University), 'Are the British More or Less European than the French?'

David Edwards (UT Professor of Government), 'How United the Kingdom: Greater or Lesser Britain?'

Michael Holroyd (British Biographer), 'George Bernard Shaw'

John Wickman (Director, Eisenhower Library), 'Eisenhower and the British'

Fall Semester 1979

Robert Palter (Philosophy), 'Reflections on British Philosophers: Locke, Hume, and the Utilitarians'

Alfred Gollin (Professor of History, University of California at Santa Barbara), 'Political Biography as Political History: Garvin, Milner, and Balfour'

Edward Steinhart (History), 'The Consequences of British Rule in Uganda'

Paul Sturges (Loughborough University), and Dolores Donnelly (Toronto University), 'History of the National Library of Canada'

Sir Michael Tippett (British Composer), 'Moving into Aquarius'

Steven Baker (UT Assistant Professor of Government), 'Britain and United Nations Emergency Operations'

Maria Okila Dias (Professor of History, University of São Paulo), 'Intellectual Roots of Informal Imperialism: Britain and Brazil'

Alexander Parker (UT Professor of Spanish), 'Reflections on *Brideshead Revisited*'

Barry C. Higman (Professor of History, University of the West Indies), 'West Indian Emigrés and the British Empire'

Gaines Post (UT Associate Professor of History), 'Britain and the Outbreak of the Second World War'

Karen Gould (UT Lecturer in Art), 'Medieval Manuscript Fragments and English 17th Century Collections: New Perspectives from *Fragmenta Manuscripta*'

John Farrell (UT Associate Professor of English), Eric Poole (HRC) and James Bieri (UT English): Round Table Discussion of Jeanne MacKenzie's new biography, *Dickens: A Life*

Joseph O. Baylen (Regents Professor of History, Georgia State University), 'British Journalism in the Late Victorian and Edwardian Eras'

Peter T. Flawn (President of UT), 'An Appreciation of Charles Dickens'

Spring Semester 1980

Annette Weiner (UT Assistant Professor of Anthropology), 'Anthropologists in New Guinea: British Interpretations and Cultural Relativism'

Bernard Richards (Lecturer in English, Oxford University), 'Conservation in the Nineteenth Century'

Thomas McGann (UT Professor of History), 'Britain and Argentina: An Informal Dominion?'

Mohammad Ali Jazayery (Director, Center for Middle Eastern Studies), 'The Persian Tradition in English Literature'

C. Hartley Grattan (UT Professor of History) 'Twentieth-Century British Novels and the American Critical Mind'

Katherine Whitehorn (London *Observer*), 'An Insider's View of the *Observer*'

Guy Lytle (UT Assistant Professor of History), 'The Oxford University Press' *History of Oxford*'

C. P. Snow, 'Reflections on *The Masters*'

Harvey Webster, '*The Masters* and the Two Cultures'

Brian Blakeley (Associate Professor of History, Texas Tech University), 'Women and the British Empire'

Stephen Koss (Professor of History, Columbia University), 'Asquith, Balfour, Milner, and the First World War'

Tony Smith (Associate Professor of Political Science, Tufts University), 'The Expansion of England: New Ideas on Controversial Themes in British Imperialism'

Stanley Ross (UT Professor of History), 'Britain and the Mexican Revolution'

Rowland Smith (Chairman, Department of English, Dalhousie University), 'The British Intellectual Left and the War, 1939–1945'

Richard Ellmann (Goldsmiths' Professor of English, Oxford University), 'Oscar Wilde: A Reconsideration and Problems of the Literary Biographer'

James Bill (UT Professor of Government), 'The United States, Britain, and the Iranian Crisis of 1953'

Fall Semester 1980

Decherd Turner (Director, HRHRC), 'The First 1000 Days'

Roger Louis (UT History), 'Britain and Egypt after the Second World War'

Alistair Horne (Visiting Fellow, Woodrow Wilson Center, Washington, DC), 'Britain and the Fall of France'

Edward Rhodes (UT Associate Professor of History), Peter Green (UT Classics), William Todd (UT History), and Roger Louis (UT History), 'Literary Fraud: H. R. Trevor-Roper and the Hermit of Peking'

Mark Kinkead-Weekes (Professor of English, Kent University), 'D. H. Lawrence's *Rainbow:* Its Sense of History'

Sir John Crawford (Vice-Chancellor, Australian National University), 'Hartley Grattan: In Memoriam'

John Stubbs (Assistant Professor of History, University of Waterloo), 'The Tory View of Politics and Journalism in the Interwar Years'

Donald L. Weismann (UT University Professor in the Arts), 'British Art in the Nineteenth Century'

Fran Hill (UT Assistant Professor of Government), 'The Legacy of British Colonialism in Tanzania'

R. W. B. Lewis (Professor of English, Yale University), 'What's Wrong with the Teaching of English?'

Charlene Gerry (British Publisher), 'The Revival of Fine Printing in Britain'

Peter Gran (UT Assistant Professor of History), 'The Islamic Response to British Capitalism'

Tina Poole (HRHRC) 'Gilbert and Sullivan's Christmas'

Spring Semester 1981

Bernard N. Darbyshire (Visiting Professor of Government and Economics), 'North Sea Oil and the British Future'

Christopher Hill (Master of Balliol College, Oxford), 'The English Civil War'

Elizabeth Heine (Assistant Professor of English, UT San Antonio), and Roger Louis (UT History), 'A Reassessment of Leonard Woolf'

Bernard Richards (Brasenose College, Oxford), 'D. H. Lawrence and Painting'

Miguel Gonzalez-Gerth (UT Professor of Spanish), 'Poetry Once Removed: The Resonance of English as a Second Language'

John Putnam Chalmers (Librarian, HRHRC), 'English Bookbinding from Caedmon to Le Carré'

Peter Coltman (UT Professor of Architecture), 'The Cultural Landscapes of Britain: 2,000 Years of Blood, Sweat, Toil & Tears to Wrest a Living from this Bloody Mud'

Thomas H. Law (former Regent University of Texas), 'The Gold Coins of the English Sovereigns'

Sidney Weintraub (Rusk Professor of International Affairs, LBJ School), James W. McKie (UT Professor of Economics), and Mary Williams (Canadian Consulate, Dallas), 'Canadian-American Economic Relations'

Amedée Turner (Conservative Member of the European Parliament), 'Integrating Britain into the European Community'

Muriel C. Bradbrook (Fellow of Girton College, Cambridge), 'Two Poets: Kathleen Raine and Seamus Heaney'

Ronald Sampson (Chief of the Industrial Development Department, Aberdeen), 'Scotland—Somewhat of a British Texas?'

Fall Semester 1981

Jerome Bump (UT Professor of English), 'From Texas to England: The Ancestry of Our Victorian Architecture'

Lord Fraser of Kilmorack, 'Leadership Styles of Tory Prime Ministers since the Second World War'

William Carr (Professor of History, University of Sheffield), 'A British Interpretation of American, German, and Japanese Foreign Policy, 1936-1941'

Iqbal Narain (Professor of Political Science and former Vice-Chancellor, Rajasthan University, Jaipur), 'The Ups and Downs of Indian Academic Life'

Don Etherington (Assistant Director, HRHRC), 'The Florence Flood, 1966: The British Effort—or: Up to our Necks in Mud and Books'

E. V. K. Fitzgerald (Visiting Professor of Economics), 'The British University: Crisis, Confusion, and Stagnation'

Robert Crunden (UT Professor of American Studies), 'A Joshua for Historians: Mordecai Richler and Canadian Cultural Identity'

Bernth Lindfors (UT Professor of English), 'The Hottentot Venus and Other African Attractions in Nineteenth-Century England'

Chris Brookeman (Professor of American Studies, London Polytechnic), 'The British Arts and Society'

Nicholas Pickwoad (Freelance Book Conservator), 'The Libraries of the National Trust'

Kurth Sprague (UT Instructor), 'John Steinbeck, Chase Horton, and the Matter of Britain'

Martin J. Wiener (Professor of History, Rice University), 'Cultural Values and Socio-Economic Behavior in Britain'

Werner Habicht (Professor of English, University of Würzburg), 'Shakespeare in Nineteenth-Century Germany'

Spring Semester 1982

Stevie Bezencenet (Lecturer in Photography, London College of Printing), 'Contemporary Photography in Britain'

Jane Marcus (UT Assistant Professor of English), 'Shakespeare's Sister, Beethoven's Brother: Dame Ethel Smyth and Virginia Woolf'

Wilson Harris (UT Professor of English), and Raja Rao (UT Professor of Philosophy), 'The Quest for Form: Britain and Commonwealth Perspectives'

Al Crosby (UT Professor of American Studies), 'The British Empire as a Product of Continental Drift'

Lord St. Brides (Visiting Scholar, University of Texas), 'The White House and Whitehall: Washington and Westminster'

Elizabeth Fernea (Senior Lecturer in English and President of the Middle East Studies Association), 'British Colonial Literature of the Middle East'

Maurice Evans (Actor and Producer), 'My Early Years in the Theater'

Joan Bassin (Kansas City Art Institute), 'Art and Industry in Nineteenth-Century England'

Eugene N. Borza (Professor of Ancient History, Pennsylvania State University), 'Sentimental British Philhellenism: Images of Greece'

Ralph Willett (American Studies Department, University of Hull), 'The Style and Structure of British Television News'

Roger Louis (UT History), 'Britain and the Creation of the State of Israel'

Peter Russell (Professor of Spanish, Oxford University), 'A British Historian Looks at Portuguese Historiography of the Fifteenth Century'

Rory Coker (UT Professor of Physics), 'Frauds, Hoaxes and Blunders in Science—a British Tradition?'

Ellen DuBois (Professor of History, SUNY Buffalo), 'Anglo-American Perspectives on the Suffragette Movement'

Donald G. Davis, Jr. (UT Professor of Library Science), 'Great Expectations—and a Few Illusions: Reflections on an Exchange Teaching Year in England'

Anthony Rota (Managing Director, Bertram Rota Ltd.), 'The Changing World of the Bookdealer'
Eisig Silberschlag (former President, Hebrew College, Visiting Gale Professor of Judaic Studies), 'The Bible as the Most Popular Book in English'

Fall Semester 1982

Woodruff Smith (Professor of History, UT San Antonio), 'British Overseas Expansion'
The Rt. Hon. George Thomas (Speaker of the House of Commons), 'Parliamentary Democracy'
Nigel Nicolson (English Historian and Biographer), 'The English Country House as an Historical Document'
Lord St. Brides (Visiting Scholar), 'A Late Leaf of Laurel for Evelyn Waugh'
Lt. Col. Jack McNamara, USMC (Ret.), 'The Libel of Evelyn Waugh by the *Daily Express*'
James Wimsatt (UT Professor of English), 'Chaucer and Medieval French Manuscripts'
Christopher Whelan (Visiting Professor, UT Law School), 'Recent Developments in British Labour Law'
Brian Wearing (Senior Lecturer in American Studies, Christchurch, New Zealand), 'New Zealand: In the Pacific, but of It?'
Robert Hardgrave (UT Professor of Government), 'The United States and India'
James McBath (Professor of Communications, University of Southern California), 'The Evolution of *Hansard*'
Paul Fromm (Professor of Economics, University of Toronto), 'Canadian–United States Relations: Two Solitudes'
John Velz (UT Professor of English), 'When in Disgrace: Ganzel's Attempt to Exculpate John Payne Collier'
Roger Louis (UT History), 'British Origins of the Iranian Revolution'

Spring Semester 1983

Sir Ellis Waterhouse (Slade Professor of Fine Arts, Oxford University), 'A Comparison of British and French Painting in the Late Eighteenth Century'
E. J. L. Ride (Australian Consul General), 'Australia's Place in the World and Her Relationship with the United States'
Edward Bell (Director of the Royal Botanic Gardens, Kew), 'Kew Gardens in World History'
The Very Rev. Oliver Fiennes (Dean of Lincoln), 'The Care and Feeding of Magna Carta'
C. V. Narasimhan (former Under-Secretary of the United Nations), 'Last Days of the British Raj: A Civil Servant's View'
Warren G. Osmond, 'Sir Frederic Eggleston and the Development of Pacific Consciousness'
Richard Ellmann (Goldsmiths' Professor, Oxford University), 'Henry James among the Aesthetes'
Janet Caulkins (Professor of French, University of Wisconsin at Madison), 'The Poor Reputation of Cornish Knights in Medieval Literature'
Werner Habicht (Professor of English, University of Würzburg), 'Shakespeare and the Third Reich'
Gillian Peele (Fellow of Lady Margaret Hall, Oxford), 'The Changing British Party System'

John Farrell (UT Professor of English), 'Scarlet Ribbons: Memories of Youth and Childhood in Victorian Authors'

Peter Russell (Professor of Spanish, Oxford University), 'A Not So Bashful Stranger: *Don Quixote* in England, 1612–1781'

Sir Zelman Cowen (Provost of Oriel College, Oxford), 'Contemporary Problems in Medicine, Law, and Ethics'

Dennis V. Lindley (Visiting Professor of Mathematics), 'Scientific Thinking in an Unscientific World'

Martin Blumenson (Office of the Chief of Military History, Department of the Army), 'General Mark Clark and the British in the Italian Campaign of World War II'

Fall Semester 1983

Anthony King (Professor of Politics, University of Essex), 'Margaret Thatcher and the Future of British Politics'

Alistair Gillespie (Canadian Minister of Energy, Mines, and Resources), 'Canadian-British Relations: Best and Worst'

Charles A. Owen, Jr. (Professor of English, University of Connecticut), 'The Pre-1400 Manuscripts of the *Canterbury Tales*'

Major-General (Ret.) Richard Clutterbuck (Reader in Political Conflict, University of Exeter), 'Terrorism in Malaya'

Wayne A. Wiegand (Associate Professor of English, University of Kentucky), 'British Propaganda in American Public Libraries during World War I'

Stuart Macintyre (Australian National University, Canberra), 'Australian Trade Unionism between the Wars'

Ram Joshi (Visiting Professor of History, former Vice-Chancellor, University of Bombay), 'Is Gandhi Relevant Today?'

Sir Denis Wright (former British Ambassador in Iran), 'Britain and the Iranian Revolution'

Andrew Horn (Head of the English Department, University of Lesotho), 'Theater and Politics in South Africa'

Philip Davies (Professor of American Government, University of Manchester), 'British Reaction to American Politics: Overt Rejection, Covert Assimilation'

H. K. Singh (Political Secretary, Embassy of India), 'United States–Indian Relations'

Roger Louis (UT Professor of History), Ram Joshi (UT Visiting Professor of History), and J. S. Mehta (UT Professor, LBJ School), 'Two Cheers for Mountbatten: A Reassessment of Lord and Lady Mountbatten and the Partition of India'

Spring Semester 1984

M. S. Venkataramani (Director of International Studies, Jawaharlal Nehru University), 'Winston Churchill and Indian Freedom'

Sir John Thompson (British Ambassador to the United Nations), 'The Falklands and Grenada in the United Nations'

Robert Farrell (Professor of English, Cornell University), 'Medieval Archaeology'

Allon White (Lecturer in English, University of Sussex), 'The Fiction of Early Modernism'

Peter Green (UT Professor of Classics), Roger Louis (UT Professor of History), Miguel Gonzalez-Gerth (UT Professor of Spanish & Portuguese), Standish

Meacham (UT Professor of History), and Sid Monas (UT Professor of Slavic Languages and History): 'Orwell's *1984*'

Uriel Dann (Professor of English History, University of Tel Aviv), 'Hanover and Britain in the Time of George II'

José Ferrater-Mora (Fairbank Professor of Humanities, Bryn Mawr), 'A. M. Turing and his "Universal Turing Machine"'

Rüdiger Ahrens (University of Würzburg), 'Teaching Shakespeare in German Universities'

Michael Brock (Warden of Nuffield College, Oxford), 'H. H. Asquith and Venetia Stanley'

Herbert Spiro (Professor of Political Science, Free University of Berlin), 'What Makes the British and Americans Different from Everybody Else: The Adversary Process of the Common Law'

Nigel Bowles (Lecturer in American Government and Politics, University of Edinburgh), 'Reflections on Recent Developments in British Politics'

Harold Perkin (Mellon Distinguished Visiting Professor, Rice University), 'The Evolution of Citizenship in Modern Britain'

Christopher Heywood (Senior Lecturer, Sheffield University), '*Jane Eyre* and *Wuthering Heights*'

Dave Powers (Curator, Kennedy Library), 'JFK's Trip to Ireland, 1963'

R. W. Coats (Visiting Professor of Economics), 'John Maynard Keynes: The Man and the Economist'

David Evans (UT Professor of Astronomy), 'Astronomy as a British Cultural Export'

Fall Semester 1984

John Henry Faulk, 'Reflections on My Sojourns in the British Middle East'

Lord Fraser of Kilmorack, 'The Thatcher Years—and Beyond'

Michael Phillips (Lecturer in English Literature, University of Edinburgh), 'William Blake and the Rise of the Hot Air Balloon'

Erik Stocker (HRHRC), 'A Bibliographical Detective Story: Reconstructing James Joyce's Library'

Amedée Turner (Member of the European Parliament), 'Recent Developments in the European Parliament'

Michael Hurst (Fellow of St. John's College, Oxford), 'Scholars versus Journalists on the English Social Classes'

Charles Alan Wright (UT William B. Bates Professor of Law), 'Reflections on Cambridge'

J. M. Winter (Fellow of Pembroke College, Cambridge), 'Fear of Decline in Population in Britain after World War I'

Henk Wesseling (Director of the Centre for the History of European Expansion, University of Leiden), 'Dutch Colonialism and the Impact on British Imperialism'

Celia Morris Eckhardt (Biographer and author of *Fannie Wright*), 'Frances Wright and *England as the Civilizer*'

Sir Oliver Wright (British Ambassador to the United States), 'British Foreign Policy—1984'

Leonard Thompson (Professor of African History, Yale University), 'Political Mythology and the Racial Order in South Africa'

Flora Nwapa (Nigerian Novelist), 'Women in Civilian and Military Rule in Nigeria'

Richard Rose (Professor of Political Science, University of Strathclyde), 'The Capacity of the Presidency in Comparative Perspective'

Spring Semester 1985

Bernard Hickey (University of Venice), 'Australian Literary Culture: Short Stories, Novels, and "Literary Journalism"'

Kenneth Hafertepe (UT American Studies), 'The British Foundations of the Smithsonian Castle: The Gothic Revival in Britain and America'

Rajeev Dhavan (Visiting Professor, LBJ School and Center for Asian Studies), 'Race Relations in England: Trapped Minorities and their Future'

Sir John Thompson (British Ambassador to the United Nations), 'British Techniques of Statecraft'

Philip Bobbitt (UT Professor of Law), 'Britain, the United States, and Reduction in Strategic Arms'

David Bevington (Drama Critic and Theater Historian), 'Maimed Rites: Interrupted Ceremony in *Hamlet*'

Standish Meacham (UT Professor of History), 'The Impact of the New Left History on British and American Historiography'

Iris Murdoch (Novelist and Philospher), and John O. Bayley (Thomas Warton Professor of English, Oxford University), 'Themes in English Literature and Philosophy'

John P. Chalmers (Librarian, HRHRC), 'Malory Illustrated'

Thomas Metcalf (Professor of History, University of California at Berkeley), 'The Architecture of Empire: The British Raj in India'

Robert H. Wilson (UT Emeritus Professor of English), 'Malory and His Readers'

Lord St. Brides, '*A Passage to India*': Better Film than Novel?'

Derek Pearsall (Medievalist at York University), 'Fire, Flood, and Slaughter: The Tribulations of the Medieval City of York'

E. S. Atieno Odhiambo (University of Nairobi, Visiting Professor, The Johns Hopkins University), 'Britain and Kenya: The Mau Mau, the "Colonial State," and Dependency'

Francis Robinson (Reader in History, University of London), 'Indian Muslim Religious Leadership and Colonial Rule'

Charles B. MacDonald (Deputy Chief Historian, US Army), 'The British in the Battle of the Bulge'

Brian Levack (UT Associate Professor of History), 'The Battle of Bosworth Field'

Kurth Sprague (UT Lecturer in English), 'The Mirrors of Malory'

Fall Semester 1985

A. P. Thornton (Distinguished University Professor, University of Toronto), 'Whatever Happened to the British Commonwealth?'

Michael Garibaldi Hall (UT Professor of History), and Elizabeth Hall (LBJ School), 'Views of Pakistan'

Ronald Steel (Visiting Professor of History), 'Walter Lippmann and the British'

Douglas H. M. Branion (Canadian Consul General), 'Political Controversy and Economic Development in Canada'

Decherd Turner and Dave Oliphant (HRHRC), 'The History of the Publications of the HRHRC'

Robert Fernea (UT Professor of Anthropology), 'The Controversy over Sex and Orientalism: Charles Doughty's *Arabia Deserta*'

Desley Deacon (Lecturer, UT Department of Government), 'Her Brilliant Career: The Context of Nineteenth-Century Australian Feminism'
John Lamphear (UT Associate Professor of History), 'The British Colonial "Pacification" of Kenya: A View from the Other Side'
Kingsley de Silva (Foundation Professor of Ceylon History at the University of Peradeniya, Sri Lanka), 'British Colonialism and Sri Lankan Independence'
Thomas Hatfield (UT Dean of Continuing Education), 'Colorado on the Cam, 1986: From "Ultra" to Archaeology, from Mr. Micawber to Mrs. Thatcher'
Carol Hanbery MacKay (UT Assistant Professor of English), 'The Dickens Theater'
Ronald Brown, Jo Anne Christian, Roger Louis (UT History), Harry Middleton, and Ronald Steel—Panel Discussion: 'The Art of Biography: Philip Ziegler's *Mountbatten*'

Spring Semester 1986

B. J. Fernea (UT English and Middle Eastern Studies), Bernth Lindfors (UT Professor of English), and Roger Louis (UT History), '*Out of Africa:* The Book, the Biography, and the Movie'
Robert Litwak (Woodrow Wilson International Center for Scholars, Washington, DC), 'The Great Game: Russian, British, and American Strategies in Asia'
Gillian Adams Barnes (UT English), and Jane Manaster (UT Geography), 'Humphrey Carpenter's *Secret Gardens* and the Golden Age of Children's Literature'
Laurie Hergenhan (Professor of English, University of Queensland), 'A Yankee in Australia: The Literary and Historical Adventures of C. Hartley Grattan'
Brian Matthews (Flinders University of South Australia), 'Australian Utopianism of the 1880s'
Richard Langhorne (Fellow of St. John's College, Cambridge), 'Apostles and Spies: The Generation of Treason at Cambridge between the Wars'
Ronald Robinson (Beit Professor of the History of the British Empire, Oxford University), 'The Decline and Fall of the British Empire'
William Rodgers (Vice-President, Social Democratic Party), 'Britain's New Three-Party System: A Permanent or Passing Phenomenon?'
John Coetzee (Professor of Literature, University of Cape Town), 'The Farm Novel in South Africa'
Ayesha Jalal, (Fellow, Trinity College, Cambridge), 'Jinnah and the Partition of India'
Andrew Blane (Professor of History, City College of New York), 'Amnesty International: From a British to an International Movement'
Anthony Rota (Antiquarian Bookdealer and Publisher), 'London Pride: 1986'
Elspeth Rostow (Dean, LBJ School), 'The Withering Away of Whose State? Colonel Qaddafi's Reflections on Nationalism at Home and Abroad, in Britain and in the Middle East'
Ray Daum (Curator, HRHRC), 'Broadway—Piccadilly!'

Fall Semester 1986

Dean Robert King and Members of the ' "Unrequired Reading List" Committee— The British Component': Round Table Discussion.
Paul Sturges (Loughborough University), 'Popular Libraries in Eighteenth-Century Britain'

Ian Bickerton (Professor of History, University of Missouri), 'Eisenhower's Middle East Policy and the End of the British Empire'
Marc Ferro (Visiting Professor of History), 'Churchill and Pétain'
David Fitzpatrick (Visiting Professor of History, Queen's University, Kingston, Ontario), 'Religion and Politics in Ireland'
Adam Watson (Center for Advanced Studies, University of Virginia, former British Ambassador to Castro's Cuba), 'Our Man in Havana—or: Britain, Cuba, and the Caribbean'
Norman Rose (Chaim Weizmann Professor of History, Hebrew University), 'Chaim Weizmann, the British, and the Creation of the State of Israel'
Elaine Thompson (Senior Fulbright Scholar, American University), 'Legislatures in Canberra and Washington'
Roger Louis (UT Professor of History), 'Suez Thirty Years After'
Antonia Gransden (Reader in Medieval History, University of Nottingham), 'The Writing of Chronicles in Medieval England'
Hilary Spurling (British Biographer and Critic), 'Paul Scott's *Raj Quartet:* The Novelist as Historian'
J. D. B. Miller (Professor of International Relations, Australian National University), 'A Special and Puzzling Relationship: Australia and the United States'
Janet Meisel (UT Associate Professor of History), 'The Domesday Book'

Spring Semester 1987

Miguel Gonzalez-Gerth (UT Liberal Arts), Robert Fernea (UT Anthropology), Joe Horn (UT Psychology), Bruce Hunt (UT History), and Delbert Thiessen (UT Psychology), 'Contemporary Perspectives on Evolution'
Alistair Campbell-Dick (Chief Executive Officer, Research and Development Strategic Technology), 'Scottish Nationalism'
Anthony Mockler (British Freelance Historian and Biographer), 'Graham Greene: The Interweaving of His Life and Fiction'
Michael Crowder (Visiting Professor of African History, Amherst College), 'The Legacy of British Colonialism in Africa'
Carin Green (UT Lecturer in Classics), 'Lovers and Defectors: Autobiography and *The Perfect Spy*'
Lord St. Brides, 'The Modern British Monarchy'
Victor Szebehely (UT Richard B. Curran Professor of Engineering), 'Sir Isaac Newton'
Patrick McCaughey (Visiting Professor of Australian Studies, Harvard University; Director, National Gallery of Victoria, Melbourne), 'The Persistence of Landscape in Australian Art'
Adolf Wood (Deputy Editor of the *Times Literary Supplement*), 'An Informal History of the *TLS*'
Nissan Oren (Visiting Professor of Political Science, The Johns Hopkins University; Kaplan Professor, Hebrew University, Jerusalem), 'Churchill, Truman, and Stalin: The End of the Second World War'
Sir Michael Howard (Regius Professor of History, Oxford University), 'Britain and the First World War'
Sir John Graham (former British Ambassador to NATO), 'NATO: British Origins, American Security, and the Future Outlook'
Daniel Mosser (Virginia Polytechnic Institute and State University), 'The Chaucer Cardigan Manuscript'
Sir Raymond Carr (Warden of St. Antony's College, Oxford), 'British Intellectuals and the Spanish Civil War'

Michael Wilding (Reader in English, University of Sydney), 'The Fatal Shore? The Convict Period in Australian Literature'

Fall Semester 1987

Peter Green (UT Professor of Classics), Winfred Lehmann (UT Temple Professor of Humanities), Roger Louis (UT Kerr Professor), and Paul Woodruff (UT Professor of Philosophy), 'Anthony Burgess: The Autobiography'
Robert Crunden (UT Professor of History and American Studies), 'Ezra Pound in London'
Carol MacKay (UT Associate Professor of English) and John Henry Faulk, J. Frank Dobie and Thackeray's Great-Granddaughter: Another Side of '*A Texan in England*'
Sarvepalli Gopal (Professor of Contemporary History, Jawaharlal Nehru University, and Fellow of St. Antony's College, Oxford), 'Nehru and the British'
Robert D. King (UT Dean of Liberal Arts), 'T. S. Eliot'
Lord Blake (Visiting Cline Professor of English History and Literature, former Provost of Queen's College, Oxford), 'Disraeli: Problems of the Biographer'
Alain Blayac (Professor of Comparative Literature, University of Montpellier), 'Art as Revelation: Gerard Manley Hopkins's Poetry and James Joyce's *Portrait of the Artist*'
Mary Bull (Oxford University), 'Margery Perham and Africa'
R. J. Moore (Professor of History, Flinders University), 'Paul Scott: The Novelist as Historian, and the *Raj Quartet* as History'
Ian Willison (Head of the Rare Books Division of the British Library), 'New Trends in Humanities Research: The *History of the Book in Britain* Project'
The Duke of Norfolk, 'The Lion and the Unicorn: Ceremonial and the Crown'
Hans Mark (Chancellor, The University of Texas System), 'The Royal Society, the Royal Observatory, and the Development of Modern Research Laboratories'
Henry Dietz (UT Professor of Government), 'Sherlock Holmes: A Centennial Celebration'

Spring Semester 1988

Lord Jenkins (Chancellor of Oxford University), 'Changing Patterns of British Government from Asquith via Baldwin and Attlee to Mrs. Thatcher'
Lord Thomas (author of *The Spanish Civil War* and *Cuba, or the Pursuit of Freedom*), 'Britain, Spain, and Latin America'
Barbara Harlow (UT English), Bernth Lindfors (UT English), Wahneema Lubiano (UT English), and Robert Wren (University of Houston), 'Chinua Achebe: The Man and His Works'
Charles Townshend (Professor of History, Keele University), 'Britain, Ireland, and Palestine, 1918–1947'
Richard Morse (Program Secretary for Latin America, Woodrow Wilson Center), 'T. S. Eliot and Latin America'
Chinua Achebe (Nigerian Novelist), 'Anthills of the Savannah'
Tapan Raychaudhuri (Reader in Indian History, Oxford University), 'The English in Bengali Eyes in the Nineteenth Century'
Lord Chitnis (Chief Executive of the Rowntree Trust and Chairman of the British Refugee Council), 'British Perceptions of U.S. Policy in Central America'
Kurth Sprague (Senior Lecturer in English), 'Constance White: Sex, Womanhood, and Marriage in British India'
George McGhee (former US Ambassador to Turkey and Germany), 'The Turning

Point in the Cold War: Britain, the United States, and Turkey's Entry into NATO'

Robert Palter (Professor of the History of Science, Trinity College), 'New Light on Newton's Natural Philosophy'

J. Kenneth McDonald (Chief Historian, CIA), 'The Decline of British Naval Power, 1918–1922'

Yvonne Cripps (UT Visiting Professor of Law), '"Peter and the Boys Who Cry Wolf": *Spycatcher*'

Emmanuel Ngara (Professor of English, University of Zimbabwe), 'African Poetry: Nationalism and Cultural Domination'

Kate Frost (UT Assistant Professor of English), 'Frat Rats of the Invisible College: The Wizard Earl of Northumberland and His Pre-Rosicrucian Pals'

B. Ramesh Babu (UT Visiting Professor of Government), 'American Foreign Policy: An Indian Dissent'

Sir Antony Ackland (British Ambassador to the United States), 'From Dubai to Madrid: Adventures in the British Foreign Service'

In the Spring Semester 1988, British Studies helped sponsor four lectures by Sir Brian Urquhart (former Under-Secretary of the United Nations) on 'World Order in the Era of Decolonization'

Fall Semester 1988

Peter Green (UT Dougherty Professor of Classics), Diana Hobby (Rice University, Editor of the *Yeats Papers*), Roger Louis (UT Kerr Professor), and Elspeth Rostow (UT Stiles Professor of American Studies), Round Table Discussion on Richard Ellman's *Oscar Wilde*

Hugh Cecil (University of Leeds), 'The British First World War Novel of Experience'

Alan Knight (UT Worsham Professor of Mexican History), 'Britain and the Mexican Revolution'

Prosser Gifford (Former Deputy Director, Woodrow Wilson Center, Washington, DC), and Robert Frykenberg (Professor of Indian History, University of Wisconsin at Madison), 'Stability in Post-Colonial British Africa: The Indian Perspective'

Joseph Dobrinski (Université Paul-Valéry), 'The Symbolism of the Artist Theme in *Lord Jim*'

Martin Stannard (University of Leicester), 'Evelyn Waugh and North America'

Lawrence Cranberg (Consulting Physicist and Fellow of the American Physical Society), 'The Engels-Marx Relationship and the Origins of Marxism'

N. G. L. Hammond (Professor of Greek, Bristol University), 'The British Military Mission to Greece, 1943–1944'

Barbara Harlow (UT English), 'A Legacy of the British Era in Egypt: Women, Writing, and Political Detention'

Sidney Monas (UT Professor of Slavic Languages and History), 'Thanks for the Mummery: *Finnegans Wake*, Rabelais, Bakhtin, and Verbal Carnival'

Robert Bowie (Former Director, Harvard Center of International Affairs and Deputy Director, Central Intelligence Agency), 'Britain's Decision to Join the European Community'

Shirley Williams (Co-Founder, Social Democratic Party), 'Labour Weakness and Tory Strength—or, the Strange Death of Labour England'

Bernard Richards (Fellow of Brasenose College, Oxford), 'Ruskin's View of Turner'

John R. Clarke (Art History), 'Australian Art of the 1960s'

Round Table Discussion on Paul Kennedy's *Rise and Fall of the Great Powers:* Alessandra Lipucci (UT Government), Roger Louis (UT Kerr Professor), Jagat Mehta (LBJ School), Sidney Monas (UT Professor of Slavic Languages and History), and Walt Rostow (UT Economics and History)

Spring Semester 1989

Brian Levack (UT Professor of History), 'The English Bill of Rights, 1689'

Hilary Spurling (Critic and Biographer), 'Paul Scott as Novelist: His Sense of History and the British Era in India'

Larry Carver (Director of the Humanities Program), 'Lord Rochester: The Profane Wit and the Restoration's Major Minor Poet'

Atieno Odhiambo (Professor of History, Rice University), 'Re-Interpreting Mau Mau'

Trevor Hartley (Reader in Law, London School of Economics, and Visiting Professor, UT Law School), 'The British Constitution and the European Community'

Archie Brown (Fellow of St. Antony's College, Oxford), 'Political Leadership in Britain, the Soviet Union, and the United States'

Lord Blake (Former Provost of Queen's College, Oxford, and Editor of the *Dictionary of National Biography*), 'Churchill as Historian'

Weirui Hou (Professor of English Literature, Shanghai University), 'British Literature in China'

Norman Daniel (British Council), 'Britain and the Iraqi Revolution of 1958'

Alistair Horne (Fellow of St. Antony's College, Oxford), 'The Writing of the Biography of Harold Macmillan'

M. R. D. Foot (former Professor of History, Manchester University, and Editor of the *Gladstone Diaries*), 'The Open and Secret War, 1939–1945'

Ian Willison (former Head of Rare Books Division of the British Library), 'Editorial Theory and Practice in *The History of the Book*'

Neville Meaney (Professor of History, University of Sydney), 'The "Yellow Peril": Invasion, Scare Novels, and Australian Political Culture'

Round Table Discussion on *The Satanic Verses:* Kurth Sprague (UT Associate Professor of American Studies), Peter Green (UT Dougherty Professor of Classics), Robert A. Fernea (UT Professor of Anthropology), Roger Louis (UT Kerr Professor), and Gail Minault (UT Associate Professor of History and Asian Studies)

Kate Frost (UT Associate Professor of English), 'John Donne, Sunspots, and the British Empire'

Lee Patterson (Professor of English, Duke University), 'Chaucerian Commerce'

Edmund Weiner and John Simpson (Editors of the new *OED*), 'Return to the Web of Words'

Ray Daum (Curator, HRHRC), 'Noel Coward and Cole Porter'

William B. Todd (UT Emeritus Professor of History), 'Edmund Burke on the French Revolution'

Fall Semester 1989

D. Cameron Watt (Stevenson Professor of International History, LSE), 'Britain and the Origins of the Second World War: Personalities and Politics of Appeasement'

Gary Freeman (UT Associate Professor of Government), 'On the Awfulness of the English: The View from Comparative Studies'

Hans Mark (Chancellor, UT System), 'British Naval Tactics in the Second World War: The Japanese Lessons'

T. B. Millar (Director, Menzies Centre for Australian Studies, London), 'Australia, Britain, and the United States in Historical Perspective'

Dudley Fishburn (Member of Parliament and former Editor of *The Economist*), '*The Economist*'

Lord Franks (former Ambassador in Washington), 'The "Special Relationship"'

Herbert L. Jacobson (Drama Critic and friend of Orson Wells), 'Three Score Years of Transatlantic Acting and Staging of Shakespeare'

Roy Macleod (Professor of History, University of Sydney) 'The "Practical Man": Myth and Metaphor in Anglo-Australian Science'

David Murray (Professor of Government, the Open University), 'Hong Kong: The Historical Context for the Transfer of Power'

Susan Napier (UT Assistant Professor of Japanese Language and Literature), 'Japanese Intellectuals Discover the British'

Dr. Karan Singh (Ambassador of India to the United States), 'Four Decades of Indian Democracy'

Paul Woodruff (UT Professor of Philosophy), 'George Grote and the Radical Tradition in British Scholarship'

Herbert J. Spiro (UT Professor of Government), 'Britain, the United States, and the Future of Germany'

Robert Lowe (Wine Columnist for the *Austin American-Statesman*), ' "God Rest you Merry, Gentlemen": The Curious British Cult of Sherry'

Spring Semester 1990

Thomas F. Staley (Director, HRHRC), 'Harry Ransom, the Humanities Research Center, and the Development of Twentieth-Century Literary Research Collections'

Thomas Cable (UT Blumberg Professor of English), 'The Rise and Decline of the English Language'

D. J. Wenden (Fellow of All Souls College, Oxford), 'Sir Alexander Korda and the British Film Industry'

Roger Owen (Fellow of St. Antony's College, Oxford, and UT Visiting Professor of Middle Eastern History), 'Reflections on the First Ten Years of Thatcherism'

Robert Hardgrave (UT Temple Centennial Professor of Humanities), 'Celebrating Calcutta: The Solvyns Portraits'

Donatus Nwoga (Professor of English, University of Nigeria, Nsukka, and Fulbright Scholar-in-Residence, University of Kansas), 'The Intellectual Legacy of British Decolonization in Africa'

Francis Sitwell (Etonian, Seaman, and Literary Executor), 'Edith Sitwell: A Reappraisal'

Robert Vitalis (UT Assistant Professor of Government), 'The "New Deal" in Egypt: Britain, the United States, and the Egyptian Economy during World War II'

James Coote (UT Professor and Cass Gilbert Teaching Fellow, School of Architecture), 'Prince Charles and Architecture'

Harry Eckstein (Distinguished Professor of Political Science, University of California, Irvine), 'British Politics and the National Health Service'

Alfred David (Professor of English, Indiana University), 'Chaucer and King Arthur'

Ola Rotimi (African Playwright and Theater Director), 'African Literature and the British Tongue'

Derek Brewer (Professor of English and Master of Emmanuel College, Cambridge), 'An Anthropological Study of Literature'

Neil MacCormick (Regius Professor of Public Law and the Law of Nations, University of Edinburgh), 'Stands Scotland Where She Should?'

Janice Rossen (Senior Research Fellow, HRHRC), 'Toads and Melancholy: The Poetry of Philip Larkin'

Ronald Robinson (Beit Professor of the History of the British Commonwealth, Oxford, and Visiting Cline Professor, University of Texas), 'The Decolonization of British Imperialism'

Fall Semester 1990

Round Table Discussion on 'The Crisis in the Persian Gulf': Hafez Farmayan (UT Professor of History), Robert Fernea (UT Professor of Anthropology), Roger Louis (UT Kerr Professor), and Robert Stookey (United States Foreign Service Officer, Retired, now Research Associate, Center for Middle Eastern Studies)

John Velz (UT Professor of English), 'Shakespeare and Some Surrogates: An Account of the Anti-Stratfordian Heresy'

Michael H. Codd (Secretary, Department of the Prime Minister and Cabinet, Government of Australia), 'The Future of the Commonwealth: An Australian View'

John Dawick (Senior Lecturer in English, Massey University, New Zealand), 'The Perils of Paula: Young Women and Older Men in Pinero's Plays'

Gloria Fromm (Professor of English, University of Illinios in Chicago), 'New Windows on Modernism: The Letters of Dorothy Richardson'

David Braybrooke (UT Centennial Commission Professor in the Liberal Arts), 'The Canadian Constitutional Crisis'

Sidney Monas (UT Professor of Slavic Languages and History), 'Paul Fussell and World War II'

James Fishkin (UT Darrell Royal Regents Chair in Ethics and American Society), 'Thought Experiments in Recent Oxford Philosophy'

Joseph Hamburger (Pelatiah Perit Professor of Political and Social Science, Yale University), 'How Liberal Was John Stuart Mill?'

Richard W. Clement (Special Collections Librarian, Kenneth Spencer Research Library, University of Kansas), 'Thomas James and the Bodleian Library: The Foundations of Scholarship'

Michael Yeats (Former Chairman of the Irish Senate and only son of the poet William Butler Yeats), 'Ireland and Europe'

Round Table Discussion on 'William H. McNeill's *Arnold J. Toynbee: A Life*': Standish Meacham (UT Dean of Liberal Arts), Peter Green (UT Dougherty Professor of Classics), Roger Louis (UT Kerr Professor), and Sidney Monas (UT Professor of Slavic Languages and History)

Jeffrey Meyers (Biographer and Professor of English, University of Colorado), 'Conrad and Jane Anderson'

Alan Frost (Professor of History, La Trobe University, Melbourne), 'The Explorations of Captain Cook'

Sarvepalli Gopal (Professor of History, Jawaharlal Nehru University, and Fellow of St. Antony's College, Oxford), 'The First Ten Years of Indian Independence'

Round Table Discussion on 'The Best and Worst Books of 1990': Alessandra Lip-

pucci (UT Lecturer in Government), Roger Louis (UT Kerr Professor), Tom
Staley (Director, HRHRC), Steve Weinberg (UT Welch Foundation Chair
in Science Theory), and Paul Woodruff (UT Thompson Professor in the
Humanities)

Spring Semester 1991

David Hollway (Prime Minister's Office, Government of Australia), 'Australia and
the Gulf Crisis'

Diane Kunz (Yale University), 'British Post-War Sterling Crises'

Miguel Gonzalez-Gerth (UT Professor of Spanish Literature and HRHRC), 'T. E.
Lawrence, Richard Aldington, and the Death of Heroes'

Robert Twombly (UT Professor of English), 'Religious Encounters with the Flesh
in English Literature'

Alan Ryan (Princeton University), 'Bertrand Russell's Politics'

Hugh Kenner (Andrew Mellon Professor of the Humanities, The Johns Hopkins
University, and Visiting Harry Ransom Professor), 'The State of English
Poetry'

Patricia Burnham (UT American Studies), 'Anglo-American Art and the Struggle
for Artistic Independence'

Round Table Discussion on 'The Churchill Tradition': Lord Blake (former Provost
of Queen's College, Oxford), Lord Jenkins (Chancellor, Oxford University),
Field Marshal Lord Carver (former Chief of the Defence Staff), Sir Michael
Howard (former Regius Professor, Oxford, present Lovett Professor of Military and Naval History, Yale University), with a concluding comment by Winston S. Churchill, M.P.

Woodruff Smith (Professor of History, UT San Antonio), 'Why Do the British Put
Sugar in their Tea?'

Peter Firchow (Professor of English, University of Minnesota), 'Aldous Huxley:
The Poet as Centaur'

Irene Gendzier (Professor of History and Political Science, Boston University),
'British and American Middle Eastern Policies in the 1950s: Lebanon and
Kuwait. Reflections on Past Experience and the Postwar Crisis in the Gulf'

John Train (*Harvard* Magazine and *Wall Street Journal*), 'Remarkable Catchwords
in the City of London and on Wall Street'

Adam Sisman (Independent Writer, London), 'A. J. P. Taylor'

Roger Louis (UT Kerr Professor), 'The Young Winston'

Adrian Mitchell (Professor of English, Melbourne University, and Visiting Professor of English and Australian Studies), 'Claiming a Voice: Recent Non-Fiction
Writing in Australia'

Bruce Hevly (Professor of History, University of Washington), 'Stretching Things
Out versus Letting Them Slide: The Natural Philosophy of Ice in Edinburgh
and Cambridge in the Nineteenth Century'

Henry Dietz (UT Professor of Government), 'Foibles and Follies in Sherlock's
Great Game: Some Excesses of Holmesian Research'

Summer 1991

Roger Louis (UT Kerr Professor), and Ronald Robinson (Beit Professor of the
History of the British Commonwealth, Oxford University, and Visiting Cline
Professor), 'Harold Macmillan and the Dissolution of the British Empire'

Robert Treu (Professor of English, University of Wisconsin, Lacrosse), 'D. H. Lawrence and Graham Greene in Mexico'

Thomas Pinney (Chairman, Department of English, Pomona College), 'Kipling, India, and Imperialism'

Ronald Heiferman (Professor of History, Quinnipiac College), 'The Odd Couple: Winston Churchill and Chiang Kai-shek'

John Harty (Professor of English, Alice Lloyd College, Kentucky), 'The Movie and the Book: J. G. Ballard's *Empire of the Sun*'

A. B. Assensoh (Ghanaian Journalist and Professor of History, Southern University, Baton Rouge), 'Nkrumah'

Victoria Carchidi (Professor of English, Emory and Henry College), 'Lawrence of Arabia on a Camel, Thank God!'

James Gump (Chairman, Department of History, University of California, San Diego), 'The Zulu and the Sioux: The British and American Comparative Experience with the "Noble Savage"'

Fall Semester 1991

Round Table Discussion on Noel Annan's *Our Age:* Peter Green (UT Dougherty Professor of Classics), Robert D. King (UT Dean of Liberal Arts), Roger Louis (UT Kerr Professor), and Thomas F. Staley (Director, HRHRC)

Christopher Heywood (Okayama University, Japan), 'Slavery, Imagination, and the Brontës'

Harold L. Smith (University of Houston, Victoria), 'Winston Churchill and Women'

Krystyna Kujawinska-Courtney (University of Lodz), 'Shakespeare and Poland'

Ewell E. Murphy, Jr. (Baker & Botts, Houston), 'Cecil Rhodes and the Rhodes Scholarships'

I. N. Kimambo (University of Dar-es-Salaam), 'The District Officer in Tanganyika'

Hans Mark (Chancellor, UT System), 'The Pax Britannica and the Inevitable Comparison: Is There a Pax Americana? Conclusions from the Gulf War'

Richard Clutterbuck (Major-General, British Army, Ret.), 'British and American Hostages in the Middle East: Negotiating with Terrorists'

Elizabeth Hedrick (UT Assistant Professor of English), 'Samuel Johnson and Linguistic Propriety'

The Hon. Denis McLean (New Zealand Ambassador to the United States), 'Australia and New Zealand: The Nuisance of Nationalism'

Elizabeth Richmond (UT Assistant Professor of English), 'Submitting a Trifle for a Degree: Dramatic Productions at Oxford and Cambridge in the Age of Shakespeare'

Kenneth Warren, M.D. (Director for Science, Maxwell Macmillan), 'Tropical Medicine: A British Invention'

Adolf Wood (Deputy Editor of the *TLS*), 'The Golden Age of the *Times Literary Supplement*'

Eugene Walter (Poet and Novelist), 'Unofficial Poetry: Literary London in the 1940s and 1950s'

Sidney Monas (UT Professor of Slavic Languages and History), 'Images of Britain in the Poetry of World War II'

St. Stephen's Madrigal Choir, 'Celebrating an English Christmas'

Spring Semester 1992

Jeremy Treglown (Critic and Author), 'Wartime Censorship and the Novel'

Toyin Falola (UT Professor of History), 'Nigerian Independence, 1960'

Donald S. Lamm (President, W.W. Norton and Company), 'Publishing English History in America'

Colin Franklin (Publisher and Historian of the Book), 'The Pleasures of Eighteenth-Century Shakespeare'

Thomas F. Staley (Director, HRHRC), *'Fin de Siècle* Joyce: A Perspective on One Hundred Years'

Sarvepalli Gopal (Jawaharlal Nehru University), '"Drinking Tea with Treason": Halifax and Gandhi'

Michael Winship (UT Associate Professor of English), 'The History of the Book: Britain's Foreign Trade in Books in the Nineteenth Century'

Richard Lariviere (UT Professor of Sanskrit and Director of the Center for Asian Studies), 'British Law and Lawyers in India'

Round Table Discussion on A. S. Byatt's *Possession:* Janice Rossen (Visiting Scholar, HRHRC), John P. Farrell (UT Professor of English), and Roger Louis (UT Kerr Professor)

William H. McNeill (University of Chicago and former President of the American Historical Association), 'Arnold Toynbee's Vision of World History'

Derek Brewer (Master of Emmanuel College, Cambridge), 'The Interpretation of Fairy Tales: The Implications for English Literature, Anthropology, and History'

David Bradshaw (Fellow of Worcester College, Oxford), 'Aldous Huxley: Eugenics and the Rational State'

Steven Weinberg (Josey Regental Professor of Science), 'The British Style in Physics'

Sir David Williams (Vice-Chancellor, Cambridge University), 'Northern Ireland'

Summer 1992

R. A. C. Parker (Fellow of Queen's College, Oxford), 'Neville Chamberlain and Appeasement'

Adrian Wooldridge (Fellow of All Souls College, Oxford, and Staff Writer for *The Economist*), 'Reforming British Education: How It Happened and What America Can Learn'

Chris Wrigley (Professor of Modern British History, Nottingham University), 'A. J. P. Taylor: An English Radical and Modern Europe'

Fall Semester 1992

Round Table Discussion on E. M. Forster's *Howards End:* The Movie and the Book. Robert D. King (UT Liberal Arts), Roger Louis (UT Kerr Professor), Alessandra Lippucci (UT Government), and Thomas F. Staley (HRHRC)

Lord Skidelsky (Warwick University), 'Keynes and the Origins of the "Special Relationship"'

Sir Samuel Falle (former British Ambassador), 'Britain and the Middle East in the 1950s'

Ian MacKillop (University of Sheffield), 'We Were That Cambridge: F. R. Leavis and *Scrutiny*'

Walter Dean Burnham (Frank G. Erwin Centennial Chair in Government), 'The 1992 British Elections: Four-or-Five-More Tory Years?'

Don Graham (UT Professor of English), 'Modern Australian Literature and the Image of America'

Richard Woolcott (former Secretary of the Australian Department of Foreign Affairs), 'Australia and the Question of Cooperation or Contention in the Pacific'

Ian Willison (1992 Wiggins Lecturer, American Antiquarian Society), 'The History of the Book in Twentieth-Century Britain and America'

Iain Sproat, (Member of Parliament), 'P. G. Wodehouse and the War'

Standish Meacham (UT Sheffield Professor of History), 'The Crystal Palace'

Field Marshal Lord Carver (former Chief of the British Defence Staff), 'Wavell: A Reassessment'

Lesley Hall (Wellcome Institute for the History of Medicine, London), 'For Fear of Frightening the Horses: Sexology in Britain since William Acton'

Michael Fry (Director of International Relations, University of Southern California), 'Britain, the United Nations, and the Lebanon Crisis of 1958'

Brian Holden Reid (King's College, London), 'J. F. C. Fuller and the Revolution in British Military Thought'

Neil Parsons (University of London), '"Clicko" or Franz Taaibosch: A Bushman Entertainer in Britain, Jamaica, and the United States c. 1919–40'

John Hargreaves (Burnett-Fletcher Professor of History, Aberdeen University), 'God's Advocate: Lewis Namier and the History of Modern Europe'

Round Table Discussion on Robert Harris's *Fatherland:* Henry Dietz (UT Government), Robert D. King (UT Liberal Arts), Roger Louis (UT Kerr Professor), and Walter Wetzels (UT Germanic Languages)

Kevin Tierney (University of California), 'Robert Graves: An Outsider Looking In, or an Insider Who Escaped?'

Spring Semester 1993

Round Table Discussion on 'The Trollope Mystique': Janice Rossen (author of *Philip Larkin* and *The University in Modern Fiction*), Louise Weinberg (UT Angus G. Wynne Professor of Civil Jurisprudence), and Paul Woodruff (UT Director of the Plan II Honors Program and Thompson Professor of Philosophy)

Bruce Hunt (UT Associate Professor of History), 'To Rule the Waves: Cable Telegraphy and British Physics in the Nineteenth Century'

Martin Wiener (Jones Professor of History, Rice University), 'The Unloved State: Contemporary Political Attitudes in the Writing of Modern British History'

Elizabeth Dunn (HRHRC), 'Ralph Waldo Emerson and Ireland'

Jason Thompson (Western Kentucky University), 'Edward William Lane's "Description of Egypt"'

Sir Michael Howard (former Regius Professor of Modern History, Oxford University, present Lovett Professor of Military and Naval History, Yale University), 'Strategic Deception in the Second World War'

Gordon A. Craig (Sterling Professor of Humanities, Stanford University), 'Churchill'

Round Table Discussion on the Indian Mathematician Ramanujan: Robert D. King (UT Rapoport Professor of Liberal Arts), James W. Vick (Vice-President for Student Affairs and Professor of Mathematics), and Steven Weinberg (UT Regental Professor and Josey Chair in Physics)

Martha Merritt (UT Lecturer in Government), 'From Commonwealth to Commonwealth, and from Vauxhall to *Vokzal:* Russian Borrowing from Britain'

Sidney Monas (UT Professor of Slavic Languages and History), 'James Joyce and Russia'

Peter Marshall (Professor of History, King's College, London), 'Imperial Britain and the Question of National Identity'

Michael Wheeler (Professor of English and Director of the Ruskin Programme, Lancaster University), 'Ruskin and Gladstone'

Anthony Low (Smuts Professor of Commonwealth History and President of Clare College, Cambridge University), 'Britain and India in the Early 1930s: The British, American, French, and Dutch Empires Compared'

Summer 1993

Alexander Pettit (University of North Texas), 'Lord Bolingbroke's *Remarks on the History of England*'

Rose Marie Burwell (Northern Illinois University), 'The British Novel and Ernest Hemingway'

Richard Patteson (Mississippi State University), 'New Writing in the West Indies'

Richard Greene (Memorial University, Newfoundland), 'The Moral Authority of Edith Sitwell'

Fall Semester 1993

Round Table Discussion on 'The British and the Shaping of the American Critical Mind—Edmund Wilson, Part II': Roger Louis (UT Kerr Professor), Elspeth Rostow (UT Stiles Professor in American Studies), Tom Staley (Director, HRHRC), and Robert Crunden (UT Professor of History and American Studies)

Roseanne Camacho (University of Rhode Island), 'Evelyn Scott: Towards an Intellectual Biography'

Christopher Heywood (Okayama University), 'The Brontës and Slavery'

Peter Gay (Sterling Professor of History, Yale University), 'The Cultivation of Hatred in England'

Linda Ferreira-Buckley (UT English) 'England's First English Department: Rhetoric and More Rhetoric'

Janice Rossen (Senior Research Fellow, HRHRC), 'British University Novels'

Ian Hancock (O Yanko Le Redzosko) (UT Professor of Linguistics and English), 'The Gypsy Image in British Literature'

James Davies (University College of Swansea), 'Dylan Thomas'

Jeremy Lewis (London Writer and Editor), 'Who Cares about Cyril Connolly?'

Sam Jamot Brown (British Studies), and Robert D. King (Linguistics), 'Scott and the Antarctic'

Martin Trump (University of South Africa), 'Nadine Gordimer's Social and Political Vision'

Richard Clogg (Professor of Balkan History, University of London), 'Britain and the Origins of the Greek Civil War'

Herbert J. Spiro (United States Ambassador, Ret.), 'The Warburgs: Anglo-American and German-Jewish Bankers'

Colin Franklin (Publisher and Antiquarian Bookseller), 'Lord Chesterfield: Stylist, Connoisseur of Manners, and Specialist in Worldly Advice'

Jeffrey Segall (Charles University, Prague), 'The Making of James Joyce's Reputation'

Rhodri Jeffreys-Jones (University of Edinburgh), 'The Myth of the Iron Lady: Margaret Thatcher and World Stateswomen'

John Rumrich (UT Associate Professor of English), 'Milton and Science: Gravity and the Fall'

J. D. Alsop (McMaster University), 'British Propaganda, Espionage, and Political Intrigue'

Round Table Discussion on 'The Best and the Worst Books of 1993': David Edwards (UT Government), Creekmore Fath (UT Liberal Arts Foundation), Betty Sue Flowers (UT English), and Sidney Monas (UT Professor of Slavic Languages and History)

Spring Semester 1994

Thomas F. Staley (Director, HRHRC), 'John Rodker: Poet and Publisher of Modernism'

Martha Fehsenfeld, and Lois More Overbeck (Emory University), 'The Correspondence of Samuel Beckett'

M. R. D. Foot (Historian and Editor), 'Lessons of War on War: The Influence of 1914–1918 on 1939–1945'

Round Table Discussion on 'Requiem for Canada?' David Braybrooke (UT Centennial Chair in Liberal Arts), Walter Dean Burnham (UT Frank Erwin Chair in Government), and Robert Crunden (UT Professor of American Studies)

Ross Terrill (Harvard University), 'Australia and Asia in Historical Perspective'

Sir Samuel Falle (British Ambassador and High Commissioner), 'The Morning after Independence: The Legacy of the British Empire'

Deborah Lavin (Principal of Trevelyan College, University of Durham), 'Lionel Curtis: Prophet of the British Empire'

Robin W. Doughty (UT Professor of Geography), 'Eucalyptus: And Not a Koala in Sight'

Al Crosby (UT Professor of American Studies and History), 'Captain Cook and the Biological Impact on the Hawaiian Islands'

Gillian Adams (Editor, *Children's Literature Association Quarterly*), 'Beatrix Potter and Her Recent Critics'

Lord Amery, 'Churchill's Legacy'

Christa Jansohn (University of Bonn) and Peter Green (Dougherty Professor of Classics), '*Lady Chatterley's Lover*'

R. A. C. Parker (Fellow of Queen's College, Oxford), 'Neville Chamberlain and the Coming of the Second World War'

John Velz (UT Professor of English), 'King Lear in Iowa: Jane Smiley's *A Thousand Acres*'

Jan Schall (University of Florida), 'British Spirit Photography'

Daniel Woolf (Dalhousie University), 'The Revolution in Historical Consciousness in England'

Fall Semester 1994

Kenneth O. Morgan (Vice-Chancellor, University of Wales), 'Welsh Nationalism'

Round Table Discussion on Michael Shelden's *Graham Greene: The Man Within*: Peter Green (UT Dougherty Professor of Classics), Roger Louis (UT Kerr Professor), and Thomas F. Staley (Director, HRHRC)

Robert D. King (Rapoport Regents Chair in Liberal Arts), 'The Secret War, 1939–1945'

Brian Boyd (Professor of English, University of Auckland), 'The Evolution of Shakespearean Dramatic Structure'

Lord Weatherill (former Speaker of the House of Commons), 'Thirty Years in Parliament'

Hans Mark (UT Professor of Aerospace Engineering), 'Churchill's Scientists'

Steven Weinberg (UT Josey Regental Professor of Science), 'The Test of War: British Strengths and Weaknesses in World War II'

Dennis Welland (Professor of English Literature and American Studies, University of East Anglia), 'Wilfred Owen and the Poetry of War'

Alan Frost (Professor of History, La Trobe University), 'The *Bounty* Mutiny and the British Romantic Poets'

W. O. S. Sutherland (UT Professor of English), 'Sir Walter Scott'

Hazel Rowley (Lecturer in Literary Studies, Deakin University, Melbourne), 'Christina Stead's "Other Country"'

Herman Bakvis (Professor of Government, Dalhousie University), 'The Future of Democracy in Canada and Australia'

Peter Stansky (Professor of History, Stanford University), 'George Orwell and the Writing of *Nineteen Eighty-Four*'

Henry Dietz (UT Associate Professor of Government), 'Sherlock Homes and Jack the Ripper'

James Coote (UT Professor of Architecture), 'Techniques of Illusion in British Architecture'

Round Table Discussion on 'The Best and Worst Books of 1994': Dean Burnham (UT Government), Alessandra Lippucci (UT Government), Roger Louis (UT Kerr Professor), Sidney Monas (UT Professor of Slavic Languages and History), and Janice Rossen (HRHRC)

Spring Semester 1995

Elizabeth Butler Cullingford (UT Professor of English), 'Anti-Colonial Metaphors in Contemporary Irish Literature'

Thomas M. Hatfield (UT Dean of Continuing Education), 'British and American Deception of the Germans in Normandy'

Gary P. Freeman (UT Associate Professor of Government), 'The Politics of Race and Immigration in Britain'

Donald G. Davis, Jr. (UT Professor in the Graduate School of Library and Information Science), 'The Printed Word in Sunday Schools in Nineteenth-Century England and the United States'

Brian Bremen (UT Assistant Professor of English), "Healing Words: The Literature of Medicine and the Medicine of Literature'

Frances Karttunen (Linguistic Research Center), and Alfred W. Crosby (American Studies and History), 'British Imperialism and Creole Languages'

Paul Lovejoy (Professor of History, York University, Canada), 'British Rule in Africa: A Reassessment of Nineteenth-Century Colonialism'

Carol MacKay (UT Associate Professor of English), 'Creative Negativity in the Life and Work of Elizabeth Robins'

John Brokaw (UT Professor of Drama), 'The Changing Stage in London, 1790–1832'

Linda Colley (Richard M. Colgate Professor of History, Yale University), 'The Frontier in British History'

Iwan Morus (University of California, San Diego), 'Manufacturing Nature: Science, Technology, and Victorian Consumer Culture'

Brian Parker (Professor of English, University of Toronto), 'Jacobean Law: The Dueling Code and "A Faire Quarrel" (1617)'

Kate Frost (UT Professor of English), ' "Jack Donne the Rake": Fooling around in the 1590s'

Mark Kinkead-Weekes (Professor of English, University of Kent), 'Beyond Gossip: D. H. Lawrence's Writing Life'

Summer 1995

S. P. Rosenbaum (Professor of English, University of Toronto), 'Leonard and Virginia Woolf at the Hogarth Press'

Maria X. Wells (Curator of Italian Collections, HRHRC), 'A Delicate Balance: Trieste 1945'

Kevin Tierney (Professor of Law, University of California at Berkeley), 'Personae in Twentieth-Century British Autobiography'

Fall Semester 1995

Brian Levack (UT Professor of History), 'Witchcraft, Possession, and the Law in Jacobean England'

Janice Rossen (Senior Fellow, HRHRC), 'The Home Front: Anglo-American Women Novelists and World War II'

Dorothy Driver (Professor of English, University of Cape Town), 'Olive Schreiner's Novel *From Man to Man*'

Philip Ziegler (London), 'Mountbatten Revisited'

Joanna Hitchcock (Director, UT Press), 'British and American University Presses'

Samuel H. Beer (Eaton Professor of the Science of Government Emeritus, Harvard University), 'The Rise and Fall of Party Government in Britain and the United States, 1945–1995'

Richard Broinowski (Australian Ambassador to Mexico and Central America), 'Australia and Latin America'

John Grigg (London), 'Myths about the Approach to Indian Independence'

Round Table Discussion on *Measuring the Mind* (Adrian Wooldridge) and *The Bell Curve* (Richard J. Herrnstein and Charles Murray): David Edwards (UT Professor of Government), Sheldon Ekland-Olson (UT Dean of Liberal Arts), Joseph Horn (UT Professor of Psychology), and Robert D. King (UT Rapoport Chair in Liberal Arts)

Paul Addison (Professor of History, University of Edinburgh), 'British Politics in the Second World War'

John Sibley Butler (UT Professor of Sociology), 'Emigrants of the British Empire'

Round Table Discussion on the Movie *Carrington:* Peter Green (UT Dougherty Professor of Classics), Robin Kilson (UT Assistant Professor of History), Roger Louis (UT Kerr Professor), Sidney Monas (UT Professor of Slavic Languages and History), and Elizabeth Richmond-Garza (UT Assistant Professor of English)

Spring Semester 1996

Kevin Kenny (UT Assistant Professor of History), 'Making Sense of the Molly Maguires'

Brigadier Michael Harbottle (British Army), 'British and American Security in the Post-Cold War'

Carol MacKay (UT Professor of English), 'The Singular Double Vision of Photographer Julia Margaret Cameron'

John Ramsden (Professor of History, University of London), ' "That Will Depend on Who Writes the History": Winston Churchill as His Own Historian'

Jack P. Greene (Andrew W. Mellon Professor in the Humanities, The Johns Hopkins University), 'The *British* Revolution in America'

Walter D. Wetzels (UT Professor of German), 'The Ideological Fallout in Germany of Two British Expeditions to Test Einstein's General Theory of Relativity'

Thomas Pinney (William M. Keck Distinguished Service Professor of English, Pomona College), 'In Praise of Kipling'

Michael Charlesworth (UT Assistant Professor of Art History), 'The English Landscape Garden'

Stephen Gray (South African Novelist), 'The Dilemma of Colonial Writers with Dual Identities'

Jeremy Black (Professor of History, University of Durham), 'Could the British Have Won the War of American Independence?'

Dagmar Hamilton (UT Professor of Public Affairs, LBJ School), 'Justice William O. Douglas and British Colonialism'

Gordon Peacock and Laura Worthen (UT Theater and Dance), 'Not Always a Green and Pleasant Land: Tom Stoppard's *Arcadia*'

Bernard Crick (Professor of Politics, University of London), 'Orwell and the Business of Biography'

Geoffrey Hartman (Sterling Professor of English, Yale University), 'The Sympathy Paradox: Poetry, Feeling, and Modern Cultural Morality'

Dave Oliphant (HRHRC), 'Jazz and Its British Acolytes'

R. W. B. Lewis (Professor of English and American Studies, Yale University), 'Henry James: The Victorian Scene'

Alan Spencer (Vice-President, Ford Motor Company), 'Balliol, Big Business, and Mad Cows'

Peter Quinn: A Discussion of His Novel, *Banished Children of Eve*

Summer 1996

Martin Stannard (Professor of English, Leicester University), 'Biography and Textual Criticism'

Diane Kunz (Associate Professor of History, Yale University), 'British Withdrawal East of Suez'

John Cell (Professor of History, Duke University), 'Who Ran the British Empire?'

Mark Jacobsen (US Marine Corps Command and Staff College), 'The North-West Frontier'

Theodore Vestal (Professor of Political Science, Oklahoma State University), 'Britain and Ethiopia'

Warren F. Kimball (Robert Treat Professor of History, Rutgers University), 'A Victorian Tory: Churchill, the Americans, and Self-Determination'

Louise B. Williams (Assistant Professor of History, Lehman College, The City University of New York), 'British Modernism and Fascism'

Fall Semester 1996

Elizabeth Richmond-Garza (UT Associate Professor of English and Comparative Literature), 'The New Gothic: Decadents for the 1990s'

Robin Kilson (UT Assistant Professor of History), 'The Politics of Captivity: The British State and Prisoners of War in World War I'

Sir Brian Fall (Principal of Lady Margaret Hall, Oxford), 'What does Britain Expect from the European Community, the United States, and the Commonwealth?'

Roger Louis (UT Kerr Professor), 'Harold Macmillan and the Middle East Crisis of 1958'

Ian Willison (former head of the Rare Books Branch, British Museum, and Editor of *The Cambridge History of the Book in Britain*), 'The History of the Book and the Cultural and Literary History of the English-Speaking World'

Walter L. Arnstein (Jubilee Professor of the Liberal Arts and Sciences, University of Illinois), 'Queen Victoria's Other Island'

Noel Annan (London), '*Our Age* Revisited'

Michael Cohen (Lazarus Philips Professor of History, Bar-Ilan University, Tel Aviv), 'The Middle East and the Cold War: Britain, the United States, and the Soviet Union'

Reba Soffer (Professor of History, California State University, Northridge), 'Catholicism in England: Was it Possible to be a Good Catholic, a Good Englishman, and a Good Historian?'

Wilson Harris (Poet and Novelist), 'The Mystery of Consciousness: Cross-Cultural Influences in the Caribbean, Britain, and the United States'

H. S. Barlow (Singapore), 'British Malaya in the late Nineteenth Century'

Donald G. Davis, Jr. (UT Professor of Library and Information Science), 'British Destruction of Chinese Books in the Peking Siege of 1900'

Round Table Discussion on the Film *Michael Collins:* Elizabeth Cullingford (UT Professor of English), Kevin Kenny (UT Assistant Professor of History), Robin Kilson (UT Assistant Professor of History), and Roger Louis (UT Kerr Professor)

A. G. Hopkins (Smuts Professor of Commonwealth History, University of Cambridge), 'From Africa to Empire'

Austin Chapter of the Society for the Preservation and Encouragement of Barber Shop Quartet Singing in America

Spring Semester 1997

Round Table Discussion on 'T. S. Eliot and Anti-Semitism': Robert D. King (UT Rapoport Chair in Jewish Studies), Sidney Monas (UT Professor of Slavic Languages and History), and Thomas F. Staley (Director, HRHRC)

Phillip Herring (Professor Emeritus of English, University of Wisconsin-Madison), 'Djuna Barnes and T. S. Eliot: The Story of a Friendship'

Bryan Roberts (UT Smith Chair in United States–Mexican Relations), 'British Sociology and British Society'

Andrew Roberts (London), 'The Captains and the Kings Depart: Lord Salisbury's Skeptical Imperialism'

Colin Franklin (London), 'In a Golden Age of Publishing, 1950–1970'

Susan Pedersen (Professor of History, Harvard University), 'Virginia Woolf, Eleanor Rathbone, and the Problem of Appeasement'

Andrew Seaman (Saint Mary's University, Halifax, Nova Scotia), 'Thomas Raddall: A Novelist's View of Nova Scotia during the American Revolution'

Gordon Peacock (UT Frank C. Erwin Professor of Drama), 'Noel Coward: A Master Playwright, a Talented Actor, a Novelist and Diarist: Or a Peter Pan for the Twentieth Century?'

Roland Oliver (Professor of African History, School of Oriental and African Studies, University of London), 'The Battle for African History, 1947–1966'

Alistair Horne (St. Antony's College, Oxford), 'Harold Macmillan's Fading Reputation'

Richard Begam (Professor of English, University of Wisconsin, Madison), 'Samuel Beckett and the Debate on Humanism'

Christopher Waters (Associate Professor of History, Williams College), 'Delinquents, Perverts, and the State: Psychiatry and Homosexual Desire in the 1930s'

Sami Zubaida (University of London), 'Ernest Gellner and Islam'

Walter Dean Burnham (UT Frank C. Erwin Chair in Government), 'Britain Votes: The 1997 General Election and Its Implications'

Fall Semester 1997

Judith Brown (Beit Professor of the History of the British Commonwealth, Oxford University), 'Gandhi—A Victorian Gentleman'

Thomas Cable (UT Blumberg Professor of English), 'Hearing and Revising the History of the English Language'

Round Table Discussion on 'The Death of Princess Diana': Judith Brown (Oxford), David Edwards (UT Professor of Government), Elizabeth Richmond-Garza (UT Associate Professor of English), Anne Baade (British Studies), Alessandra Lippucci (UT Government), and Kevin Kenny (UT Associate Professor of History)

David Hunter (Music Librarian, Fine Arts Library), 'Handel and His Patrons'

Anne Kane (UT Assistant Professor of Sociology), 'The Current Situation in Ireland'

James S. Fishkin (UT Darrell K. Royal Regents Chair in Ethics in American Society), 'Power and the People: The Televised Deliberative Poll in the 1997 British General Election'

Howard D. Weinbrot (Vilas Research Professor of English, University of Wisconsin, Madison), 'Jacobitism in Eighteenth-Century Britain'

J. C. Baldwin, M.D. (Houston), 'The Abdication of King Edward VIII'

Kenneth E. Carpenter (Harvard University), 'Library Revolutions Past and Present'

Akira Iriye (Professor of History, Harvard University), 'Britain, Japan, and the International Order after World War I'

Anthony Hobson (London), 'Reminiscences of British Authors and the Collecting of Contemporary Manuscripts'

David Killingray (Professor of History, University of London), 'The British in the West Indies'

Alan Knight (Professor of Latin American History, Oxford University), 'British Imperialism in Latin America'

Round Table Discussion on King Lear in Iowa: The Movie '*A Thousand Acres*': Linda Ferreira-Buckley (UT Associate Professor of English), Elizabeth Richmond-Garza (UT Associate Professor of English), Helena Woodard (UT Assistant Professor of English), and John Velz (UT Professor of English)

Timothy Lovelace (UT Assistant Professor of Music) and the Talisman Trio

Spring Semester 1998

Richard Ollard (Biographer and Publisher), 'A. L. Rowse: Epitome of the Twentieth Century'

Round Table Discussion of Arundhati Roy's *The God of Small Things:* Phillip Herring (HRHRC, Professor Emeritus of English, University of Wisconsin), Brian Trinque (UT Economics), Kamala Visweswaran (UT Anthropology), and Robert Hardgrave (UT Government)

Jonathan Schneer (Professor of History, Georgia Institute of Technology), 'London in 1900: The Imperial Metropolis'

Trevor Burnard (Senior Lecturer in History, University of Canterbury, New Zealand), 'Rioting in Goatish Embraces: Marriage and the Failure of White Settlement in British Jamaica'

Felipe Fernández-Armesto (Oxford University), 'British Traditions in Comparative Perspective'

Michael Mann (Professor of Sociology, University of California, Los Angeles), 'The Broader Significance of Labour's Landslide Victory of 1997'

Dane Kennedy (Professor of History, University of Nebraska at Lincoln), 'White Settlers in Colonial Kenya and Rhodesia'

Round Table Discussion on 'Noel Annan, Keynes, and Bloomsbury': Jamie Galbraith (UT LBJ School), Elspeth Rostow (UT LBJ School), and Walt Rostow (UT Professor of Economics and History)

Lisa Moore (UT Associate Professor of English), 'British Studies—Lesbian Studies: A Dangerous Intimacy?'

James Gibbs (University of the West of England), 'Wole Soyinka: The Making of a Playwright'

Marilyn Butler (Rector of Exeter College, Oxford), 'About the House: Jane Austen's Anthropological Eye'

R. J. Q. Adams (Professor of History, Texas A&M University), 'Britain and Ireland, 1912–1922'

John M. Carroll (UT Asian Studies), 'Nationalism and Identity in pre-1949 Hong Kong'

Round Table Discussion on the Irish Referendum: Anne Kane (UT Sociology), Kevin Kenny (UT History), Roger Louis (UT Kerr Professor), and Jennifer O'Conner (UT History)

Fall Semester 1998

Louise Hodgden Thompson (UT Government), 'Origins of the First World War: The Anglo-German Naval Armaments Race'

John P. Farrell (UT Professor of English), 'Thomas Hardy in Love'

Carol MacKay (UT Professor of English), 'The Multiple Conversions of Annie Besant'

Roy Foster (Carroll Professor of Irish History, Oxford University), 'Yeats and Politics, 1898–1921'

Robert Olwell (UT History), 'British Magic Kingdoms: Imagination, Speculation, and Empire in Florida'

Sara H. Sohmer (Lecturer in History, Texas Christian University), 'The British in the South Seas: Exploitation and Trusteeship in Fiji'

Helena Woodard (UT Associate Professor of English), 'Politics of Race in the Eighteenth Century: Pope and the Humanism of the Enlightenment'

D. A. Smith (Grinnell College), 'Impeachment? Parliamentary Government in Britain and France in the Nineteenth Century'

Round Table Discussion on the Irish Insurrection of 1798: Robert Olwell (UT History), Lisa Moore (UT English), and Kevin Kenny (UT History)

Robert D. King (UT Rapoport Regents Chair of Jewish Studies), 'The Accomplishments of Raja Rao: The Triumph of the English Language in India'

Donald G. Davis, Jr. (UT Professor of Library and Information Science and History), 'Religion and Empire'

A. D. Roberts (Professor of History, School of Oriental and African Studies, University of London), 'The Awkward Squad: African Students in American Universities before 1940'

Chaganti Vijayasree (Professor of English, Osmania University, Hyderabad), 'The Empire and Victorian Poetry'

Martha Deatherage (UT Music), 'Christmas Celebration: Vauxhall Gardens'

Spring Semester 1999

Round Table Discussion on *Regeneration,* Pat Barker's Trilogy on the First World War: Betty Sue Flowers (UT Professor of English), Roger Louis (UT Kerr Professor), and Paul Woodruff (UT Professor in the Humanities)

Alistair Campbell-Dick (Founding Member of British Studies and Director of Cybertime Corporation), 'The Immortal Memory of Robert Burns'

Hugh Macrae Richmond (Professor of English and Drama, University of California at Berkeley), 'Why Rebuild Shakespeare's Globe Theatre?'

Ralph Austen (Professor of History, University of Chicago), 'Britain and the Global Economy: A Post-Colonial Perspective'

Jerome Meckier (Professor of English, University of Kentucky), 'Aldous Huxley's American Experience'

Peter Marsh (Professor of History, Syracuse University), 'Joseph Chamberlain as an Entrepreneur in Politics: Writing the Life of a Businessman Turned Statesman'

Roger Adelson (Professor of History, Arizona State University), 'Winston Churchill and the Middle East'

Margot Finn (Associate Professor of History, Emory University), 'Law, Debt, and Empire: The Calcutta Court of Conscience'

Fred M. Leventhal (Professor of History, Boston University), 'The Projection of Britain in America before the Second World War'

Larry Siedentop (Fellow of Keble College, Oxford University), 'Reassessing the Life of Isaiah Berlin'

Ross Terrill (Research Associate in Government, Harvard University), 'R. H. Tawney's Vision of Fellowship'

Juliet Fleming (University Lecturer of English, Cambridge University), 'The Ladies' Shakespeare'

Elizabeth Fernea (UT English and Middle Eastern Studies), 'The Victorian Lady Abroad: In Egypt with Sophia Poole and in Texas with Mrs. E. M. Houstoun'

Richard Schoch (University of London), 'The Respectable and the Vulgar: British Theater in the Mid-Nineteenth Century'

Ferdinand Mount (Editor, *TLS*), 'Politics and the *Times Literary Supplement*'

Fall Semester 1999

Round Table Discussion on the Boer War, 1899–1902: Barbara Harlow (UT Professor of English), John Lamphear (UT History), and Roger Louis (UT Kerr Professor)

Sharon Arnoult (Assistant Professor of History, Southwest Texas State University), 'Charles I: His Life after Death'

Kenneth O. Morgan (Fellow of Queen's College, Oxford and former Vice Chancellor, University of Wales), 'Lloyd George, Keir Hardie, and the Importance of the "Pro-Boers"'

Richard Cleary (UT Architecture), 'Walking the Walk to Talk the Talk: The Promenade in Eighteenth-Century France and England'

Keith Kyle (Journalist and Historian), 'From Suez to Kenya as Journalist and as Historian'

Malcolm Hacksley (Director of the National English Literary Museum, Grahamstown, South Africa), 'Planting a Museum, Cultivating a Literature'

Ben Pimlott (Warden of Goldsmiths College, University of London), 'The Art of Writing Political Biography'

Geraldine Heng (UT Associate Professor of English), 'Cannibalism, the First Crusade, and the Genesis of Medieval Romance'

A. P. Martinich (UT Philosophy), 'Thomas Hobbes: Lifelong and Enduring Controversies'

Round Table Discussion on Lyndall Gordon's *T. S. Eliot: An Imperfect Life:* Brian Bremen (UT Associate Professor of English), Thomas Cable (UT Blumberg Professor of English), Elizabeth Richmond Garza (UT Professor of Comparative Literature), and Thomas F. Staley (Director, HRHRC)

Shula Marks (Professor of History, School of Oriental and African Studies, University of London), 'Smuts, Race, and the Boer War'

Round Table Discussion on the Library of the British Museum: William B. Todd (English), Irene Owens (Library and Information Science), and Don Davis (Library and Information Science and Department of History).

Henry Dietz (UT Professor of Government), '*The Hound of the Baskervilles*'

Spring Semester 2000

Susan Napier (UT Associate Professor of Asian Studies), 'The Cultural Phenomenon of the Harry Potter Fantasy Novels'

Round Table Discussion on *Dutch: A Memoir of Ronald Reagan:* A Chapter in the 'Special Relationship'?: Roger Louis (UT Kerr Professor), Harry Middleton (Director of the LBJ Library), and Elspeth Rostow (LBJ School)

Norman Rose (Chaim Weizmann Chair of International Relations, Hebrew University, Jerusalem), 'Harold Nicolson: A Curious and Colorful Life'

Charlotte Canning (UT Theater History and Theory), 'Feminists Perform Their Past'

John Ripley (Greenshields Emeritus Professor of English, McGill University), 'The Sound of Sociology: H. B. Tree's *Merchant of Venice*'

Sergei Horuji (Russian Academy of Sciences), 'James Joyce in Russia'

Janice Rossen (Biographer and Independent Scholar), 'Philip Toynbee'

Max Egremont (Novelist and Biographer), 'Siegfried Sassoon's War'

Paul Taylor (Professor of International Relations, London School of Economics and Political Science), 'Britain and Europe'

Lord Selborne (President, Royal Geographical Society), 'The Royal Geographical Society: Exploration since 1830'

Craig MacKenzie (Department of English, Rand Afrikaans University, Johannesburg), 'The Mythology of the Boer War: Herman Charles Bosman and the Challenge to Afrikaner Romanticism'

Peter Catterall (Director, Institute of Contemporary British History, London), 'Reform of the House of Lords'

Bernard Porter (Professor of Modern History, University of Newcastle), 'Pompous and Circumstantial: Sir Edward Elgar and the British Empire'

Craufurd D. Goodwin (James B. Duke Professor of Economics, Duke University), 'Roger Fry and the Debate on "Myth" in the Bloomsbury Group'

Jamie Belich (Chair in History, University of Auckland), 'Neo-Britains? The "West" in Nineteenth-Century Australia, New Zealand, and America'

Round Table Discussion on Norman Davies, *The Isles:* Sharon Arnoult (Midwestern State University, Wichita Falls), Raymond Douglas (Colgate University), Walter Johnson (Northwestern Oklahoma State University), David Leaver (Raymond Walters College, Cincinnati), and John Cell (Duke University)

Fall Semester 2000

Round Table discussion on Paul Scott, the Raj Quartet, and the Beginning of British Studies at UT—Peter Green (UT Dougherty Professor of Classics), Robert Hardgrave (UT Professor of Government and Asian Studies), and Roger Louis (UT Kerr Professor)

Suman Gupta (The Open University), 'T. S. Eliot as Publisher'

Jeffrey Cox (University of Iowa), 'Going Native: Missionaries in India'

Kevin Kenny (Boston College), 'Irish Nationalism: The American Dimension'

Joseph Kestner (University of Tulsa), 'Victorian Battle Art'

James E. Cronin (Boston College), 'From Old to New Labour: Politics and Society in the Forging of the "Third" Way'

Gerald Moore (Mellon Visiting Research Fellow, HRHRC), 'When Caliban Crossed the Atlantic'

Richard Howard (Shakespearean Actor, London), '"Health and Long Life to You": A Program of Irish Poetry and Prose Presented by an Englishman, with Anecdotes'

Stephen Foster (Northern Illinois University), 'Prognosis Guarded: The Probable Decolonization of the British Era in American History'

Frank Prochaska (University of London), 'Of Crowned and Uncrowned Republics: George V and the Socialists'

Robert H. Abzug (UT History and American Studies), 'Britain, South Africa, and the American Civil Rights Movement'

Paula Bartley (Visiting Research Fellow, HRHRC), 'Emmeline Pankhurst'

Thomas Jesus Garza (UT Associate Professor of Slavic Languages), 'A British Vampire's Christmas'

Spring Semester 2001

Betty Sue Flowers (UT Distinguished Teaching Professor), 'From Robert Browning to James Bond'

Larry Carver (UT Professor of English), 'Feliks Topolski at the Ransom Center'

Oscar Brockett (UT Distinguished Teaching Professor), 'Lilian Baylis and England's National Theatres'

Linda Levy Peck (George Washington University), 'Luxury and War'

R. James Coote (UT Architecture), 'Architectural Revival in Britain'

Adam Roberts (Oxford University), 'Britain and the Creation of the United Nations'

Mark Southern (UT Professor of Germanic Studies), 'Words over Swords: Language and Tradition in Celtic Civilization'

Round Table discussion on Ben Rogers, *A Life of A. J. Ayer:* David Braybrooke (UT Government and Philosophy), Al Martinich (UT History and Philosophy), David Sosa (UT Philosophy), and Paul Woodruff (UT Plan II and Philosophy)

Bartholomew Sparrow (UT Government), 'British and American Expansion: The Political Foundations'

Jose Harris (Oxford University), 'Writing History during the Second World War'

Charles Loft (Westminster College), 'Off the Rails? The Historic Junctions in Britain's Railway Problem'

Dan Jacobson (University of London), 'David Irving and Holocaust Denial'— Special Lecture

Dan Jacobson (University of London), 'Self-Redemption in the Victorian Novel'

George S. Christian (UT British Studies), 'The Comic Basis of the Victorian Novel'

Paul Taylor (London *Independent*), 'Rediscovering a Master Dramatist: J. B. Priestley'

Fall Semester 2001

Round Table Discussion on Ray Monk's Biography of Bertrand Russell, *The Ghost of Madness*—Al Martinich (UT History and Philosophy), David Sosa (UT Philosophy and British Studies), and Paul Woodruff (UT Plan II and Philosophy)

Alex Danchev (Keele University), 'The Alanbrooke Diaries'

Robert M. Worcester (LSE and Market Opinion Research International), 'Britain and the European Union'

Martha Ann Selby (UT Associate Professor of Asian Studies), 'The Cultural Legacy of British Clubs: Manners, Memory, and Identity among the New Club-Wallahs in Madras'

Roger Owen (Harvard University), 'Lord Cromer and Wilfrid Blunt in Egypt'

James Loehlin (UT Associate Professor of English), 'A Midsummer Night's Dream'

Jeffrey Meyers (Biographer), 'Somerset Maugham'

Elspeth Rostow (UT LBJ School), 'From American Studies to British Studies— And Beyond'

Nicholas Westcott (British Embassy), 'The Groundnut Scheme: Socialist Imperialism at Work in Africa'

Round Table Discussion on 'The Anglo-American Special Relationship': Gary Freeman (UT Government), Roger Louis (UT Kerr Professor), Elspeth Rostow (UT American Studies), and Michael Stoff (UT History)

Christopher Heywood (Sheffield University), 'The Brontës: A Personal History of Discovery and Interpretation'

James Bolger (New Zealand Ambassador and former Prime Minister), 'Whither New Zealand? Constitutional, Political, and International Quandaries'

R. J. Q. Adams (Texas A&M University), 'Arthur James Balfour and Andrew Bonar Law: A Study in Contrasts'

Ferdinand Mount (Editor, *Times Literary Supplement*), 'British Culture since the Eighteenth Century: An Open Society?'

James Loehlin (UT English), 'A Child's Christmas in Wales'

Spring Semester 2002

Round Table Discussion on Adam Sisman, *Boswell's Presumptuous Task:* Samuel Baker (UT English), Linda Ferreira-Buckley (UT English), Julie Hardwick (UT History), and Helena Woodward (UT English)

A. G. Hopkins (UT History), 'Globalization: The British Case'

Susan Napier (UT Professor of Asian Studies), 'J. R. R. Tolkein and the Lord of the Rings: Fantasy as Retreat or Fantasy as Engagement?'

Wilfrid Prest (Adelaide University), 'South Australia's Paradise of Dissent'
Tom Palaima (UT Professor of Classics), 'Terence Rattigan's *Browning Version*'
Alan H. Nelson (University of California at Berkeley), 'Thoughts on Elizabethan Authorship'
Penelope Lively (London), 'Changing Perceptions of British and English Identity'
Hans Mark (UT Professor of Aerospace Engineering), 'The Falklands War'
David Butler (Oxford University), 'Psephology—or, the Study of British Elections'
Robert L. Hardgrave (UT Professor of Government), 'From West Texas to South India and British Studies'
Geoffrey Wheatcroft (London), 'The Englishness of English Sport'
Eileen Cleere (Southwestern University), 'Dirty Pictures: John Ruskin and the Victorian Sanitation of Fine Art'
Jamie Belich (Auckland University), 'A Comparison of Empire Cities: New York and London, Chicago and Melbourne'
Churchill Conference—Geoffrey Best (Oxford), Sir Michael Howard (Oxford), Warren Kimball (Rutgers), Philip Ziegler (London), Roger Louis (UT Kerr Professor)
Catherine Maxwell (University of London), 'Swinburne's Poetry and Criticism'
Round Table Discussion on Churchill and the Churchill Conference: Rodrigo Gutierrez (UT History), Adrian Howkins (UT History), Heidi Juel (UT English), David McCoy (UT Government), Joe Moser (UT English), Jeff Rutherford (UT History), Bill Livingston (UT Senior Vice-President), and Roger Louis (UT Kerr Professor)

Fall Semester 2002

James K. Galbraith (UT LBJ School of Public Affairs), 'The Enduring Importance of John Maynard Keynes'
Michael Green (University of Natal), 'Agatha Christie in South Africa'
Sumit Ganguly (UT Asian Studies), 'Kashmir: Origins and Consequences of Conflict'
Margaret MacMillan (University of Toronto), 'At the Height of His Power: Lloyd George in 1919'
Douglas Bruster (UT English), 'Why We Fight: *Much Ado About Nothing* and the West'
John Darwin (Oxford University), 'The Decline and Rise of the British Empire: John Gallagher as an Historian of Imperialism'
Kevin Kenny (Boston College), 'The Irish in the British Empire'
David Wallace (University of Pennsylvania), 'A Chaucerian's Tale of Surinam'
Peter Bowler (Queen's University, Belfast), 'Scientists and the Popularization of Science in Early Twentieth-Century Britain'
Bernardine Evaristo (London), "A Feisty, Funky Girl in Roman England'
Frank Moorhouse (Australia), 'Dark Places and Grand Days'
David Cannadine (University of London), 'C. P. Snow and the Two Cultures'
Round Table Discussion on 'Edmund S. Morgan's Biography of Benjamin Franklin'—Carolyn Eastman (UT History), Bruce Hunt (UT History), Roger Louis (UT Kerr Professor), Alan Tully (UT History)
Mark Lawrence (UT History), 'The Strange Silence of Cold War England: Britain and the Vietnam War'
Tom Cable (UT English), 'The Pleasures of Remembering Poetry'

Spring Semester 2003

Round Table Discussion on 'W. G. Sebald—*Rings of Saturn*': Brigitte Bauer (UT French and Italian), Sidney Monas (UT History and Slavic Languages), Elizabeth Richmond-Garza (UT English and Comparative Literature), Walter Wetzels (UT Germanic Studies)

Diana Davis (UT Geography), 'Brutes, Beasts, and Empire: A Comparative Study of the British and French Experience'

Colin Franklin (Publisher), 'Rosalind Franklin—Variously Described as "The Dark Lady of DNA" and "The Sylvia Plath of Molecular Biology"'

Sidney Monas (History and Slavic Languages), 'A Life of Irish Literature and Russian Poetry, Soviet Politics and International History'

Neville Hoad (UT English), 'Oscar Wilde in America'

Selina Hastings (London), 'Rosamond Lehman: Eternal Exile'

Bernard Wasserstein (Glasgow University), 'The British in Palestine: Reconsiderations'

Anne Chisholm (London), 'Frances Partridge: Last of the Bloomsberries'

Philip Morgan (The Johns Hopkins University), 'The Black Experience and the British Empire'

Jeremy duQuesnay Adams (Southern Methodist University), 'Joan of Arc and the English'

Didier Lancien (University of Toulouse), 'Churchill and de Gaulle'

Avi Shlaim (Oxford University), 'The Balfour Declaration and its Consequences'

Martin J. Wiener (Rice University), 'Murder and the Modern British Historian'

Winthrop Wetherbee (Cornell University), 'The Jewish Impact on Medieval Literature: Chaucer, Boccaccio, and Dante'

Philippa Levine (University of Southern California), 'Sex and the British Empire'

Summer 2003

Donald G. Davis, Jr. (UT History and School of Information), 'Life without British Studies is Like . . .'

Kurth Sprague (UT English and American Studies), 'Literature, Horses, and Scandal at UT'

David Evans (UT Astronomy), 'An Astronomer's Life in South Africa and Texas'

Tom Hatfield (UT Continuing Education), 'Not Long Enough! Half a Century at UT'

Fall Semester 2003

Richard Oram (HRHRC), 'Evelyn Waugh: Collector and Annotator'

Round Table Discussion on 'Booker Prize Winner James Kelman: Adapting a Glasgow Novel for the Texas Stage': James Kelman (Glasgow), Mia Carter (UT English), Kirk Lynn, and Dikran Utidjian

Simon Green (All Souls College, Oxford University), 'The Strange Death of Puritan England, 1914–1945'

Elizabeth Richmond-Garza (UT English and Comparative Literature), '*Measure for Measure*'

Lewis Hoffacker (US Ambassador), 'From the Congo to British Studies'

A. P. Thornton (University of Toronto), 'Wars Remembered, Revisited, and Reinvented'

Deryck Schreuder (University of Western Australia), 'The Burden of the British Past in Australia'

Robert Mettlen (Lamar Centennial Professor), 'From Birmingham to British Studies'

Paul Schroeder (University of Illinois), 'The Pax Britannica and the Pax Americana: Empire, Hegemony, and the International System'

Ferdinand Mount (London), 'A Time to Dance: Anthony Powell's *Dance to the Music of Time* and the Twentieth Century in Britain'

Brian Bond (University of London), '*Oh! What a Lovely War:* History and Popular Myth in Late-Twentieth Century Britain'

Wendy Frith (Bradford College, England), 'The Speckled Monster: Lady Mary Wortley Montagu and the Battle against Smallpox'

Harry Middleton (UT LBJ Library), 'The Road to the White House'

Jeremy Lewis (London), 'Tobias Smollett'

Christian Smith (Austin, Texas), 'Christmas Readings'

Spring Semester 2004

Round Table Discussion on 'The Pleasures of Reading Thackeray': Carol Mackay (UT English), Judith Fisher (Trinity University), George Christian (British Studies)

Thomas F. Staley (HRHRC), ' "Corso e Recorso": A Journey through Academe'

Patrick O'Brien (London School of Economics), 'The Pax Britanica, American Hegemony, and the International Order, 1793–2004'

Michael Wheeler (former Director of Chawton House Library), 'England Drawn and Quartered: Cultural Crisis in the Mid-Nineteenth Century'

Walter Wetzels (UT Germanic Studies), 'Growing Up in Nazi Germany, and Later American Adventures'

Kathleen Wilson (State University of New York, Stony Brook), 'The Colonial State and Governance in the Eighteenth Century'

Elizabeth Fernea (UT English and Middle Eastern Studies), 'Encounters with Imperialism'

Chris Dunton (National University of Lesotho), 'Newspapers and Colonial Rule in Africa'

Miguel Gonzalez-Gerth (UT Spanish and Portuguese), 'Crossing Geographical and Cultural Borders—and Finally Arriving at British Studies'

Peter Stansky (Stanford University), 'Bloomsbury in Ceylon'

Round Table Discussion on *The Crimson Petal and the White:* John Farrell (UT English), Betty Sue Flowers (LBJ Library), Roger Louis (UT Kerr Professor), Paul Neimann (UT English)

Ann Curthoys (Australian National University), 'The Australian History Wars'

Martha Ann Selby (UT Asian Studies), 'Against the Grain: On Finding My Voice in India'

Steven Isenberg (UT Visiting Professor of Humanities), 'A Life in Our Times'

Summer 2004

Carol Mackay (UT English), 'My Own Velvet Revolution'

Erez Manela (Harvard University), 'The "Wilsonian Moment" in India and the Crisis of Empire in 1919'

Scott Lucas (Birmingham University), ' "A Bright Shining Mecca": British Culture and Political Warfare in the Cold War and Beyond'

Monica Belmonte (US Department of State), 'Before Things Fell Apart: The British Design for the Nigerian State'

Dan Jacobson (London), 'Philip Larkin's "Elements"'
Bernard Porter (University of Newcastle), "'Oo Let 'Em In? Asylum Seekers and Terrorists in Britain, 1850–1914'

Fall Semester 2004

Richard Drayton (Cambridge University), 'Anglo-American "Liberal" Imperialism, British Guiana, 1953–64, and the World Since September 11'
David Washbrook (Oxford University), 'Living on the Edge: Anxiety and Identity in "British" Calcutta, 1780–1930'
Joanna Hitchcock (University of Texas Press), 'An Accidental Publisher'
Alan Friedman (UT English), '*A Midsummer Night's Dream*'
Antony Best (London School of Economics), 'British Intellectuals and East Asia in the Inter-War Years'
John Farrell (UT English), 'Beating a Path from Brooklyn to Austin'
Christopher Middleton (UT Liberal Arts), 'Relevant to England—A Reading of Poems'
Gail Minault (UT History and Asian Studies), 'Growing Up Bilingual and Other (Mis)adventures in Negotiating Cultures'
Roger Louis (Kerr Professor of English History and Cultures), 'Escape from Oklahoma'
John Trimble (UT English), 'Writing with Style'
Niall Ferguson (Harvard University), 'Origins of the First World War'
James Hopkins (Southern Methodist University), 'George Orwell and the Spanish Civil War: The Case of Nikos Kazantzakis'
James Currey (London), 'Africa Writes Back: Publishing the African Writers Series at Heinemann'
Sidney Monas (UT History and Slavic Languages), 'A Jew's Christmas'
Geoffrey Wheatcroft (London), '"In the Advance Guard": Evelyn Waugh's Reputation'

Spring Semester 2005

Katharine Whitehorn (London), 'It Didn't *All* Start in the Sixties'
Gertrude Himmelfarb (Graduate School of the City University of New York), 'The Whig Interpretation of History'
Kurt Heinzelman (English and HRHRC), 'Lord Byron and the Invention of Celebrity'
Brian Levack (History), 'Jesuits, Lawyers, and Witches'
Richard Cleary (Architecture), 'When Taste Mattered: W. J. Battle and the Architecture of the Forty Acres'
Edward I. Steinhart (Texas Tech University), 'White Hunters in British East Africa, 1895–1914'
Don Graham (English), 'The Drover's Wife: An Australian Archetype'
A. C. H. Smith, (London) 'Literary Friendship: The 40-Year Story of Tom Stoppard, B. S. Johnson, and Zulfikar Ghose'
Paul Woodruff (Philosophy and Plan II), 'A Case of Anglophilia—And Partial Recovery: Being an Account of My Life, with Special Attention to the Influence of England upon My Education'
Toyin Falola (History), 'Footprints of the Ancestors'
Robert Abzug (History) 'Confessions of an Intellectual Omnivore: The Consequences on Scholarship and Career'

Deirdre McMahon (Mary Immaculate College, University of Limerick), 'Ireland and the Empire-Commonwealth, 1918–1972'

James Coote (Architecture), 'Building with Wit: Sir Edwin Lutyens and British Architecture'

Jay Clayton (Vanderbilt University), 'The Dickens Tape: Lost and Found Sound before Recording'

Christopher Ricks (Oxford University), 'The Force of Poetry: Shakespeare and Beckett'

Summer 2005

Blair Worden (Oxford University), 'Poetry and History of the English Renaissance'

Robert Bruce Osborn (British Studies), 'The Four Lives of Robert Osborn'

Alessandra Lippucci (Government), 'Perseverance Furthers: A Self-Consuming Artifact'

William H. Cunningham (former President of the University of Texas), 'Money, Power, Politics, and Ambition'

David V. Edwards (Government), 'Friendly Persuasion in the Academy'

Elizabeth Richmond-Garza (English), 'A Punk Rocker with Eight Languages'

Richard Lariviere (Liberal Arts), 'Confessions of a Sanskritist Dean'

Fall Semester 2005

Celebration of 30th Anniversary and Publication of *Yet More Adventures with Britannia*

Robert D. King (UT Jewish Studies) , 'T. S. Eliot Reconsidered'

Round Table Discussion on 'The London Bombings': James Galbraith (LBJ School), Elizabeth Cullingford (UT English), Clement Henry (UT Government), Roger Louis (UT Kerr Professor)

Dolora Chapelle Wojciehowski (UT English), 'The Erotic Uncanny in Shakespeare's *Twelfth Night*'

Karl Hagstrom Miller (UT History), 'Playing Pensativa: History and Music in Counterpoint'

James D. Garrison (UT English), 'Translating Gray's *Elegy*'

Miguel Gonzalez-Gerth (UT Spanish and Portuguese), 'Another Look at Orwell: The Origins of *1984*'

Round Table Discussion on 'The Imperial Closet: Gordon of Khartoum, Hector McDonald of the Boer War, and Roger Casement of Ireland': Barbara Harlow (UT English), Neville Hoad (UT English), John Thomas (HRHRC)

Guy Ortolano (Washington University in St. Louis), 'From *The Two Cultures* to *Breaking Ranks:* C. P. Snow and the Interpretation of the 1960s'

Catherine Robson (UC Davis), 'Poetry and Memorialization'

Round Table Discussion on 'Britain and the Jewish Century': Lauren Apter (UT History), Robert D. King (UT Jewish Studies), Sidney Monas (UT History and Slavic Languages)

Hans Mark (UT Aerospace Engineering), 'Churchill, the Anglo-Persian Oil Company, and the Origins of the Energy Crisis: From the Early 20th Century to the Present'

Randall Woods (Arkansas), 'LBJ and the British'

Richard Gray (London), 'Movie Palaces of Britain'

Samuel Baker (UT English), 'The Lake Poets and the War in the Mediterranean Sea'

Thomas F. Staley (HRHRC), 'Graham Greene and Evelyn Waugh'

Gary Stringer (Texas A&M), 'Love's Long Labors Coming to Fruition: The John Donne Variorum Donne'

Caroline Elkins (Harvard), 'From Malaya to Kenya: British Colonial Violence and the End of Empire'

Grigory Kaganov (St. Petersburg), 'London in the Mouth of the Neva'

Graham Greene (London), 'A Life in Publishing'

John Davis (Oxford), 'Evans-Pritchard: Nonetheless a Great Englishman'

Barry Gough (Wilfrid Laurier University), 'Arthur Marder and the Battles over the History of the Royal Navy'

Ivan Kreilkamp (Indiana), ' "Bags of Meat": Pet-Keeping and the Justice to Animals in Thomas Hardy'

James Wilson (UT History), 'Historical Memory and the Mau Mau Uprising in Colonial Kenya'

Anne Deighton (Oxford), 'Britain after the Second World War: Losing an Empire and Finding a Place in a World of Super Powers'

Steve Isenberg (UT Liberal Arts), 'Auden, Forster, Larkin, and Empson'

Harriet Ritvo (MIT), 'Animals on the Edge'

Peter Quinn (NY), 'Eugenics and the Hour of the Cat'

Dan Jacobson (London), 'Kipling and South Africa'

Michael Charlesworth (UT Art and Art History) and Kurt Heinzelman (UT English), 'Tony Harrison's "v."'

Peter Stanley (Australian War Memorial), 'All Imaginable Excuses: Australian Deserters and the Fall of Singapore'

Selina Hastings (London), 'Somerset Maugham and "Englishness"'

James W. Vick (UT Mathematics), 'A Golden Century of English Mathematics'

John O. Voll (Georgetown), 'Defining the Middle East and the Clash of Civilizations'

James Loehlin (UT English), 'The Afterlife of Hamlet'

Daniel Topolski (London), 'The Life and Art of Feliks Topolski'

John Darwin (Oxford), 'The British Empire and the British World'

David Cannadine (University of London), 'Andrew Mellon and Plutocracy across the Atlantic'

John Lonsdale (Cambridge), 'White Settlers and Black Mau Mau in Kenya'

Kate Gartner Frost (UT English), 'So What's Been Done about John Donne Lately?'

John Summers (Harvard), 'The Power Elite: C. Wright Mills and the British'

Marrack Goulding (Oxford), 'Has It Been A Success? Britain in the United Nations'

Priya Satia (Stanford), 'The Defence of Inhumanity: British Military and Cultural Power in the Middle East'

Don Graham (UT English), 'Burnt Orange Britannia: A Missing Contributor!'

Spring Semester 2007

Bernard Porter (Newcastle University), 'Empire and British Culture'

Paul Sullivan (UT Liberal Arts Honors Program), 'The Headmaster's Shakespeare: John Garrett and British Education'

Round Table Discussion on *The Queen*: Elizabeth Cullingford (UT English), Karen King (UT American Studies), Roger Louis (UT Kerr Professor), Bryan Roberts (UT Sociology)

Martin Francis (University of Cincinnati), 'Cecil Beaton's Romantic Toryism and the Symbolism of Wartime Britain'

Susan Crane (Columbia University), 'Animal Feelings and Feelings for Animals in Chaucer'

Michael Charlesworth (UT Art History), 'The Earl of Strafford and Wentworth Castle'

Adam Sisman (London), 'Wordsworth and Coleridge'

Jenny Mann (Cornell University), 'Shakespeare's English Rhetoric: Mingling Heroes and Hobgoblins in *A Midsummer Night's Dream*'

David Atkinson (Member of Parliament), 'Britain and World Peace in the 21st Century'

Bertram Wyatt-Brown (University of Florida), 'T. E. Lawrence, Reputation, and Honor's Decline'

Roger Louis (UT Kerr Professor), 'All Souls and Oxford in 1956: Reassessing the Meaning of the Suez Crisis'

Indivar Kamtekar (Jawaharlal Nehru University), 'India and Britain during the Second World War'

Cassandra Pybus (University of Sydney), 'William Wilberforce and the Emancipation of Slaves'

Stephen Howe (University of Bristol), 'Empire in the 21st Century English Imagination'

Geoffrey Wheatcroft (London), 'The Myth of Malicious Partition: The Cases of Ireland, India, and Palestine'

Charles Rossman (UT English), 'D. H. Lawrence and the "Spirit" of Mexico'

Kenneth O. Morgan (House of Lords), 'Lloyd George, the French, and the Germans'